DOES CONQUEST PAY?

Princeton Studies in International History and Politics

DOES CONQUEST PAY?

THE EXPLOITATION OF OCCUPIED INDUSTRIAL SOCIETIES

Peter Liberman

PRINCETON UNIVERSITY PRESS   PRINCETON, NEW JERSEY

Copyright © 1996 by Princeton University Press
Published by Princeton University Press, 41 William Street,
Princeton, New Jersey 08540
In the United Kingdom: Princeton University Press,
Chichester, West Sussex
All Rights Reserved

Library of Congress Cataloging-in-Publication Data

Liberman, Peter, 1962–
Does conquest pay? : the exploitation of
occupied industrial societies / Peter Liberman.
p. cm. — (Princeton studies in international history and politics)
Includes bibliographical references and index.
ISBN 0-691-02986-5
ISBN 0-691-00242-8 (pbk.)
1. Military occupation—Economic aspects.
2. Military occupation—Economic aspects—Case studies.
I. Title II. Series.
JX5003.L53 1995
325'.32'0904—dc20   95-17925 CIP

This book has been composed in Sabon Typeface

Princeton University Press books are
printed on acid-free paper and meet the guidelines
for permanence and durability of the Committee
on Production Guidelines for Book Longevity
of the Council on Library Resources

Second printing, and first paperback printing, 1998

http://pup.princeton.edu

Printed in the United States of America

3 5 7 9 10 8 6 4 2

Contents

Figures and Tables

FIGURES

TABLES

Preface and Acknowledgments

"DOES CONQUEST PAY?" is a controversial but little-studied question in international politics. That conquerors can harness captured economies is a longstanding premise of realist balance-of-power strategy and theory. But the virulence of nationalism, the correlation between development and democracy, the long postwar peace, and finally the collapse of the Soviet Empire have suggested to many observers that conquest no longer pays. The importance of economic resources to power means that the truth of the matter is relevant to the likelihood of expansion and the need for balancing strategies like containment. Yet the study of resource "cumulativity" has been confined to historical works on specific occupations and empires.

This book will argue that invaders can, in fact, make conquest "pay" in the limited sense that they can exploit seized industrial economies for their own purposes. To demonstrate this, I have assembled evidence on the imperial revenues, policing costs, and productivity of several twentieth-century occupations and empires. The evidence shows that modern societies can be mobilized intensively in the short run or controlled and "farmed" in the long run. This is true, however, only for ruthless oppressors. Invaders who are morally, internationally, or economically constrained from applying coercion and repression find their attempts at exploitation foiled by massive popular opposition.

Understanding why and when conquest pays, despite the power of nationalism, requires analyzing the sources of collaboration and resistance. It is the economic and political behavior of a nation's leaders, bureaucracies, firms, and individual citizens that determines the profitability of conquest. The variety of important actors and circumstances make this an extremely complex subject. But patterns of collaboration and resistance appear to reflect different levels of coercion, repression, and modernization. To explain this, I draw on theories of coercion and collective action, combined with basic features of modernization. These theories and the evidence suggest, in contrast to commonly held notions, that modern industrial societies are in many respects more vulnerable to coercion and repression than less-developed ones.

Collaboration, resistance, and their impact on economic extraction need interdisciplinary study. Interactions between invaders and invaded often resemble relations among states and have important ramifications for the quality of life in the international system. But rule by invaders or their proxies is also close to the subject of comparative politics, political sociology, and political economy. Although none of these fields has specifically addressed the profitability of conquest, they all offer relevant theoretical insights. For evidence, I have relied on specialized histories and governmental reports on individual occupations and conquests. By abstracting a few key measures and causes from their rich accounts of extraordinarily complex events, and by using the comparative method to test specific hypotheses, it is possible to identify and explain simple, recurring patterns not fully revealed by prior historical research.

This book does not try to cover all consequences of conquest. By defining "profitability" narrowly, in terms of the economic benefits and costs provided or imposed directly by the conquered societies themselves, I leave aside external and noneconomic costs and benefits, such as the war costs of taking territory and defending it from outside powers, the losses caused by economic sanctions, the strategic advantages of eliminating neighboring enemies, and the utility of captured military manpower. Conquest usually does not pay in the larger reckoning, as Napoleon, Hitler, and other aggressors learned, because conquerors are usually vanquished in the end by defensive alliances. But the exploitability of captured industrial economies is by itself important and poorly enough understood to merit separate study.

This book also does not grapple with the atrocities and suffering resulting from conquest and empire, however horribly momentous they may be. Conquerors have committed some of the most evil crimes of genocide, torture, slavery, oppression, and discrimination in history. My purpose here, though, is to measure the profitability of conquest and identify its causes. Besides noting the coercion and repression applied to make the conquest of nationalistic societies pay, I will not explore the vast human costs that were also involved. I hope such a focused analysis will not be misread as an effort to sanitize or condone conquest, coercion, repression, or worse. Rather, it is a modest attempt to contribute to knowledge that may help prevent their recurrence.

This book would not have been possible without the help of many teachers, colleagues, and institutions. My greatest debt is to Barry Posen, who first suggested this topic to me and has been an inspiring mentor. Kenneth Oye, Douglass Forsyth, and Stephen Van Evera provided incisive criticism and suggestions at crucial stages of the project. Steve's persistent prodding was especially instrumental in helping me to clarify my ideas and writing.

For comments and advice on earlier drafts of one or more chapters, I thank James Alt, Suzanne Berger, Tom Christensen, Joshua Cohen, Andrew Cortell, Neta Crawford, Michael Desch, Steven Flank, Aaron Friedberg, John Gillingham, Carl Kaysen, Beth Kier, Jon Kirshner, Jonathan Mercer, Steven Miller, Alan Milward, Ramon Myers, Robert

Keohane, Jaroslav Krejčí, Kevin Oliveau, Mark Peattie, Laura Reed, Alan Rousso, David Rowe, Richard Samuels, Jack Snyder, Ray Taras, Brian Taylor, Alice Teichova, Kenneth Waltz, and Werner Warmbrunn. Extra thanks are due to the historians among this group for their generous help across disciplinary lines.

I would also like to thank Colin Borstal, Edward Guernica, and Robert Lane Greene for research assistance, Lee Liberman and David Nelson Blair for editorial help, and Malcolm DeBevoise and Beth Gianfagna for shepherding the manuscript through publication.

Financial support for this work was provided by MIT's Defense and Arms Control Studies Program, the Ford Foundation's Program in Western Security and European Society, the John D. and Catherine T. MacArthur Foundation, the John M. Olin Institute for Strategic Studies, and Tulane University's Committee on Research. The DACS Program at MIT and the Ford and Olin programs at Harvard University's Center for International Affairs provided stimulating intellectual environments for most of the research and writing of this book. I am grateful to their staffs and especially their directors, Jack Ruina and Harvey Sapolsky of MIT, Richard Eichenberg of the Ford Program, and Samuel P. Huntington of the Olin Institute. I also thank my colleagues and students at Tulane University for their ideas and patience while I completed this book.

Portions of this book originally appeared as "The Spoils of Conquest" and are reprinted with permission from *International Security* 18, no. 2 (Fall 1993), published by MIT Press. Copyright (c) 1993 by President and Fellows of Harvard College and the Massachusetts Institute of Technology. I thank the journal and its publishers for permission to use the material here.

Finally, I am deeply grateful to my parents and to Sarah Soffer for their love and moral support. Sarah's laugh also helped me keep my sanity while I was spending so much time studying terrible events. This book is dedicated to her.

DOES CONQUEST PAY?

CHAPTER 1

Does Conquest Pay?

DOES CONQUEST PAY in the modern era? Can invading powers mobilize the economic resources of occupied industrial societies? Or do nationalistic societies frustrate invaders by imposing high costs and denying economic gains? What factors influence the size of imperial profit margins, and why? These questions are the subject of enduring disagreement among policymakers, analysts, and scholars. Many have found it self-evident that industrial nations are potentially cumulative or transferable economic resources. Others have believed just as firmly that the conquest of modern societies is economically futile. These diametrically opposite opinions lie at the root of longstanding debates in foreign policy and international relations theory.

Nevertheless, these questions have never been subjected to systematic analysis. Claims on one side or the other are rarely supported with more than casual hypotheses and anecdotal data. Political scientists have analyzed the ability of states to mobilize domestic resources, as well as the causes of imperialism and "overexpansion" (i.e., expansion despite negative marginal returns).[1] Historians have studied particular cases of exploitation but have focused their comparative efforts on preindustrial empires.[2] The gains to conquerors from eliminating potential enemies and using conquered territory—as well as the losses suffered at the hands of imperial rivals and defensive coalitions—have been studied extensively by international relations historians and theorists.[3] But whether the conquest of industrial economies pays, *aside from* the costs of conquering territory and the costs imposed by retaliating third parties, is more controversial, as shall soon become clear.

This book attempts to measure and explain the profitability of conquest by examining several historical episodes of hostile occupation through the lenses of social-science theory. Germany occupied and tried to mobilize Belgium and Luxembourg during the First World War. After that war, the victorious Allies partially occupied and attempted to extract reparations from Germany, forcefully in the Ruhr operation of 1923–24. Nazi Germany successfully mobilized Western Europe during World War II. Meanwhile, Japan had constructed a passive and economically dynamic empire out of Taiwan, Korea, and Manchuria. The end of the second great conflagration found the Soviet Army in Central and Eastern

Europe, where it remained until 1989. Each of these episodes has been studied individually by historians, but determining how thoroughly industrial economies can be harnessed by foreign occupiers, as well as identifying the factors that affect mobilization, requires comparative analysis.

THE ARGUMENT

In this book I will argue that ruthless invaders can, in fact, successfully exploit industrial societies, at least for short periods of time. Control over industrial societies, moreover, can be maintained for longer periods at relatively low expense. Also, the available evidence does not show that foreign domination per se precludes economic growth, although multinational empires are unlikely to be as robust as comparably sized and developed nation-states. Conquest does not always pay; nationalism ensures that conquerors unwilling to engage in coercion and repression will face massive political and economic resistance. But determined conquerors can put a lid on nationalism, if not eradicate it, and cultivate or exploit their new domains on demand.

In arguing that conquest pays, I mean only that a conqueror or occupier can extract a large percentage of the economic potential of industrial nations. Nationalism and "people power" alone cannot prevent ruthless states from extracting large imperial profits (revenues net of collections costs) from occupied industrial societies. In other words, industrialized economies are "cumulative" resources—the economies of captured nations can be added to a conqueror's total economic base.[4] This is not to say that conquest is profitable when all of its geopolitical consequences are considered (see table 1-1). The balance sheets evaluated in this book do not consider the costs of military conflict or economic sanctions imposed by states outside the empire, the benefit of neutralizing potentially hostile neighbors, or the utility of strategic territory. Mainly because other states balance against aggressors, conquest usually leads to disaster. Nor are industrial societies *fully* cumulative resources; if they were, conquerors could mobilize occupied economies as completely and efficiently as their own. The extraction rates (profits taken as a percentage of the nation's economic potential) that can be reached are not as high as the resource-mobilization rates that nation-states can achieve domestically. But industrial societies are cumulative enough that conquerors can greatly increase their mobilizable economic base through expansion.

An explanation can be found in the sources of collaboration and resistance. Nationalism ensures that modern societies detest foreign domination, not to mention exploitation. But hostility and discontent are not enough to generate resistance. Coercion works, especially against socie-

TABLE 1-1
Conquerors' Costs and Benefits

	Costs	Benefits

Internal	Administration
	Policing
	Decreased trade with
	   conquered region[a]
		Tribute and plunder
		Military collaboration
		Military bases
		Increased trade with
		   conquered region[a]

External	Initial military victory
	Wars with balancing states
	Trade sanctions by
	   balancing states
		Elimination of potential
		   enemies

[a] All trade effects depend in part on external factors.

ties unable to organize themselves for collective action. Since conquerors generally have superior coercive capabilities to militarily defeated societies and can repress social self-organization, they can compel defeated societies to collaborate politically and economically.

Moreover, industrialization and other facets of socioeconomic development do not increase the bargaining position of occupied societies. While modernization does increase the potential for collective action, it also increases the efficiency of social coercion and repression. The result is that with a relatively small investment in the instruments of domination, and with an economic strategy that creates incentives for collaboration, ruthless conquerors—but only ruthless ones—can make defeated modern societies pay a large share of their economic surplus in tribute. Modernization increases nations' social surplus, but without significantly increasing the costs of the coercion, repression, and administration needed to maintain and extort it.

These findings suggest that the conquest of industrial regions by an expansionist state can result in a drastic and possibly enduring shift in the international distribution of capabilities, lending support to realist arguments for balancing against expansionists. Another implication is that industrial empires, though less efficient than nation-states, are economically and politically durable as long as they are commanded by ruthless regimes. Since expansion can be self-reinforcing, moreover, the international system is more war-prone than many optimists claim. If conquest and empire have become less common in the modern age, we should be thankful for other causes of peace, like deterrence and democracy. In addition, guerrilla-based and civilian-based defenses are unlikely to work or even to be implemented by modern societies against coercive and repressive conquerors.

CONTENDING VIEWS

The cumulativity of resources is a matter of longstanding disagreement in the international relations field. But it has rarely generated open debate, because scholars' and policymakers' opinions on the subject are usually buried assumptions in complex theoretical and policy arguments. As a result, claims on either side are rarely specific. It is difficult to tell whether those who believe that conquest pays think that conquered economies are worth a comparable loyal province (that is, 100 percent cumulative) or worth only half (50 percent cumulative). The critics of this view are just as vague, suggesting alternatively that conquered economies are a liability, a net wash, or simply less cumulative now than in the past. Others argue that even when conquest pays initially for any given empire, at some point in size and time, the costs eventually exceed the benefits.[5] Still, there is a clear divergence of opinion about the cumulativity of resources, particularly for industrial economies.

Imperial rulers and propagandists, unsurprisingly, have typically believed that conquest pays. In ancient Greece, Pericles claimed that "the strength of Athens came from the money paid in tribute" by her allied satellites throughout the Aegean, payments that matched Athenian domestic tax revenues. Athenians' imperialism was fueled, according to their rivals, by their confidence that "the farther they go the more they will get."[6] Even the rise of nation-states in Europe can be seen as a repeating cycle of conquest, consolidation, and resource extraction.[7]

But the notion that conquest pays also informs a long tradition of balance-of-power thinking by realist statesmen and scholars. Statesmen and strategists have often urged their nations to build up against and contain expansionists on the assumption that conquest adds to expansionists' power while eliminating potential members of defensive alliances. For example, Foreign Secretary Edward Grey of Great Britain wanted his country to stand by France and Russia in World War I, for if these nations were defeated, "Germany would wield the whole power of the continent."[8] American realists' arguments for joining the war against Hitler were based on this premise as well, especially after France's defeat in the summer of 1940 focused their attention on the geopolitical significance of a Nazi-dominated Europe. At least a year before Pearl Harbor and Hitler's declaration of war, President Roosevelt himself had worried that "if Great Britain goes down, the Axis powers will control the continents of Europe, Asia, Africa, Australia, and the high seas—and they will . . . bring enormous military and naval resources against this hemisphere."[9] This view was echoed throughout the policy media before and during the war. In the April 1941 *Foreign Affairs*, an economist calculated that the estimated annual shipbuilding capacity of countries now under Nazi rule . . . , plus that of Japan, plus that of Italy, was about 2,300,000 gross tons at the outbreak of the war. . . . Nazi conquest of the British Isles [would add] about 2,500,000 gross tons. . . . If that is a good estimate, it would take us more than four years to overtake totalitarian shipbuilding capacity, *supposing that they stood still.*[10]

Similarly, Walter Lippmann argued that the United States had to defeat Hitler because "the potential military strength of the Old World is enormously greater than that of the New World."[11]

After the war, Stalin's domination of Eastern and Central Europe provoked fears that he had succeeded Hitler as a contender for European hegemony. Realists in and out of government supported a policy of containment, on the assumption that the Soviet Union could mobilize conquered industrial economies for war against the United States.[12] George Kennan, a key architect of the policy, explained that containment was necessary to assure "that no single Continental land power should come to dominate the entire Eurasian land mass . . . become a great sea power as well as land power . . . and enter . . . on an overseas expansion hostile to ourselves and supported by the immense resources of the interior of Europe and Asia."[13] In the same vein, a 1948 National Security Council report stated that "there are in Europe and Asia areas of great potential power which if added to the . . . Soviet world would enable the latter to become so superior in manpower, resources and territory that the prospect for the survival of the United States as a free nation would be slight."[14] Containment, like the U.S. participation in the war against Hitler, was inspired by moral and economic motives as well. But even at the end of the cold war, its chief goal was still "to prevent any hostile power or group of powers from dominating the Eurasian land mass."[15]

This focus on Eurasia stemmed from the belief that the wealthier the conquest, the more wealth and power gained—in other words, industrial economies were cumulative power resources. Kennan thus argued for limiting containment to the protection of only those "centers of industrial and military power" outside the United States and Russia—that is, Great Britain, Germany and Central Europe, and Japan—that have the "requisite conditions of climate, of industrial strength, of population and of tradition" capable of generating significant "amphibious power."[16] In 1951 Secretary of State Dean Acheson justified the deployment of additional U.S. troops to Europe by noting that "outside our own country, free Europe has the greatest number of scientists, the greatest industrial production, and the largest pool of skilled manpower in the world. It has a tremendous shipbuilding capacity, essential to control of the seas."[17] U.S. policy toward Japan was informed by similar reasoning. "If Japan, the principal component of a Far Eastern war-making complex, were added to the Stalinist bloc," argued a 1949 NSC report, "the Soviet Asian base could become a source of strength capable of shifting the balance of world power to the disadvantage of the United States."[18] And while the United States also made commitments to geopolitically insignificant nations during the cold war—due to beliefs in falling dominoes, bandwagoning, and the monolithic nature of communism—critics of global containment continued to argue for defending Western Europe, Japan, and the Persian Gulf.[19]

Most balance-of-power theorists share the strategists' premise that economic resources are cumulative. Formal theorists explicitly state their assumption that resources are "freely transferable" and are fully absorbed by victorious powers.[20] The same thinking is evident in traditional theorizing about international politics. The British geographer Halford Mackinder wrote in 1904 that the political consolidation of the Eurasian continent "would permit the use of vast continental resources for fleet-building, and the empire of the world would then be in sight."[21] Mackinder's early speculations gave little credit to the impediment of national loyalties: "Were the Chinese . . . organized by the Japanese, to overthrow the Russian Empire and conquer its territory, they might constitute the yellow peril to the world's freedom just because they would add an oceanic frontage to the resources of the great continent, an advantage as yet denied to the Russian tenant of the pivot region."[22] Nicholas Spykman, an American political scientist and a devotee of Mackinder's geopolitics, agreed that expansionists throughout history made "each new conquest the stepping stone for further enlargement. Power tends to grow and diffuse through wider areas, and the states in the vicinity have the choice between collective defense and ultimate absorption."[23] Hans Morgenthau gave more credit to national character and morale as sources of power. But he also thought that conquest "without prospects for speedy recovery usually breaks the will to resist of the conquered people" and "amounts to a piecemeal change in the power relations in favor of the imperialistic nation."[24] One can find the same premise in Kenneth Waltz's explanation of the priorities in U.S. foreign policy: "Only Japan, Western Europe, and the Middle East are prizes that if won by the Soviet Union would alter the balance of GNPs and the distribution of resources enough to be a danger."[25]

But the notion that GNPs can be transferred between capitals like money wired between banks has long had its critics. Adam Smith's *The Wealth of Nations*, published in the same year that the American colonists declared their independence, concluded with a diatribe against maintaining the "showy equipage" of colonies that "contribute neither revenue nor military force towards the support of an empire."[26] Smith thought that empire drained the mother country because the costs of seizing and defending colonies from imperial rivals typically exceeded the low revenues collected from them.

Subsequent critics advanced a more ambitious claim, that even cheap and unopposed conquest among modern states did not pay. The British free-trade advocate Richard Cobden argued in 1849 that where "one empire will take possession, by force of arms, of its neighbor's territory . . . the accession of territory would be a source of weakness, not of strength."[27] On the eve of World War I, Norman Angell's *The Great Illusion* popularized the notion that "the exaction of tribute from a conquered people has become an economic impossibility."[28] Political scientists and economists resuscitated Angell's claims starting in the early 1960s.[29] Klaus Knorr argues that "the conquest of territory for economic reasons has become an anachronism."[30] One economist claims that "the extent to which the conquest of new territory added to the economic strength of the conqueror is questionable," and another agrees that "much of the surplus that accrues to modern populations is simply not available to a conqueror."[31]

These "quagmire" theorists also claim that conquest among *modern* nations is especially unprofitable. Angell believed that, while colonial exploitation was still possible, the property rights upon which industrial society had been built precluded economic exploitation. Later writers have stressed the impact of nationalism, a phenomenon unique to developing and modern societies. For example, Robert Gilpin's *War and Change in World Politics* (1981) argues that in the premodern era, "the size of the economic surplus from agriculture and imperial tribute was principally a function of the extent of territorial control. Therefore, other things being equal, the greater the territorial extent of an empire . . . the greater the power of the empire."[32] But in the modern world, according to Gilpin, the nation-state proved a more efficient unit of political and economic organization because it commands the loyalty of nationalistic populations. By contrast, empires "were able to enlist and secure the loyalty of only a small fraction of their inhabitants . . . [accounting] for the ultimate fragility of empires in the face of internal revolts and external pressures."[33] Other theorists have updated Angell's economic argument with reasons why new possibilities for economic noncooperation inhere in modern forms of production.

The opposing positions about the cumulativity of resources correspond roughly to two traditions of international relations thought, realist and liberal. The resource-cumulativity view underlies old realist tenets about the importance and likelihood of balancing against expansionists, the utility of military power, and the war-proneness of the international system. The quagmire view has a classical liberal pedigree, going back to Cobden, Angell, and even earlier liberal economists, who used it to make archetypical liberal arguments against imperialism, for isolationism and disarmament, and in support of the notion that war among developed nations had become obsolete.

But particular claims about the cumulativity of resources are not entailed by the core axioms of realist and liberal international theory, and the correlation between the claims and the schools is far from perfect. Since the central idea of realism is that the international system is an anarchic, self-help arena, realists like Klaus Knorr and Robert Gilpin can argue without inconsistency that conquered industrial nations are not cumulative resources. (Still, realist balance-of-power strategists and theorists contradict their own assumptions about "economic prizes" by claiming, as does Kenneth Waltz, that "force is always on the side of the governed."[34]) Core liberal doctrines about the shared costs of trade barriers and war and the pacific effects of trade also do not entail specific presumptions about the cumulativity of resources. Thus the liberal philosopher Jeremy Bentham could argue that while overseas imperialism was economically futile, continental conquest paid: "The new property, being contiguous, is laid on his old property. . . . the inhabitants, as many as he thinks fit to set his mark on, go to increase his armies; their substance, as much as he thinks fit to squeeze from them, goes into his own purse."[35] While there is a definite correspondence of beliefs about the cumulativity of resources to realism and liberalism, these beliefs cannot be neatly pigeon-holed into such diverse schools of thought.

WHY THE CUMULATIVITY OF RESOURCES MATTERS

Two important debates in international relations theory depend at least in part on whether conquest pays. Analyzing the cumulativity of resources should help us understand when states should balance against expansionists and should help us predict when they will do so. Understanding the likelihood of war also requires analyzing the cumulativity of resources. In addition, research on foreign domination and resource cumulativity helps answer two other questions: How great is the potential of modern "people power" to frustrate detested rule? Can this potential be tapped by guerrilla or nonviolent defenses?

Analyzing the cumulativity of economic resources is essential for measuring both the power of empires and the impact of expansion on the international balance of power. This is because of the importance of economic resources as a source of military power. "The outcome of all the major, lengthy wars among the Great Powers," observes Paul Kennedy, "repeatedly points to the crucial influences of productive economic forces—both during the struggle itself, and during those periods between

wars when differentiated growth rates cause the various Powers to become relatively stronger or weaker."[36] Assuming that modern great powers have the will and skill to translate economic capacity into military
force, and are economically self-sufficient, most international relations
theorists use Gross National Product (GNP) as a rule-of-thumb measure
for power.[37]

If industrial societies are fully cumulative resources—if, in other
words, they can be fully mobilized by a conqueror at trivial cost—their
absorption adds substantial increments of power to the empire. To the
extent that conquest pays, realist arguments for balancing gain support,
and states are more likely to respond to aggression with arms buildups,
alliances, containment policies, or war. But if the conquest of modern
societies is economically futile, balancing becomes both less important
and less likely. Just as the cumulativity-of-resources premise motivates
balancing strategies, the opposite quagmire view has been used to criticize
them. Cobden's version quoted earlier appears in a critique of British
intervention against Russia in the Crimea, and Angell's *Great Illusion*
served as the bible of interwar British isolationists. Similarly, critics of the
U.S. entry into World War II argued that internal resistance by the occupied societies would have minimized German and Japanese gains from
conquest.[38] And containment has been criticized on the grounds that the
Soviet Union could not mobilize a conquered Western Europe for war
against the United States.[39]

Since this book supports the premise that industrial resources are cumulative for ruthless conquerors, it adds to the case for power-balancing
strategies. But the assessment and prediction of such strategies depends
on other factors as well. Gaining economic resources is not the only wor-
risome result of expansion; a conqueror's gain of bases alone, or its loss
of potential allies, may warrant a reaction.[40] Geopolitical analyses must
also take into account factors like proximity; one could plausibly argue
that even a Eurasian empire could not project its power efficiently enough
to threaten a distant, ocean-moated United States.[41]

Even more important is the nuclear revolution, which makes conquest
both less likely and less consequential. Since countries with survivable
nuclear forces can devastate any attacker, the probable costs of aggression outweigh any possible gains. At the same time, a conqueror's growing economic strength might not threaten other nuclear-armed powers,
whose ability to deter depends more on survivable nuclear forces than
relative power. Accordingly, cold war isolationists argued that France
and Britain could deter a Soviet invasion of Western Europe without U.S.
assistance, and that the United States could deter or defend against invasion by even a Eurasian hegemon.[42] On the other hand, some theorists
have argued that nuclear weapons do not make geopolitical calculations

wholly obsolete. The "stability-instability paradox" argument holds that since even nuclear-armed states might prefer surrender to mutual destruction, old-fashioned conventional aggression remains viable.[43] Moreover, economic size remains a desired source of power, if only because it affects states' spending levels on research and development of future technologies that might someday undo mutual assured destruction. But even if nuclear weapons do disconnect security from economic size, knowing the cumulativity of resources is essential to understanding balancing in regions with neither nuclear weapons nor nuclear-armed allies. It also helps us evaluate the utility of nuclear deterrence. Since, as this book will show, industrial economies are highly cumulative, states should balance more strenuously in a nonnuclear world than in a nuclear one.

The cumulativity of resources has important implications for a second set of concerns, those involving the causes of imperial expansion and war. While many theories of imperialism attempt to explain the occurrence of *unprofitable* expansion, nations also expand when it pays to do so.[44] The supposed unprofitability of conquest has thus been used to explain why, "in the modern era, expansion by means of the world market economy and extension of political influence have largely displaced empire and territorial expansion as a means of acquiring wealth."[45] Since the cumulativity of resources increases states' appetite for neighboring real estate, it also increases the likelihood of war, both among imperialist rivals as well as between imperialists and defenders of the status quo.[46] Conversely, the view that conquest no longer pays has been used to explain a supposed secular decline in war among developed countries and to predict its continued obsolescence. This idea is distinct from—though typically advanced as part of—the more general war-does-not-pay argument, which also includes the high costs of modern warfare.[47]

It should be noted that the link between resource cumulativity and war presupposes constant or inadequate balancing behavior. But if states believe that expansion pays, they will also try harder to deter the expansion of rivals. Thus as states' possessions become more attractive to burglars, their security systems become more robust, reducing the total effect on the likelihood of war. But states can bolster deterrence only as far as their resources permit, and even increased spending may not enhance deterrence when offensives are easy. If conquest pays, those lacking the necessary resources or allies to deter are more likely to be gobbled up. Weak states are often sheltered by alliances, but these alliances will not be extended and strengthened in direct proportion to the profitability of conquest. States balance inadequately, because they tend to buck-pass in multipolar systems, because they sometimes fail to recognize threats in time to deter them, and because even prompt balancing can fail to deter. The uncertainties, misperceptions, and inefficiencies in international politics make it unlikely that balancing behavior would fully compensate for the temptation of easily exploitable territories.[48]

Since, as this book will argue, conquest still pays, peace must be due to other causes, such as system structure, the costliness of modern—and especially nuclear—warfare, or the spread of liberal values.[49] Conflict is going to be likely when these sources of peace are absent, as they are in Eastern Europe or in the Balkans, where Bosnian military-industrial assets have fuelled Serbian expansionism.[50] Modern nations cannot rely on their nationalism and development alone as sufficient deterrents to aggression.

Analyzing the cumulativity of resources also sheds light on the significance of "people power" and on the conditions under which societies can frustrate and overthrow tyrannical rule. Thus it should not only help us understand the durability and power of empires—an embarrassing subject, given the recent failure to predict the collapse of the Soviet Empire—but also that of all authoritarian regimes.[51] Collaboration and resistance have similar causes, whether the despots involved are foreign or native, the main difference being that nationalism is a more potent motivator of political hostility than the resentments, anger, and hopes that fuel domestic rebellions. But despite ongoing scholarly debates over the relative importance of discontent and opportunity in causing rebellious collective action, and over the impact of modernization on authoritarian rule, research in these fields has concentrated exclusively on domestic cases.[52] Examining the pacification and exploitation of foreign peoples adds insight into the stability and durability of all detested tyrannies.

The recent wave of democratization and imperial collapse has prompted many observers to conclude that societal resistance made these changes inevitable. But by showing that nationalism and development do not present insurmountable obstacles to ruthless tyrants, this book demonstrates that coercion and repression can control and exploit modern societies, even where all legitimacy is lacking and discontent is extreme. This lends weight to the role of strategic opportunity in rebellious collective action, provides insight into the stability of modern authoritarian and totalitarian political systems, and explains such puzzles as why foreign-imposed regimes could survive for forty years in East Germany but not in Afghanistan. It also suggests that future Orwellian nightmares are not an intrinsic impossibility.

Studying collaboration and resistance is also necessary to evaluate strategies to mobilize social discontent against foreign domination or domestic tyranny. Some strategists argue that guerrilla tactics enable rebels to impose high costs on occupying armies and to sabotage economic collaboration.[53] Others contend that preparation and training in nonviolent, civil disobedience can economically and politically paralyze invaded countries and thus deny a conqueror any gains.[54] Proponents of both types share quagmire assumptions about the power potential of civil society, but rather than claim that conquest is always unprofitable, they argue that preparation and training in national resistance would make it so.[55] However, by focusing entirely on strategies, these writers have neglected to develop a viable theory explaining resistance successes and failures (resulting in rather cursory dismissal by mainstream security analysts).[56] This study shows that the strategies overlook more fundamental causes of resistance and collaboration and are thus unlikely to work against determined oppressors who command loyal militaries.

CASES AND METHOD

This book analyzes four short occupations: the German occupation of Belgium and Luxembourg during World War I, the Franco-Belgian occupation of the Ruhr-Rhineland in 1923–24, the German occupation of Western Europe during World War II, and the Soviet occupation of East Germany 1945–53. It also examines two long-term empires: the Japanese Empire of 1910–45 and the Soviet–East European Empire of 1945–89. Each case study attempts to answer the following questions: Where conquerors attempted to intensively mobilize their conquests, how well did they succeed? What factors determined the size of the imperial profit margin? Finally, did foreign domination strangle economic productivity?

These cases were selected according to four basic criteria, in addition to the requirement of data availability. First, the conquered societies must be nationalistic vis-à-vis the conqueror, since it is nationalism that supposedly generates enough political hostility to make foreign rule impracticable. Thus post-Anschluß Austria, which shared a common language and culture with Germany, is not included in the chapter on Nazi-occupied Europe. Second, because modernization is also alleged to generate resistance, the subject economies should be relatively modern (see table 1-2). A third criterion for the shorter-occupation cases is that there is attempted extraction, whether as peacetime tribute, mobilization for war, or postwar reparations. Benevolent occupations obviously do not provide good test cases. One must not dismiss cases where conquerors hesitated to exploit because they anticipated failure, but in most cases intentions are transparent. Thus the fact that the United States neglected to mobilize postwar West Germany and Japan tells us little about the profitability of conquest.[57] Finally, cases were selected to ensure that there is variation in the factors that affect the profitability of conquest: coercion, repression, and level of development. Since there is less variation in the

TABLE 1-2
Development Level of the United States in 1980 and Case-Study Countries
(In 1980 U.S. Dollars)

	GDP per Capita		GDP per Capita
United States 1980	11,360	Germany 1922	1,845
East Germany 1980	5,910	Belgium 1913	2,406
Czechoslovakia 1980	4,740	Luxembourg 1913	1,976
Hungary 1980	4,390	Taiwan 1938	752
Poland 1980	3,730	Korea 1938	484
Denmark 1937	3,254	Manchukuo 1938	394
Netherlands 1937	3,221		
Belgium 1937	2,829		
Norway 1937	2,676		
France 1937	2,586		
Czechoslovakia 1937	1,948		

Sources: Figures for 1980 from Paul Marer, *Dollar GNPs of the U.S.S.R. and Eastern Europe* (Baltimore: Johns Hopkins Press for the World Bank, 1985). Interwar figures from Mark Harrison, "GDPs of the USSR and Eastern Europe: Towards an Interwar Comparison," *Europe-Asia Studies* 46, no. 2 (1994): 248, 253, and Angus Maddison, *The World Economy in the 20th Century* (Paris: OECD, 1989), appendices B and C. Japanese Empire figures from Toshiyuki Mizoguchi and Mataji Umemura, *Basic Economic Statistics of Former Japanese Colonies, 1895–1938* (Tokyo: Toyo Keizai Shinposha, 1988), 231–39, and Kang Chao, *The Economic Development of Manchuria*, Michigan Papers in Chinese Studies, no. 43 (Ann Arbor: Center for Chinese Studies, University of Michigan, 1983), 34, and interpolated to 1980 dollars using Maddison, *World Economy in the 20th Century*, appendices A, B, C. Pre-World War I Belgium figures based on ibid. Pre-World War I Luxembourg based on Robert Summers and Alan Heston, "A New Set of International Comparisons of Real Product and Price Levels Estimates for 130 Countries, 1950–1985," *Review of Income and Wealth* 34, no. 1 (March 1988): 16, and Grand Duchy of Luxembourg, Ministère de l'Économie, *Statistiques historiques, 1839–1989* (Luxembourg: Service Central de la Statistique et des Études Économiques, 1990), 102.

last variable (due to the interest in industrial societies), some additional less-developed cases are also briefly considered.

It is also useful to examine nations long subjugated but not intensively exploited, for these should shed additional light on whether conquest does in fact strangle industrial productivity. Conquerors often refrain from full-tilt exploitation, which would harm local economic growth. When confident of peace, all rulers decrease extraction rates in order to fatten their domain and increase the total economic capacity that can be milked later in time of war.[58] The examples studied here are the Japanese Empire and the Soviet–East European Empire. (Now that archives in the former Soviet Union are opening, important evidence on the "domestic" Soviet empire may soon come to light as well.) Japan prior to 1941 and the Soviet Union during most of the cold war were attempting to build up their colonies and satellites, although the significance of these episodes is weakened by a low level of development in the former and the inefficient economic policies in the latter.

The small number of episodes involving industrial empires—most colonies achieved independence before becoming industrialized—necessitates careful comparison among cases.[59] Examining cases in depth makes it possible to use actors' perceptions and motivations to corroborate the hypotheses that appear to be supported by economic data. Careful analysis is also necessary to assess how imperial profits are affected by coincidental or external factors. No one imagines that it can be profitable to conquer any economy ruined by invasion, scorched-earth measures, stupid occupation policies, or military and economic warfare waged by third parties. Conversely, one would expect greater profits from countries with ideological "fifth-columns" predisposed to collaboration. Careful, structured case-study analysis can help control for such idiosyncratic factors.

Finally, for source material I rely almost entirely on the substantial body of published historical research on empires and occupations. Statistics and studies produced by governmental agencies are also used, in some cases requiring archival research. But my goal here is not to unearth new historical facts, but instead to test generalizations through comparative analysis. This approach was necessitated by the number of countries and periods analyzed here, but there remains much to be learned about the questions raised here by further historical research.

A ROAD MAP

Before proceeding to these cases, it is essential to identify the conditions that affect the profitability of conquest. The next chapter reviews the arguments that have been advanced to support the claim that the conquest of modern societies is economically futile, and shows that theories of coercion, collective action, and basic facts about modernization predict just the opposite.

Chapters 3 through 7 are devoted to historical episodes of occupation and conquest, in an effort to measure the profitability of conquest and to test these contending hypotheses. Nazi-occupied Western Europe is analyzed first, because it provides several very well documented cases of the occupation and attempted exploitation of relatively modern and nationalistic nations. This chapter finds strong evidence that ruthless conquerors can reap large short-term profits. Comparisons among the cases and with some other Nazi-occupied countries also support the hypothesis that modernization increases exploitability, and help rule out alternative explanations for collaboration, such as ideological predispositions. The next two chapters turn to the German occupation of Belgium and Luxembourg during World War I and to the Franco-Belgian occupation of the Ruhr in 1923–24. In both episodes the outcomes were mixed, but the difference between success and failure was determined by the amount of coercion—specifically, economic coercion—the occupiers were able to apply. These chapters provide further evidence that conquest can pay, but they show that coercion is a necessary condition.

The final two chapters investigate additional questions. Since the Japanese sought to fatten rather than exploit their possessions until the outbreak of World War II (when economic data is too vague to measure resource flows), the case of the Japanese Empire is most useful for examining the efficiency with which empires can maintain economic development and political control in subjugated nations over the long term. The Soviet–East European Empire is analyzed in the final case-study chapter for the same purpose, but it also provides an additional example of the economic mobilization of an occupied industrial economy—Soviet reparations from East Germany, 1945–53. The evidence these chapters provide on long-term profitability is not entirely conclusive. Japan's experiment in imperial development was derailed by World War II, and the Soviet experiment was distorted by inefficient centralized planning. Still, the imperial growth and pacification in these cases further support the view that industrial economies are cumulative.

CHAPTER 2

When Does Conquest Pay?

UNDERSTANDING WHY and under what conditions conquest pays requires a theory about the sources of resistance and collaboration. This is because the behavior of conquered peoples greatly influences the revenues and collection costs of empire. Resistance—whether by whole nations, administrative agencies, political parties, unions, and businesses, or by individual workers, technicians, scientists, bureaucrats, and all other citizens—reduces revenues and imposes costs. But if a conquered nation collaborates fully with the invader, then it can be taxed and mobilized as efficiently as a loyal ally or province, and the cumulativity of resources will be 100 percent.

Resistance can reduce extraction rates and cumulativity either by withholding or by reducing a society's economic surplus. Mobile capital can usually be plundered by occupation armies with minimal collaboration. But loot is a one-time gain and making conquest pay for any length of time requires exploiting continued production. A nation could theoretically maintain economic production but refuse to pay tribute or to sell goods and services to the invaders. Failing that option, it could still frustrate a conqueror's economic goals by suppressing its own production, whether by strikes, self-sabotage, deliberate slowdowns, Schweikan bumbling, or even a devolution to subsistence farming. Imperial costs are also affected by resistance. Guerrilla warfare and assassination draw blood and necessitate more expensive imperial police forces, and even nonviolent refusal to obey the invader's political demands would increase the invaders administrative expenses.[1]

Regardless of a nation's attitude, potential extraction rates depend on its level of economic development. Rich countries have big purses, while undeveloped economies by definition produce little more than what they need to keep them going. Consider the fact that Americans on average produce about $11,404 per year in goods and services, while Ethiopians produce only $325.[2] Wealth increases the amount of resources states can tax from their societies, whether to pay for highways or battleships. Even the strongest twelfth-century states could not mobilize 2 percent of GNP; by World War II, Britain could spend nearly 50 percent of GNP on the war alone.[3]

But whether the great wealth generated by modern industrial societies can be harnessed by conquerors depends on whether the vanquished peoples resist or collaborate. Believers in the cumulativity of resources have made little effort to show that collaboration is inevitable. Quagmire theorists, at least, have argued that nationalism provides a strong motive for resistance, and that socioeconomic development provides opportunities. But although nationalism is a powerful desire, coercion and repression sharply limit the opportunities for popular resistance by modern societies. Theories of coercion and of collective action, developed and tested in research on international and domestic politics, explain why.

This chapter begins by exploring how nationalism and other domestic political circumstances influence the preferences of vanquished populations. Theories of coercion and collective action are then used to infer hypotheses about the effects of coercion, repression, and development on the likelihood and intensity of resistance and collaboration. Hypothesized effects of time, size, and trade patterns will also be investigated, followed by a discussion of how claims about the profitability of conquest can be tested.

HYPOTHESES ON RESISTANCE AND COLLABORATION

Nationalism

Nationalism is the main obstacle to the exploitation of conquered societies. The desire to be governed by members of one's own culture entails hatred of foreign domination and provides a potent motivation for political and economic resistance. Robert Gilpin claims that "the imperial game of territorial conquest for the sake of exploitation [was] discovered by Napoleonic France to be costly in an age of nationalism," while Richard Rosecrance thinks that it was only in the nineteenth century that nationalism had become sufficiently virulent to make foreign rule impracticable.[4] Nationalism can also occur in developing, pre-industrial societies; indeed, the insurrections against foreign empires and intervening powers in less developed countries like Algeria and Vietnam seem to have been the original inspiration for postwar writers' doubts about the profitability of conquest. As Knorr points out, "The French required only thirty thousand men to subdue Algeria in 1830. In 1962, they could not subdue her with a force twenty times as large."[5] But all students of nationalism agree that this political ideology is inherent in modern industrial societies and is nearly impossible to eradicate once it has taken root.

Nationalism is associated with level of development for several reasons. Peasants living in small, isolated, agrarian communities that speak local dialects have little stake in the cultural credentials of far-off rulers. But these communities dissolve as industrializing states provide mass education to create a basically literate and numerate workforce, while the population seeks education to compete for the growing number of factory and service jobs in growing urban areas. Because they depend on their proficiency in a shared culture for economic advancement, citizens of modernizing and modern societies prefer rulers who share and thus will protect their language and other traits subject to discrimination.[6] The increasing scale and complexity of modern warfare also leads states to promote literacy and inculcate nationalist loyalties in their populations.[7] Both education and loyalty were essential qualities for building competitive mass armies, from the Napoleonic era onward. Regardless of the original impetus behind increasing literacy and geographical mobility, they further intensify popular demand for mass media and communications, which accelerates the process of cultural standardization.[8]

Conversely, anything that undermined a people's patriotism would also weaken the will to resist. "Fifth columns"—a term used to describe the greatly exaggerated saboteurs within nations hostile to Nazi Germany—motivated by nationalistic or ideological affinity to the invaders might provide a corps of ready collaborators. Nationalism is the stronger of the forces, and there is much more evidence of foreign invasions supported by national irredenta than of those supported by other ideological movements. But the prominent role of ideological quislings in both Nazi-occupied Western Europe and Soviet-occupied Eastern Europe makes plausible the notion that certain political predispositions may facilitate collaboration.[9]

Even where there is no faction predisposed toward collaboration, discord among and within subordinate nations may undermine the solidarity needed for resistance and help the invaders "divide and rule."[10] For example, Nazi threats to hand over Serbian lands to Croatia, which was certainly willing to absorb them, reportedly had persuasive effect with the Serbian puppet regime during World War II. On the other hand, a history of conflict between ethnic or ideological factions would have honed organizational and fighting skills that could be turned against a common enemy. Thus the Chinese communists and nationalists set aside their long quarrel in 1936 in order to combat the Japanese, Germany failed to play Flemish and francophone Belgians off each other during both world wars, and Tito managed to combine Croats, Serbs, and Muslims in his anti-Nazi partisan forces. In cases of foreign domination, nationalists—even those of different ideological or ethnic stripe—usually recognize the invaders as the chief obstacle to their treasured autonomy.

Coercion and Repression

Coercion is the use of demands and threats to persuade a target—whether a state, a social group, or an individual—that resistance is more costly than compliance. Its effectiveness depends on the perceived capability and resolve of the bully for inflicting harm and on how much suffering the target is willing to endure rather than give in. Thus the capabilities and resolve of both sides are important to the outcome. The logic of coercion, supported by research on threats in international and domestic politics, suggests that ruthless conquerors should be able to compel the political and economic collaboration of defeated societies at low cost.

In models of international bargaining, coercion by the ruthless and strong should be easy against the militarily weak, who can neither protect their populations from harm nor retaliate.[11] Although sovereign nations generally ally against threatening states, weak and vulnerable ones often jump on the bandwagon of aggressors.[12] Defeated and occupied nations are the most weak and vulnerable of all; unsurprisingly, Thomas Schelling begins his textbook analysis of interstate coercion by recounting the pacification methods of an ancient Persian conqueror.[13] Because a prolonged struggle means devastation to the subjects but not to the conqueror, the latter usually has better leverage. Of course, greater resolve can compensate for lesser capabilities. Physical vulnerability is irrelevant to those, like the Israelites at Masada and the Melians against Athens, who prefer death to foreign domination and exploitation. But when survival ranks as a higher priority than sovereignty and prosperity, collaboration is likely.

Bargaining models in international relations theory generally assume that nations are unitary, rational actors. This is useful for analyzing intraimperial relations to the extent that institutions, social groups, and individuals in defeated societies behave as if they are motivated by the national interest. "Satellite" or "puppet" regimes can fit this description. While some may act out of opportunistic, class-based, ideological, or other narrow interests, patriotic officials, bureaucrats, and civil servants will worry about the harm to their societies that resistance could incur.[14] When conquerors threaten public goods such as national treasures, public buildings, transportation services, or other shared economic, social, and moral values, collaboration is often the lesser evil for the nation as a whole.

But when stripped of legitimate governments, defeated nations behave less like unitary actors and more like groups and individuals seeking to promote their own self-interests. Threats can still be effective, but they must be targeted against these disparate groups and actors rather than against the nation as a whole. Most research on the causes of domestic rebellion suggests that coercion succeeds on this level as well. While the leading theories of the 1960s and early 1970s stressed economic and psychological discontent,[15] these theories failed to explain the fact that history is full of unhappy, frustrated, and oppressed peoples who fail to rebel.

In contrast, "resource-mobilization" researchers have shown that resistance is a purposive political activity, which occurs only when social contenders have enough political resources relative to the state to provide a good chance of success.[16] States that are highly repressive—that is, that institutionalize coercion through brutally enforced antiresistance decrees—face very low levels of resistance.[17] Throughout history, the eruption of rebellion and revolution has typically followed the emergence of cracks in state coercive power, resulting from lack of resolve, defeat in war, or governmental divisions.[18] Studies of modern authoritarian regimes report that "no transition can be forced purely by opponents against a regime which maintains the cohesion, capacity, and disposition to apply repression."[19] Nationalism would generate greater political hostility than these independent autocracies typically face. But this research demonstrates that hostility does not always result in politically and economically effective resistance.

Resource-mobilization theorists assume that rebellious groups act rationally on the basis of an unspecified combination of private *and* public costs and benefits. But if individuals are motivated exclusively, or even mainly, by private costs and benefits, the likelihood of collective action diminishes greatly. When public goods—that is, goods that many others will share regardless of whether they help provide it—require many contributors to be realized, rational, self-interested individuals will not pay their share.[20] Those who cannot change things with their own actions, and who will enjoy the fruits of change whether they try or not, have little incentive to try. Thus when national liberation requires widespread action, this "free-rider problem" will result in levels of resistance far lower than the national interest would predict. Since the expected private benefits of resistance are small, the private costs need not be very high for individuals to prefer shirking, no matter how fervently they desire national liberation.

The free-rider problem can be surmounted by governments, unions, underground resistance movements, or close-knit communities that reward participation and punish free riding, in other words, that provide selective incentives. Government officials in defeated countries are never permitted to organize resistance, although they can use selective incentives to motivate collaboration. In small, close-knit communities, social sanctions against defectors facilitate collective action, explaining the importance of cohesive villages in peasant rebellions and revolutions.[21] Absent such communities, opposition organizations are essential for distributing selective incentives.[22] This explains the importance of organizations to mobilizing resistance, which has been long recognized by revolutionary organizers and the regimes trying to extirpate them, as well as by resource-mobilization theorists.[23] Of course, organizations do more than just provide selective incentives; by coordinating people with diverse skills and resources, they also increase each individual's effectiveness.

If all individuals were motivated purely by narrow self-interest, collective action would be virtually nonexistent, because organizations and communities can rarely outbid the state in the provision of selective incentives. Nationalism is alien to the thinking of true egoists, who will take no action unless the rewards outweigh the costs and risks. But many people are motivated to some degree by common goals or a sense of personal integrity, with the strength of these motivations varying among different individuals. Combined with the fact that there is power and safety in numbers, this explains why a "critical mass" of participants is often needed to spark widespread collective action.[24] A small revolt by the most patriotic may convince the next most patriotic that the public and private benefits of rebellion now exceed the costs. Repressive regimes aim to preclude critical masses from developing; if they are successful, resistance will remain very low.

What can be deduced from theory and research on coercion and collective action about the profitability of conquest? First, the conqueror's capability and resolve to inflict harm increases collaboration and the profitability of conquest and empire. Since there is almost always a great imbalance of coercive resources between victors and conquered countries, resolve is the key variable. Because threats alone are cheap, if the conqueror's resolve is so obvious that no one dares test it, costly and destructive reprisals can be employed sparingly. The costs of surveillance then exceed those of force. As Schelling put it, "A well-behaved occupied country . . . may be one in which latent violence is used so skillfully that it need not be spent in punishment."[25]

Few conquerors are constrained by moral reservations, but some have worried about the reactions of other powers to their cruelty. Deterring and suppressing resistance also requires loyal officials and military forces who will not flinch at carrying out brutal and morally repugnant policies. Military defection has played an important role in domestic revolutions, but armies are more apt to sympathize with their own compatriots than with foreign subjects. Modern occupation armies have had little difficulty in maintaining their own internal discipline; indeed, some have engaged in wanton atrocities and genocide involving cruelties far exceeding those needed for pacification and exploitation.

Second, targeting the membership and especially the leadership of independent societal organizations is an especially efficient use of repression. If the motivation and multiplier effect supplied by organizations are absent, the private expected benefits of individual resistance actions will be small, and tyrants will not need to make the expected private costs of resistance actions very high. Thus resistance will be minimized, if conquerors supervise all independent associations and suppress any showing signs of opposition activity, including unions or relief organizations that could feed striking workers and their families.

Indigenous administrative institutions represent a special case, because they can be useful for maintaining the political and economic order necessary if conquest is to be profitable. By putting their local expertise and authority at the service of a conqueror, collaborating administrators facilitate the imperial policing and taxing of their own countries. But the value to the conqueror of these services enables puppet regimes to bargain for greater rights and living standards. In addition, the conqueror must monitor indigenous administrations closely to prevent them from fomenting rebellious collective action. Greater loyalty with less monitoring is feasible with direct rule through colonial administrators or, in hybrid cases, through combinations of traitorous quislings and conscientious civil-servants, but only at a cost of lower expertise and legitimacy.

Third, expectations of liberation—for example, if the occupier is embroiled in a closely fought international war—can heighten resistance and reduce collaboration. Conversely, the apparent hopelessness of liberation increases collaboration at the expense of resistance. This is due partly to the fact that the national and individual consequences of resistance or collaboration depend on who will be ruling just over the horizon. The feasibility of liberation also affects the potential contribution of resistance. For example, if the occupier is embroiled in a closely fought international war, resistance that would otherwise appear futile might appear just damaging enough to tip the balance in favor of friendlier powers. But an increasing marginal effectiveness for individual resistance still will rarely make resistance a cost-effective choice for most individuals. And if liberation appears inevitable, whether because the occupier is about to be defeated in war or has credibly committed to withdrawal, resistance becomes unnecessary.

Finally, coercion is most cost-effective in resource extraction when combined with low cost, positive incentives for collaboration. Expropriating a nation's entire surplus leaves it little incentive to produce more than subsistence. But if only a fixed percentage or amount of production is taken, the nation has an incentive to maintain productivity. Assuming that boycotts can be prevented, nations would have to deny themselves the economic fruits of their own activity in order to deny them to the conqueror. The population would face the harshest consequences of its own self-sabotage, strikes, and slowdowns. It is thus unsurprising that the greatest self-sabotage in history, scorched-earth retreats by Tsar Alexander before Napoleon's onslaught and by Stalin before Hitler's, was committed not by occupied societies but by retreating rulers.

The same logic applies even more at the micro level, where surveillance and the application of force is more costly. Plundering households and businesses at gunpoint takes vast physical force for marginal material gain; the transaction costs involved in such crude exploitation are extremely great. For the same reason, slavery is also inefficient for most modern kinds of production.[26] As Robert Dahl argues, "compulsion and coercion are often damaging to incentives. In an advanced economy, long-run performance under threat or coercion is less productive at all levels than a more willing performance based on voluntary compliance."[27] But when tribute is used to buy goods and services from a conqueror's new subjects, ordinary exchange replaces coercion as the mechanism of exploitation. Successful conquerors are more like bank robbers than cat burglars; instead of going door-to-door, they extort tribute from defeated regimes, residual finance ministries, or national banks. A conqueror who preserves the market becomes just another customer with a great deal of cash, which is no less enticing for being ill-gotten.

When individual productivity and willingness to deal with the conqueror are rewarded through normal market mechanisms, obtaining economic collaboration does not require holding a gun to everyone's head. Strikes, sabotage, boycotts, and foot-dragging by individual firms and workers, unless supported by strike pay or relief networks, involve at a minimum lost private income. Free-riding individuals will value that private income over the marginal contribution of their resistance to liberation. Even if it is in their national interest to resist, firms will compete for profits and workers will compete for salaries. Coercion can stimulate competition further, and at low cost, by adding selective threats to pillage the least productive firms or to conscript the least productive workers for forced labor.

Modernization

The effects of modernization on the cumulativity of resources are complex and controversial. Modernization level refers to a variety of intercorrelated socioeconomic features, including urbanization, literacy, proportion of nonagricultural labor, radios or telephones per capita, and GNP per capita, the latter being the most commonly used single measure. Quagmire theorists contend that modern societies are uniquely indigestible, not only because they are inherently nationalistic but also because industrialization increases civil society's bargaining leverage against authoritarian regimes. But basic observations about modernization, illuminated by theories of coercion and collective action, suggest otherwise. Because modernization of conqueror and conquered increase the efficiency of coercion and repression, modern economies are cumulative resources for ruthless expansionists.

Modernization increases conquerors' bargaining leverage in several ways. In contests of violence, modern societies have little chance because development usually centralizes control over coercive resources and always facilitates the quick deployment of this power over large regions. Tyrants can more easily monopolize coercive resources within their borders because the division of labor in modern societies grants the state a real monopoly on violence, legitimate or not.[28] In the eighteenth century, a population armed with rifles, like the American colonists, could do considerable damage to an occupying army. But after centuries of relying entirely on their state to protect them, from criminals as well as from conquerors, ordinary people's skills and tools for violence have not kept pace with those of modern militaries, police, and paramilitary forces. Artillery, machine guns, armored vehicles, and explosives are for obvious reasons difficult to obtain and to produce clandestinely. Unless weapons and training are supplied externally, modern societies will be unable to impose high costs on conquerors.

In addition, the ease of communication and transportation in modern societies allows tyrants to use their coercive resources efficiently.[29] One of the chief obstacles to imperial expansion throughout history has been the difficulty of collecting information and projecting power (the "loss-of-strength gradient") over long distances and natural barriers. But modern communication links and technologies, urbanization, roads, and mechanized means of transport facilitate the surveillance and sanctioning of resistance. As Morgenthau observed shortly after World War II, "Today the government of a world empire, appraised . . . by radio, would send within a few hours a squadron of bombers and a score of transports loaded with parachutists, mortars, and tanks, weapons of which it has a monopoly or near monopoly, to the revolting city and squelch the revolt with ease."[30] Evidence for this is provided by studies of guerrilla warfare, which typically conclude that modern societies, and particularly urban areas, do not provide a hospitable environment for armed resistance.[31] As a result, modern despots can economize on the administrative bureaucracies and police forces they disperse throughout their dominions.

It is one thing to bring overwhelming force to bear efficiently throughout an empire, but quite another to sustain and mobilize continued economic life. Quagmire theorists believe that modern societies can not be compelled to surrender their surpluses. This is possible, according to Rosecrance, because "highly developed economies are much more dependent upon social cooperation and obedience to the rulers of the state than are primitive or transitional economic systems."[32] International relations theorists may have borrowed this idea from theories of democratization. Dahl's *Polyarchy* contends that "economic development itself generates the conditions of a pluralistic social order," in part because advanced economies "automatically distribute political resources and political skills to a vast variety of individuals, groups, and organizations."[33] Highly trained workers "can refuse to use their skills," according to Robert Bates, "leaving governments that have invested in their education with a declining economy."[34] With a hostile workforce, preventing sabotage and slack working requires considerable attention and expertise. High information costs necessitate costly supervision.[35] Productivity may fall from demoralization in addition to deliberate resistance. A worker's efficiency is motivated not only by his or her pay but also by personal identification with the job, especially in sophisticated tasks and after his or her salary has reached the point of diminishing returns.[36] Thus one economist concludes that "seizing gold, rubber, minerals, lumber, or other natural resources must be surely less costly than enlisting sufficient cooperation from an enslaved population to produce electronic parts, computer programs, or reliable transportation."[37]

This picture, however, ignores the fact that most conquerors can manipulate sanctions and incentives so completely that societies will see collaboration as the best policy. Rich nations have centralized financial institutions, providing easy targets for the equivalent of bank robbery on a national scale. Their very wealth provides an additional hostage for compliance, and thus greater vulnerability to coercion. While all conquerors can resort to the age-old terror tactics of murder, rape, and slavery, cunning ones can also threaten modern societies' plentiful industrial capital, national treasures, or consumer goods and services. Modernization provides a wide range of vulnerable and highly valued property and services that can be threatened by administrative mismanagement, not to mention deliberate reprisals. Social collaboration is essential to modern productivity, but this only means that defeated societies will collaborate when their welfare depends on it.

It is conceivable that a subject society could be so dedicated to resistance that it would be willing to abandon all wealth and consumption beyond that needed for raw survival, just to deny its economic surplus to the invader. But the high degree of specialization and interdependence within modern national economies make it generally impossible for nations to revert to subsistence production. Modern urban workers do not have backyard gardens to fall back on, and the ingrained division between industrial and agricultural production in modern societies makes a return to the land difficult even without the interference of a repressive conqueror. To avoid starvation, labor in industry, services, and commercial agriculture must either produce for the market or collect unemployment relief.[38] The latter is possible only under unusual circumstances (see chapters 4 and 5); when relief distribution is suppressed, modern societies must work or starve.

Modernization has complex effects on free-riding. Although modern societies lack the socially cohesive communities that can support collective action, urbanization and infrastructure facilitate the formation of opposition organizations. As Marx and Engels argued in *The Communist Manifesto*, "the improved means of communication that are created by modern industry and that place the workers of different localities in contact with one another" are essential "to centralize the numerous local struggles, all of the same character, into one national struggle between classes."[39] But urbanization and infrastructure also enhance state surveillance and policing capabilities.[40] In addition to allowing tyrants to rapidly extinguish outbreaks of active defiance, as mentioned above, a modern communications infrastructure also facilitates the repression of underground organizations and of crowds. Thus while modern societies have a high *potential* for collective action, repression is also more efficient.

Some theorists have argued that as societies continue to develop, their communication infrastructures tend to give greater advantages to the opponents of authoritarian rule. According to Stephen Van Evera, the productivity of highly developed societies depends on free access to information, which in turn "requires a free domestic press, and access to foreign publications, foreign travel, personal computers, and photocopiers." Since the repression needed to maintain political control requires banning these "critical elements of the economic fabric," foreign domination impoverishes modern "information" economies.[41] But while modern economies undoubtedly depend on communication, few economically important practices and technologies are inherently subversive. It is conceivable that despotic regimes could promote the communication of economic and scientific data while suppressing political organization and dissent. Moreover, the subversive potential of information technologies must be weighed against their contribution to state surveillance. Bar codes, magnetic stripes, miniature microphones, video cameras, and computerized data banks—if not photocopiers—all have more Orwellian than libertarian applications. Thus information dependence does not have a strong effect on the cumulativity of highly developed economies.

Size, Time, and Trade

In discussions of the profitability of conquest, other factors have been suggested to constrain the cumulativity of resources: size, time, and lost trade. Regarding size, some argue that the expansion and durability of all great powers is governed by a U-shaped cost curve.[42] Growth is initially facilitated by positive returns to scale in political control and economic extraction, but eventually the marginal costs of further expansion exceed the marginal benefits. This curve results partly from the reaction of balancing coalitions but also from such internal factors as the geographical loss-of-strength gradient and the administrative difficulty of governing and exploiting numerous hostile peoples.

Time also works against empires and great powers, it is sometimes argued. Gilpin provides two reasons.[43] First, the economic, technological, and organizational skills of the conqueror tend to diffuse to the conquered, increasing the latter's relative power. Second, domestic pressures lead the dominant nation to consume rather than invest the fruits of victory, and this newfound affluence corrodes its martial and industrial spirit.

Although made plausible by the rise and decline of empires and great powers throughout history, these hypotheses lack a strong deductive basis when applied to the modern era. It has already been pointed out that modernization has decreased the costs of power projection and information collection, greatly reducing if not eliminating this element of the U-shaped cost curve. Moreover, the diffusion of economic and other skills from the dominant nation would not weaken its grip as long as it continued to monopolize coercive resources and to apply repression. Tendencies toward administrative inefficiency, decadence, or internal political liberalization that undermined the dominant nation's ruthlessness and administrative integrity would certainly diminish the cumulativity of resources and the viability of empire. But the likelihood and pace of these processes remain poorly understood.

Trade effects are another source of imperial gain or loss worth considering. To the extent that conquest hampers productivity and growth, opportunity costs from foregone trade may arise. If the withering colonies would otherwise have traded freely with the conqueror, then conquerors lose the gains from trade and investment that they would have enjoyed had they opted for peace over aggression. Quagmire theorists often claim that opportunity costs are a major liability of conquest. Rosecrance, for example, writes that after the Industrial Revolution "there was no sense in using military force to acquire power and wealth when they could be obtained more efficiently through peaceful economic development and trade."[44] However, much of the force of this argument is based on two sorts of external costs, war costs and loss of trade outside imperial dominions.

Even those gains and losses resulting from intra-imperial trade are still partly external because they depend on the likelihood that each conquered nation would have raised barriers in the absence of conquest. If an open trading system can be assumed, then conquest results in opportunity costs from lost trade with the withering colonies. But if a closed system is assumed, then conquerors reap positive gains from trade. Conquest assures access to markets and resources that might otherwise be curtailed by trade barriers, and even weak economies can make better trading partners than protectionist ones. In fact, some modern expansionists have been motivated almost exclusively by the desire for autarky, and hardly at all for imperial tribute.[45]

These hypotheses about size, time, and trade will not be systematically analyzed in this book for several reasons. Vagueness about the point in size and time where economies of scale end and the marginal costs mount makes testing virtually impossible, especially with the mostly brief occupations and empires examined here. The value of the internal gains and losses in trade are overlooked because they too are likely to emerge over long periods of time, with the gradual accumulation of low growth rates. In addition, these gains and losses cannot be conceptualized or measured independently of external factors, and thus they depend not only on cumulativity of resources but on the expected future likelihood, intensity, and duration of war and trade barriers.[46]

To sum up, the cumulativity of resources depends mainly on whether conquered populations resist or collaborate. Cumulativity is diminished to the extent that resistance withholds revenues, undermines productivity, and/or increases collection costs. It is also reduced if the repression needed to combat resistance also harms productivity. The hypothesized causes of resistance and economic stagnation, some supporting the quagmire view and others supporting the resources-are-cumulative view, are summarized in table 2-1.

If nationalism and modernization cause resistance and inherently reduce economic performance, as the quagmire theorists claim, then industrial economies can never be very cumulative. But if coercion and repression work and are efficient against modern societies, then industrial economies are highly cumulative, although only if the conqueror is ruthless.

Even then, however, they are not likely to be fully cumulative. However efficient, coercion and repression still involve a permanent economic drain that free nations do not suffer. Furthermore, although the theory of collective action assumes a rational, self-interested population, most soci-

TABLE 2-1
Hypotheses on Resistance and Productivity

Quagmire Hypotheses

1. Nationalism causes political hostility, which causes resistance and lowers productivity.

2. Modernization increases resistance, especially in economic and administrative sectors dependent on highly skilled workers.

3. Repression reduces productivity, especially in modern, communication-dependent economies

Coercion Hypotheses

1. Coercion (implicit or explicit threats of reprisals) against societies and repression (institutionalized coercion against individuals) decrease resistance.

2. The efficiency of coercion and repression in suppressing resistance and eliciting collaboration are enhanced by the:

    i. subjects lack of coercive resources

    ii. banning of opposition organizations and crowds

    iii. apparent ruthlessness of the conqueror

    iv. apparent permanence of the conquest

    v. use of low-cost incentives for collaboration

3. Modernization does not increase the costs of the coercion, repression, and administration needed for control and exploitation.

4. Coercion and repression do not reduce productivity, as long as incentives for efficient production are preserved.

Time, Size, and Trade Hypotheses

1. At some stage, political and social change in the conquering state and the diffusion of its skills increase resistance.

2. At a certain point, declining returns to scale in power-projection and administration increase resistance.

3. Conquest provides trading gains if captured societies remain productive and if there otherwise would have been high barriers to international trade. Conversely, conquest results in trading losses if captured societies decline economically and if there otherwise would have been low barriers to international trade.

---

eties have an unknown share of irrational and ultrapatriotic citizens ready to sacrifice their lives to impose costs on a conqueror. These factors reduce the performance, and certainly reduce the growth rates, of conquered economies.

CONCEPTUAL AND MEASUREMENT ISSUES

A few definitions are needed for analyzing the cumulativity of resources. Imperial profits can be defined as extracted resources less the costs of administration and repression. All extorted current output of goods and services should be counted as "extracted resources," not just arms and munitions. Economic resources are fungible, and everything extracted from occupied societies that would otherwise have to be produced in the conqueror's economy frees up labor, raw materials, and plant for military purposes. Plundered loot, even of great value to the conqueror, is a one-time gain that damages local productivity and should be considered separately. Resources are easiest to measure when they are purchased with tribute payments, although adjustments must be made for inflation and black-market purchases.[47] In some empires, such as Japan's, resources were extracted through hundreds of private and state investments; although a concerted research effort would produce important results, this study falls back on less precise surrogate measures.[48] Finally, the value of autarky is also set aside, for it depends on counterfactual assumptions about the openness of the trading system.

Measuring imperial costs involves a difficult double-counting problem. Occupation armies, though not administrators and police, often have external as well as internal roles. While they are sometimes used for pacification, they typically spend much of their time training, defending borders from outside attack, or preparing for further expansion. Since occupation armies (or even those simply nearby) can serve two purposes, the apportionment of their cost is somewhat arbitrary. Because their mere presence has a deterrent effect on would-be rebels, the fact that an army devotes only one tenth of its energies to pacification does not mean that an army one tenth the size could control the same territory. On the other hand, to the extent these armies are able to leave or fight external foes, their local deterrent effect might be considered a free side-benefit of strategic deployments and might not involve any internal cost at all. Thus measuring the costs of occupation armies requires analyzing their internal and external roles.

Extraction rates compare net profits to local economic potential. Economic potential should be used rather than actual output levels, so that declining productivity is not concealed. For example, a conqueror mobilizing 50 percent of a nation's current GNP is not doing very well if resistance and repression have reduced production by 90 percent. Based on economic potential, the extraction rate is only 5 percent, a figure more relevant to resource cumulativity. In the case of shrinking productivity, a workable measure for a nation's economic potential is its preconquest national income.[49]

Resource cumulativity compares the extraction rates achieved in conquered nations to the military mobilization rates of comparable, independent nations. For establishing a benchmark for complete mobilization, military spending rates in total warfare are the most relevant figures. Since maximum extraction rates increase with development, the benchmark should be based on rates achieved by countries at the same

TABLE 2-2

World War II Mobilization of the United States, Britain, Germany, and Italy
(Percentage of Wartime and 1939 National Income)

	United States		Britian		Germany		Italy	
	Current	Prewar	Current	Prewar	Current	Prewar	Current	Prewar
1939	2	2	8	8	24	24	12	12
1940	3	3	31	36	36	36	25	25
1941	14	18	41	50	44	45	35	35
1942	40	55	43	53	52	55	36	35
1943	53	79	47	60	60	70	44	40
1944	54	82	47	56	—	—	—	—

Sources: Mark Harrison, "Resource Mobilization for World War II," *Economic History Review*, 2d ser., 41 (1988): 184–85; Vera Zamagni, *The Economic History of Italy, 1860–1990* (Oxford: Clarendon Press, 1993), 255; Brian R. Mitchell, *International Historical Statistics: Europe, 1750–1988*, 3d ed. (New York: Stockton Press, 1992), table J1.

Note: Net national product at factor cost, except for Italian income, measured at market prices.

stage of development as the conquered nations. Even among equally modern countries, however, considerable variation occurs due to complex political and economic conditions (see table 2-2). During World War II, for example, Britain mobilized an average of 51 percent of prewar national income (1940–44), Germany averaged 52 percent (1940–43), the United States averaged 72 percent (1942–44), while Italy averaged only 34 percent (1940–43). Because the mobilization process increased total economic output in Britain, Germany, and especially the United States, their mobilization as a proportion of prewar income was higher than current mobilization. The U.S. case is rather extraordinary, due to the fact that war mobilization snapped the economy out of the Depression. This effect was less pronounced in Germany and Italy, both of which had started rearming earlier and had already recovered fully from the Depression. Italian GNP, moreover, declined 12 percent between 1939 and 1942, explaining its lower mobilization as a proportion of prewar income.[50] Despite the cross-national and longitudinal variation in mobilization rates, such data provides a ballpark range for assessing resource cumulativity.

The data on net profits is often inadequate to draw a balance sheet. In such cases, other measures of collaboration and resistance must be used as surrogate measures for the dependent variable. For instance, evidence of continued productivity and low guerrilla resistance imply high profit, extraction rate, and resource cumulativity, while assassinations, riots, rebellions, sabotage, strikes, boycotts, and declining productivity suggest the opposite.

The main causal variables explored in the case studies are modernization, nationalism, coercion, and repression. Modernization level is most easily measured by GNP per capita, although other features relevant to the model, such as urbanization, should also be considered. Nationalism can be crudely gauged according to modernization level and linguistic/cultural differences between conqueror and conquered. A tradition of nationalistic education and propaganda, used to generate support for military service, is also likely to increase nationalistic fervor.

Measuring coercion with precision is difficult, because threats can be implicit as well as explicit. In addition, the wide variety of hostages and reprisals—ranging from killing, burning, or pillaging to decrees that all boycotting businesses will be shut down ("work for the conqueror or don't work at all")—do not lend themselves to simple measurement. Repression is a generally recognizable form of coercion, because the "criminalization" of opposition activity requires publicized decrees and laws. Sanctions can range from the denial of educational and professional opportunities to imprisonment, torture, and execution. But the level of coercion and repression depends on the chances of being caught as well as the severity of the sanctions. If surveillance is so effective that most resisters are apprehended, use of physical violence may be quite rare, even though coercion and repression are very high. Although precise quantitative measures are difficult to establish, it is possible to make rough qualitative assessments (for example, whether all opposition organizations are banned) and to detect changes in the overall level of threat.

The case studies attempt to demonstrate a relationship between coercion, repression, and modernization, on the one hand, and the cumulativity of resources (and related measures), on the other. The primarily macrotype data they examine, however, is less well suited to tracing the hypothesized causal mechanisms. In particular, it is difficult to demonstrate the extent of free riding. The best theory-testing research on rational-choice models of revolution has shown that selective-incentive-providing political entrepreneurs or cohesive communities increase the likelihood of rebellious collective action.[51] This is difficult to show for conquered modern societies, where political entrepreneurs are imprisoned and cohesive communities rare. Variations in repression, moreover, change incentives for nations and individuals in the same direction, making it difficult to distinguish macro and micro effects. That said, this study will try to show, at least anecdotally, cases of free riding and collective action that conform to rational-choice theory, which in turn warrant greater pessimism about the profitability of conquest.

Before attempting these measures, each of the case-study chapters begins with an analysis of the invader's aims. This helps establish the economic strategy of the conqueror, which is essential for interpreting each case. Reviewing aims also makes it possible to check whether conquerors believed that conquest paid and whether this was recognized as an incentive for conquest. The debates about containment and defense strategies depend on the reality of the profitability of conquest rather than what states believe about it. But much of the interest in this question arises from its relevance to international peace, and here perceptions matter. Even if conquest did not pay at all, international stability would still suffer if all states still believed it did, just as it suffered from the widespread delusion that the offense was dominant prior to World War I.[52]

CHAPTER 3

Nazi-Occupied Western Europe, 1940–1944

IN THE SPACE of three short years, from 1938 through 1941, Hitler conquered nearly all of Europe. The course of this expansion began with the
annexation of Austria in March 1938 and of the Czech Sudetenland after
Munich. Hitler invaded the Czech rump of Bohemia-Moravia in March
1939, attacked Poland in September, and seized Denmark and Norway in
April 1940. Then, in a victory that stunned the world, the German Army
swept into the Netherlands, Belgium, Luxembourg, and France in May,
losing fewer than one hundred thousand men.[1] Yugoslavia and Greece
were seized in the spring of 1941; in June, Hitler turned on the Soviet
Union, where the tidal wave of conquest was stemmed just short of Moscow. This empire was ruthlessly exploited for years of grinding warfare
against Britain, the Soviet Union, and the United States.

Occupied Western Europe provides a critical test of the view that nationalism and industrialization make conquest economically futile. Before the outbreak of World War II, Norway, Denmark, the Netherlands,
Belgium, France, and the Czech provinces of Bohemia and Moravia had
strong national identities and relatively modern economies.[2] If this view
were correct, conquest should have been an economic disaster for Germany. But Germany succeeded in mobilizing all these societies during the
war. They were compelled to supply tribute and labor, which either directly supported military logistics and operations on the periphery of
Fortress Europe or were funneled into the German war economy. Most
of these countries experienced economic decline, but as a result of continental raw material shortages more than of passive resistance. In addition, expenses for maintaining internal order were remarkably low once
Europe's militaries had been defeated and disarmed. The mere proximity
of troops preparing for battle with the Allies, combined with repression
by German and native collaborating police, effectively deterred active
resistance.

German success was possible only with extensive collaboration by the
native administrative machinery and populations of each occupied country. The commonalities of collaboration throughout occupied Europe,
moreover, suggest that it was not due to idiosyncratic anticommunist or
pro-German predispositions. Rather, Nazi ruthlessness gave Europeans
good reason to believe that collaboration was a lesser evil to resistance,

while economic control provided positive incentives for economic cooperation and productivity. Isolated by repression, firms and workers acted
in their own narrow self-interests, which dictated working for German
orders. The case of Nazi-occupied Western Europe, then, provides strong
evidence that ruthless conquerors can profit, at least in the short term, by
seizing industrial nations.

This chapter does not dwell on the consequences of Nazi domination
outside Western Europe, except for brief comparisons to the Balkans.
Austria is passed over because its cultural and linguistic closeness to the
German Reich makes it a weak test case. Occupied Eastern Europe and
Russia are also poor tests because there Nazi racial ideology dictated
rampant plunder, deportation, enslavement, indiscriminate massacres,
and systematic genocide.[3] Hitler initially ordered that "all attempts to
establish orderly conditions [in Poland] must be avoided; 'Polish chaos'
must be allowed to flourish."[4] Economic exploitation was further im-
paired in the Soviet Union by the Red Army's scorched-earth retreats, but
even the factories found intact were heavily plundered.[5] Of course, the
Nazis also killed 6 million European Jews and 3.3 million Soviet prisoners of war.[6] It is impossible to comment on the material consequences of
these policies without dwelling on the immense human tragedy they
caused. But by destroying potential resources and by making cooperation
no more palatable than resistance, they were also economically self-de-
feating. The "Final Solution" and economic mismanagement reached
into every corner of occupied Europe. But German occupation policy was
far more attuned to the economic requirements of the ongoing war in
Western Europe, and to a lesser extent in Serbia and Greece, than in Eastern Europe.

This chapter first reviews Nazi aims in occupied Europe, showing that
although capturing foreign industrial capacity was not high among
Hitler's initial war priorities, he sought during the war to mobilize it and
planned to keep it following victory. I then assess German profits from
occupied Western Europe, and in the rest of the chapter show that German success depended on level of development, coercion, and repression,
and was constrained primarily by continental coal shortages.

NAZI AIMS IN OCCUPIED EUROPE

Hitler's war was clearly a war of conquest.[7] Rearmament, the restoration
of pre–World War I borders, and the annexation of German-speaking
Austria and Sudetenland appealed to mainstream German aspirations.
For Hitler they were simply preparations for a campaign of unlimited, if
opportunistic, territorial expansion. Hitler's life mission was to make

Germany a world power capable of vying for world dominion. To become a world power, he baldly declared in *Mein Kampf*, Germany had to conquer a vast *Lebensraum* ("living space") that would provide the strategic depth, agricultural lands, and raw materials comparable to those commanded by the United States. Lebensraum would provide Germandom with a geopolitical springboard for further expansion by future generations.

In Hitler's worldview, German power would ultimately rest on the proliferation and spread of the Aryan race rather than on the mobilization of conquered peoples. Soil for colonization by German farmers, rather than industrial complexes, was the main focus of Nazi expansionism. Hitler did not thirst to command non-Aryan peoples, whom he thought would fall by the wayside as Germandom expanded. The first step in this blueprint called for an assault on "inferior races." Slavic and Jewish *"Untermenschen"* would be removed, subjugated, or exterminated to make room for German Lebensraum in Eastern Europe and Russia.

Hitler initially attacked Western Europe less to capture its economic potential than to protect his western flank in preparation for the conquest of the East. His original plans for the West were far more vague than for the East but appear to have involved German economic hegemony rather than annexation (except for Alsace-Lorraine, which was to be restored to the Reich).[8] But Hitler's appetite grew with each victory. After the summer of 1940, Hitler planned to Germanize and Nazify the Nordics, Dutch, and Flemish, and to herd the French and the Belgian Walloons (a "race of degenerates" but still better than Untermenschen) into a small, Mediterranean satellite state. Had Germany won the war, Hitler would have tried to establish an empire in Europe that included the Netherlands, Belgium, northern and western France, Norway, Denmark, probably Sweden and Switzerland, Austria, Croatia, northern Italy, Poland, Czechoslovakia, the Baltics, Ukraine, and Russia up to the Urals.[9]

If Hitler's initial balance-of-power calculations regarding the West fastened on defeating potential attackers and controlling their territory, economic gains were never ignored. Detailed plans were drawn up on the eve of each invasion for the seizure of arms, strategic raw materials, and even arms industries. In the case of Austria and the Sudetenland, Hitler was tempted by the reservoir of German-speaking military manpower, along with raw materials, labor, and industrial capacity.[10] The Germans invaded rump Czechoslovakia "to increase German war potential by the exploitation of industry there," according to Hermann Goering, commander of the German Air Force and initially the chief war-economy official.[11] Knocking a powerful enemy out of the war was the main rea-

son for invading France, although economic considerations came somewhat more to the fore in the decision to take neutral Belgium and the
Netherlands.[12]

Economic policy in the occupied Western territories was soon geared
toward military-economic mobilization. As Goering put it in September
1940:

> The aim is the strengthening of German war potential. For this purpose all
> mines, iron works, rolling mills, firms producing primary materials, and also
> important manufacturing firms such as machine-tool factories, locomotives
> and wagon works, and so on should be used at their full capacity and firms
> unimportant for war shall have their production reduced or be closed. Raw
> materials important for war which will not be used, as well as machine tools
> . . . will be transported to the homeland. The consumption of the population
> is to be shrunk to the lowest possible level.[13]

Only Denmark, which was treated until mid-1943 as a "model protectorate" (because of the Danes' peaceful acquiescence to the German invasion
and their privileged status in Nazi racial theory), was spared immediate
exploitation. Germany increased the level of mobilization over time, in
part because of the difficulty of rapidly organizing six nations with a combined population exceeding Germany's, but also possibly because of
evolving expectations about the course of the war. Especially after the
quick defeat of France in 1940, Hitler was unrealistically optimistic about
his ability to rapidly subdue Britain and the Soviet Union. Historians are
still debating whether this "Blitzkrieg" strategy resulted in Germany's
relaxed mobilization of its domestic and conquered economies in the period before failure to defeat the Soviet Union by the autumn of 1941, or
if instead initially sluggish output was due entirely to mismanagement.[14]

Whatever Germany's initial plans, the eventual reality of total war dictated the total mobilization of all resources at Germany's disposal. Germany preferred to produce completed armaments domestically and in the
Czech Protectorate; as German war economy czar Albert Speer put it, if
the French could not develop a strong armaments industry before the
war, then German "endeavors to make an armaments industry out of
French industry will also be impossible."[15] West European nations did
provide Germany with weapons components, fortifications, and other
goods with direct military uses, but most other kinds of economic contributions were also useful to the German war effort. And because the region surpassed Germany in population and national product and produced almost as much electricity, over two-thirds as much steel and
motor vehicles, and a third as much coal (see table 3-1), it represented a
potentially huge addition to German military-industrial power.

TABLE 3-1
West and Central European Population and Industrial Output, 1938

	Population (millions)	Coal (millions of tons)	Steel (millions of tons)	Electricity (gigawatt hours)	Vehicles (thousands)	GDP[a] (b $1980)
France	42.0	47.6	7.9	20.1	227	107.6
Czechoslovakia	14.6	34.7	2.3	3.6	13	30.2
Netherlands	8.7	13.7		3.5		28.3
Belgium	8.4	29.6	3.1	5.4		23.8
Denmark	3.8			1.1		12.4
Norway	2.9	.3		9.2		8.0
Total	80.4	125.9	13.3	42.9	240	210.3
Germany	68.6	369.2	19.8	49.0	338	190.2
Percentage of Germany	117	34	67	88	71	111

Sources: Mitchell, *International Historical Statistics: Europe*, tables A5, D2, D9, D25, D27; Harrison, "GDPs of the USSR and Eastern Europe," tables 2, 5.

[a] For 1937.

A "EUROPEAN WAR ECONOMY"

In fact Nazi Germany succeeded dramatically in mobilizing Western Europe for its war effort against the Allies. Germany used more than a third of Western European economic potential and absconded with much loot and foreign labor besides. In contrast, the costs of control represented only a few percent of Germany's total gains. German success, moreover, was limited more by the lack of European coal and other natural resources than by resistance. Few West Europeans collaborated enthusiastically and few resisted. But by passively acquiescing to German demands and by trying to carry on business as usual, administrators, business, and labor all became part of the German war machine.

Extraction through Tribute

Pillage and slave labor, the most visible and notorious forms of Nazi profit, represented a small part of the economic value of conquered Europe. Germany's chief gains were bought from continued production with funds extorted from the indigenous administrations of every occupied country. Like sovereign nations mobilizing for war, the occupied countries shifted resources from domestic consumption to pay for military spending. In this case, however, the military doing the spending was the German Wehrmacht. As the German armistice negotiators told their Vichy counterparts, "France was going to be made to lower her standard of living and to bring it to a level analogous to Germany."[16] Denmark, which remained the showpiece of the Nazi "New Order" until anti-Nazi demonstrations in the summer of 1943, was the only exception, and a temporary one at that.[17]

Tribute was collected in three forms: occupation costs, clearing deficits, and forced bond-sales. German occupation authorities demanded regular payments of "occupation costs" ("matricular contributions" in the case of the Czech Protectorate) from each country.[18] These sums were much greater than the actual costs of the occupation armies, and Germany used the surplus to buy goods and services for its war effort. Exports to Germany were also financed with borrowed funds. Indigenous administrations had to pay their own exporters while the amounts were chalked up as "clearing deficits" in Berlin, on the unlikely presumption of postwar repayment.[19] German agencies also spent Reichsmarks in the Czech Protectorate and the Netherlands, which were recovered by forced sale of German treasury bonds. The Czech and Dutch regimes had to compensate holders of Reichsmarks with domestic currency and hand over the marks to Germany in return for bonds that had as little real value as the clearing accounts.

The indigenous administrations of every occupied country collaborated fully with German financial depredations. French negotiators fretted that the demanded "occupation costs" payments would enable the Germans "to buy the whole of France," but after a few protests they caved in.[20] Vichy unilaterally lowered its payments from 400 to 300 million francs per day in May 1941. But German authorities countered by making greater use of the clearing mechanism and, in November 1942, they forced Vichy to increase its daily payments to 500 million francs.[21] Belgium and the Netherlands failed to offer even this degree of resistance, although their obligations too were unilaterally increased to cover higher German expenditures. By agreeing to German demands for occupation costs and clearing arrangements, collaborating administrations effectively put their finance ministries, central banks, and taxation systems at Germany's service. Thus France and the other occupied economies were compelled to become Germany's economic allies.

Throughout occupied Europe, tribute was spent on a wide array of goods and services. Most were not strictly military, in part because Germany preferred to build its own weapons. But nearly all kinds of production are useful to a fully mobilized war economy. Western European textiles were used by Germany for parachutes, rags, and uniforms, and hides and furs also helped to dress the German soldier; lumber went into German barracks and other construction projects in France and in the

TABLE 3-2
Occupation Costs and Credits, through March 1944 (Millions of Marks)

	Occupation Costs	Clearing	Total
France	27,935	7,128	35,063
Netherlands	7,767	4,260	12,027
Bohemia-Moravia[a]	2,314	3,400	5,714
Belgium	5,311	3,982	9,293
Norway	5,044	−143	4,901
Denmark	1,446	1,088	2,534
Total	49,817	19,715	69,532

Sources: Forschungsstelle für Wehrwirtschaft, "Finanziellen Leistungen"; Bank for International Settlements, *Fourteenth Annual Report* (Basle, 1944), 149.

[a] Incomplete estimate, for reasons explained in the text.

East. Even consumer-goods production in the occupied territories, some directly for the Wehrmacht and the rest to keep the German arms workers happy, allowed the transfer of 1–1.5 million German workers (3–5% of the total) from consumer goods to armaments industries in 1943 alone.[22]

A rough measure of the dimensions of German exploitation is the sum total of the financial contributions of the occupied territories. An October 1944 report by the German Research Office for Military Economy (Forschungsstelle für Wehrwirtschaft) under the Supreme Command calculated these through March 1944.[23] The report is particularly useful because it takes account of inflation, black market premiums, arbitrary exchange rates, and export tariffs to evaluate the actual purchasing power of the financial transfers (see table 3-2). Except insofar as they hampered economic productivity, inflation and black-marketeering did not cut into the financial transfers, which were pegged according to what the local economy could bear.

France, having by far the largest economy, provided the greatest contribution to the German war economy in absolute terms. But France was not the most intensively exploited. Table 3-3 approximates the average mobilization rates in each country by taking Germany's annual gains as a proportion of each country's prewar national income.

The estimate for the Bohemian-Moravian burden appearing in table 3-2 and subsequent tables must be considered highly tentative. The Forschungsstelle für Wehrwirtschaft report inexplicably omitted Bohemian-Moravian clearing deficits, treasury bills, and credits covered by local banks. Of these, only the clearing deficits can be established from other sources, and have been included in the tables. Some estimate the other payments reached 6.9 billion Reichsmarks by the end of the war, and if most of this amount had accumulated by the end of March 1944, the Bohemian-Moravian contribution to the German war economy would

TABLE 3-3
Mobilization of Western Europe for the Nazi War Economy

	Average Annual Transfer[a] (bil. marks)	1938 Nat'l Income[b] (bil. marks)	Avg. Mobilization Rate (percentage)
Netherlands	3.1	7.2	44
Belgium	2.4	5.5	44
Norway	1.3	3.0	42
France	9.4	30.8	30
Bohemia-Moravia[c]	1.4	4.5	30
Denmark	.6	3.4	19
Total	18.2	54.4	33

Sources: Forschungsstelle für Wehrwirtschaft, "Finanziellen Leistungen"; Bank for International Settlements, *Fourteenth Annual Report* (Basle, 1944); Colin Clark, *The Conditions of Economic Progress*, 3d ed. (London: Macmillan, 1957); J. Krejčí, "The Bohemian-Moravian War Economy," in *Economic History of Eastern Europe*, ed. Kaser and Radice, 2:458.

[a] Averages calculated on the basis of periods from military surrender through March 1944.

[b] National income unit is net national product at factor cost. Income data is converted into German Reichsmarks according to the 1940 purchasing power rates used by the Forschungsstelle für Wehrwirtschaft. French income is reduced 5 percent to compensate for the loss of Alsace-Lorraine. Czech income from 1940.

[c] Incomplete estimate.

have been about double the amount shown.[24] On the other hand, a considerable but unknown percentage of Czech payments were used by the state-owned Reichswerke to buy out existing shares in major Czech armament, iron, steel, and coal enterprises.[25] Transfer of ownership has long-term economic advantages, but it does not represent additional mobilization of current production. Because of these uncertainties and omissions, further research is needed to more reliably estimate Czech payments and mobilization.[26]

Pillage and Slave Labor

In addition to the financial transfers, Germany also gained from loot and foreign labor. The overall policy of "milking" Western Europe (as opposed to the East, where plunder took precedence) did not preclude considerable looting, especially early in the war. There is little reliable data on the value of German plunder, but it was clearly considerable, at least in France. The French commission assigned to evaluating France's wartime losses estimated that booty amounted to a seventh of all industrial products, a quarter of the raw materials, and a tenth of the foodstuffs taken from France by the Germans.[27]

Obvious targets for plunder were captured military equipment and stockpiles. These were not essential to economic production in the occupied areas but were dangerous to leave around and could bolster German military strength. Hitler seized from rump Czechoslovakia over 1,500 airplanes, 2,000 artillery pieces (with 3 million shells), 500 anti-aircraft guns, 470 tanks, and 1 million rifles (with 1 billion rounds), equipment that proved useful in the subsequent invasions of Poland and France.[28] Victory in 1940 resulted in an even greater arms bonanza, as the French surrendered all of their nonnaval arms and munitions, including 1,700 surviving military aircraft.[29] French tanks (many of them modified into mobile assault guns) supplied German panzer brigades, 7,000 World War I–vintage "75s" equipped coastal batteries on the Atlantic beaches, and light tanks and aircraft were sold off to German allies.[30]

Raw material stockpiles also fell prey to seizure, often easing critical bottlenecks in the German war economy. The capture of Austrian and Czech raw material stockpiles—as well as finished goods, gold, and foreign-currency reserves—helped Germany pay for sorely needed raw material imports before the outbreak of war.[31] Approximately $622 million dollars in gold was ultimately seized from treasuries of occupied Europe.[32] The pillage of raw material stocks was soon halted in these countries in order to increase their industrial output, but the practice continued on an even greater scale in Western Europe. Western Europe's stocks of nonferrous metals, such as copper, lead, tin, nickel, zinc, magnesium, and tungsten, probably prevented serious bottlenecks in German armament production in 1941.[33] Liquid fuel stocks seized in France alone amounted to 10 percent of Germany's 1941 consumption.[34] Toward the end of the war, the increasingly desperate Germans began pillaging church bells, bronze statues, and even brass door knobs for their copper.

The Germans also preyed on West European industrial infrastructure, carting home industrial, transport, and agricultural equipment of all kinds.[35] France, for example, was stripped of over half of its railway wagons, a fifth of its locomotives, and over a third of its buses and trucks.[36] French wagons and locomotives increased the German supply by 45 percent and 15 percent, respectively, helping the German Railway to overcome a severe transportation crisis in the winter of 1941–42 as supply lines stretched deep into Russia.[37] But while pillaging gained Germany badly needed goods, it hampered production in the occupied territories, much of which was going to Germany anyway. Whether from vindictiveness, overconfidence, internal German rivalries, or sheer greed, excessive pillaging stripped occupied Europe of equipment that would have been more useful there than in Germany.[38]

Another means of German gain was the labor siphoned out of occupied Europe and put to work in German factories.[39] Polish prisoners of war and conscripted civilians added 700,000 workers to the German economy, and were joined by 924,000 French prisoners of war after the

TABLE 3-4

Foreign Workers in Germany, Fall 1943

	POWs	Civilian	Total	Percentage of all FWs	Percentage of home pop.
Soviet Union	496,000	1,716,000	2,212,000	32	1.2
Poland	29,000	1,621,000	1,650,000	24	4.8
France	739,000	649,000	1,388,000	20	3.3
Bohemia-Moravia	—	286,000	286,000	4	3.8
Belgium	53,000	228,000	281,000	4	3.4
Netherlands	—	256,000	256,000	4	3.0
Serbia	94,000	45,000	139,000	2	2.9
Italy	—	117,000	117,000	2	0.3
Others	54,000	427,000	481,000	7	
Total	1,465,000	5,345,000	6,810,000	100	

Sources: Homze, Foreign Labor, 195. Population figures from Mitchell, International Historical Statistics: Europe, table A5; and E. A. Radice, "Territorial Changes, Population Movements and Labor Supplies," in Economic History of Eastern Europe, ed. Kaser and Radice, 2:309-28.

fall of France. Germany immediately began recruiting West European labor, especially skilled workers. By the end of 1940, 220,000 civilians from the western occupied nations were working in Germany; a year later, the number had grown to almost 300,000. The flow of volunteers dwindled in 1942, after the unemployment that had been caused by the invasion dried up, despite policies intended to free up additional labor, such as withholding unemployment benefits, lengthening the work week, and closing down "unessential" enterprises.[40]

Germany then began deporting workers for forced labor in German factories. The German foreign labor czar, Fritz Sauckel, began combing through Dutch and Belgian factories, without indigenous cooperation, although the Dutch secretary-general for social affairs authorized the release of labor records.[41] In France, Pétain's prime minister Pierre Laval managed to put off Sauckel until February 1943, when he instructed French labor agencies to provide employment data and personnel to the German recruiters and imposed sanctions against conscription evaders.[42] The total foreign labor force in Germany increased from 1.2 million in 1940 to 7.1 million—or a fifth of the total labor force—in 1944.[43] Only a third of these were West Europeans in 1943, but they represented a sizable proportion of their domestic labor forces (see table 3-4).

The productivity of foreign workers was just as important to the German war economy as their numbers. One might expect nationalistic foreigners to work as slowly and negligently as they possibly could, especially those (a third in German industry) working in arms factories. Yet, despite becoming 20 percent foreign, overall labor productivity in Germany rose more than 15 percent between 1940 and 1943.[44] This was mainly due to the reorganization of the German war economy implemented by Hitler's armaments czar, Albert Speer, during 1942–43, as well as to greater mechanization and longer working hours. But the increase in productivity would not have been possible if a fifth of the workforce had been significantly noncompliant.

Indeed on average foreign workers from Western Europe were 80 percent as efficient as German workers in equivalent jobs.[45] Productivity varied by treatment, period of the war, nationality, gender, and POW/civilian status. Within industry, foreigners were used predominantly for heavy manual labor, like mining, steel processing, construction, or routine, assembly-line tasks.[46] But the Germans also attempted to exploit foreigners' skills, by offering higher pay for complex work and the opportunity to avoid more arduous alternatives. By late in the war, Daimler-Benz was using a 45 percent foreign workforce to manufacture aircraft engines, trucks, and tanks. Although foreign workers were paid less than their German counterparts, their productivity was good overall.[47] A 1942 Krupp survey rated French skilled and unskilled POWs at 92 percent and 79 percent of their German counterparts; their civilian compatriots were rated at 84 percent and 78 percent, respectively.[48] And at an I. G. Farben chemical plant, "entire divisions were handed over to French personnel from the chemist in charge, down to supervisors and workers. The results fully came up to expectations."[49] Historians agree that forced labor was critical to the maintenance of the German war economy and marvel at how "the Germans brought millions of unwilling persons, many of whom were personally mistreated, into a strange country, presented them with grim living circumstances, and then molded them into productive workers."[50]

Germany profited from foreign workers, voluntary as well as forced, whose wartime wages were far lower than the normal, "free" value of their labor. Foreign workers at Krupp in Essen earned on average 90 percent of their German coworkers' salaries; POWs were paid 68 percent.[51] Of course, they found it just as difficult as Germans to find consumer goods in Germany, and were subject to the same forced savings that helped pay for the war. Their labor thus cost Germany little more than the food, clothing, shelter, and occasional black-market cigarettes needed to sustain them. Given that their compatriots back home were consuming only two-thirds as much grain, two-fifths the potatoes, and a third of the meat they ate before the war, their real income must have been no more than half their prewar income.[52] Thus the use of French labor in Germany, for example, increased Germany's total gain by about 8 percent of French wartime payments to the occupiers.[53]

Costs of Control

Controlling Western Europe cost Germany only a fraction of its gains. The great majority of German personnel in occupied Europe were soldiers, but they devoted themselves almost entirely to coastal defense, air and naval attacks on the Allies, and training—hardly at all to counterinsurgency or policing. As Joseph Goebbels noted in September 1943, "The divisions now in the British Isles were keeping a large number of German divisions immobilized in the West."[54] This is reflected in the concentration of troops along the coasts, rather than near population centers, as well as in an increase in numbers as D-Day loomed. After defeating France, for example, the German Army in France declined steadily to 500,000 (or 11 per thousand inhabitants) by 1942, before climbing back up to 800,000 in mid-1944.[55] About 450,000 German troops (or 150 per thousand inhabitants) were required to cover Norway's long coastline, while only 65,000 (8 per thousand) were deployed in Holland.[56] Without the threat of a second front, Germany would have spent much less on military forces in Western Europe without risking rebellion.

The administrators and police required to govern occupied Western Europe were tiny in comparison. The total number of German civilian and military police in the occupied territories—including the occupied East, Balkans, and Italy—was 246,000 in 1943.[57] Further research is needed to establish their regional distribution, but anecdotal evidence— one source cites 10,000 German civil and military police in the Netherlands, another mentions 6,000 military police in France—suggests they were thinly distributed in occupied Western Europe.[58]

Even fewer were the German administrators required, less than 15,000 in all of Western Europe (see table 3-5). Thus, the main cost of control was the armies. Even if all German soldiers are counted, despite their mainly extra-imperial activity, controlling Western Europe (except for Norway) was cheap for Germany. Indeed, there were more Frenchmen working in Germany than Germans occupying France. Vichy's armistice negotiators calculated that the "occupation costs" would sustain an army of 18 million men; the actual costs of all German personnel in France at the end of 1941 could not have exceeded 5 percent of France's average annual payments. German official sources suggest that personnel expenses reached 14 percent of French financial contributions later in the war, while in the Netherlands they amounted to about 7 percent.[59]

German control costs were low because armed resistance failed to materialize. Armed guerrillas were virtually nonexistent in Denmark, Holland, Belgium, and Czechoslovakia, and only marginally active in the mountainous regions of France and upper Italy.[60] Estimating total num-

TABLE 3-5
German Administrative Personnel in
Occupied Territories

	Fall 1941	End of 1942
France	1,489	
Netherlands	1,596	
Belgium	1,166	
Norway	806	
Protectorate	9,362	1,884
Denmark	89	

Sources: Werner Best, "Die deutschen Aufsichtsverwaltungen in Frankreich, Belgien, den Niederlanden, Norwegen, Dänemak, und im Protektorat Böhmen und Mähren,"
September 1941, Records of German Field Commands, National Archives, T501/101/1367; Mastny, Czechs under Nazi
Rule, 201.

bers remains problematic. The necessary secrecy of underground movements during the war precluded systematic counting and after liberation
people tended to exaggerate their participation in resistance. But it is clear
that, while active resisters gradually increased over the course of the war,
they remained few. In France, for example, active resisters numbered only
around four hundred thousand, or just 2 percent of the French adult population. Most of these were unarmed and joined just before the liberation.[61] Resistance movements were smaller still in the rest of Western
Europe. Although the method of counting may be different from that
used by historians of the French resistance, historians of the Dutch resistance figure that there were only twelve hundred full-time resisters in the
Netherlands, or less than a tenth of 1 percent.[62]

Guerrillas survived in occupied Europe mainly by avoiding confrontation with the Germans. Assassinations and ambushes were rare, not-
withstanding the communist slogan "à chacun son Boche (to each his
German)". In fact, German records indicate that only fifty thousand Germans perished from partisan attacks, nearly all of these in occupied Russia.[63] Rare attempts to seize and hold territory near the end of the war
proved suicidal, especially in urban areas. Fifteen thousand guerrillas and
two hundred thousand civilians perished in the Warsaw uprising.[64] The
Paris uprising on the eve of liberation, according to resistance historian
M. R. D. Foot, "was really almost as much farce as triumph," while the
rebellion in Naples was "a four days' massacre."[65]

The only significant impact on German military power, other than providing the Allies with intelligence, was slowing German troop movements
toward Normandy following D-Day. Saboteurs attacked French and Bel-

gian railways on the eve of the June 1944 landings, making thousands of railway cuts and disabling locomotives at a rate comparable to Allied bombing.[66] German divisions forced to march were slowed further by hit-and-run ambushes. The Second SS Panzer Division ("Das Reich"), for example, though losing only thirty-five men, lost ten days—some attributable to Allied air attacks—in their march to Normandy from southern France.[67] Even this limited success depended on the support smuggled to the underground by the Allies during the war. So many arms, radios, explosives, and advisers were parachuted into Western Europe by Britain's Special Operations Executive (SOE) that the Allied Command concluded, "Without the organization, communications, material, training and leadership which SOE supplied . . . 'resistance' would have been of no military value."[68]

Pacification was so successful and required so few German personnel because of police collaboration in each occupied country. Each collaborating administration was compelled to issue decrees outlawing acts of resistance like sabotage and assassination. The Germans found native police forces generally cooperative and efficient in enforcing these decrees, although as the war progressed they worried about their reliability in repressing mass anti-German demonstrations or rebellions.[69] The Dutch police appear to have been especially compliant instruments of German rule. The head of German security in Amsterdam testified after the war that "the main support of the German forces in the police sector and beyond was the Dutch police. Without it, not 10 per cent of the German occupation tasks would have been fulfilled."[70] A wartime (and thus more reliable) report by the German military authority in occupied France noted that "if nearly half of all saboteurs between 21 August 1941 and 14 March 1942 have been caught (46 culprits for 109 attacks) this has largely been thanks to the energetic efforts of the French police."[71] According to historian Robert Paxton, "As many Frenchmen participated in 1943–44 in putting down 'disorder' as participated in active resistance."[72] Police collaboration was not uniformly total. While the entire Dutch police helped deport all but 20,000 of 140,000 Dutch Jews, Denmark and Belgium refused all cooperation with the Final Solution.[73] Vichy authorized the use of census data and French police in rounding up Jews, and took other anti-Semitic initiatives not even demanded by the Nazi overlords. When it reversed this policy in mid-1943, the Milice (a quasi-official militia) continued to help the SS root out French Jews.[74] But the police of every occupied country assisted the occupiers in the repression of active resistance, the main important requirement for the German war effort.

Germany's gains from pillage and slave labor probably exceeded its control costs. Thus the mobilization rates provided in table 3-3 and the weighted average of 33 percent of national income provide a ballpark estimate of German imperial profits. To put these rates in perspective, consider that in 1939 French military spending reached 23 percent of national income.[75] Thus the Nazis mobilized French resources more fully than had the Third Republic on the eve of war. The most appropriate benchmark for evaluating the cumulativity of resources would be the rates attained by comparably developed and fully mobilized contenders. As mentioned in Chapter 2, Britain mobilized an average of 51 percent of prewar national income during World War II, Germany averaged 52 percent, the United States averaged 72 percent, while Italy averaged only 34 percent. Since U.S. GNP/capita was significantly higher than Western Europe's, and Italy's significantly lower, Germany and Britain are the best benchmarks. West European mobilization averaged two thirds of Britain's and Germany's. Conquered Belgian, Dutch, and Norwegian GNP was worth about 80 percent of a belligerent's GNP. France and the Protectorate were worth about 58 percent, and Denmark was worth only 37 percent. Although Western Europe was not fully mobilized, Hitler clearly succeeded in fashioning a "European War Economy."

PATTERNS OF ECONOMIC PRODUCTIVITY

These extraction rates appear all the more impressive if one considers the fact that Germany had to mobilize Western Europe without organizational preparation and with a continental shortage of coal, problems that the belligerents did not face in mobilizing their own economies for war. Germany was simply not administratively geared up to begin the full mobilization of European capacity in the summer of 1940, and delays were aggravated by mismanagement and anarchy in procurement. Thus the financial transfers increased over time (table 3-6). These increases, which were moderated only slightly by low wartime German inflation, still exaggerate the early mobilization levels, since the flow of tribute initially exceeded Germany's rate of spending.[76] By the end of 1941, Germany had saved up almost 65 billion francs, or seven months' worth of French payments.[77] Germany stepped up contracting to Western European industries after the winter of 1941–42, but while Speer's rationalization measures tripled German munitions production between early 1942 and late 1943, interagency competition continued to plague West European procurement.[78] Speer began to address these problems in 1943, but by then it was too late.[79]

Since Germany had access to virtually unlimited tribute, its mobilization of the occupied territories was limited chiefly by the wartime decline

TABLE 3-6

Average Monthly Financial Transfers, July 1940–March 1944
(Millions of Marks)

	1940–41	1941–42	1942–43	1943–44
France	648	751	855	959
Belgium	115	205	233	245
Netherlands	116	305	280	470
Norway	91	143	80	109
Bohemia-Moravia[a]	64	86	148	177
Denmark	38	34	47	137
Total	1,112	1,524	1,643	2,097

Sources: Forschungsstelle für Wehrwirtschaft, "Finanziellen Leistungen";
Bank for International Settlements, *Report for 1944*.

[a] Incomplete estimate.

in their total economic output. Norway and the Netherlands maintained higher levels of output than France and were also mobilized more completely by Germany (see Table 3-7). Norway's productivity is understated by income indices, because the Allies seized four fifths of its merchant shipping, which had provided over 10 percent of its national income before the war.[80] The relationship between output and extraction rates is imperfect, especially for Denmark (the "model protectorate") and Bohemia-Moravia (where data on extraction remains incomplete). But these latter two countries show that exploitative occupation does not preclude the maintenance or even surpassing of prewar production levels.

The relatively sharp decline in French activity was largely due to wartime raw material shortages, mainly of coal. Coal was the primary energy source of European industry in peacetime, and during the war, as John Gillingham has shown, the continental coal supply "provided a ceiling for economic activity in German-dominated Europe."[81] This ceiling was lower for some countries than for others, and France lost more than a third of its coal supply during the war.[82] Before the war, Belgium and the Netherlands had been roughly self-sufficient in coal, but France had imported about 30 percent of her annual consumption, mainly from Britain and Germany.[83] Rather than make up for lost British coal, Germany fed its prior surplus to its superheated war economy and took part of French, Belgian, and Dutch output besides.[84] French general industry in 1942 obtained only 63 percent of its prewar coal consumption, small industry and engineering received only 45 percent, and steel works and other metallurgical industries only 40 percent. As a result, overall industrial activity fell to 60 percent of prewar levels in 1942 and down to 55 percent in the following year.[85] In contrast, Belgian coal consumption remained at

TABLE 3-7
Real National Income (Percentage of 1938) and Average Extraction Rates, 1940–1944

	1940	1941	1942	1943	1944	Avg.	Average Extraction Rate
Norway[a]	91	93	90	88	83	89	42
Netherlands	88	83	76	74	50	74	44
France	88	70	63	59	50	66	30
Bohemia-Moravia[a]	95	95	98	101	101	98	30?
Denmark	86	81	83	92	102	89	19

Sources: Table 3-4 above; Krejčí, "Bohemian-Moravian War Economy," 468; Odd Aukrust and P. J. Bjerve, *Hva kriegen kostet Norge* (Oslo: Dreyers, 1945), 45; Cornelis A. van Bochove and Wim van Sorge, "Constant Wealth National Income: Accounting for War Damage with an Application to the Netherlands, 1940–45," *Review of Income and Wealth* 35 (June 1989), 205; Institute National de la Statistique et des Etudes Economiques [INSEE], *Annuaire statistique, 1966* (Paris: Imprimerie Nationale, 1967), 561; Mitchell, *International Historical Statistics: Europe*, table J1.
[a] Index based on 1939.

over 78 percent of prewar levels in 1941 and 69 percent in 1943.[86] Norwegian industry consumed 70–80 percent of its prewar supply of coal, and Dutch coal consumption hardly fell at all.[87]

German leaders, believing their own economy the most efficient in Europe, naturally diverted to it European fuel (German coal and coke consumption increased by 50 percent during the war), as well as other raw materials and foreign labor.[88] This belief may have been based partly on concerns about nationalism, but there were other reasons for it as well. The German military-industrial base had been the most productive in Europe before the war, and it had considerable excess capacity during the war.[89] Transportation costs and vulnerability to strategic bombing also militated against diverting Ruhr coal to France. In general, shorter distances and greater prewar economic integration favored Bohemia-Moravia (whose prewar trade with Germany amounted to 17.3 percent of its national income), the Netherlands (9.6 percent), and Belgium (8.2 percent) over France (1.5 percent).[90]

The fact that economic sectors better supplied with coal, or less dependent upon it, performed relatively well during the occupation also supports the interpretation that coal shortages affected German profits far more than did national resistance. Germany's heavy reliance on French railways for the movement of troops and the delivery of goods to Germany meant that the railway would receive a disproportionate share of France's coal allotment. Supplied with 75 percent of prewar levels in 1942, the railroads managed to sustain prewar levels of traffic, despite losing more than half its wagons and a fifth of its locomotives and workforce.[91] Agriculture also performed well in all of Western Europe.[92] French agriculture, for example, maintained 75 percent of prewar production, despite the loss of 10 percent of its cultivated land, and 13 percent of its farmers, 22 percent of its horses, half its fertilizers, almost all liquid fuel and spare mechanical parts.[93] Production was probably even higher than official statistics indicate, because unreported foodstuffs had a lucrative outlet on the black market. Incidentally, Germany was a major beneficiary of continued French production. By reducing French food rations to about half the healthy number of calories, Germany was able to skim 15–20 percent of bread grains, meat, and dairy products produced in France during the war.[94]

European extractive industries also performed relatively well. French bauxite output, 80 percent of which ended up in German aircraft, even surpassed prewar levels in 1943, thanks mainly to increased manpower.[95] French and Luxembourg iron ore was mined at 70 percent, 75 percent, and 95 percent of prewar levels in 1941, 1942, and 1943, respectively.[96] France alone provided, in 1943, about a quarter of the total supply of ore available to Germany.[97] Coal output increased slightly in France, while dropping only 8 percent in the Netherlands and 17 percent in Belgium over 1940–43.[98] The decline in Belgian coal mining resulted mainly from the loss of Belgian miners to the Ruhr, shortages of supplies like pit-props, wear and tear on machinery, and malnutrition, which affected the productivity of German and British miners during the war as well.[99]

If one takes into account continental coal shortages, the removal of 3–4 percent of the population of the occupied countries, the looting of equipment and stocks, and finally Allied bombing, this does not leave much of a role for national resistance in reducing West European economic output. In fact boycotts, sabotage, and strikes were rare and ineffective during the occupation. German orders for goods were virtually never refused, even when they were of direct and obvious value to the German war effort. The Skoda Works and other Czech arms plants churned out high-quality tanks for Germany throughout the war.[100] Although they realized that Germany preferred to purchase arms components rather than completed weapons, Vichy and Dutch officials forbade only the latter (although the Belgians forbade both).[101] French construction companies readily built air bases, coastal fortifications (the "Atlantic Wall"), and thirty-foot-thick submarine pens.[102] Industrial collaboration even extended to technologically sophisticated products. For example, Dutch firms built radios for the Luftwaffe and even received a development contract for new submarine components.[103] The extensive collaboration of the Belgian electronics industry even led the German conglomerate AEG to fret about its Belgian competition.[104]

Sabotage was virtually nonexistent in the first two years of the occupation.[105] Incidents grew as the war dragged on, and resistance veterans'

memoirs describe hundreds of small successes.[106] But their total cost to
Germany was small, even in France, where sabotage was most widespread. Optimists compare the effect of industrial and railway sabotage
on French economic performance to the damage inflicted by strategic
bombing, but the latter had only a marginal effect on the French economy
until mid-1944.[107] When Albert Speer was questioned after the war about
the impact of the French resistance on German exploitation, he retorted:
"What French resistance?"[108] The preeminent historian of the French
and Norwegian economies under occupation, Alan Milward, concludes
that "it is extremely difficult to find cases where important resistance activity was economically effective and also justifiable as an investment
choice."[109]

Strikes were also too small and infrequent to hamper economic performance. Brief and mainly apolitical strikes broke out sporadically, beginning in the fall of 1942. But the only major strikes occurred in 1944,
when it was too late to make a dent in German imperial profits.[110] The
thousands of Frenchmen who joined the partisans in the French countryside were the only workers successfully able to withhold their labor from
the Germans, but most of these had been driven away from their jobs by
Germany's ill-considered labor draft. Speer begged Hitler to restrain
labor conscription in 1943, arguing that "it is imbecility if I call up one
million men in France. . . I end up with two million workers less there and
fifty to a hundred thousand more in Germany."[111]

Thus labor resistance had to take the form of working slowly and
poorly rather than refusing to work at all. This type of resistance, inherently secretive and diffuse, and difficult to distinguish from all the waiting
around for materials and fuel is hard to assess. Historians of the period
believe that slack-working was common, but "subtle and indirect."[112]
One specialist on the French automobile industry finds that "absentee-
ism, turnover, lack of discipline, and resistance (including even a few
strikes) had a conspicuous likeness to those of the prewar period."[113]
Further research is needed to document the extent and economic effects of
passive workplace resistance. But the wartime performance of the Western European economies, considering all their material difficulties, suggests it was not very great. The fact that Bohemia-Moravia and Denmark
maintained prewar levels of economic activity shows that nationalism is
insufficient to reduce a country's economic surplus.

COERCION, REPRESSION, AND MODERN SOCIETIES

German success in mobilizing occupied Western Europe was due to Nazi
coercion and repression and the level of development of the defeated societies. This is evident, first, in the ruthless and calculated use of terror by

the Nazi invaders. Nazi terror hardly needs elaboration here, but its impact is evident in administrators' and populations' recognition that at least a modicum of political and economic collaboration was a lesser evil than resistance. Second, the only plausible alternative explanation of collaboration—European elites' desire to support the Nazi war on Bolshevism—does not hold up under close scrutiny. Third, anecdotal evidence suggests that individual firms collaborated energetically in the pursuit of their own narrow self-interests. Fourth, national resistance was lower, and German economic profits were higher, in the more developed regions of Nazi-occupied Europe.

Coercion and Collaboration

Every West European administration traveled down the path of collaboration without straining very hard against the Nazi leash. Some went further than others, but all went well beyond the minimal policing and financial collaboration needed for Germany to make conquest pay. German occupation authorities presented European civil servants with a simple choice: obey or resign. Many did resign rather than collaborate, and the Germans purged others who they considered unreliable or hostile. But the vast majority of European officials, bureaucrats, and civil servants stuck to their posts and obeyed. They often dragged their feet, especially in hunting down Jews, communists, and forced-labor evaders. But they dutifully assisted in the overall exploitation and policing of their countries.

Native administrations collaborated simply because they believed that it was in the best interest of their societies to do so. They recognized that collaboration helped the Germans, but they thought it a lesser evil than the reprisals, chaos, and hardship that would result from resistance. Hitler's capacity to torment subject peoples was made quite obvious to the rest of Europe by his treatment of Poland. After invading in September 1939, Hitler annexed the western third of the country, and by the end of 1940 had deported three hundred thousand Poles, murdered thousands more, and given their property to German colonists. The remainder of German-occupied Poland was initially to be used as a dumping ground for Jews and other deportees, and "Polish chaos" was deliberately exacerbated.[114]

Although the threat of "Polandization" lay behind all negotiations between victor and vanquished, the Germans reserved their most vicious coercive threats to deter armed attacks on themselves. Each assassinated German official or soldier was "avenged," according to a policy of collective responsibility, by the immediate execution of dozens of natives selected from local prisons or even randomly off the streets. The number slain depended on the rank of the German victim and the time elapsed until the perpetrators were identified. In one extreme case, the assassination of Reinhard Heydrich, then the chief German official in the Czech Protectorate, by Allied-trained paratroopers was met by the slaughter of thirteen hundred Czechs. At the funeral, Hitler told President Emil Hacha that he would deport the entire population if it failed to support the German war effort. According to Hitler's own chilling account of this episode:

> At this, Hacha collapsed like a pricked balloon, as did also his colleagues. After a pause, they asked whether they might—at least partially and with appropriate discretion—make use of this communication in their own country. As I consider the Czechs to be industrious and intelligent workers and am most anxious to see political stability restored in their country—and particularly in view of the presence therein of two great and most important German armaments factories—I acceded to their request.[115]

Such high costs turned émigré governments, most underground resistance groups, and even the Allies against assassinating Germans, at least until the Allied landing.[116]

Threatened reprisals compelled the occupied countries to police themselves. Collaborating administrations also sought to prevent actions that, while targeted against the occupier, caused collateral damage to domestic welfare, such as railway sabotage. But in the face of German threats, the distinction between German interests and native interests blurred. So they also outlawed anything that might provoke a violent reaction—assassination, sabotage, underground resistance organizations, and even strikes, demonstrations, anti-German statements and writings. For example, the Dutch secretaries-general denounced their

> fellow countrymen who have obviously not understood the gravity of the current situation. In their blindness they believe they can damage the occupying power by acts of sabotage, although in reality they can only damage the *interests of the Dutch people*. This cannot be permitted. Understand that the German authorities cannot tolerate incorrect conduct on the part of the Dutch population and realize above all that the life of many people is brought into great danger by ... the actions of reckless and criminal elements.[117]

The general welfare nearly always seemed better served by the lesser evil of collaboration, even if this meant obvious assistance to German interests. West European police forces and judiciaries were thus drawn into assisting German control and repression.

To achieve their economic policies, Germany used the lesser and more flexible threats of plunder, labor conscription, internal blockades, or more direct German control to coerce native administrations. Officials could drag their feet at the margins of German ultimatums, but on matters of any importance they had to comply or resign. Most complied because they believed that they would be replaced by incompetent, unprincipled, and/or German personnel. Abdication would thus lead to an erosion or even collapse of governmental services. Collaborating officials and functionaries obeyed German demands because they believed that there was no other way to maintain the smooth functioning of government so essential to the public good. For example, the Dutch secretary-general for economics, Hans Max Hirschfeld, believed that extensive collaboration was the only way "to secure essential supplies for the population and maintain the country's economic and social structure," despite its help to the Germans.[118] After the war, he justified this attitude by pointing out that resistance would have led much earlier to the kind of chaos and suffering of the 1944-45 "hunger winter," brought on in part by a Dutch railway strike.[119] In France, the World War I hero Marshal Pétain surrendered to the Germans and then volunteered to serve as France's "shield," because "to deprive France of her natural defenders [French government] in a period of general disorder is to deliver her to the enemy, it is to kill the soul of France—it is, consequently, to make her revival impossible."[120] Each of the vanquished nations of Western Europe faced the same dilemma and made the same choice.

Wartime popular support for at least a modicum of collaboration and postwar clemency for many leading collaborators suggests that such statements were not simply rationalizations. Even before the war, the Dutch and Belgian governments had decided that collaboration was preferable to resistance in the event of military occupation. Directives in civil servants' desks instructed them to take no action against an occupying power, but rather continue their work to promote peace, order, and the general welfare. They were to resign only if they believed their services to the occupier outweighed their services to the population. In the minds of most Dutch and Belgian officials, this dictated collaboration.

The subject peoples also recognized that collaboration was in their best interest. The French responded with nearly unanimous adulation and gratitude to Pétain's armistice. Even those countrymen far from Hitler's reach agreed, and only a few far-flung colonies and a small percentage of military personnel abroad defected to Charles de Gaulle in 1940.[121] The Dutch also supported a rapid return to normalcy.[122] And in Belgium, "three-quarters of the population gave the impression of having rallied, or being largely resigned, to the New Order, and it is permissible to believe that if Germany had [promised an independent, satellite status] . . . the overwhelming majority of public opinion would have . . . enter[ed] full-fledged the path of collaboration with Germany behind the banner of Axis hegemony."[123]

Condemnation of collaboration was reserved mainly for labor conscription and political arrests, not for the more economically significant forms of collaboration. Although angry mobs on the dawn of liberation were not very discriminating, postwar tribunals were sympathetic to those who had served German interests without participating in the most heinous Nazi policies. Hirschfeld, for example, even got his pension, despite having ignored the government-in-exile's demands that he refuse to participate in labor conscription and "excessive" requisitions.[124] Most historical studies of the period conclude that basic political and economic collaboration was an inevitable response to German coercion, because "it enabled a majority of a subject population to lead comparatively normal lives throughout the occupation and to survive."[125]

The increase in resistance over time, to the point where it posed at least an irritation to the Germans, can also be explained by coercion theory. The numbers of West Europeans engaged in active resistance to German rule gradually increased over the course of the war as the shock of sudden collapse and the seeming inevitability of total German victory gradually wore off. In the summer of 1940, German victory appeared complete and irreversible. This conviction waned, however, as the BBC broadcasted into occupied Europe news of German reversals on the Eastern Front, Anglo-American landings in North Africa, Italy's surrender, and finally the Normandy landings. The turning of the war against Germany gave occupied societies reason to think that resistance that had earlier seemed futile might now tip the scales in favor of the Allies, and that the Germans might be too preoccupied to dish out reprisals.

Historians commonly attribute the increases in resistance to two other factors as well. The German attack on the Soviet Union in June 1941 thrust European communists, always sympathetic to the Soviet cause and now viciously persecuted, into resistance. This effect should not be overstated, however, because resisters came from all classes and ideologies.[126] More significant was the forced labor conscription, which drove thousands of Frenchmen underground in 1943.[127] Both of these factors may be explained at least partially by coercion theory, which requires that collaboration be made more tolerable than resistance for threats to work. While the costs and risks of joining the resistance remained high, they were not all that much worse than the alternatives of political persecution or industrial slavery in a foreign land.

European "Fifth Columns"?

If idiosyncratic factors, like ideological predilections or domestic cleavages, were responsible for European collaboration with Nazi Germany, then German success would have been a historical accident rather than an inevitable consequence of coercion. Thus one quagmire theorist claims that "the Nazis had one particular factor in their favor, the hatred of Bolshevism on the part of the European right. Collaboration was facilitated by some common ideological dispositions."[128] This interpretation deserves careful scrutiny because of the notorious record of collaborationist excesses in Nazi-occupied Europe. Norway's collaborating administration was directed by Norwegian fascists under Vidkun Quisling, who had attempted a coup during the German invasion. The French regime in Vichy, if not fascist, was fiercely anticommunist. In December 1942, Prime Minister Pierre Laval even proclaimed that "Victory for Germany will save our civilization from sinking into communism. Victory for the Americans would be a triumph for Jewry and communism. . . . I, for my part, have made my choice."[129]

But there are good reasons to discount the effect of the European far right on the success of German exploitation. There were very few indigenous fascists in Western Europe before and during the war, and most of these were nationalist as well as anti-communist, and thus not pro-German per se. In addition, while fascists gained real power in only a couple collaborating regimes, mainstream officials and bureaucrats collaborated just as obediently on policies essential to the Nazi war effort.

The weakness of the West European radical right on the eve of the war is evident in the most recent elections held in each country. Quisling's National Union drew about 2 percent of the Norwegian vote in 1936 elections; the Danish National-Socialist Workers Party (DNSAP) fared about as well in 1939.[130] Czech fascists also won 2 percent of the vote in prewar elections, although 3.5 percent of the population of the Protectorate considered themselves German.[131] The Dutch National Socialist Movement (Nationaal-Socialistische Beweging, or NSB), led by Anton Mussert, earned 4 percent of the 1937 vote and was hemorrhaging members on the eve of the war.[132] Belgium's Catholic Rexist party gained more than 11 percent of the vote in 1936, but lost support once the fascistic objectives of its leader, Leon Degrelle, became apparent, gaining only 4 percent in 1939. To this one might conceivably add the 7 percent won by the right-wing Flemish National League (Vlaamsch Nationale Verbond, or VNV), but these supporters were attracted more by the promise of Flemish autonomy than by anticommunism per se.[133] In France, Jacques Doriot's French People's Party (Parti Populaire Français or PPF) had only about fifty to sixty thousand members on the eve of the war.[134]

Fascist movements remained highly unpopular throughout the war, with no more than 2 percent of their societies: 43,000 members in Norway's National Union, 100,000 in the Dutch NSB, at most that many in the Belgian VNV and Rex, and 150–200,000 total in France's PPF, People's National Rally (Rassemblement National Populaire), and the Militia (Milice).[135] Motives for joining these parties, as well as the SS legions, were as often opportunistic as ideological; the French Milice, for example, was filled with unemployed hoodlums seeking to escape forced labor.[136] A scattering of Europeans (27,000 Dutch, 6,500 Norwegians, 15,000 Belgians, 7,000 Danes, and 10,000 Frenchmen) actually volunteered to don SS or Wehrmacht uniforms.[137]

Ironically, European reactionaries and fascists were ardent nationalists as well as die-hard anticommunists. They were more willing to engage in "collaborationist" policies (political and religious persecution and the like) that suited their own right-wing domestic agenda, but they also believed that cooperation would earn concessions and eventual autonomy from Hitler.[138] While they might have preferred German rule to domestic communist rule, claims that an Allied victory would mean the triumph of communism in Europe are difficult to take at face value. The Anglo-Americans were closer to Western Europe than was Stalin (they seized North Africa in November 1942, months before the turning point in the East at Stalingrad in February 1943), and it is hard to imagine how Anglo-American victory could have promoted communism. If European nazis really feared German defeat, it was because they knew they would be punished for their past treachery if the Allies liberated Europe.

Regardless of the motives and behavior of the European far right, its limited role is demonstrated by the fact that the administrations of occupied Europe were run primarily by mainstream politicians and bureaucrats. Except in the annexed territories, such as Sudetenland, Alsace-Lorraine, and Luxembourg, German victory left the local governments and national bureaucracies and civil services of the vanquished nations intact. Changes occurred at high levels, but fascist stooges gained immediate leadership only in Norway, where the German Reichskommissar handpicked a new administration from Quisling's National Union. Vichy's Marshal Pétain was right of center but no fascist. In Belgium and the Netherlands, fleeing ministers left in charge their department heads, or "secretaries-general"—all mainstream conservatives. Over the course of the occupation, only a few fascists were foisted upon the Dutch, Belgian, and French administrations.[139] The same Czech government headed by Emil Hacha that had succeeded that of Eduard Benes after Munich remained in office after the German invasion, although under especially tight supervision. In Denmark, the cabinet and parliament remained intact, at least until August 1943, when they abdicated leadership to the secretaries-general.[140]

This was due in part to a deliberate German policy not to politically promote indigenous fascists, outside of Norway. From the German perspective, the domestic unpopularity and administrative inexperience of these fringe groups made them less efficient than the occasionally foot-dragging politicians and civil servants from the conservative mainstream. As a German diplomat reported from Paris in 1943, "We have inhibited the rise to power of political groups and ideologies related to us. . . . We have wanted instead a government to preserve peace and order, the most efficient contribution of labor, the highest possible production for our war needs."[141]

Whatever Germany's calculations, the differences in leadership among the native administrations of occupied Western Europe appear not to have affected their willingness to pay tribute or police their countries. Belgium and the Netherlands were mobilized just as fully as Quisling's Norway. The fact that France was the least intensively exploited except for Denmark suggests that Laval's declared wish for German victory was not particularly useful to the German war economy. Nor did French pre-war parliamentary instability, which is often taken as evidence of French disillusionment with democracy, result in a particularly high degree of mobilization. Belgium and the Netherlands enjoyed domestic political stability before the war, had tiny nazi parties, and were administered throughout the war by mostly mainstream officials; yet they were among the most intensively exploited.[142]

In sum, Europe did not unite voluntarily to defeat Soviet Bolshevism or in disgust with democracy. While native fascists served Hitler's cause in various ways, they remained a small minority in the administrations and societies of occupied Europe. Collaboration, at least on the imperially vital matters of finance and policing, was pursued by mainstream politicians and supported by the majority of citizens, in the belief that collaboration was in their societies' best interest. If ideologically motivated "collaborationism" in occupied Europe was an artifact of prewar fascist currents, the basic collaboration required for German profits was dictated by naked coercion. Resistance meant reprisals and economic disruptions, and abdication meant the progressive deterioration of the governmental services so essential to modern societies. Rather than abdicate, then, mainstream politicians, bureaucrats, and civil servants chose to participate in Nazi repression and exploitation.

Collective Action

Repression increased the costs of individual resistance efforts, but it also effectively prevented the formation of organizations that could promote anti-German collective action. Indigenous administrations were compelled to organize their societies for collaboration while being forbidden from organizing them for resistance. The German occupiers, with the assistance of native police forces, outlawed and ruthlessly repressed all

demonstrations, political parties, public criticism, and underground organizations directed against their rule. Assassins, underground leaders,
and saboteurs were rooted out, often betrayed by rewarded informers
and compelled to talk by torture.[143] The largest and most centrally organized underground movements, such as the Czech Obrana Naroda, established before the war by military officers, were the most quickly dis-
assembled, but few resistance groups evaded Gestapo penetration.[144]
German infiltration into the French resistance contributed to the capture
of a quarter of SOE airdrops of arms and explosives in 1942, and half in
1943.[145] And because occupation authorities forbade any but the most
insignificant organizations from distributing unemployment relief in the
occupied territories, industrial labor had to work to get both the currency
and ration tickets needed to put food on the table.[146]

Repression ensured that no resistance organizations would emerge
capable of rewarding resisters or punishing free-riders. As a result, each
citizen of the occupied countries was free to act in his or her narrow
self-interest. From the individual's point of view, to resist was to take a
deadly risk in order to make a single pin prick in the German jackboot.
Millions of pin pricks might have made a difference. But since one's
own contribution was so small, it was rational to sit back and let others
stick out their necks. After all, even if resistance did successfully hasten
liberation, everybody would enjoy the results whether or not he or she
participated.

The overall low degree of resistance and high economic performance
suggests that most individuals followed their own, rather than national,
interests. By fully mobilizing the occupied nations, the Nazis left them
little incentive to be productive. Since so few goods were produced for
domestic consumption, it is difficult to see how any industrial worker
could see that his or her productivity was in the national interest. Detailed
productivity comparisons among sectors and firms being exploited to different degrees by the Germans are needed to provide more conclusive
evidence. But the continued activity of intensively exploited sectors—such
as armaments, metallurgy, mining, chemicals, and construction—suggests that firms and workers were striving to protect their own individual
welfare without much regard to national interest.

Anecdotal evidence of self-interested behavior abounds. Although the
Belgian secretaries-general forbade the sale of weapons components to
the Germans, the Belgian Fabrique Nationale agreed to produce its famous small arms on the condition that the Germans "take over" its factory in Liège with only seventy-nine supervisors. The same attitude was
shown by Cockerill Steel, which accepted a German Navy order for gun
barrels thinly disguised as "tubes."[147] Vichy's attempts to negotiate limits
on German procurement of bauxite, iron, and aircraft components were

outflanked by French companies' eagerness to cut individual deals with German agencies and firms.[148]

The French automotive industry provides additional examples of profit-maximizing and competitive behavior. Of the "big four"—Renault, Citroën, Peugeot, and Berliet—only Peugeot was eventually taken over by the Germans.[149] The managements of the other companies worked hard to fill German orders throughout the war with minimal supervision by a handful of German engineers and guards. One reason was fear of pillaging. According to one of his aides, Louis Renault "didn't like the Germans. Why would he like them? He never liked anyone. But he was afraid they would take his machines. . . . He gave them everything in order to keep it all."[150] Citroën's management resolved more magnanimously that "duty commands us to stay and not abandon Citroën's employees."[151]

But these companies responded to the market as well as to coercion. Louis Renault regularly pleaded with the Germans for orders: "My will is to give you material of the best possible quality, given our metal supply. We will make everything that you want. Tomorrow, we will make more tank turrets if you want, but please order more trucks. Help us through this difficult period. We have done at least as much as Ford to help you. We are ready to do still more, but don't strangle us."[152] Renault was bitterly angry that the Royal Air Force had singled out his factories for bombing, while sparing those of Peugeot and Citroën.[153] After one particularly devastating Allied raid in 1943, his director-general argued that the factories must rapidly resume producing tank parts and trucks for the German Army because otherwise "their labor and material will little by little be removed and put at the disposition of more active factories. Our activity will be progressively reduced to the profit of other enterprises ready to do work."[154]

Threats of pillage were not needed at all for Marius Berliet, who ran France's fourth largest automotive company. The Berliet factories were located in Lyon, which remained out of reach of German looters until the south of France was occupied in November 1942. Later, Berliet took advantage of the German labor draft to rid his factories of union leaders, slack-workers, and communists. He explained after the war that the possibilities for German gain from his energetic truck production "were subtleties I didn't consider. In any case we were not at war since there was an armistice. I saw matters only as an industrial leader."[155]

West European industrialists recognized the value of their contribution to the German war effort, but they collaborated nevertheless. If all had refused to work, they could have significantly affected German profits. German repression precluded any organized collusion among them, and none were willing to sacrifice themselves for the greater good. Most businesses believed that resistance was pointless, not only because of the threat of requisition but because of the readiness of competitors to collaborate. The overall lack of labor resistance mentioned above suggests that the same dynamic stimulated employee productivity as well. Since industrial managers maintained their usual vigilance against poor performance and sabotage, workers not performing up to par risked losing wages or jobs, or being deported for forced labor in Germany.

One additional fact provides further support for the impact of the collective goods problem. In all of France, the most courageous examples of resistance to the deportation of Jews occurred in small, close-knit villages. As mentioned in Chapter 2, studies of peasant rebellions have shown that the social cohesiveness of small villages facilitates collective action. The isolated Protestant communes of the Haute Loire, Hautes Alpes, and the Tarn were unique in the risks they took to offer shelter and aid to Jewish refugees. The most celebrated of these is Chambon-sur-Lignon, the "safest place for Jews in Europe," whose villagers maintained a solid front even under intense Gestapo pressure.[156]

Effects of Modernization: Comparisons to Poland, Greece, and Serbia

The extent of German profits and the lack of significant political and economic resistance by West European bureaucrats, business, and labor all point to the cumulativity of industrial resources. But the effects of modernization can be examined only by comparing the performance of Germany's conquests. Table 3-8 ranks the occupied countries by their level of modernization and compares the average yearly amount that citizens of the occupied countries were compelled to contribute ("occupation costs" plus "clearing deficits") to the German war economy. As the table makes clear, Germany was able to mobilize the more modern economies—Norway, Belgium, Netherlands, and France—much more intensively than the less modern ones—Poland, Greece, and Serbia.

The difference in mobilization rates is due mainly to the far greater economic surplus produced by modern societies. While destructive racial policies and plunder further reduced Nazi gains from Poland, poverty put a low ceiling on the potential exploitation of all the less developed regions. But it also appears that political and economic resistance were more prevalent in the less developed countries. As mentioned above, mining in occupied Western Europe maintained near prewar levels. In Serbia, by contrast, a workforce fleeing to the countryside and persistent sabotage attacks decreased coal output in 1943 by more than a third.[157] Greek industrial output declined to less than 25 percent of prewar levels in 1942

TABLE 3-8

European Modernization Levels and Per Capita Contributions to
the German War Economy

	GNP/Capita (1980 dollars)	Urban Pop. (percentage in cities > 20,000)	Telephones (per 1000)	Annual Burden/ capita (marks)
Germany	2,736	50	60	602
Norway	2,676	28	80	391
Belgium	2,829	51	50	285
Netherlands	3,221	52	50	353
France	2,586	45	39	234
Bohemia-Moravia[a]	1,948	21	14	183?
Greece	1,373	25	7	27[b]
Polish General Gov't[a]	1,372	24	9	108
Serbia[a]	1,275	10	4	45

Sources: GNP per capita data for 1937 from Harrison, "GDPs of the USSR and Eastern Europe," 248, 253. Burden per capita figures based on table 3-3; Klein, *Germany's Economic Preparations*, 256; Mitchell, *International Historical Statistics: Europe*, table A5; and Radice, "Territorial Changes," 309–28. Urbanization data for 1940 from United Nations, Department of Economic and Social Affairs, *Growth of the World's Urban and Rural Population, 1920–2000* (New York: United Nations, 1969), 105–6. Telephone data for 1938 from Henry Barbera, *Rich Nations and Poor in Peace and War: Continuity and Change in the Development Hierarchy of Seventy Nations from 1913 through 1952* (Lexington, Mass.: Lexington Books, 1973), 147–48.

[a] Czechoslovakian development data used for Bohemia-Moravia, Polish data used for the general government, and Yugoslavian data used for Serbia. This introduces a downward bias in the development indices for Bohemia-Moravia, which was the most developed province of Czechoslovakia. (The Czech workforce was 66 percent nonagricultural in 1948, compared to 37 percent in Slovakia. Jaroslav Krejčí, *Social Change and Stratification in Postwar Czechoslovakia* [London: Macmillan, 1972], 29.)

[b] This figure understates the Greek burden by around 25 percent because payments to the Italian co-occupiers, a third of those provided to the Germans prior to Spetember 1943, have not been included. Little is known about the exploitation of the one million Greek inhabitants of the Bulgarian zone, so they are not counted in the table.

and to less than 20 percent in 1943.[158] And while farmers in the more developed areas of Europe continued to sell their crops on the open market, with only moderate diversion to black market channels, Serbian, Polish, and Greek farmers reverted to subsistence farming, eliminating much of their agricultural surplus.[159] In Greece, declining production, hoarding, and shortages were worsened by an occupation policy that set occupation-cost payments according to German military requirements rather than the Greek government's capacity to pay, resulting in one of the worst cases of hyperinflation in history.[160]

Armed resistance was also more common in the less developed countries. In the Protectorate, according to one historian, the "concentration of population in industrial cities [and] the dense communication system" helped make "the work of Nazi security troops much easier than it was in Poland or Norway."[161] As mentioned earlier, guerrilla resistance was greater in France than in Belgium and the Netherlands, especially in France's rural mountainous regions. It was greater still in Yugoslavia, where partisans were 250,000 strong and still growing in early 1944— 1.7 percent of the population, or almost twice the proportion in France. Tito's guerrillas moreover controlled a significant amount of Yugoslavian territory and tied down several German divisions, neither of which was ever achieved in occupied Western Europe.[162] The Greek resistance, while less strong than that in Yugoslavia, also appears to have caused greater inconvenience to the Germans than did West European partisans. Resisters destroyed important chrome, nickel, and bauxite mines in 1943–44, killed more than two thousand German soldiers, and wounded another four thousand. One German division and another briefly were deployed in Greece specifically for counterinsurgency action in mid-1944.[163]

CONCLUSIONS

The case of Nazi-occupied Western Europe provides powerful evidence for the cumulativity of industrial economies. Hitler's "hostile takeover" of European nations enabled him to mobilize a European war economy for the duration of the war. In stark contrast to what quagmire theorists would predict, nationalistic and industrialized nations failed to withhold, eliminate, or even significantly reduce their economic surpluses. Through financial transfers alone, Germany was able to mobilize annually 42–44 percent of Dutch, Belgian, and Norwegian economic potential, 30 percent in the case of France, and that or more from Bohemia-Moravia. Germany spent only a small fraction of these profits on occupying and administering its conquests, and it gained huge amounts of booty and cheap labor in addition. When compared to the wartime mobilization of the most productive belligerents, it appears that the Czech Protectorate was fully mobilized for the German war effort and France was about half mobilized. Belgium, the Netherlands, and Norway fell in between.

Conquest permitted profits far beyond what Germany would otherwise have secured in trade, even assuming, implausibly, that Western Europe would have remained neutral in an Anglo-German or Soviet-German war. Nazi Germany traded coal for Swedish iron ore throughout World War II on extremely favorable terms thanks to German coercion. But conquest and the extortion of tribute allowed Germany to take French ore, and much else besides, for nothing.[164]

German successes seem all the more dramatic in light of the fact that the continental coal supply was insufficient to run European industry at full capacity. The readiness of industrialists to fill German contracts and the relatively strong performance of well-supplied sectors suggest that Germany would have mobilized occupied Europe, and especially France, even more successfully with more coal and less mismanagement.

European collaboration was dictated by German coercion. The commonalities of collaboration in each occupied territory, the mainstream political backgrounds and public justifications of most administrative collaborators, reliance on prewar directives, and popular support all suggest that financial and police collaboration was a rational response to German domination rather than a right-wing, anti-Bolshevik crusade. Yet, in choosing the lesser evil, Western European nations contributed to the German war economy and—were it not for the Allies—to their own future enslavement.

The emphasis of some quagmire theorists on the obstacles to exploitation presented by modernization appears profoundly misguided in light of this history. Nazi profits from Western Europe were due precisely to its relatively high level of development. Germany extracted far more resources per capita from its industrialized than agrarian conquests, and active resistance to Nazi rule was far more intense in the latter than in the former.

Only industrial countries generate the kind of huge economic surpluses Nazi Germany was able to squeeze from occupied Western Europe. West Europeans each contributed far more economically to the Nazi war economy than did Poles, Balts, Ukrainians, Russians, Yugoslavians, or Greeks, because their economies were more productive. Modernization facilitated exploitation in other ways. By enriching West European societies, modernization gave them much to lose from German "reprisals" against resistance efforts. West European administrations collaborated to preserve governmental services required by advanced societies. The prospect of organizing national strike-pay systems in the face of German opposition was so dim that few appear even to have considered it. Industrialists collaborated to keep their capital. Labor, having no backyard plots or relief to fall back upon, stayed at jobs they needed to feed their families.

Modernization also made West European societies vulnerable to repression. Without the ability to organize opposition, they became utterly passive. If strategies of resistance were in fact in the national interest, atomizing repression ensured that firms and citizens would have little individual incentive to stick out their necks. The heroic rebels of wartime Europe were motivated by principle rather than interest, but their small number suggests that most people are not.

Hitler's success over a period of four years does not prove that Germany could have maintained control, profit, and productivity in occupied Europe indefinitely. George Kennan, who traveled through most of occupied Europe in 1940–41, believed that Nazi ideology, based as it was on the glorification of the German people, could never appeal to more than a small minority of non-German Europeans. Thus,

> the Germans were faced with a dilemma, either to try to remain permanently in military occupation of most of the remainder of Europe, something which was physically almost impossible and would inevitably lead to the disaffection of large elements in their own military forces; or to accommodate themselves in some way to regimes . . . which would pursue aims by no means identical, and at times even in conflict, with those of German national socialism.[165]

But it is difficult to say if and when the German Army and the SS, which were capable of the most hideous crimes against humanity, would have become "disaffected" by a prolonged occupation of foreign lands.[166] It should be remembered that the failed army plot to assassinate Hitler in 1944 was intended to avert to the imminent national catastrophe of total defeat, not successful German imperialism.

West Europeans, for their part, appeared willing to collaborate indefinitely. Hitler's "Germanization" programs were unlikely to stamp out their national identities, but continued coercion and repression would probably have compelled continued compliance. Collaboration was not merely a tactical maneuver for weathering the storm of a brief German occupation. The vast majority of Europeans, indeed much of the world, saw German victory as complete and irrevocable in June 1940. Administrators, business, and labor embarked on collaboration as an adjustment to the perceived new political realities of a German-dominated Europe. Resistance increased over time, but only in reaction to the growing prospects for liberation, and then providing at most a minor irritation to German political and economic objectives. If the German Army had remained a loyal and brutal instrument of Nazi policy and the Allies had not come to the rescue, occupied Europe might still be working for the Germans today.

CHAPTER 4

Belgium and Luxembourg, 1914–1918

BY THE TIME Germany's 1914 offensive against France stalled at the battle of the Marne, the German Army had occupied Belgium, northern France, and Luxembourg. Over the next four years, Germany attempted to mobilize these relatively industrialized regions for its draining struggle against the Allies. The military call-up and flight from the front at the outbreak of the war stripped northern France of its male labor force and thus hamstrung its wartime economic potential.[1] But Belgium and Luxembourg provide useful test cases of the profitability of conquest.[2]

Occupied Belgium was at best marginally profitable for Germany. On one hand, the costs of control were low. Neither the German Army in the military zones (East and West Flanders), nor the general government ruling the rest of Belgium, faced any active resistance, permitting Germany to rule the country with a minimum of personnel.[3] Despite the fact that this was a closely matched war in which the future independence of Belgium was at stake, the occupied populations were unable or unwilling to engage in guerrilla warfare to affect its outcome. But a four-year passive resistance campaign limited Germany's economic gains by paralyzing every important Belgian industry other than coal. Germany in the end had to satisfy itself with large-scale plundering of raw material stocks, scrap metal, and industrial equipment.

The story was very different in the small but metallurgically important Grand Duchy of Luxembourg, whose mines, foundries, and steel mills churned out iron ore, iron, and steel for the German war machine. This was because economic circumstances permitted Germany to apply greater coercion and to offer greater incentives for collaboration to Luxembourg than to Belgium. Since Belgium was a net food importer and the Central Powers were themselves struck by famine, Germany allowed a neutral relief organization to bring food through the Allied blockade to Belgium and northern France and to distribute it unmolested. This relief amounted to a form of strike pay, enabling the Belgians to survive without working for Germany. In contrast, the citizens of Luxembourg, denied access to imported relief, had to sing for their supper. This pair of cases thus provides further evidence of the importance of coercion and positive incentives to securing collaboration. And Luxembourg provides another counterexample to the claim that industrial economies will refuse to surrender their economic surplus.

GERMAN AIMS

Although Imperial Germany bears a considerable burden of war guilt, it did not begin World War I as a war of conquest. However, its ambitions grew increasingly expansionistic during the war, presenting a formidable obstacle to any compromise peace. Meanwhile, Germany's immediate objective in the occupied territories was to harness them as much as possible to the German war effort.[4]

The German Kaiser Wilhelm II declared upon the outbreak of the war that "it is no lust of conquest that inspires us."[5] Indeed, territorial ambitions do not appear in the foreground of any belligerent's motives in July–August 1914, although rival imperialisms had exacerbated the long-standing tensions in Europe prior to the war. Austro-Hungarian aggrandizement in the Balkans—the 1908 annexation of Bosnia-Herzegovina and the 1914 invasion of Serbia that precipitated World War I—was motivated more by nervousness about South-Slav nationalism than by naked greed. Russo-German antagonism had been exacerbated by Berlin's economic and military ventures in Turkey, whose control over the Dardanelles had been long coveted in Moscow. French readiness to fight Germany stemmed in part from French ambitions to regain Alsace-Lorraine.[6] Finally, German-French and especially German-British relations had been chronically aggravated by German demands for overseas colonies, a "place in the sun" alongside the other European empires.[7]

This German quest for world power has been interpreted by the German historian Fritz Fischer and his followers as proof of German guilt for the outbreak of the war. Clearly there were many influential advocates in prewar Germany for aggressive continental and colonial expansion, and a feverish propaganda campaign had spread Social Darwinist fears and aspirations for overseas empire and Lebensraum.[8] German expansionists prior to World War I argued that Germany had to expand to survive: "The continental expansion of German territory [and] the multiplication on the continent of the German peasantry . . . would form a sure barrier against the advance of our enemies."[9] But there is little evidence that the German government was so bewitched by these ambitions as to gamble war for them. As Chancellor Bernhard von Bülow told his Kaiser in 1908: "There would be nothing for us to gain in the conquest of any fresh Slav or French territory. If we annex small countries to the Empire we shall only strengthen those centrifugal elements which, alas, are never wanting in Germany."[10] His successor Bethmann Hollweg agreed, apparently sharing the Angell-esque view of his trusted adviser, Kurt Riezler, that "wars between great powers [would] no longer be started because of the rewards to be gained from them, but only from necessity."[11]

"Necessity" arose for Germany from the rising power of Russia and the declining power of Austria-Hungary. Bethmann Hollweg took grave risks in July 1914 to prop up his seemingly tottering ally because he and his military advisers saw war now as better than a future conflict against even worse odds: "In a sense it was a preventive war. But the war was hanging over us anyway, two years later it would have come even more dangerously and unavoidably."[12] Smashing Russian power would have required driving back the Russian border, but initial plans called for a cordon sanitaire rather than extensive German expansion.[13]

If the fruits of conquest were not an important aim before the war, they became so during it. As German troops approached the Marne, Bethmann Hollweg drew up a set of demands for nothing less than continental hegemony and overseas empire for Germany. His "September Program" required that "Belgium, even if allowed to continue to exist as a state, must be reduced to a vassal," meaning that it must demilitarize, cede Liège, Verviers, and its colonies to Germany; allow German control of Belgian railways and ports; and "become economically a German province" via an enforced customs union. Germany would also obtain France's African colonies and advance the Alsace-Lorraine border to include the Vosges Mountains and the "ore-field of Briey, which is necessary for the supply of ore for our industry." France would also be bound economically to Germany by a treaty that "secures the French market for our exports and makes it possible to exclude British commerce from France" and would have to pay a war indemnity "high enough to prevent France from spending any considerable sums on armaments in the next 15–20 years." Plans for Russia were not yet so focused, but it "must be thrust back as far as possible from Germany's eastern frontier and her domination over the non-Russian vassal peoples broken." By eliminating France and Russia as great powers, the war would achieve "security for the German Reich in west and east for all imaginable time."[14] German aims continued to grow with the German Army's conquest of western Russia, from a slight incursion of the Prussian border into Russian Poland, with Austrian suzerainty over Poland, to the attachment of the Baltics and Poland to the Reich.

Escalating German, as well as Allied, territorial ambitions presented an insurmountable obstacle to a negotiated peace, even though many of the misconceptions leading to war had been dispelled after 1914. Woodrow Wilson offered repeatedly to mediate talks between the Entente and the Central Powers on the basis of a return to the status quo ante.[15] But Germany was never willing to accept such terms, as Bethmann Hollweg made clear in a May 1915 Reichstag speech: "The greater the danger which we have to face from the ring of enemies around us . . . the more necessary is it for us to hold out until we have fought for and achieved all possible real guarantees and safeguards that none of our enemies will again dare appeal to arms, alone or in company."[16] Of course the blame for prolonging the war must be shared by Allied insistence on victory and compensation as well.

Wartime expansionism grew from a range of motives held by various domestic interests in Germany. Some scholars argue, in a variation on the social-imperialism theme, that promises of victory and great gains were deemed necessary to mobilize the population for the war and deflect criticism of the monarchy.[17] But the Reichstag's July 1917 resolution calling for "peace without annexations or indemnities" more accurately reflected the rank-and-file's preferences.[18] The increasingly dominant German High Command led the expansionist charge, demanding outright annexation of any strategic territories it had seized, and the German Navy insisted on keeping the Channel coastline as a springboard for threatening Britain. But in addition to achieving military security "for all time," Germany sought economic security and prestige. Heinrich Class and his Pan-German League were interested mainly in gaining vast depopulated farmland for peasant settlement—a forerunner of Nazi Lebensraum.[19] German industry, severed from its world market opportunities by Allied blockade and the threat of protracted economic warfare, now sought an economically unified European market that it could dominate free from British competition.[20] It was even more insistent on the annexation of mineral deposits: the coal fields of northern France and upper Silesia, and especially the French iron-ore fields of Longwy-Briey. A delegation of prominent industrialists told the chancellor in 1917 that they were prepared to carry on the war for another ten years for Longwy-Briey, and in January 1918 they were still insisting that it was "an absolutely vital necessity for the future development of the German iron and steel industry."[21]

Germany's appetite for foreign real estate was tempered somewhat by the prospect of political struggles with the people who lived there. Annexation posed the problem of how to integrate them into the Reich's constitutional structure. Alsace-Lorrainers had grumbled interminably since 1871 about their lack of representation in the Reichstag, and Poles and Belgians were even more remote culturally. The Pan-German League advocated massive depopulation and German settlement, but this was accepted in official circles only for small bits of territory destined for annexation, like the Polish frontier strip. German officials thought that making Belgium, Poland, and the Baltics "vassal-states" was the ideal compromise, offering "the advantages of annexation without its inescapable domestic political disadvantages."[22] Belgium and Poland were to be permitted "to enjoy their national life to the full" with independent national institutions, subject only to German military and economic control.[23]

TABLE 4-1
Population and Industrial Output of Germany, Belgium, and Luxembourg, 1913

	Population (millions)	Coal (millions of tons)	Iron Ore (millions of tons)	Iron (millions of tons)	Steel (millions of tons)
Germany	67.0	277.2	28.6	16.8	17.6
Belgium	7.6	22.8	0.0	2.5	2.5
Luxembourg	0.3	0.0	7.3	2.5	1.3
Belgium and Luxembourg as Percentage of Germany	12	8	26	30	22

Source: Mitchell, *International Historical Statistics: Europe*, tables A5, D2, D7, D8, D9.

The wartime governor general of Belgium, Ferdinand von Bissing, having a more realistic view of what indefinite German control would require, recommended permanent restrictions on rights of association, assembly, and the press.[24] The possibility of Germanization appeared somewhat more feasible in the Baltics, where ethnic Germans amounted to about 7 percent of the populations.[25] Still, Kaiser Wilhelm objected to annexations even here in order to avoid "a second Alsace-Lorraine."[26]

Actual German policy in the occupied territories was driven by the exigencies of war. This involved not only preventing any threat to German lines of communication, but also economic mobilization. In late August 1914, War Minister Erich von Falkenhayn proposed that Germany "so exploit [Belgium] militarily, economically, and financially that it covers in large part the needs of our Army. The land should materially relieve our own Fatherland, and must thus be treated as conquered territory."[27] By November, the German Army had already exhausted its weapons and ammunition reserves. The increasing economic demands of the war only magnified the urgency of exploitation of territories that represented potentially significant additions to the German war economy (see table 4-1).

Germany's most serious problem was a manpower shortage. Military mobilization stripped labor from factories in July and August, causing an immediate slump in industrial production to two-thirds of prewar levels.[28] The German Army had to release arms workers from military service to cope with an October 1914 munitions crisis; a series of measures followed to mobilize more labor.[29] Germany also desperately needed raw materials and transportation equipment. The Allied blockade cut off raw material imports, causing shortages immediately in nonferrous metals and nitrogen, and subsequently in lubricants and textile fibers. Production was also held up in the winter of 1916–17 because the rail network could not supply factories with the necessary coal; even after this transport crisis eased, a lack of miners constrained the coal supply. Coal and steel remained in short supply until the end of the war.[30]

Although labor, raw material, and transportation shortages were the main constraints on German armament production, Germany also sought briefly to expand its industrial capacity between September 1916 and February 1917. In August 1916 the new Supreme Command doubled and tripled production targets for ammunition, artillery, mortars, machine guns, aircraft, and fortification materials. In addition to the usual call for a more intensive mobilization of manpower and materials, the Hindenburg Program planned the construction of new blast furnaces and arms factories. Most of these new projects were abandoned when it became clear that the raw material supply would be inadequate to run them.[31] Still, Belgium and northern France together had ample labor, coal, and iron for steel production.[32]

GERMAN GAINS AND LOSSES

Germany failed to mobilize Belgium more than partially, but it succeeded in Luxembourg. Although German administrative and policing costs were low in both countries, Belgian industry and labor refused for the most part to work for the German war economy. As a result, the factories of Belgium lay idle throughout the war, leaving Germany no better option than pillage on a massive scale. Only in Luxembourg, and in the case of Belgian coal mining, did Germany succeed in mobilizing captured industrial resources.

Gains from Production

Germany extorted massive tribute payments from Belgium, but financial disarray during the war makes it impossible to use these to draw up a balance sheet. Belgium's leading financial consortium, the Société Générale, paid 40 million francs per month (later increasing to 60 million) in "war contributions" from December 1914 to the armistice, totaling 2.3 billion Belgian francs by the end of the war.[33] The German authorities also spent 4 billion marks (the mark being decreed convertible into francs at the prewar rate) in Belgium. Strict commercial restrictions prevented Belgian holders of marks from buying German goods during the war. Indeed, to keep the marks spent in Belgium from filtering back into Germany, the General Government periodically confiscated the mark holdings in Belgian banks, with a dubious promise of future repay-

TABLE 4-2

Industrial Output of Belgium, 1913–1918 (Millions of Tons; Except for Stone, Measured by Millions of Francs)

	1913	1914	1915	1916	1917	1918
Coal	22.8	16.7	14.2	16.9	14.9	13.9
Pig-iron	2.5	1.5	0.1	0.1	0.0	0.0
Steel	1.4	0.9	0.1	0.1	0.0	0.0
Stone	70.6	45.6	12.1	19.5	10.3	10.8
Semifinished iron and steel	0.8	0.4	0.1	0.2	0.1	0.1
Zinc	0.2	0.1	0.1	0.0	0.0	0.0

Source: Belgium, Ministère de l'Industrie, du Travail et du Ravitailement, Administration des Mines, *Extrait de la statistique des industries extractives et métallurgiques en Belgique pour les années 1913–1918* (Bruxelles: Narisse, 1919), 4–25.

ment.[34] Although Luxembourg was spared having to pay war contributions, the 200 million Reichsmarks left in Luxembourg at the end of the war amounted to the same thing.[35] But the absence of reliable wartime price indices makes this financial data inconclusive. The German mobilization of Belgium and Luxembourg is thus best evaluated by examining wartime production data.

Germany's failure in Belgium is immediately evident from the fact that Belgian industrial production fell to 37 percent of prewar levels in 1915, and to 29 percent by 1918 (see table 4-2).[36] German financial depredations in Belgium proved meaningless because the prostrate country refused to produce much worth buying. The most important exception was the collaboration of Belgian coal mining, which maintained output at 60–75 percent of prewar levels. The decline in output was due to a labor force that had decreased 13 percent by 1916 and 23 percent by 1917, while diminishing in productivity by 15 percent—not much considering miners' malnourishment and shortages of horses, mine-timber, and hoisting ropes.[37]

The Germans took control of coal distribution by establishing a Central Coal Office, to which all Belgian mines were required to sell their coal. This agency sold about half of the coal in Belgium (falling to 40 percent in 1918), and reserved the rest for the German Army, the military railroads, and for export to nearby neutral states (less than 10 percent).[38] Although Belgian coal was not exported to Germany, it saved Germany from having to haul scarce Ruhr coal to the front; exports, moreover, bought Germany desperately needed Dutch, Swiss, and Scandinavian goods.[39]

The rest of Belgium's economic potential remained largely unexploited. There was some activity, especially when the output was not of

TABLE 4-3

Industrial Output of Luxembourg, 1913–1918 (Millions of Tons)

	1913	1914	1915	1916	1917	1918
Iron ore	7.3	5.0	6.1	6.8	4.3	3.1
Pig-iron	2.5	1.8	1.6	2.0	1.5	1.3
Steel	1.3	1.1	1.0	1.3	1.1	0.9

Sources: Faber, *Métallurgie du Luxembourg*, 147, 149, 151; Hemmer, *Economie du Grand-Duché*, vol. 1:80.

obvious immediate military use. Industry in the general government collaborated more fully than in the operations zones, where the German Army was the only German customer.[40] In 1917 and the first half of 1918, Belgium exported nearly 900 million francs worth of glass, stone, ceramics, phosphates, and sugar, 83 percent going to Germany and the rest mainly to the Netherlands. Exports in 1915 and 1916 were much higher, although value figures are not available.[41] The goods Germany exported from Belgium to neutral countries were worth twice the value of the Dutch cereals, fodder, and industrial raw materials returned to Belgium.[42] The difference in Dutch goods was siphoned off to Germany.

In sharp contrast to Belgium, Luxembourg "became a cog in the German war machine."[43] Its mines and forges lost their Italian and German labor at the outset of the war, but a sufficient number of natives took their place to keep the total work force from dropping sharply.[44] Higher-than-prewar labor productivity in 1915 and 1916 enabled near-prewar levels of industrial production (see table 4-3).[45] The 13 percent decline in Luxembourg's steel production over 1915–17 was less than the 19 percent drop in German output over the same period, both declines being due to coal shortages.[46] There were no anti-German boycotts, and labor refused to work only during a single, five-day general strike in June 1917, at a time when industrial strikes were breaking out in the belligerent countries as well.[47] Although there is little data on wartime resource flows, total German control over Luxembourg's trade and limited local demand make it unlikely that any of Luxembourg's industrial output escaped the German war economy.[48]

Germany extracted this production not through direct tribute or taxation, but by forced savings. Luxembourg's enterprises and subjects were paid for their labor with German Reichsmarks, which had become legal tender at the outset of the occupation. But Luxembourg's inability to freely import foodstuffs and consumer goods, from Germany and other neutrals, reduced the actual value of these earnings. Food prices rose more rapidly than wages or industrial-goods prices, so the savings that did accumulate were captured by farmers and entrepreneurs rather than labor.[49]

Pillage and Forced Labor from Belgium

Unable to get Belgian factories to work, the German authorities resorted to a campaign of industrial plunder. They first pillaged raw-material stocks, requisitioning entire holdings in the warehouses of commercial centers. Thousands of machine tools were seized for use in German armaments and munitions plants, and a few factories were even entirely dismantled for shipment to Germany.[50] The German Army also seized 40 percent of Belgium's horses, whose value amounted to half of Germany's total gains (estimated at 800 million francs by Governor General von Bissing) by November 1916.[51]

In 1917 Germany began to devour Belgian and French industrial plant on a massive scale. Von Bissing opposed this policy because "a squeezed lemon affords no juice and a slaughtered cow gives no more milk."[52] But Belgium was not affording much milk anyway, and von Bissing's ambitions to farm the Belgian economy in the long run clashed with Germany's dire wartime needs. A panoply of new military and private agencies thus began stripping factories systematically in the operations zones in early 1917 and in the rest of Belgium by mid-year.[53] By the end of the war, the Germans had destroyed 151 Belgian factories, shipped home 43,000 tons of scrap iron, 50,000 tons of scrap lead, and 24,000 machines, and had stored another 12,000 machines in holding dumps within occupied territory.[54] The loss to Belgium was magnitudes greater than Germany's gain. Even the equipment that arrived in Germany intact was allocated poorly, and greedy German industrialists were able to get French and Belgian machinery for which they had no immediate need.[55] Still, the failure to exploit Belgian productivity and labor meant that plunder was probably the source of Germany's greatest gains.[56]

Germany tried to remove Belgian labor as well as plant, deporting idle workers for work in the labor-starved Fatherland.[57] Around a half million Belgians were unemployed in the spring of 1915, with hundreds of thousands more underemployed.[58] At first the general government was more concerned about the politically destabilizing potential of such idleness than the economic-opportunity costs, and it even permitted locally organized public works projects. In June 1915 German iron and steel industrialists established the German Industry Bureau to recruit volunteers, but only twenty-six thousand Belgians had taken industrial jobs in Germany by September 1916.[59] In addition, nearly forty-six thousand Belgian prisoners of war were compelled to work in German mines and factories. Although not highly productive and requiring extensive supervision, they and 1.6 million other prisoners of war (mainly Russians, 20 percent of whom were employed in industry) "constituted a considerable economic asset for the war economy of the Reich."[60]

TABLE 4-4
Belgians Working Directly for Germany in January 1918

In Germany	
Volunteers	90,000
Civilian prisoners	1,800
Prisoners of war	38,800
Deportees	11,800
Total	142,400
In Belgian operations zones	
Railroad operation and repair	105,858
Trade and industry	100,000
Construction and roads	4,543
Other	19,517
Total	229,918
Grand total	372,318

Source: Passelecq, *Deportation et travail forcé*, 349.

But Germany's growing labor shortage in 1916 intensified pressure to obtain more Belgian labor, if not by wages then by force. German industrialists presented their case for civilian labor conscription at a September 1916 meeting in the War Ministry. Chemicals magnate Carl Duisburg urged the Supreme Command to "open up the great human reservoir of labor in Belgium," while the electrical industrialist and war-economy official Walter Rathenau claimed that "by compulsion Germany can get 700,000 workers for her own industry."[61]

Starting in October, civilians in the general government were deported to Germany, and those in the operations zones were pressed into forced labor on military works.[62] But the civilian deportation program was a failure. The Germans allocated inadequate administrative resources for identifying unemployed, healthy, industrial workers. Despite the imprisonment of numerous mayors and judges, municipal officials refused to help identify suitable deportees, forcing German officials to go from town to town rounding up able-bodied men with little screening for health, skills, or employment status. Rail and camp accommodations for the 61,000 deportees were so brutal that 800 perished, and another 13,150 had to be sent back due to sickness.[63] German employers feared resistance and sabotage and were hesitant in the end to take them on, so a majority of deportees never left holding camps.[64] Those who did "worked only with ill will and insuperable apathy."[65] An outcry in the Reichstag and in the Netherlands and other neutral states persuaded Germany to halt the deportations in February 1917 and to send the conscripts back home.

The exploitation of Belgian labor did intensify somewhat, however. In the military zones, sixty thousands Belgians and French grouped in "Civilian-Worker Battalions" slaved over fortifications, roads, railways, and barracks.[66] Belgians also volunteered in increasing numbers for work in German railroads and industry in the military zones, and for industry and mining in Germany proper. Having obtained only thirty thousand Belgians in its first sixteen months of operation, the German Industry Bureau enrolled another fourteen thousand in the three months after deportations began.[67] Another twelve thousand deportees signed work contracts in Germany, and continued to work there as "volunteers" after the deportation program had ended. By the end of the war, about 5 percent of the Belgian population was working directly for German enterprises, 2 percent in Germany and another 3 percent in the Belgian operations zones (see table 4-4).

Costs of Control

Germany pacified the occupied territories easily. Except for initial and greatly exaggerated reports of Belgian partisans, German troops and authorities felt no threat from the occupied populations of Belgium and Luxembourg. These reports resulted in, or perhaps were invented to justify, a vicious army rampage that left five thousand Belgian civilians dead and several towns and cities devastated by fire.[68] But in the aftermath, the German Army hardly had to lift a finger to pacify occupied territory. The governor-general's civil administration chief, von der Lancken, reported to Berlin in September 1916 that nothing in Belgium even remotely approached rebellion, and Belgians refrained from making any physical attacks on German troops or administrators throughout the war.[69] They even obeyed German demands to turn in all firearms.[70] The crowning achievements of Belgian resistance were the 170 issues of the underground newspaper and an underground railway that helped thirty thousand Belgians escape to join the Allies.[71]

The costs of controlling the occupied territories do not appear to have been high, despite a lack of indigenous administrative collaboration at the national level. Belgian cabinet ministers had escaped to London, and the governor-general staffed new departments of general administration, finance, education, commerce and industry, and justice with German administrators (the interior, agriculture, and public works departments remained mainly Belgian, under German supervision).[72] German officials also replaced the main Belgian provincial and district administrators, but they left all municipal governments intact. Minor Belgian officials continued at their posts, and after a brief strike, most state employees, such as police and postal workers, returned to their positions or were replaced by other Belgians.[73] The number of German bureaucrats in the civil administration was thirty-five hundred in 1918, while the military staff, responsible for maintaining internal order, had only two hundred officers and fourteen hundred soldiers, mainly older men.[74] The six massive German armies along the front, in occupied France and southwestern Belgium (East and West Flanders), may have had a deterrent effect in the general government. But it appears that only five thousand Germans were actively involved in the administration and garrisoning of its 5 million inhabitants.

Costs for controlling Luxembourg were probably lower. The government of Luxembourg, which continued to hold office under German occupation, protested the occupation and insisted on maintaining its neutrality throughout the war. But aside from refusing to cooperate with martial-law measures taken by German troops, such as rounding up escaped prisoners of war, the government collaborated coolly with the invaders.[75] So did the population, which a commanding general praised as "quiet and correct."[76] German authorities had to intervene only once, to repress the June 1917 general strike.[77]

EXPLAINING COLLABORATION AND RESISTANCE

The passivity of the Belgian and Luxembourg peoples can be explained by the threat of German reprisals for active resistance. Physical force, however, was insufficient to compel more than a small degree of economic collaboration. But where people had to work to eat, as in Luxembourg, or to stay warm, as in coal-dependent Belgium, they did.

The "rape of Belgium" by the German Army in August 1914 made it perfectly clear to the Belgians that the slightest guerrilla activity would be met with vicious reprisals. For the rest of the occupation, few Belgians were willing to incur the wrath of, in the words of the American ambassador (and maudlin novelist) Brand Whitlock, "this dread thing, this monstrous anachronism, modern science yoked to the chariot of autocracy and driven by the cruel will of the pagan world."[78] The lesson was also not lost on the citizens of Luxembourg. Prime Minister Paul Eyschen's mid-August 1914 proclamation warned against any act of active resistance, because "such a senseless deed would not only endanger [the resister's] own life but also the property and life of his fellow citizens."[79] Even those who despised the Germans agreed that passivity was the best way to avoid the "hurricane of wartime destruction" that had struck Belgium.[80] But even had the "rape of Belgium" not occurred, in the words of one historian, "a temporary acceptance of German rule was a matter of common sense since noncooperation entailed the risk of anarchy as metropolitan modern citizens will define anarchy—namely, the standstill of civilized life when postal and banking services, hospitals and schools, streetcars and order police, all cease to function."[81]

The Germans tried to use coercion for economic gain as well. Explicit threats of destructive plunder were sufficient to extort lump sums in cash from individual municipalities during the first months of the war. It was the threat to continue these depredations that persuaded the Société Générale to pay a monthly tribute starting in January 1915.[82] Threats of pillage without compensation pressured Belgian firms to sell their stocks for worthless paper money. Coercion was also aimed directly at industrialists boycotting the German Army. Those who continued their boycott after the dismantling campaign began in 1917 faced a much graver threat of losing their entire capital stock, machines, structures, and all. This persuaded many previously reluctant employers to cooperate.[83] The general government boasted in a 1918 bulletin about the new attitude of the battered iron industry: "Where in some cases difficulties arose, pointing out the disagreeable consequences for the factories almost always sufficed to make them compliant."[84]

But most Belgian industrialists were prepared to lose their factories and even suffer incarceration or forced labor rather than collaborate. And even where management agreed to collaborate or where factories were taken over by German agents, Belgian labor refused to work. Workers, like their employers, defiantly invoked their national duty and their protection by international law, which expressly prohibited compelling services that contribute to the occupier's military effort. They simply walked off the job.[85] Passive resistance thus crippled the Belgian industrial economy.

Raw material shortages would have limited production anyway, but to higher levels than actual wartime activity. The Allied blockade cut Belgian metallurgical, metal-working, and textile industries off from their peacetime suppliers of metal ores and fibers.[86] But ample iron ore was available in mineral-rich northern France if only the Germans could have mobilized Belgian labor to exploit it.[87] Even sectors with no supply problems refused to collaborate. The entire personnel of the Belgian railways, officials as well as employees, refused to work under German orders or for German accounts, so German soldiers were required to organize the transport of men and materiel to the front.[88] Most machine factories refused to repair German railroad equipment, and most quarries refused to cut stone that the German Army wanted for trench-building.[89]

Although the resistance of Belgian labor was impressive, it was possible only because of the lack of German economic control, which itself arose out of rather unique circumstances: An inviolable and unconditional supply of free food allowed Belgian industrial labor to remain idle. Ironically, it was a shortage of Belgian and German foodstuffs that compelled German authorities to tolerate this situation. Densely populated and highly industrialized, prewar Belgium had imported three-quarters of its wheat supply and much of its livestock feed and fats. Germany had nothing to spare; its own people were pushed to the brink of starvation by domestic shortages and the Allied blockade.[90] German officials hardly enjoyed the prospect of Belgian starvation, even if only out of self-interest. An American observer noted at the end of October 1914 that "the people are so hungry, and so desperate that . . . they are liable to attack the German soldiers at any moment, which would mean another terrible and useless sacrifice of the Belgian people." At the same time the Liège City Council was warning of riots, because "the people will rather die fighting than starving."[91] But rather than further squeeze its own population, the German government declared that Belgian suffering would be the fault of the Allies and their blockade. French and British leaders for their part relished Germany's dilemma and refused to slacken the pressure of the blockade on Germany.

A solution to this impasse appeared in the form of an international relief effort led by Herbert Hoover.[92] Hoover negotiated a deal with the belligerents allowing his Commission for Relief in Belgium (CRB) to ship food (provided mostly by the U.S., French, and British governments) into Belgium and northern France. The Allies agreed to let food through the blockade, but only with guarantees that it would not feed German mouths and that the occupiers would not take local produce that the CRB would then have to replace. The Germans accepted these conditions in October 1914. Over the course of the war, CRB ships, bearing the CRB flag and huge, illuminated "Belgian Relief" signs to ward off Allied warships and German submarines, carried 4 million tons of foodstuffs to Belgium and northern France.[93] (The flags, informal treaties, and immunities of the CRB inspired a British official to call it a "piratical state organized for benevolence.")[94] Food supplies were distributed by the locally organized National Food and Relief Committee (Comité Nationale de Secours et d'Alimentation), with forty thousand full-time employees and another eighty-five thousand assistants.[95] The Germans generally kept their part of the bargain and refrained from meddling with the unconditional distribution of relief. Periodic interference, like the August 1915 general government decree forbidding relief for strikers, brought immediate Allied threats to shut down the entire program and hasty German concessions.[96]

By feeding unemployed industrial labor, including those put out of work by the anti-German boycott, the CRB allowed Belgians to refuse German orders without sentencing themselves or their families to starvation. The availability of relief in Belgium also increased the incentives of conscripted workers to behave stubbornly, for work in Germany, in addition to all its other hardships, offered Belgians poorer rations than they could get doing little or nothing at home. This connection between relief and passive resistance was recognized by both the general government and the Allies. The German minister of trade and labor in the general government called the foodstuffs shortage "a terrible misfortune" that forced Germany to accept the CRB's "poisonous dowry."[97] Hoover also stressed this in his pleas to the Allies to support the relief effort:

> From an economic point of view the war will be won not by compelling the Germans to give up 6 per cent of their breadstuffs to the Belgians, but by the pressure on the other 94 per cent. . . . On the other side of the balance sheet, the Belgians are on strike; their attitude keeps a considerable number of Germans off the fighting line; their passive resistance in refusing to work arsenals and machine-shops and railways is a service to the allies. . . . Assuming that the Germans should in the last resort change their minds and feed the desperate and starving population, they certainly would only do so upon receiving in return the services of this population.[98]

Indeed, the Allies even went so far as to secretly supplement CRB relief with smuggled cash to reward striking Belgian railmen and mechanics.[99]

Germany's bargain with the CRB also weakened its ability to repress Belgian self-organization. The German authorities closed down all newspapers (because they refused to submit to censorship) and banned public meetings, anti-German activities, and open expression of patriotic sentiments. Violators were subject to the harsh judgments of German military tribunals, which included heavy fines, imprisonment, forced-labor, and deportation to German prison camps. About one thousand Belgians, beyond the five thousand who perished in the August 1914 terror, were executed for engaging in anti-German resistance.[100] But the Germans, as required by the CRB accord, permitted the National Food and Relief Committee to spread throughout occupied Belgium, meet regularly, and remain in direct contact with the population through its stores and soup kitchens. Although prohibited from overt political activity, the mere existence of the committee provided Belgian society with an element of autonomous organization. As Henri Pirenne wrote: "The Belgians' cooperation in the face of their shared misery maintained among them the awareness of their common destiny and the will to remain united. . . . All parties rallied spontaneously around the Comité. Its weekly meetings were the only assemblies where the Belgians could freely discuss their affairs, fostering—even under the cover of charity—patriotic and civic feelings."[101] In other words, the committee provided the organization and selective incentives necessary for the provision of collective goods. It thus put additional pressure on Belgian industrialists and labor to cooperate with each other rather than with the invaders.

But the variations in passive resistance within Belgium, and between Belgium and Luxembourg, show that material support was more decisive than organizational support. The CRB did not supply coal, an important military commodity, to Belgium. Since the Germans could have easily shut down Belgian coal mines in the event of a boycott, the Belgians had to collaborate with the occupiers to obtain any fuel for themselves. Knowing full well that it helped the German war effort, and with the blessing of the exile Belgian government, Belgium produced coal for Germany on the condition that a substantial percentage was consumed domestically.[102] Also, worsening living conditions in Belgium (daily bread rations dropped from four hundred grams in late 1916 to three hundred grams in 1917) enticed an increasing number of volunteers into Germany and German-run plants in Belgium, even after the deportations ceased.[103] Although grossly inflated, currency earned working for the Germans allowed desperately hungry souls to buy an extra meal on the black market. As Pirenne observed, "The occupation was too long, the miseries too cruel—total passive resistance by the working class would have required superhuman heroism."[104]

Luxembourg experienced little repression, but unlike Belgium it had to work to eat. Uncertain of Luxembourg's true loyalties, Britain and France vetoed Luxembourg's entreaties for CRB support. Luxembourg was thus thrown back on its own resources, which were inadequate to provision such a densely populated area, and on whatever foodstuffs it could obtain through commerce with Germany and neutral countries. Germany, moreover, insisted that Luxembourg obtain all its imports through German central offices.[105] As one historian put it, "For food the government was simply 'bound hand and foot' to Germany."[106] Germany was thus in a strong position to obtain a maximum amount of Luxembourg steel for a minimal amount of food.

Iron and steel magnates collaborated because they feared the effects of prolonged unemployment on their workers, were concerned about maintaining possession of their factories, and wanted even to turn a profit.[107] Labor also realized that unemployment would have meant starvation; as a machinist pointed out in opposition to the June 1917 strike, "We are materially too poor and don't have enough determined workers."[108] Hunger forced workers back to the mines and factories after only five days. Attempts to establish a national strike fund foundered, at least in part due to direct German intervention but also due to the inadequacy of national resources.[109] Indigent families could apply for a dole, but it only covered a quarter of the cost of basic rations.[110]

Because of its cultural similarities to Germany, Luxembourg does not provide the strongest test of the claim that nationalistic societies will resist exploitation. Although French was used in legal and official proceedings, Luxembourg newspapers were mainly in German, and the colloquial language, Westmoselfränkisch, is a Westphalian-German dialect.[111] Its government remained neutral, never going into exile or declaring war on Germany, as did Belgium. But Luxembourg did have a distinct national identity. Contemporary observers report widespread popular hostility to the German invaders, and even the *Frankfurter Zeitung* admitted that the populace was decidedly pro-French.[112] Overall, then, Luxembourg's political passivity and economic collaboration provide further evidence that conquest pays.

CONCLUSIONS

The contrasts between Belgian and Luxembourgeois productivity, between Belgian coal mining and other industries, and between overall Belgian collaboration in the early and the late stages of the occupation, all point to the importance of economic coercion in determining the profitability of conquest. Holding a bayonet to each worker was impracticable. But in the cases of Belgian coal mining and Luxembourg, the occupier provided irresistible incentives for work. To procure coal for themselves, Belgians had no alternative but to deal with the Germans. Germany made a "work or freeze" threat against Belgium, and Belgium complied. German control over Luxembourg's food supply allowed it to make a more potent "work or starve" threat, with considerably greater results. Germany was unable to do the same in Belgium because of the availability of relief for the unemployed.

The fact that German restraint stemmed ultimately from German and Belgian food deficits also shows that under conditions of economic warfare, states must have a well-balanced supply of resources in the territories they control to maintain economic output. Import-dependent conquests cannot be fully mobilized unless the conqueror or other trading partners can compensate for lost sources of supply. But it would be improvident to assume that all conquerors are as economically vulnerable as World War I Germany. Some are more autarkic, whether because of their size or their ability to substitute materials, and others have conquered more self-sufficient regions.

This set of cases thus provides additional evidence for the cumulativity of industrial resources. Luxembourg was an industrialized and at least moderately nationalistic nation that was forced to collaborate economically with despised invaders. Belgium was highly nationalistic, yet where it had to collaborate to procure coal for winter warmth, it did so. If Germany had controlled sufficient food resources to feed the Belgians, it would never have permitted the distribution of relief that was so crucial to passive resistance. It seems likely that in such a case, Germany could have exploited the Belgian economy almost as fully during the First World War as it did during the Second.

CHAPTER 5

The Ruhr-Rhineland, 1923–1924

REPARATION, like imperial tribute, consists of economic resources extorted from vanquished nations. The main difference is that reparations are justified by victors, fairly or unfairly, as legitimate and finite compensation for war damages and costs caused by criminal aggression. But few defeated nations are so burdened by war guilt that they happily surrender the demanded sums. Most must be militarily occupied or threatened for reparations to be extracted. Since cases of forced reparations extraction are analogous to other cases of conquest and economic mobilization, they add to our knowledge about the profitability of conquest.

Over the course of 1923 and 1924, France and Belgium occupied Germany's industrial Ruhr Valley to collect reparations for the damage inflicted on them in World War I. The first phase of the occupation, from January through September 1923, resembled the German occupation of Belgium during World War I. The occupied population took no violent steps to expel the intruders but used passive resistance to frustrate resource extraction. This passive resistance campaign, known as the *Ruhrkampf* ("Ruhr struggle"), worked while it lasted, but it depended on support from the rest of Germany. When this support dried up, resistance collapsed, allowing the occupiers to extract massive reparations during the second phase of the occupation. Comparing the two phases of the Ruhr occupation, like comparing World War I Belgium and Luxembourg, provides further evidence of the importance of coercion to the profitability of conquest.

FRANCO-BELGIAN AIMS

At the end of World War I, France sought lasting guarantees of security against Germany. Though defeated and territorially pruned, Germany remained the most industrially dynamic and populous country in Western Europe. France, while triumphant, had lost a generation of men, mortgaged its financial future, and seen its industrial northern region devastated. The French had won the war, but now they feared losing the peace. Their foremost demand was to recover Alsace-Lorraine, the provinces lost to Germany in 1871. The French state also needed economic relief for reconstruction and for paying off its crushing war debts, and it sought to shift this burden to Germany. A third goal was to weaken Germany further by long-term demilitarization and by the separation of the Rhineland into an autonomous state under permanent French influence. Finally, France tried to secure promises of future wartime military and economic cooperation by the victorious powers to prevent any revival of the German threat.[1]

At the Paris Peace Conference, the British and Americans supported the return of Alsace-Lorraine but rejected French proposals for Rhenish autonomy and for a permanent anti-German alliance. The British, who overestimated French strength and underestimated Germany's potential for resurgence, feared that France wished to exploit the Allied victory to achieve its own hegemony on the continent. The idealistic Americans were even less sympathetic to French security fears. Detaching the left bank of the Rhine from Germany was hardly consistent with Woodrow Wilson's insistence that "peoples and provinces must not be bartered about from sovereignty to sovereignty."[2]

The Allies agreed for the moment on the necessity of reparations.[3] Britain and Belgium had also been economically exhausted by the war, and public opinion there as in France demanded that Germany pay for their war debts and reconstruction costs. "We must squeeze the Germans until the pips squeak," declared Sir Eric Geddes, first lord of the British admiralty, in 1919.[4] An interim payment of 20 billion gold marks, in cash and in kind, was fixed in the Versailles Treaty, and in early 1921 the Allies presented Germany with a 50 billion gold-mark bill, payable over a thirty-six-year period to France (52 percent), Britain (22 percent), Italy (9.5 percent), Belgium (8 percent), and other claimants.

France and Belgium were especially keen on reparations paid in coal. Cash transfer was difficult for a state as financially unsteady as Germany and resulted in currency devaluation. In addition, the transfer of German manufactures, even if useful for the national economy, would hurt French and British producers of the same goods, who were already clamoring for protection against foreign competition.[5] Coal, on the other hand, was in desperate demand in France. France had been a net coal importer before the war, and its dependence on coal imports was increased by the absorption of Alsace-Lorraine's iron and steel complex as well as the destruction of French coal mines by retreating German troops. France's fifteen-year possession of the Saar's low-grade coal mines helped only somewhat. France had to import 50 percent of its coal during 1919; 70 percent of that was bought from Britain at astronomical prices.[6] The Versailles Treaty obliged Germany to deliver 7 million tons of reparations coal to France per year for ten years, plus millions more to compensate for the lost output of the damaged French mines; Belgium and Italy were to receive 12.5 million tons. In August 1919, the Allies granted a temporary reduction from 3.3 million to 1.7 million tons per month, until German output had recovered.[7]

The Versailles Treaty was to be guaranteed by a prolonged occupation of the Rhineland, the region between the Rhine River and Holland, Belgium, and France. German recalcitrance on reparations would be deterred, the Allies thought, by the threat to extract them directly from the Rhineland or the neighboring Ruhr Valley, Germany's industrial heartland. But although the German government was forced to accept the terms of the Versailles Treaty, it doggedly resisted full implementation. Chancellor Wilhelm Cuno initially balked at Allied proposals at the 1921 London Conference, agreeing to the "London Schedule" only after the Allies occupied the Ruhr ports of Duisburg, Ruhrort, and Düsseldorf and confiscated their customs receipts.[8] But after paying the billion gold marks in cash demanded by the London ultimatum, the German government again failed to make full payments through mid-1922, and coal deliveries fell short by one fifth. In July, the German government requested a complete moratorium on cash payments through 1924.

The justification given by German officials was that their country was simply incapable of paying the amounts demanded. This position, echoed by John Maynard Keynes's famous diatribe against the Versailles Treaty in *The Economic Consequences of the Peace* (1920), became the conventional wisdom in Anglo-American historiography for decades afterward.[9] German Economics Ministry officials did sincerely doubt Germany's ability to pay,[10] but the French believed that Germany could pay and only lacked the requisite will, a position that has gained support from recent historical research.[11] The reparations demanded at Versailles were not far out of proportion to German economic potential: 6–7 percent of German national income was not much more than the 5.6 percent of French national income that Prussia had demanded and received during the five years following the Franco-Prussian War of 1870.[12] The fact that Germany's per capita coal consumption was higher than France's, while its coal deliveries were consistently short, is additional evidence of the capacity to pay. Berlin did have acute difficulties obtaining loans in the aftermath of World War I. But it would spend more funding resistance in 1923 than it had in three years of reparations payments.[13]

Although German politicians and popular opinion denied the war guilt upon which the harsh peace had been premised, German policy was not wholly cynical and evasive. Rather, a domestic political stalemate prevented Berlin from raising the taxes necessary to meet Allied demands.[14] Whatever the motive, the Cuno government believed it could compel a reduction of the reparations bill. Foreign Minister Walter Rathenau advocated in March 1922 a policy of testing the Allies to see "how far the ice is capable of bearing the load," because "a policy of fulfillment pure and simple could not lead to modification" of the treaty.[15] If the Allies replied with punitive measures, a halt of coal deliveries would frustrate their economic aims and split the anti-German coalition. The French and Belgian economies were already strained, and prescient German industrialists thought an impasse would make the franc fall.[16] And British reparations fervor had noticeably cooled since Versailles, raising hopes that Britain might restrain the French, especially after a brief struggle "demonstrated" German insolvency once and for all.

The French resolved to make the Germans yield.[17] President Raymond Poincaré hoped that a brief occupation of the Ruhr would result in rapid acquiescence, just as the customs operation had in 1921. This time occupiers would seize coal and coal taxes, the latter alone being worth more than Germany's total reparations deliveries in 1922.[18] French planners reasoned that the Weimar government would rather give in than endure foreign control of Ruhr coal. But if coercion failed against Berlin, the French would try to squeeze reparations directly from the occupied territory, in which 11 million Germans produced 70 percent of Germany's coal and 80 percent of its steel.[19] Resource extraction would not only fulfill French needs but would show the German government that the French could prolong the occupation if necessary. Jacques Seydoux, the French Foreign Ministry's undersecretary of commerce, anticipated a net profit of 700 million gold marks per year.[20] But Finance Minister Charles de Lasteyrie warned that "everything depends on the attitude of the German authorities and their reaction to the measures of the occupation."[21]

A secondary objective of at least some French officials was a revival of the longstanding plan to separate the Rhineland from Germany. Gen. Joseph Degoutte, the French commander of the Allied occupation force, argued in May 1922 that a Rhineland economically severed from Germany would soon separate politically, "as a ripe fruit falls from a tree."[22] But Poincaré, who anticipated stiff British opposition to further dismemberment of Germany, saw Rhenish separatism as a card to play in the reparations battle rather than an end in itself.[23]

As it turned out, Britain after 1921 was no longer willing to support French efforts to collect reparations. Doubts had grown in London about Germany's ability to pay, as had interest in a rapid German recovery that would stimulate British exports. The British were also concerned about the survival of the Weimar democracy, while the French worried about German revival in any shape or form.[24] Finally, the British suspected that "France was endeavoring to re-establish that supremacy in Europe which she had exercised from time to time in her history."[25] Belgium supported France, but fear of a sharp break with the British and the Versailles framework, combined with financial dependence on American loans, would prove a critical constraint on France's ability to extract resources from Germany.

RESISTANCE AND SUBMISSION

On January 11, 1923, General Degoutte and about seventeen thousand French and Belgian troops escorted three hundred tax collectors and engineers of the Interallied Control Mission for Factories and Mines (Mission Interalliée de Contrôle des Usines et des Mines or MICUM) into the Ruhr.[26] MICUM was authorized to impose licenses, tariffs, and taxes and to supervise the distribution of Ruhr coal and coke. But the occupiers were met by near total passive resistance, orchestrated by Berlin with little advance preparation but with broad support from local officials, industrialists, and unions. The sale or delivery of coal to the occupiers was specifically prohibited, and severe fines and prison sentences were decreed for paying taxes, tariffs, or licensing fees to any foreign power.[27] Customs officials who had worked efficiently for the Allies in 1921 now deserted their posts. The state-run rail and canal network in the Ruhr and Rhineland refused to transport Ruhr coal or anything else to Belgium or France. Coal-laden trains commandeered by occupation troops were abandoned by German railroad workers, and by early February the entire rail network in occupied territory was on strike.

The occupiers attempted to collect reparations directly by looting coal and other goods, but this required a means to transport the booty back to France and Belgium. Despite incidental sabotage (325 attacks resulting in fifty derailments), skeletal rail service was slowly established by 17,500 French and Belgian technical troops, assisted by only a few thousand of the 170,000 German railway employees.[28] Mine by mine, the occupiers used Polish and some local German workers to seize and load stockpiled coal.[29] Daily coal deliveries crept up from one thousand tons in February to eleven thousand tons in May, to fifteen thousand tons in September. But this was still a small fraction of Ruhr capacity (6 percent) and less than half of the amount of reparations coal Germany had been delivering before the occupation.[30] Even these low levels were unsustainable because the mines halted production once they realized that it would be seized by the occupiers (see figure 5-1). MICUM responded by taking over several mines and cokeries, but these produced marginal results.[31] Over the course of the passive resistance campaign, France and Belgium were able to extract only a quarter of 1922 German coal deliveries. Even French hawks were calling it "the Verdun of the peace battle."[32]

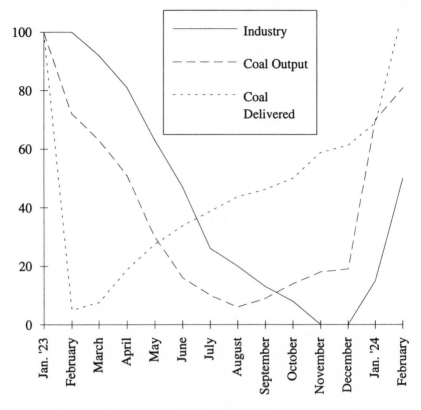

Figure 5-1.
Industrial Output, Coal Output, and Reparations-Coal Deliveries of the
Ruhr-Rhineland, January 1923–February 1924 (percentage of 1922 average). *Source*: France, Armée du Rhin, *Un an d'occupation: L'Oeuvre
franco-belge dans la Ruhr en 1923* (Düsseldorf: Imprimerie de
l'Armée du Rhin, February 1924), 84–85.

Passive resistance entailed high costs as well as low gains for the occupiers. French and Belgian casualties were few, over half occurring when
a sabotaged troop train derailed, killing twelve.[33] But to police and administer the occupied territories, the French had to increase their Rhineland occupation force from 80,000 to a total of 140,000 in the expanded
occupied region. (Belgian troops remained around 10,000 throughout.)[34]
This meant that about one Allied soldier was deployed for every ninety
German citizens in occupied territory. The expenses of the occupation
force, the railway, and MICUM combined with the low harvest of Ruhr
production meant that the French and Belgians were earning nothing
from the occupation and probably had taken a net loss.[35]

The occupation began to reap profits, however, as the passive resistance campaign collapsed during the autumn of 1923. Railway workers returned to work in mid-October, including sixty thousand who had been deported for disobedience.[36] Coal output and deliveries from MICUM-run mines increased immediately, but the real turning point was the agreement of Ruhr industry in late November to pay MICUM coal taxes plus 18 percent of new coal and 35 percent of new coke output.[37] As industrial production revived quickly in early 1924, the occupiers began exploiting other industries as well. By imposing a general turnover tax on all major industries in the Ruhr and Rhineland, they financed the delivery of reparations lumber, chemicals, tools, automobiles, aluminum, and other products. The region finally had become, it seemed, a "reparations province."[38]

By the end of August 1924 net profits reached 721 million gold marks (see table 5-1), an average of around 8 percent of the economic potential of the occupied territories over the course of the whole occupation.[39] But since the occupiers had been losing money until the end of the Ruhrkampf, the extraction rate during the second half of the occupation was closer to double that figure.[40] The collapse of passive resistance appeared to many, in Marshal Foch's words, as "Armistice once again."[41] But while the French and Belgians had finally achieved their initial goal of controlling and taxing Ruhr coal, the MICUM accords could not be continued for long because the Reich was now bankrupt and its industrialists could only briefly shoulder the entire reparations burden.[42] Still, the French and the Belgians had succeeded, if only briefly, in mobilizing occupied Germany for their own gain.

THE ROLE OF COERCION AND REPRESSION

It was intensified economic coercion that broke German resistance in the autumn of 1923 and dictated economic collaboration during the following year. The French and Belgians lacked the necessary leverage in the first phase of the occupation due to their own weak economic policy combined with external support for resistance from Berlin. But by imposing a blockade around occupied Germany, they effectively shut down its boycotting industrial complex. Berlin supported passive resistance by issuing laws against collaboration and by distributing unemployment relief to the industrial work force, but the paralysis of Germany's industrial heartland devastated the entire economy. This took a mounting toll on the German people, especially in the occupied territories. By autumn 1923 Berlin and the occupied populations preferred to collaborate economically rather than continue the struggle.

Although they could not immediately harness Ruhr-Rhenish industry,

TABLE 5-1

Ruhr Occupation Balance Sheet, January 1923–August 1924

(Millions of Gold Marks)

Payments		Goods	
Customs	172.6	Coal and coke	362.1
Coal tax	132.8	Industrial material	27.8
Licenses	100.1	Coal by-products	26.6
Paper marks seized	81.7	Nitrates	24.7
Exploitation of forests	30.5	Wood	20.3
Regie profits	72.3	Sugar	10.8
Diverse charges	11.3	Dyes	8.6
Total payments	601.3	Canal barges	7.6
		Other	22.1
Expenses		Total goods	510.6
Occupation troops	304.0	Net Balance	
Coal seizures and mining	67.6		
Civil administration	17.3	Goods + payments	1111.9
Other	2.0	Total expenses	−390.9
Total expenses	390.9	Net profit	721.0

Source: Weill-Raynal, Réparations allemandes, 3:220–23.

the French and Belgians had no difficulty shutting it down. By establishing a customs barrier around occupied Germany at the end of January 1923, MICUM could require the payment of taxes on all Ruhr exports.[43] Producers refusing to pay taxes to MICUM were effectively stripped of all outside markets. Ruhr industry tried to keep going, drawing on its own financial resources as well as subsidies from the Reich, but little could be done without trade outlets. Stocks of coal accumulated at the pit-heads, and metallurgy suffered from lack of ores.[44] Even this diminished production was halted once the occupiers began looting stocks. Retailers were subject to the same pressure, since shops refusing to sell to occupation troops were also closed down. The MICUM-run mines, though producing little, demonstrated French and Belgian resolve to prolong Germany's suffering indefinitely. As Poincaré put it in February, they would show the Germans that "quite apart from the suffering we inflict upon them, we are capable of achieving a long, stable and remunerative occupation."[45]

Military control allowed the occupiers to turn the German boycott into a general strike but failed to prevent the German government from providing financial subsidies to the unemployed. The French and Belgians could not seize more than a fraction of the Reichsmarks smuggled into the occupied area. These funds, distributed clandestinely by employers and private associations, enabled an idle workforce to continue buying food, which the French still allowed freely into occupied Germany. By the end of June 1923, the subsidies amounted to nearly one billion gold marks.[46]

But time was on the side of the French and Belgians. Unoccupied Germany, already financially unsteady and now severed from its industrial heartland, could not maintain this level of subsidies for long. Berlin resorted to printing paper marks to cover its ever-widening deficits, resulting in extreme hyperinflation. The collapse of the mark in turn undermined the relief effort, indeed the entire economy, as neither German nor foreign farmers would sell their foodstuffs for worthless paper. Growing hungry, the population began to turn against the government. General Degoutte predicted in July that "the day Berlin is no longer able to finance the resistance, the patriotism of the Rhine and Ruhr populations will cease to have a hold on them."[47] In fact, labor and business in the occupied territories were beginning to warn the government that they had no alternative but to strike a deal with the invaders.

On September 26, Chancellor Gustav Stresemann, who had replaced Wilhelm Cuno in August, revoked the passive resistance decrees. But since he continued to hold out on sanctioning reparations payments (by refusing to promise reimbursement to Ruhr industry), conditions continued to worsen. The rise of left-radical movements in Saxony and Thuringia and right-radical movements (including Hitler's Beer Hall Putsch on November 8–9), along with demonstrations by French-backed separatists in the Rhineland, pushed Stresemann toward the MICUM accords. This chaos would probably have compelled even greater concessions had it not simultaneously aroused British, American, and even Belgian anxieties about the course of the occupation.[48]

Threatened reprisals against the occupied population were used effectively to deter active resistance. At first, Berlin had secretly supported a campaign of sabotage against rail lines in heavy use by the occupiers.[49] Degoutte's forces replied by imposing curfews, banning road traffic, and tightening the barrier between occupied and unoccupied Germany. This turned German opinion against active resistance, and Cuno denounced all sabotage in July.[50]

Repression was rather mild, at least compared to the martial law experienced by the Belgians and French under German rule during World War I. The occupiers tracked down and punished suspected saboteurs, achieving some success thanks to the collaboration of rewarded informants. In the course of the struggle, the occupiers killed 132 German citizens, imprisoned 4,124, and expelled 172,000 from occupied territory.[51] There was a certain amount of press censorship, but meetings and demonstrations were permitted unless they grew especially vitriolic. German unions and other organizations were thus able to apply their ordinary techniques of monitoring and rewarding or sanctioning rank-and-file discipline.

More important, the German government continued to exercise influence in occupied Germany despite the deportation of thousands of officials from occupied territory. Many major industrialists were initially willing to pay coal taxes and export tariffs (if not out-of-pocket reparations) to MICUM, for example, until they were sternly forbidden by Berlin.[52] Germany's passive resistance decrees could not be enforced immediately, but since France disavowed any annexationist plans, it was clear that German law would be enforced in the near future. Potential collaborators thus had more to fear from German prisons than French ones. Berlin reminded Ruhr businesses of this by publishing black lists, based on clandestine surveillance, of those to be punished.[53]

But black lists and threatened penalties were insufficient to sustain passive resistance when the population approached the brink of starvation in autumn 1923. Nor could Berlin control the extent of collaboration once it became clear that some degree of collaboration was inevitable. While Stresemann was still trying to restrain Ruhr industrialists, he was surprised to learn that a group led by Otto Wolff, accounting for about 15 percent of Ruhr output, had cut a separate deal with MICUM in early October.[54]

Historian Marc Trachtenberg has argued convincingly that a different economic policy would have obtained much better results for the occupiers.[55] Seydoux and other mid-level French officials had advanced in 1922 a contingency plan for imposing a new currency in the occupied territories. Replacing the German Reichsmark would have vitiated Berlin's subsidies, providing the occupiers with financial control and ample spending money. A Rhenish mark would have required substantial capital backing (some of which Rhenish bankers were willing to provide as the Reichsmark disintegrated) and possibly control over the food supply to make sure that the new currency would be the only legal tender for buying food. Such a considerable investment of capital and administration nevertheless would have been more cost-effective than taking over German railroads and mines. Passive resistance would have been broken more quickly, and greater reparations could have been extracted over a longer period. But Poincaré preferred a strategy of gradual pressure. He feared British and possibly Belgian opposition to occupation measures that diverged from the Versailles settlement, especially to measures hinting of permanence. Poincaré also hesitated to raise taxes for funding a Rhenish currency and feared that using food as a weapon would hinder his side strategy of weaning Rhinelanders from the Reich. Poincaré failed, according to Trachtenberg, "not because success was impossible, but because he had no clear idea of what his aims were and what it would take to achieve them."[56]

French policy ultimately foundered in the face of Anglo-American opposition. Throughout the occupation, the British had registered their passive disapproval by abstaining from all decisions in the Inter-Allied Rhineland High Commission (the agency established by the Versailles Treaty to administer the Rhineland occupation).[57] But London grew increasingly irritated by the MICUM accords, which raised the possibility of a Franco-German coal and steel bloc, and by French support for Rhenish separatism. German economic woes also convinced the British that Allied reparations ambitions had to be scaled down drastically. Over the course of 1923, they resurrected an American proposal from the previous year to convene an interallied committee of experts to reevaluate the whole reparations and war-debts problem.[58] Poincaré assented to this plan on October 19, not long after the end of passive resistance. At the outset he insisted that the size of the reparations debt was not to be questioned, and that the scope of the investigation be limited to the restoration of German finances. With France's stranglehold on the Ruhr-Rhineland intact and the MICUM accords in full swing, Poincaré hoped finally to engage Anglo-American capital in a financially workable solution to the reparations and war-debts stalemate.[59]

But his bargaining position was undermined by the precariousness of French state finances, to which the Ruhr struggle expenses had added the final straw. Instead of raising taxes to pay for postwar reconstruction, the French government had resorted to inflationary deficit spending in the expectation of imminent German reparations. The Ruhr struggle exacerbated this situation. The loss of the coal Germany had been supplying hurt French industrial production. More importantly, French and foreign creditors lost confidence in France's ultimate ability to collect; the resulting speculation against the franc caused it to fall by almost a third against the dollar during 1923. Mounting inflation and its implications for French bond holders were politically disastrous for the government. But when Poincaré turned to London and New York financiers to rescue the franc, he discovered that their condition for credit was a deep reduction of Germany's reparations debt. By the time the Dawes Committee arrived at its lenient reparations plan in April 1924, Poincaré had no alternative but to accept.[60] As historian Stephen Schuker has argued, the French government's inability to "cope with the difficult but not necessarily unmanageable problems of domestic public finance undermined the success of the Ruhr occupation and, at a critical moment, fatefully weakened the nation's power to impose a satisfactory reparations settlement."[61] The Dawes Plan replaced the MICUM accords in September 1924, and the occupation of the Rhineland ended less than a year later.

CONCLUSIONS

The Ruhrkampf of 1923 paralleled the passive resistance in occupied Belgium during World War I. In both cases, a nationalistic mass movement, nourished by external support and by self-organization, effectively blocked the foreign extraction of economic resources. This case even more strongly confirms the dependence of passive resistance on external support, because as the flow of relief dried up half way through the occupation, so did the Ruhrkampf. When the citizens of occupied Germany could no longer eat without working, they went back to work.

The Ruhrkampf is perhaps the favorite example of popular-resistance strategists for demonstrating the potential of people power. If a largely improvised campaign could achieve so much, the argument goes, it would have been far more effective with better strategies, preparations, and training.[62] But this overlooks the inescapable dependence of the resistance on the subsidies, which could not withstand the occupiers' blockade and the Reich's bankruptcy. In addition, the French and Belgians could have implemented a more effective occupation policy. Germany had tolerated the external support of idle masses in occupied France and Belgium during World War I, and the French and Belgians returned the favor in 1923. But by sealing off occupied from unoccupied Germany and replacing the mark with a new currency, the occupiers could have applied economic coercion more efficiently. The Ruhr-Rhineland would then have been forced to resume production and commerce quickly in order to feed its inhabitants. As Seydoux argued in 1922, control over the currency and food supply would have permitted a smoother and more durable means of extracting resources than France actually achieved.

But the occupiers' policy was moderated by a desire to work within the Versailles framework and to avoid alienating Britain. The resulting vacillation led Lord Balfour to observe in 1925 that the French "are so dreadfully afraid of being swallowed up by the tiger, but yet they spend all their time poking at it."[63] Given that by 1923 the British had stopped taking French reparation demands seriously, France should have either abandoned its reparations claims or pursued a more independent and decisive occupation policy. Even Poincaré's policy would have produced more durable results if France had not been already mired in serious, and to a considerable extent, self-inflicted financial difficulties. However, the fact that France was able to crush the Ruhrkampf and exploit occupied Germany, even for a limited period, is evidence for the cumulativity of industrial resources. For if national resistance fails against a timid and economically weak conqueror, what chance does it have against a ruthless and strong one?

CHAPTER 6

The Japanese Empire, 1910–1945

THE JAPANESE EMPIRE differs from previously analyzed episodes of conquest in both duration and level of development. Japan built it up over a half century by conquering and then developing backward, agrarian societies. When first seized—Taiwan in 1895, Korea in 1905, and Manchuria in 1931—they contained virtually no industrial development. If resources were to be mobilized from these conquered regions, they first had to be developed. But Japan managed to create an economically booming and politically submissive empire, and thus greatly increased the economic resources available for wartime mobilization. Although further expansion, into China and Southeast Asia, ultimately plunged Japan into an unwinnable and devastating war, the Japanese Empire supports the cumulativity-of-resources thesis in three ways. First, Japan demonstrated that it is possible to achieve high rates of industrial development in conquered nations. Second, despite Japan's haste and concern for autarky, much of this development appeared quite efficient. Third, although Japan's conquests were initially agrarian societies, their rapid modernization did not result in effective political or economic resistance.

This chapter first shows how Japanese imperialism came to focus on economic goals. Japan's success in developing Taiwan, Korea, and Manchuria and then in mobilizing them for World War II are discussed next, followed by an analysis of the profitability and opportunity costs of Japanese investments. The final section documents the Japanese use of repression and economic incentives to eliminate resistance and encourage collaboration, and analyzes the effects of modernization on the profitability of the empire.

JAPANESE IMPERIALISM

Japanese imperialism was initially motivated by a quest for territorial bulwarks against foreign invasion. But economic objectives became increasingly important after World War I and the Depression, when Japanese leaders began to think that expansion was necessary to assure Japanese economic and military security. Japan ultimately sought to carve an empire out of East Asia that would provide an economic base for peacetime prosperity and for waging total war. Militarized domestic politics had a major role in Japan's irrational overexpansion, which resulted in disastrous struggles against China and the United States. But the ambition to control and exploit the economic resources of other nations, whatever its origins, played a significant role in Japanese imperialism.

The Meiji oligarchs who seized power in 1868 understood the importance of industrial might to military power. Under the slogan of "rich country, strong army," they launched a crash modernization effort by copying Western military, educational, and economic institutions. Until they had succeeded in bolstering Japanese power, however, they remained cautious about imitating Western imperialism as well. At first, their greatest concern was that a rival power might try to seize the Korean Peninsula, which their Prussian military adviser called a "dagger pointed at the heart of Japan."[1] Japan very nearly invaded Korea in 1873, but those mindful of Japan's weakness and fearful of Western intervention prevailed after a bitter internal quarrel.[2] Japan finally declared war on China in 1894 to eliminate its main competitor on the peninsula. A decisive victory forced China's withdrawal from Korea, payment of an indemnity, and the cession of Taiwan. This acquisition had little economic allure, and was intended to preclude territorial encroachment by one of the European empires. Indeed, Prime Minister Ito Hirobumi thought that "we may have to spend on the lands more than we can reap from them."[3]

When Japan went to war over Korea again a decade later, its motives were still chiefly territorial. Russia had become the leading threat by building railways and stationing troops in Manchuria, leasing the nearby Liaotung Peninsula from China, and currying the favor of the Korean court. But Japanese aims also included keeping protectionist Russia from closing Korea and Manchuria to Japanese exports.[4] Victory over Russia in 1905 left Japan with a protectorate in Korea, a sphere of influence and ownership of Russian railways in southern Manchuria, the southern half of Sakhalin (renamed Karafuto), and the Liaotung (renamed Kwantung) leasehold. Japan gradually increased its grip on Korea and annexed it in 1910.[5]

In the following decades, economic security became a more important goal of Japanese imperialism. As Japan industrialized, it became increasingly nervous about its dependence on foreign markets and raw material supplies. Even the British Foreign Office thought in 1921 that Japan "stands little chance of industrial survival unless she can obtain control over the resources of China."[6] Japan also now had enough capital to contemplate investment in China. But the Japanese remained hesitant to antagonize the Western powers by pursuing privileged colonial markets.[7] Two international developments intensified Japanese anxieties and ambitions over the course of the 1920s. First, Japan's existing privileges in China, which had been enlarged during World War I, were threatened by Chiang Kai-shek's consolidation of power in south and central China.[8] Second, Japan's access to world markets and resources seemed suddenly more precarious in the wake of the 1929 collapse of international trade. Trade with the colonies held up better than extra-imperial trade during the ensuing depression, leading many in Japan's political and economic elite to conclude that a large economic trading bloc was needed to protect their country from Western and Chinese "economic warfare." Politicians, military officers, and mass newspapers now regularly referred to Manchuria—which contained four-fifths of Japanese investment and most of Japan's trade in China—as Japan's "economic lifeline."[9]

The military was a particularly strong advocate of economic autarky, but for security reasons. Japanese war planners observed that the European powers had fought World War I by totally mobilizing their own economies and attempting to blockade those of their enemies. This held dire implications for resource-poor Japan, especially in light of Germany's famine and final collapse. These planners concluded that for Japan to survive another war with a great power, it would have to expand to gain control of resource-rich territories.[10] Expansion was feasible because conquest would pay for itself; as the popular army slogan put it, "War can maintain war."[11]

While the Western powers gradually gave way to Chiang Kai-shek on the treaty port system (with the exception of Shanghai and Hong Kong), Japan resolved to secure its position in Manchuria. It supported a south Manchurian warlord from 1921 and then assassinated him in 1928, when he proved too independent. His son and successor, unsurprisingly, established ties to Chiang, and in September 1931 the Kwantung Army on its own initiative proceeded to "establish order" throughout Manchuria. None of the great powers reacted, so Tokyo sanctioned the fait accompli and established the new puppet state of Manchukuo.[12]

Japan's initial economic policy in the colonies was to restrict industries that would compete with Japanese manufactures.[13] But in the 1930s, the crash development of mining and heavy industry began in the colonies and Manchukuo. Nevertheless, Japan's own industrial expansion in the 1930s further increased its dependence on foreign raw materials, especially iron ore, coal, oil, tin, bauxite, and several ferro-alloys.[14] Coal- and iron-rich North China became the next target of Japanese expansion.[15] Japan proceeded by negotiating for economic and political rights with Chiang, while actively subverting his authority in the region; in mid-1935, Koumintang troops were expelled from North China.[16] But Chiang was determined to oppose the 'Manchukuo-ization' of North China, and he moved forces northward after arranging a truce with the Communists in 1936. When local Chinese troops revolted against the Japanese in July 1937, Tokyo resolved to smash Chiang in what it thought would be a three-month campaign.[17]

Dissenters, including the original Kwantung Army conspirators, argued that Japan needed several years of peace to consolidate its economic gains in Manchukuo, and advocated withdrawing from North China to avoid a war "like what Spain was for Napoleon, an endless bog."[18] They were right. Even after Japanese forces had occupied northern and central China's principal cities and towns, Chiang fought on from the interior, assisted by Anglo-American support via Burma and French Indochina. Making matters worse, the protracted fighting required increased imports of iron, oil, and machinery, while the outbreak of war in Europe in 1939 reduced Western trade with Japan.[19]

But the German successes of 1940 provided an opening to drive the Western powers out of Southeast Asia and create an autarkic "Greater East Asia Co-Prosperity Sphere." The Japanese were especially hungry for Indonesian oil, which would end their abject fuel dependence on the United States. Despite the assumption that captured wells and refineries would be totally wrecked, Japanese war planners expected to obtain 30 million barrels of Indonesian crude oil (out of a total demand of 35 million) by 1943; the new conquests would also provide rubber, bauxite, tin, nickel, and copper.[20] With the United States threatening to cut off its oil supplies unless Japan retreated from China, and with the French and Dutch prostrate and the British under siege from Germany, Japan launched its attack on Pearl Harbor. However irrational this gamble, the chief goal was to utilize newly conquered domains to "establish the foundation for a long war."[21]

Tokyo had no definite conception of the political structure it would ultimately establish in East Asia in the event of victory, but the wartime slogans of "Asia for the Asians" and "co-prosperity" were pure propaganda. Colonial administrators had long planned for the very gradual and paternalistic economic, cultural, and political integration of Taiwan and Korea with Japan. In Manchukuo, the puppet regime of China's "last emperor," Pu-Yi, was actually run by the Kwantung Army, but the long-term objectives appeared to be the same as for the colonies. Puppet regimes established in North China, Inner Mongolia, and Central China appeared to be nascent Manchukuos. Japanese ambitions appear somewhat more restrained for the rest of China and Southeast Asia, which might have been granted some domestic autonomy within an enforced military and economic alliance with Japan.[22] As it was, the international climate, the brevity of Japanese rule, and the huge dimensions of the task precluded much more than minimal military control.

Once embroiled in war, Japanese immediate policies were "to fulfill the demand for resources vital to the prosecution of the present war, to establish at the same time an autarkic Greater East Asia Co-Prosperity Sphere, and to accelerate the strengthening of the economic power of the empire."[23] But the geographic sprawl of the empire meant that its conquests could not be held for long, and even if Japan had been able to mobilize all of Greater East Asia, it would have remained a military-industrial pygmy compared to the United States. Thus the attempt to achieve ultimate economic security plunged Japan into the ultimate national disaster.[24]

PROFITABILITY OF EMPIRE

Taiwan, Korea, and Manchuria were backward agrarian societies when conquered by Japan. To make them economically useful, Japan applied the same modernization model that had worked so well in Japan, minus the military, political, and advanced educational institutions. The result was astonishing growth rates, unparalleled in the history of empire. By expanding agricultural and mining output in these regions, Japan increased its economic self-sufficiency. Whether Japanese investment in the empire was as productive as foregone alternatives is less clear. But, after describing Japan's success in developing its conquests, I will argue that circumstantial evidence suggests that much, if not all, of Japanese imperial development was profitable.

Colonial Development

Under Japanese rule, annual GDP growth averaged 3 percent in Korea and 4 percent in Taiwan and Manchuria (see figure 6-1).[25] These were very high rates by prewar standards for less developed Asian countries, which averaged just over 1 percent between 1913 and 1952.[26] Development was coordinated by the colonial administrations of Taiwan and Korea, and by the Kwantung Army in Manchukuo. The colonial administrations closely regulated and in many cases provided incentives for the extension of Japanese big business (zaibatsu) to the colonies. Semiofficial companies, such as the Oriental Development Corporation, were active in Korea and Taiwan, but as in Japan did not dominate the private economy.[27] The Kwantung Army's stranglehold over all aspects of Manchurian development, in contrast, discouraged zaibatsu investment. Capital was raised instead through bonds, with returns guaranteed by Manchukuo or Japan, and combined with government capital into semiofficial companies.[28]

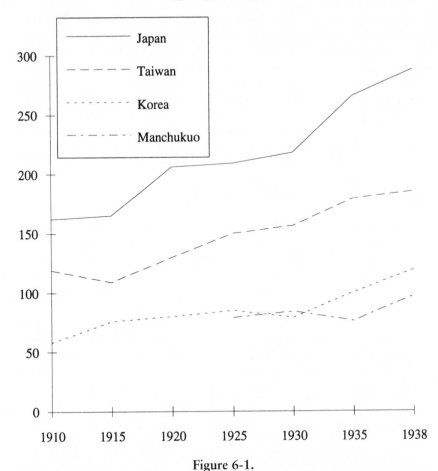

Figure 6-1.
Per Capita Gross Domestic Expenditure in the Japanese Empire, 1910–1938 (constant 1934–1936 yen). *Source*: Mizoguchi and Umemura, *Basic Economic Statistics*, 231–39; Chao, *Economic Development of Manchuria*, 34.

The first steps in development were property reforms and the building of a market infrastructure. A comprehensive land survey facilitated the systematic taxation of property, including lands once exempted by feudal privileges. Commercial infrastructure was improved by the construction of railways, roads, telegraph networks, harbors, and warehouses, the standardization of currency and measures, and the availability of credit.[29] Railways were given especially high priority, because they not only connected newly opened resources to ports but were also militarily useful for combating both external attack and internal rebellion.[30]

To improve agricultural productivity, research bureaus for evaluating and disseminating information about seeds and fertilizers were established, and Japanese capital permitted the clearing and irrigation of new lands for cultivation.[31] High irrigation investments in Korea and Taiwan paid off in a doubling of rice production, with the increases all exported to Japan. Sugar-cane introduced to tropical Taiwan soon weaned Japanese consumers from Indonesian imports.

In the 1930s, Japan began encouraging industrial development in the empire. Maximizing steel and chemical output within the empire required locating heavy industries—and the Japanese managers and technicians directing investment and production—near the raw materials, energy, and cheap local labor they fed upon.[32] The growth of industrial production was impressive.[33] Korean iron ore output increased from 0.6 million tons in 1930 to 1 million tons in 1940; almost half was shipped to Japan, but by 1940 Korea was producing 240,000 tons of pig-iron. Over the same period, Manchurian coal nearly doubled (from 10 to 20 million tons), iron ore more than tripled (from nearly 1 million tons to 3 million tons), as did pig-iron (from a third of a million tons to 1 million). Steel production was getting under way in Korea by 1940, and had already reached more than half a million tons in Manchuria.[34] Korean chemical industries, which produced fertilizers and explosives, grew from 16 percent to 30 percent of Korea's total manufacturing output.[35] Although Taiwanese industry concentrated on sugar refining, Taiwan was producing a sixth of Japan's aluminum consumption in 1940.[36]

Japanese also cultivated "human resources" as a means of expanding the productivity of conquered populations. Improved health and medical care reduced mortality rates significantly.[37] Schools proliferated in the 1930s, designed to mold the colonial populations into economically useful and indoctrinated subjects. Much of the investment in education would be reaped only by the postwar inheritors of the empire, but the improvements during the period of Japanese rule reveal the seriousness of modernization policy. Whereas before Japanese rule only a small percentage got any education at all, half of all Taiwanese children and a third of all Korean and Manchurian children were attending primary schools by 1940. Secondary schools, which focused on vocational training, also proliferated in the colonies, and a few universities were even established.[38]

Wartime Mobilization

On the eve of Pearl Harbor, Japan was still investing heavily in the modernization of the empire, planning to reap the rewards of "co-prosperity" long into the future. This development paid off during the war for the

TABLE 6-1

Coal, Aluminum, Iron, and Steel Production in Korea,
Taiwan, and Manchukuo, 1937–1944
(Thousands of Tons)

	Coal	Aluminum	Iron	Steel
1937	19,073	2.78	988	454
1938	21,606	5.56	1,122	611
1939	27,275	11.12	1,285	636
1940	30,055	15.27	1,307	650
1941	33,720	23.70	1,384	676
1942	33,125	25.30	1,698	805
1943	34,288	35.58	1,862	951
1944	34,317	30.14	1,358	538

Sources: Cohen, *Japan's Economy in War*, 163; Myers, *Japanese Economic Development*, 283; SCAP, *Mineral Resources of Japan Proper*, 19; SCAP, *Iron and Steel Metallurgy of the Japanese Empire*, 39–40, 53.

Japanese, who could rely heavily on their own possessions for the raw materials of war. From 1941 through 1944, a third of the pig-iron and aluminum, half of the coal, and a tenth of the steel in Japanese hands were produced beyond the home islands. In addition, two-thirds of the iron ore smelted in Japan was imported, and a third of the empire's electric power and half of its magnesium lay in the periphery by 1944.[39]

This could only have been possible with the continued expansion of mining and industrial output in Japanese possessions. Table 6-1 summarizes the wartime production of coal, iron, steel, and aluminum in Korea, Taiwan, and Manchukuo. These territories, along with occupied North China, also produced increasing amounts of mineral ores, electrical power, chemicals, textiles, machinery, and even motor vehicles, despite U.S. bombing raids starting in 1943.[40] Although national income series are lacking for wartime Korea or post-1941 Manchuria, it appears that overall production increased well into the war. By 1941 Manchurian GDP had increased by 14 percent from 1939 levels.[41] Taiwanese national income increased by 29 percent in real terms between 1938 and 1942, but fell to 88 percent and 60 percent of 1938 levels in the next two years, probably due to the tightening U.S. blockade.[42]

Japan also mobilized slave labor and military manpower from its empire. By the end of the war, over two hundred thousand Koreans had been conscripted into the Japanese Army and Navy. Hundreds of thousands more were drafted for forced labor in Japanese coal mines, construction, and manufacturing; Koreans comprised a third of all miners in Japan, and reportedly worked at 80 percent of Japanese productivity. Forced labor was also rampant in Korea itself.[43] Most horrifying of all was the enslavement of seventy thousand Korean "comfort women" in military brothels throughout the empire.[44]

Japan's ability to mobilize its conquests depended on intra-imperial shipping, which was very vulnerable to U.S. submarine warfare. Tojo's February 1943 announcement that Japan's oil problem had been solved by new Indonesian supplies was premature, as the blockade was just starting to bite. Oil shipped to Japan fell accordingly from 14.5 million barrels in 1943 to 5 million barrels in 1944, with profound effects on Japanese war-making ability.[45] Shipping shortages also limited the amount of Chinese coking coal going to Japan and Manchuria starting in late 1943, which in turn limited steel production. Japan's attempt to alleviate the transportation bottleneck by shifting blast furnaces to the continent came too late,[46] and steel production in the Japanese Empire fell as a result, from a peak of 8.8 million tons in 1943 to 6.5 million tons in 1944 to 0.8 million tons in the first quarter of 1945.[47]

Efficiency and Opportunity Costs

Rapid growth in the empire was necessary to Japan's quest for economic autarky. Japan unquestionably sank massive resources into its new domains to achieve the high industrialization rates of the 1930s. To the extent that these resources were used inefficiently, empire involved significant opportunity costs. Unfortunately, the present state of historical research on the Japanese Empire does not permit a definitive evaluation of its profitability. Imperial revenues were extracted through returns on private and public investments rather than from easily measured tribute or taxes. The huge number of investments makes measuring Japanese profit an immensely difficult undertaking, and makes suspect, for example, one historian's undocumented claim that Japanese investment in Korea over 1910–23 earned about 18 percent in interest and profits.[48] Account must also be taken, moreover, of the drain on the Japanese treasury posed by state subsidization of certain sectors (about which data has not been compiled) and by the administration and garrisoning of the empire (discussed below).

But there are several important indications that the empire was, or might have become, a profitable venture. The first kind of evidence is the judgment of academic specialists and of Japanese officials. U.S. officials in the 1930s liked to believe that Japan's expansion into Manchuria was an uphill struggle against "natural economic forces."[49] But the most detailed prewar study of the Japanese and Manchurian economies criticized the "inclination to write off what has been done in Manchukuo as having only strategic importance and no permanent constructive value," since "the improvement of transportation facilities and the development of forestry and mineral resources will be to a very large extent useful in a peacetime economy."[50] As for Taiwan and Korea, an economic historian has recently concluded that they were exploited with "considerable success."[51]

Japanese officials agreed with this assessment after the war, when defeat and political reorganization had dispelled earlier militaristic biases. Commenting on the $20 billion in assets stranded in the former empire, a Japanese Foreign Ministry study noted wistfully that "it cannot help but be a blow to the future Japanese economy that these investments have been lost when they are about to bear fruit one by one."[52] The same study also worried that "the loss of such monopolistic markets will deprive Japan of the benefit of reinforcing its competitiveness in other free markets by making a monopolistic profit in these areas into a foothold."[53]

Further evidence for imperial profitability can be found in the fact that labor in the empire was cheap and apparently productive. Per capita consumption increased by only 20 percent in Taiwan and 40 percent in Korea between 1910 and 1940, lower than the corresponding increases in per capita national product, 55 percent in Taiwan and 105 percent in Korea.[54] An illustration of this is the fact that although they grew rice in ever greater quantities, rice consumption by Taiwanese and Koreans fell over the course of Japanese rule and had to be supplemented with cheaper and inferior grains.[55] Nor did consumption keep pace with the 21 percent increase in Manchukuo's per capita GDP between 1929 and 1941.[56] Labor costs were held artificially low by administrative manipulation of the agricultural market. Farmers were required to sell rice and sugar cane to a small number of licensed refineries, mills, and exporters, whose monopsony position kept prices down.[57] The native populations were also exploited through land taxes, sales taxes (for example, on alcohol and sugar), monopoly profits (for example, on opium, salt, tobacco), and tariffs for government services, like railways.[58]

Historians have hardly begun to examine the question of labor productivity. But one study of the Manchurian coal mines at Fushun suggests it was at least adequate. According to the author, rapid expansion "was undoubtedly achieved due to the co-operation given by the Chinese engineers and laborers. . . . labor control was achieved relatively smoothly for the management of a modern gigantic coal mine."[59]

Records of intra-imperial trade provide additional useful evidence, but profitability cannot be directly inferred from trade balances. This is because trade balances do not reflect profits that, instead of being repatriated, are reinvested in industry or spent on other imperial projects. Japan's farming strategy meant that most profits were plowed back into its possessions. According to some experts, for example, between a half and four-fifths of total Korean capital formation came from reinvested profits mobilized from within the colony.[60] Imports from Japan may also have represented military spending by Japan proper, since Korea and especially Manchukuo by the late 1930s had become advance military supply bases for the Japanese Army.[61]

Furthermore, although capital inflows are reflected in trade balances as they are invested, the returns may not appear until years later. When the pace of development is as intense as it was in Korea and Manchukuo, new investments on infrastructure and factories would be expected to outstrip the return on past investments. In fact, Japan invested more capital in Manchukuo in a decade than Britain had invested in India during two centuries of imperial rule.[62] Japanese settlers owned the most fertile 20–25 percent of farmland, and Japanese corporations owned over 90 percent of the large factories.[63] These investments were made with the expectation of profits for many years to come, profits reaped by the Taiwanese, Korean, and Chinese inheritors after the war.[64]

Thus the fact that Korea and Manchukuo had persistent import surpluses from Japan does not mean that they were economic liabilities.[65] But Taiwan's export surpluses, accumulating to 750 million yen by 1937, do indicate that Japan's oldest possession was a highly profitable investment.[66] From the 1920s, Taiwanese growth was financed primarily by Taiwanese savings, by Japanese companies based in Taiwan, and by the colonial government. Growth had become self-generating, and a clear surplus was being transferred to Japan proper.[67]

Economic efficiency varied across the empire. Some investments were quite profitable, while others received tax breaks, protective tariffs, subsidies, guaranteed returns, or assured government demand, all in the interest of autarky. Cheaply grown colonial rice was more profitable than Taiwanese sugar, which was protected by tariffs to reduce dependence on Javanese sources.[68] Another contrast can be seen in the Nitchitsu chemical corporation, which had built a massive and profitable fertilizer/explosives complex in northern Korea by the mid-1930s, but diversified into less efficient but governmentally subsidized strategic industries in the latter half of the decade.[69] This problem was particularly acute in Manchukuo, where the Kwantung Army's command-economy approach scared off the traditional zaibatsu from participating at all and resulted in wasteful imbalances in Manchurian development[70]

It would be wrong, however, to assume that protection and subsidization were indefinite costs of autarky. Japan in the 1930s was pioneering the art of state-directed industrial policy. It intervened in the market to nourish strategic industries in the home islands as well as in the colonies, just as it has intervened to promote high-technology industries in the postwar period.[71] Manchukuo's state-controlled development even had its analogues in Japanese public utilities.[72] And if strategic trade policy is gaining increasing adherents in today's open world economy, it made even more sense in the protectionist environment of the 1930s.

More research is needed into the economic productivity of Japan's imperial development. But existing studies have failed to find any evidence that labor resistance was a significant obstacle to efficiency, except in North China, where guerrillas attacked railways (though without halting steady increases in Japanese traffic).[73] Instead, they stress the compromises inherent in crash development, a policy that nevertheless achieved astounding rates of growth in the empire.

Costs of Control

Imperial profitability depends not only on the productivity of economic investments, but also on the expense of guarding them from hostile populations. In the Japanese Empire, the political apparatus included Japanese occupation armies and partly Japanese, partly native colonial governments. Pacification required considerable initial expenditures on political repression. But once the conquests had been consolidated, the everyday costs of control were too low to drain either Japanese budgets or colonial productivity.

Conquest entailed costly pacification campaigns against local rebels. Taiwanese guerrillas put up such a fierce battle between 1895 and 1898 that the oligarchs considered selling their new possession to France for 100 million yen.[74] Within but a few years of annexation, Japanese troops had eradicated an initial seventy thousand insurgents in Korea (even assuming no double counting, this amounted to a half of 1 percent of the population).[75] The Japanese faced greater and more protracted guerrilla resistance in Manchuria. But the 360,000 "bandits" there in 1932 were reduced to 20–25,000 by 1935, and to 7,300 by 1938. They had been completely eradicated by 1941.[76] Otherwise, Japan faced no violent resistance in these territories until the end of the empire.

After the consolidation of control, it was maintained mainly by colonial police forces. But these forces were not very large, and most of their energies were devoted to suppressing nonpolitical crime, as well as assisting in local administrative duties like population and land surveys, tax collection, information dissemination, and labor and military conscription during the war.[77] The low cost of repressing nationalistic resistance is evident in the fact that the police per capita in Korea and Taiwan was roughly the same as in Japan proper, about 1 per thousand in 1940.[78] The still larger colonial bureaucracies (the Korean general government had 82,870 employees, or 3.6 per thousand in 1940) had a primarily economic role, evident in large increases during the crash industrialization of the late 1930s (the proportion in 1935 was only 2.5 per thousand).[79]

Costs were reduced by the recruitment of indigenous personnel. By the end of Japanese rule, natives comprised about half of the administrative personnel in Taiwan, Korea, and Manchuria, particularly in the lower ranks. The proportions of natives serving in the police forces were a sixth, a third, and almost nine-tenths, respectively.[80] Costs were also reduced by the self-policing of indigenous village leaders.[81] Another low-cost aid to effective Japanese rule were Japanese settlers, who made up 5 percent of Taiwan's population, 2.5 percent of Korea's, and 1.3 percent of Manchukuo's.[82] But they did not represent an additional economic liability, for most—other than the administrators already noted—were productively involved in farming or business.

Japanese troops in Korea (46,000 men, or 2 per thousand Koreans) and in Taiwan (about 23,000, or 4 per thousand) were relatively small.[83] Moreover, once the initial pacification period was through, they played little role in domestic repression. (The Japanese military police were merged into the civil police after 1919.)[84] Military forces were responsible for defending the empire from external attack, and for occasional offensive actions, like the Korea Army's participation in the 1931 invasion of Manchuria. The Kwantung Army in Manchukuo was proportionately larger, growing from 164,000 in 1935 (almost 5 per thousand) to 270,000 in 1939 (7 per thousand), but it was deployed to balance against the Soviet Far Eastern Army, which increased from 230,000 to 570,000 during the same period.[85] After the initial pacification effort, the remaining Manchurian insurgents were hunted down by a force of 40,000 native mercenaries, trained and commanded by Kwantung Army officers.[86]

In sum, the total personnel required to control Taiwan, Korea, and Manchuria were not high in proportion to the local populations. Tax revenues more than covered administrative budgets; for example, regular administration and policing expenses ranged between 80 and 86 percent of Korean revenues between 1936 and 1938, and between 56 and 68 percent of Manchukuoan revenues between 1937 and 1941.[87] This was probably also the case for Taiwan, where direct subsidies from Japan had ended by 1904 (in Korea, they declined from 24 percent to only 3 percent of the Government-General's budgets between 1910 and 1937).[88] It thus does not appear that the costs of repression were very significant in Taiwan, Korea, and Manchuria, at least in comparison with the economic gains.

Thus, although Japanese foreign policymaking was deluded by many myths in the years leading up to the attack on Pearl Harbor, belief in the cumulativity of resources was not one of them. Empire paid handsomely for Japan, at least until the invasion of China in 1937.[89] Consistent with this conclusion, although only circumstantial proof of it, is Japan's economic growth in the decades leading up to World War II (figure 6–1). Between 1915 and 1940, Japan's real GNP more than doubled, growing at an average annual rate of 3.7 percent. Growth in the 1930s, during the period of heavy investment in Korea and Manchukuo, averaged an astounding 4.6 percent, and this occurred at a time when the other industrialized countries were mired in depression.[90] Growth tapered in the late 1930s, but this was due chiefly to increased military spending and economic controls during the war.[91]

In contrast to Taiwan, Korea, and Manchuria, occupied China between 1937 and 1945 was indeed an "endless bog." Communists based in the remote Shensi Province infiltrated easily behind Japanese lines after 1937 and worked with the poverty-stricken peasants to increase agricultural production and defend against Japanese requisitions of grain and labor.[92] Peasant support in return allowed a great increase in guerrilla numbers, from 50,000 in 1937 to 400,000 in 1940.[93] While maintaining a powerful grip on the occupied towns and cities, Japanese troops—which increased from 400,000 in 1939 to 750,000 by 1943—were able to control only a quarter of the vast area and less than half of the 183 million Chinese behind Japanese front lines.[94] The guerrillas were strongest in North China; in Central China, the Koumintang-Communist rivalry and the less desperate food situation allowed much greater Japanese success in rural pacification. Puppet regimes established in North China, Inner Mongolia, and Central China provided some assistance to the Japanese but were unable to compete with the Communists for peasant support.[95] In frustration, the Japanese resorted to a scorched-earth policy against villages suspected of harboring guerrillas. The onslaught set the Communists back over 1941–42, but ultimately drove the peasantry more solidly into their ranks, which reached 500,000 by 1945.[96]

The Communist guerrillas generally refrained from attacking Japanese urban strongholds, except in the unsuccessful autumn 1940 "Hundred Regiments Offensive." For its part, the Japanese Army focused on pursuing and blockading Chiang's Nationalist forces. But the guerrilla threat to smaller garrisons and railways created a steady drain on the Japanese war effort. Economic gains in China were also not particularly impressive. Although Japan was able to dramatically increase coal and iron production in China for its own war economy, occupied China was too poor and rebellious to exploit systematically. Requisitions of peasants' cash crops led to the widespread adoption of diversified, subsistence agriculture.[97] This meant mass starvation by Chinese peasants, but it also frustrated

Japanese efforts to mobilize an agricultural surplus from China. As a result, the army failed here to make conquest pay for war, reminding a Japanese Foreign Ministry official in 1938 of "an octopus eating its own tentacles."[98]

COLLABORATION AND RESISTANCE

Despite levels of development that would predict moderately intense nationalism, significant resistance to Japanese domination failed to arise in Korea, Taiwan, and Manchuria. After initial periods of armed revolt, the populations remained submissive to Japanese rule. Political repression stamped out the Korean independence movement of 1919, and nothing analogous even appeared in Taiwan or Manchuria. Level of development did not correspond, over time or cross-nationally, with levels of resistance, even as police repression remained more-or-less constant. Japan was unable to fully control, much less mobilize, the two hundred million Chinese conquered after 1937. But Japan's prior experience in Taiwan, Korea, and Manchuria suggests that if it had not also been waging a war against Chiang Kai-shek and, later, the United States, China too might have eventually shared their fate.

The populations of Taiwan, Korea, and Manchuria were somewhat, though not highly, nationalistic vis-à-vis the Japanese. Japanese propaganda about "Asia for Asians" presupposed an imaginary common ethnic identity. While sharing some linguistic and religious traits, Koreans and the ethnic Chinese of Taiwan and Manchuria were no closer culturally to the Japanese than British are to Germans.[99] Nationalism was evident in brief but widespread revolts against the Japanese conquest and in the massive Korean protests of 1919.

However, the comparatively low level of development in all three societies meant that they were not highly nationalistic. If considerable urbanization and proletarianization occurred during the period of Japanese rule, most of the colonized remained peasant farmers who rarely traveled from their villages and had little knowledge of national affairs. However, Korea, Taiwan, and Manchuria were at least as developed as other less developed countries noted for fierce nationalistic resistance, such as North China during World War II and Vietnam and Algeria somewhat later (see table 6-2).

Whatever nationalism developed in Taiwan, Korea, and Manchuria, it was successfully contained by Japanese repression. After Japan consolidated control in the colonies, the only significant challenge was the massive pro-independence demonstrations in Korea that began on March 1,

TABLE 6-2

Development Indicators for Japanese Empire, 1938,
and South Vietnam and Algeria, 1958

	GDP/Capita (U.S. 1980 dollars)	Urbanization (Percentage of population in cities over 20,000)	Telephones (per 1,000 pop.)
Taiwan 1938	752	21	6.0
Korea 1938	484	13–19	3.4
Manchuria 1938	394		
South Vietnam 1958	190	14	0.9
Algeria 1958	468	24	14.4
Japan 1938	1,405	39	19.4

Sources: Japanese Empire income estimates based on Mizoguchi and Umemura, *Basic Economic Statistics*, 231–39; Chao, *Economic Development of Manchuria*, and Angus Maddison, *World Economy*, appendices A, B, C. Vietnamese and Algerian income estimates from United Nations, *Yearbook of National Accounts Statistics, 1964* (New York: United Nations, 1965), 389–92, adjusted to 1980 dollars with a standard GNP deflator. Urbanization data from United Nations, *Growth of the World's Urban and Rural Population, 1920–2000* (New York: United Nations, 1969), 105–6; and Edward Mason, et al., *The Economic and Social Modernization of the Republic of Korea* (Cambridge: Harvard University Press, 1980), 80. Telephone data from American Telephone and Telegraph, *Telephone Statistics of the World*, 1938 and 1958.

1919. Despite the outlawing of all agitation against Japanese rule, about 1 million Koreans (or 5 percent of the population) from all regions and occupations participated in the March First Movement. Initially peaceful protests escalated to rioting, and bloody clashes between Japanese forces and Korean mobs ensued over the following months. But once the movement had been crushed, Korea would remain quiet for the remainder of Japanese rule.[100] In Manchuria, guerrilla resistance persisted through the 1930s, but had dwindled to insignificance by the end of the decade. Active resistance failed entirely to materialize in Taiwan. The small political movements that did surface there lobbied for political and educational equality with the Japanese colonists, or at most, limited autonomy within the empire.[101] Indeed, the Taiwanese rebelled only in 1947, against Chiang Kai-shek's reimposition of Chinese rule.[102]

Collaboration, in contrast, was widespread. Colonial bureaucracies, headed by appointed Japanese governors, swept away the indigenous ruling institutions and elites in Taiwan and Korea.[103] In Manchukuo, the Japanese relied on native provincial administrations that were left intact.[104] But throughout the empire, locals readily provided much of the bureaucrats and policemen in the Japanese-run administrations. There were ten to twenty native applicants for every patrolman opening in

Korea and Taiwan, and the Taiwanese police could report in 1937 that they "not only have no problem in getting the number of men needed but also are able to freely select the well-qualified ones."[105] Native landlords and businessmen paid taxes and sold goods and services to the Japanese authorities, and simply by running their plantations and companies they helped tax and mobilize native laborers as well. The magnitude of economic collaboration is reflected in the fact that 60 percent of the top, postwar South Korean companies were founded by men with some kind of colonial business experience.[106] During the war, leading Korean businessmen even found themselves giving speeches like "Korean Student Soldiers Enlist in a Bright Tomorrow" and "Dying for a Righteous Cause: The Responsibility of Imperial Citizens is Great," which insisted that "your sacrifice will not be in vain . . . a sacrifice for this peninsula that gave you life, and with it, this peninsula will attain the qualifications [necessary] for imperial membership; thus it may be said that the future of Korea rests solely on your course of action."[107]

Japanese success was due to a combination of coercion, repression, and incentives for collaboration. The Japanese authorities left no doubt about the consequences of mass resistance. As the first governor general of Korea made painfully clear, "Japan will just suppress such rebellion with force. This will not hurt Japan; only Koreans will suffer."[108] The initial pacification campaigns in each new conquest provided vivid evidence of Japanese power and ruthlessness. So did the bloody suppression of the March First Movement with twenty thousand arrests, two thousand Korean casualties, and the use of torture to root out the movement's leaders.[109] Gloating twenty years later about its victory over "the so-called independence agitation," the general government concluded that "the strengthening of the police and the popular awakening to the utter futility of the movement have done much to stop intrigues and also made collective demonstrations practically impossible." It also warned that "any attempting to interfere with this bond of union [between Japan and Korea] will be strictly repressed and severely dealt with."[110]

Collective action was further restricted by the surveillance of social organizations, which were immediately banned upon suspicion of political activity. Meetings, speeches, and publications not sponsored by colonial agencies were rarely permitted, and even then were closely monitored and censored. Firearms and explosives were tightly controlled.[111] Prior to 1919, Korean churches had remained a means of national communication outside of Japanese control, and it was in this organizational space that the March First Movement was secretly coordinated. In its aftermath, the police force was increased and a new "thought-police" branch established. Some leeway was given to strictly cultural publications and organizations in Taiwan and Korea in the 1920s, but even this was terminated with the intensification of assimilationist policies after 1935.[112] As industrial labor increased during the 1930s, unions were outlawed as well. Through the establishment of efficient colonial police states, the Japanese successfully atomized fledgling colonial city-dwellers and kept a close watch on the countryside.

As is so often the case, it is difficult to distinguish the individual and national motivations for collaboration with conquerors. Japanese ruthlessness, determination, and successful empire-building made it difficult for conquered subjects even to imagine liberation. Historians agree that nationalist movements and resistance were simply not realistic.[113] But collaboration also had its financial rewards. Native bureaucrats, police, and businessmen flocked to work for the Japanese, not out of any affection for their haughty overlords but to earn a living. Landlords and businessmen were particularly assiduous supplicants to Japanese authorities, bankers, and merchants, who held many of the keys to financial success. As Carter Eckhart has shown in the case of Korea, the incentives wielded by the Japanese inclined native elites "to think first of their class interests ... and only secondarily, if at all, of a national struggle against the Japanese."[114] Obtaining Japanese capital, subsidies, technology, and labor control required utter obedience and even assimilation to Japanese culture.

While Japanese possessions remained for the most part pre-industrial societies, their rapid modernization over the period of Japanese rule failed to increase resistance. Between 1915 and 1940, nonagricultural labor increased from 11 percent to 25 percent in Korea, from 29 percent to 39 percent in Taiwan, and to 25 percent in Manchuria.[115] Over roughly the same period, the proportion of urban population grew from 4 percent to 13 percent in Korea and from 7 percent to 21 percent in Taiwan.[116] But anti-Japanese resistance seemed only to flag over time. In Korea, the average annual number of political offenses prosecuted in the colonial courts declined steadily from 35 cases per million Koreans in 1920–24, to 21 cases in 1925–30, to 13 in 1930–34, to 5 in 1935–40; over this same period the number of police per capita also declined slightly.[117] After 1940, intensified mobilization and Japanization measures increased both crime and police numbers in Korea. Wartime economic hardships combined with labor and military conscription and intensified Japanization increased unrest (political offenses climbed back up to 10 per million, and the police force increased 20 percent), but the Japanese Home Ministry claimed to be satisfied with Korea's participation in the war effort.[118] In Taiwan, police per capita declined gradually throughout the period of Japanese rule. Despite the fact that this trend continued after 1940, crime also declined during the war.[119]

In fact, despite brutal methods, the Japanese even seemed to be having some success in culturally assimilating the Taiwanese and Koreans. Primary schools throughout the empire trained children in Japanese language, imperial ideology, and eventually Shintoism.[120] By 1945 more than half of all Taiwanese and nearly a fifth of all Koreans were conversant in Japanese.[121] Japanese education did not necessarily result in acceptance of Japanese culture, particularly since the Japanese refused to extend equal economic or political rights to native populations. But native elites in both colonies increasingly welcomed assimilation. By the end of the war, a tenth of the Taiwanese population had voluntarily adopted Japanese surnames.[122] Thousands throughout the empire participated in pro-Japanese associations and turned out at rallies celebrating Japanese military victories.[123]

Although hostility to Japan was greater in Korea than in Taiwan, well-to-do Koreans also sought to assimilate. For example, a Korean businessman who had been a leading nationalist in 1919 declared two decades later that the Japanese "national character is deep-rooted, strong, and has come down from high-above [that is, from the divine emperor]. I do not think, however, that either the Korean people or the Chinese people have been formed from such a center."[124] Japanese authorities, planning for the military mobilization of the entire empire after 1937, banned the Korean language from schools and newspapers and compelled most Koreans to adopt Japanese surnames and Shinto rituals.[125] Forced Japanization and other wartime brutalities stamped an enduring bitterness into the hearts of Korean people, but whether their culture would have survived a Japanese victory is hard to say.

A simple connection between modernization and resistance does not hold up in cross-national comparisons either. Taiwan was the most modern Japanese possession in terms of nonagricultural labor, education levels, urbanization, and per capita income, but it was also the most submissive. Taiwan's slightly higher number of *Japanese* police per capita, its conquest at an earlier stage of development (unlike in Korea, prior to the establishment of state-run schools), its higher living standards, and its longer exposure to Japanese rule and language also may have been important.[126] Interestingly, a disproportionately high number of police per capita were required to control the relatively few (135,000) primitive aborigines occupying the undeveloped half of Taiwan.[127]

The greatest resistance to Japanese rule was in North China, the least modern area controlled by Japan (85 percent of Manchuria's per capita GDP in the early 1930s and less than 60 percent of it by 1941).[128] Within North China, guerrillas flourished in remote rural areas with poor roads and communications, which impeded monitoring and access by Japanese forces. North China's rebels also benefited from a relatively close unoccupied sanctuary in Shensi Province, more hospitable weather and terrain, and the ongoing struggle between the Japanese and Chiang Kai-shek. Chinese village communities were probably more cohesive than those in immigrant-heavy Manchuria, and it is possible that Japanese troops were spread more thinly in China than in Japan's prior conquests.[129] One would not want to conclude that backwardness was sufficient for rebellion—Japan after all did successfully pacify Taiwan and Korea at very early stages of development. More research is needed to explain why Japan pacified Taiwan, Korea, and Manchuria so much more easily than North China. But modernization did not appear to help the subjects of the Japanese Empire to assert their own nationhood.

CONCLUSION

Industrialized but resource-poor nations are inherently vulnerable to protectionism in time of peace and to blockade in time of war. In light of the lessons of World War I and the Depression, Japanese leaders sought to redress its vulnerabilities through territorial expansion. They proceeded, with increasing recklessness, to carve an autarkic and prosperous empire out of East Asia. China resisted its own dismemberment with the support of the Western powers, whose own colonies or trading interests were at stake in the region. The China War and a U.S. embargo meant that by 1941 Japan's quest for economic security produced the opposite. And Japan's final desperate bid to overcome its dependence on the West by seizing Southeast Asia was doomed to fail, due to U.S. military-industrial superiority and Japan's vulnerability to naval blockade.

But the failure of Japan's empire-building was due almost entirely to war with China and the United States, not to internal liabilities. Despite a continuing dependence on foreign oil, scrap iron, nonferrous metals, and machinery, Japanese conquests did increase its geopolitical might. Even before Pearl Harbor, Japan had vastly expanded its supply of food, coal, iron, and aluminum. If Japan's expansionism had not resulted in an unwinnable war, the empire would have added greatly to its economic self-sufficiency and ability to wage protracted war.

The empire also appeared to be profitable; if not "co-prosperous" then prosperous for Japan at least. Japan did have to invest its own resources to modernize its captured economies. It had to create an economic surplus in Taiwan, Korea, and Manchukuo before it could exploit that surplus. But most of the investments appeared to be profitable. Cheap and compliant labor and natural resource endowments outweighed the costs of maintaining political control. The waste and inefficiency in the empire, mainly in Manchuria, were due more to haste and overcentralized control; state-sponsored development in Korea and Taiwan was both effective and profitable. The fledgling nationalism and industrialization of the Japanese Empire thus did not appear to present a constraint on economic performance or Japanese profit.

Up to 1937, Japan had had little difficulty in pacifying its conquests, and it maintained smooth, repressive control over populations nearly equaling its own in size. Contrary to what the quagmire view of conquest would predict, rapid modernization did not help the Taiwanese, the Koreans, or the Chinese Manchurians to seriously challenge Japanese profits or control. After the 1919 demonstrations in Korea, a slight increase in police expenditures apparently persuaded most Koreans that "the wisest thing seemed to be to adjust themselves to the situation."[130] Despite unrelenting Japanese discrimination, Koreans, Taiwanese, and Manchurians appeared increasingly resigned to accept their role in the Japanese Empire. And the fact that Japan finally overextended itself in China does not provide any support for the quagmire view, since China was at the time more backward economically than Japan's other possessions.

Of course, these societies remained little industrialized compared to the other cases examined in this study. With work forces still only 25–40 percent nonagricultural in 1940, Taiwan, Korea, and Manchuria were in some ways still less modern than 1850 France, in which half the labor force was nonagricultural.[131] Their low level of development makes these possessions less than ideal test cases for the quagmire view of conquest. It is possible that continued modernization would have eventually caused economic and political resistance. But the fact that the trends interrupted by World War II were toward a wealthy, prosperous empire should give pause to anyone believing that empires are inherently uneconomic.

CHAPTER 7

The Soviet Empire, 1945–1989

BY THE TIME the smoke cleared at the end of the Second World War, Stalin's Red Army had nearly restored Soviet borders to czarist dimensions and had occupied Eastern Europe as well. Installing loyal communist regimes and backing them with threats of force, the Soviet Union assumed informal control over the region Mackinder once called the "pivot of history." Because the cold war stayed "cold," Eastern Europe was never mobilized for war. But the Soviet Union for several years sought to extract reparations, and throughout the cold war wanted to maintain control and cultivate industrial growth there. Thus Eastern Europe—especially the more developed and strategically significant "northern tier" countries of East Germany, Czechoslovakia, Poland, and Hungary, examined in this chapter—offers intriguing cases for analyzing the cumulativity of resources.

The massive East German reparations supplied to the Soviet Union over eight years provide important evidence for the short-term cumulativity of resources. But in the longer run, the economic utility of the northern tier countries depended on their passivity and economic growth. Pacification was quite effective as well as efficient, at least if Soviet military power in Europe is assumed to have had a primarily external role. This allowed the Soviet Union forward military bases, guaranteed trading partners, and even subservient militaries at low cost. On the other hand, although economic growth was high early on, it tapered off dramatically in the last two decades of the cold war. But this was due to the inefficient central planning systems imposed on each of these countries, rather than to social resistance to foreign domination.

If the evidence has somewhat ambiguous implications for the long-term cumulativity of resources, it does not support the conclusion, contrary to much current thinking, that Eastern Europe became an economic quagmire. The end of reparations in the early 1950s, Soviet subsidies during the late 1970s and early 1980s, and the final escape from Soviet hegemony in 1989–90 seem to some observers as evidence for long-term unprofitability. But reparations appear to have been terminated less to appease East German society than to begin the process of rebuilding the periphery of the empire. Nor were the Soviet subsidies provided to quell unrest; these were probably either rewards for military contributions to

the Warsaw Pact or artifacts of a rigid trading system. Finally, the dissolution of the Soviet Empire was permitted because it was costing too
much in Western antipathy, had become less essential for Soviet security
in the nuclear era, and was irreconcilable with Soviet domestic liberalization.

SOVIET AIMS IN EASTERN EUROPE

Historians still debate Stalin's ultimate territorial aspirations, as well as
the relative mix of fear and greed that inspired them. At one end of the
spectrum, and in the Truman administration's view, the Soviet Union
sought "to impose its absolute authority over the rest of the world."[1]
Thus Stalin was as ambitious as Hitler, if somewhat more cautious. This
has been inferred not only from his postwar grab of Eastern Europe but
also from his 1939 pact with Hitler and seizure of eastern Poland and
Romania, the Baltic countries, and Finnish borderlands, as well as
Stalin's paranoid megalomania and contempt for human life. This view
suggests that only Western pressure kept Stalin from annexing Eastern
Europe outright as he did the Baltics, and that only rigorous containment
stood in the way of further aggrandizement.

Revisionists, in contrast, saw the Soviet Union as a more typical great
power, expanding primarily to assure its own security.[2] After nearly
being annihilated during World War II and having paid a massive blood
price to defeat Hitler, the Soviet Union was exhausted and vulnerable to
U.S. military, industrial, and nuclear might. Stalin thus saw Eastern Europe not as a springboard for the conquest of all Eurasia, but as a bul-
wark against a resurgent Germany and an ideologically hostile West.
Since free elections in Eastern Europe would have produced anti-Soviet
governments, and since outright annexation might have provoked another war, informal control through puppet regimes appeared the best
way to protect Soviet security. Accordingly, an unsympathetic and over-
reacting United States bears its share of guilt for the cold war. This interpretation has been inferred from Stalin's difficulty in finding allies and
his need to buy space and time in 1939, from Soviet relative military
weakness after the war, and from past Soviet experience of Western anticommunism.

The general aims of Stalin's successors are also debated, though to a
lesser extent. Some sovietologists believed the Soviet state to be expansionistic by nature, either because its leaders shared Stalin's lust for
power, adhered to an inherently aggressive Marxist-Leninism, or needed
foreign exploits to earn domestic legitimacy. But most would agree that
Nikita Khruschev and Leonid Brezhnev were less paranoid and less ag-

gressive than Stalin and that their primary goals were security for the Soviet state and peaceful coexistence with the West.[3]

Regardless of where the frontiers of their ambitions lay, every Soviet regime until that of Mikhail Gorbachev believed that control over Eastern Europe was critical to Soviet power. The spread, or at least the preservation, of communism outside the Soviet Union may also have been thought to enhance the ideology's domestic prestige. But most historians deem the security motive paramount. Thus Brezhnev reportedly told Czech leaders in 1968, while crushing their liberalization movement, that the postwar division of Europe would be "permanent" because it guaranteed the security gained by Soviet sacrifices during the Second World War.[4]

In addition to offering a territorial buffer between the West and the Soviet homeland, East Germany, Czechoslovakia, Poland, and Hungary also provided economic security in the form of guaranteed trading partners and an industrial base that could be mobilized in the event of another world war. This base could be mobilized for other purposes as well, and Stalin resolved to extract reparations to reconstruct an economy ravaged by years of grinding warfare on Soviet soil.[5] At Yalta in February 1945, Stalin demanded half of a proposed total of $20 billion in German reparations. Accepting this "as a basis for discussion" over British objections, the Americans subsequently opposed such heavy reparations, particularly from current production. At Potsdam the Allies could agree only that each power would dismantle and remove industrial plant from its own occupation zone. In recognition of its sacrifices, the Soviet Union was also granted a quarter of the equipment removed from the Western zones, as well as all German assets in eastern Austria, Hungary, Romania, Bulgaria, and Finland.[6]

As the United States backpedaled on reparations, Stalin began to extract his demanded share independently. East Germany was ripe for the picking because its industry had been built up intensively during the war and had suffered relatively little bombing damage.[7] Although heavy reparations would hamstring East German growth, two other factors beyond Soviet reconstruction needs favored a heavy "milking" strategy. First, growing U.S.-Soviet discord in 1947 led to an apparent "war scare" in the Soviet Union that lasted through 1951.[8] Declaring that war with the West was imminent, Stalin increased military-industrial mobilization, sacrificing consumption and stable long-term growth in both the Soviet homeland and the satellites. Arms production increased sevenfold in Czechoslovakia between 1948 and 1953, and Polish officials later looked back at this period as a "half-war economy."[9]

Second, as long as the German question remained unresolved, exploiting the Soviet zone at the expense of growth made additional sense. Just how likely withdrawal seemed to Stalin is the subject of debate among historians, hinging largely on whether a demilitarized, neutral, and reunified Germany would have seemed preferable to a division that left the greater part of Germany in an anti-Soviet alliance.[10] On one hand, it seems doubtful that a man as suspicious as Stalin would have trusted mere agreements to demilitarize and neutralize Russia's hereditary enemy. On the other hand, the initial uncertainties of the new bipolar era and of U.S. reactions might have kept him open to the possibility. In fact, he floated proposals for German reunification through April 1952. These may have been merely cynical efforts to forestall West German remilitarization. But reunification was at least plausible because at least one member of the Soviet interregnum, Lavrenti Beria, and probably Georgii Malenkov as well, recommended it in May 1953, although they were overruled by the rest.[11] (Perhaps not coincidentally, Beria and Malenkov were both believers in the efficacy of nuclear deterrence, which reduces the importance of territory and economic size to security.)

Soviet motives for terminating reparations in 1953, providing subsidies in the 1970s and early 1980s, and cutting Eastern Europe loose in the late 1980s are relevant to drawing lessons about resource cumulativity. If these steps were compelled by the impossibility or unprofitability of extracting resources and maintaining control, as Valerie Bunce and others argue, they would count as evidence against long-term cumulativity. Bunce posits that because East European workers had "considerable resources to transform anomic anger into cohesive concerns and cohesive actions," they could demand ever-increasing living standards as a condition of political passivity. Downturns in the state-controlled economy violated this "social contract," imperiling the satellite regimes and necessitating weaker and more generous Soviet policies. Thus social power in effect halted reparations, turned Eastern Europe into a Soviet quagmire, and perhaps indirectly resulted in liberation from Soviet rule.[12]

In reality, as this chapter will show, East European civil societies remained quite weak. There were other compelling reasons for each of these policy shifts. The conditions originally sharpening Soviet reparations demands on East Germany—the need for reconstruction, the war scare, and the possibility of relinquished control—all had evaporated by the early 1950s. Successful economic reconstruction and a nuclear program producing a detonation in 1949 reduced the need for crash mobilization. So did the end of the "war scare," evident in Stalin's emphasis beginning in 1952 on "peaceful coexistence" rather than "inevitable conflict." In fact, a "New Course" of decreased military-industrial mobilization in the Soviet Union and its satellites was adopted shortly after Stalin's March 1953 death.[13] Soviet incentives to rebuild East Germany in particular were also increased by the diminishing possibility of German neutralization and reunification, especially after the Western powers granted the Federal Republic sovereignty and a military role in Western defense in May 1952.

As a result of these considerations, the Soviet leadership was planning to scale back East German reparations even *before* the June 17, 1953, uprising.[14] Hungarian and Romanian reparations had been scaled back as early as December 1947.[15] In June 1952 a large number of Soviet enterprises (the principal means of exploitation, explained below) were sold back to the Germans.[16] In mid-April 1953, one of the first decisions of Stalin's successors was to plan a reduction in German reparations.[17] In May, Vladimir Semyonov, the chief Soviet political official in East Germany, urged Moscow to "lighten the economic burdens on the GDR and create more favorable conditions for socialist construction in the GDR."[18] On June 4, the East German leadership was informed that reparations would soon be reduced.[19] Thus the June 17 uprising merely precipitated a long-planned change. The only way in which nationalistic resistance limited resource extraction was through emigration, an "exit" option unique in Eastern Europe that was closed finally by the Berlin Wall.

The subsidization of Eastern Europe in the 1970s also cannot be explained by resistance and unrest. If the Soviet Union was concerned about political stability, Poland should have received the most subsidies, while glacially placid East Germany, Czechoslovakia, and Bulgaria hardly needed any. In fact, East Germany received the largest subsidies, followed by Czechoslovakia, Poland, Bulgaria, Hungary, and Romania; East Germany also received the most subsidies per capita, followed by Bulgaria, Czechoslovakia, Hungary, Poland, and Romania.[20] East European instability was alleviated only by temporary Soviet loans and aid. The subsidies do correlate cross-nationally with defense spending rates and thus may have been rewards or compensation for the loyalty of geopolitically important allies.[21] But the changes in subsidies over time—including their disappearance in 1983–84—reflected changing world oil prices rather than changing East European defense spending rates. This suggests that the subsidies were simply an artifact of institutionalized trading agreements that were difficult to change. Future research will undoubtedly clarify Soviet purposes, but it is doubtful that maintaining political stability was prominent among them.

By urging reform on East European regimes and by renouncing the Brezhnev Doctrine of socialist internationalism in the late 1980s, Gorbachev effectively allowed the dissolution of the empire. If, like Western observers, he foresaw neither the pace nor the extent of the 1989–90 communist collapse in Eastern Europe, he nevertheless must have been resigned to the loss of Soviet hegemony, so obviously underpinned by the ever-present threat and intermittent use of military intervention. While

Gorbachev's calculations about the empire in the late 1980s are not fully known, it is doubtful that the costs of the empire were an important consideration. As will be shown below, the subsidies were small—less than half of East European military spending—and dwindling in the late 1980s. Rather, Gorbachev's primary concern was to solve Soviet domestic economic problems, which had been compounded by high military spending and economic isolation. Ending the cold war and improving relations with the West would not only dampen the arms race, but would also open foreign economic barriers. "New thinking" about international politics suggested, moreover, that control over Eastern Europe could be relinquished without endangering Soviet security.

The first element of new thinking was the recognition that states balance against threatening expansionists. Domination over Eastern Europe combined with offensive military forces and geographic proximity was largely responsible for the fact that the Soviet Empire was ringed by adversaries of much greater combined strength.[22] Gorbachev's predecessors had failed to understand this because they believed that capitalist states were inherently aggressive toward socialist ones and that the pursuit of a favorable "correlation of forces" would compel other states to bandwagon with the Soviet Union. New thinking suggested that Soviet security problems had been largely self-inflicted, and that letting Eastern Europe go would fragment and reduce the military power arrayed against the Soviet Union.[23]

The Gorbachev regime also reevaluated the nuclear revolution. Nuclear deterrence had long decreased the importance to Soviet security of East European territory, armies, and military-industrial capacity. Although the Soviet Union first acquired a survivable intercontinental nuclear deterrent in the 1960s and achieved nuclear parity in the 1970s, it took time for the significance of the nuclear revolution to take hold. Stalin himself denied that nuclear weapons had transformed war. Khrushchev's enthusiasm for nuclearizing the Soviet military met stiff resistance from the High Command, and under Brezhnev Soviet doctrine went the other way, toward preparing for nonnuclear or limited nuclear war.[24] But Gorbachev's generation, which had little or no direct experience of World War II, appears to have concluded that nuclear deterrence was enough.[25]

The change in policy toward Eastern Europe also may have been motivated by new liberal ideals. If Gorbachev was at heart a democrat and valued "freedom of choice" for its own sake, this would explain why he opposed further interventions to uphold Soviet hegemony and communist rule and why he urged liberalizing reforms on East European regimes. Even if he was concerned solely with Soviet domestic reform, he may have believed that he could not introduce freedom of speech and democratic reforms at home without permitting liberalization—and consequently political opposition to communist rule—in Eastern Europe as well.[26]

In sum, the reduction and termination of reparations, the provision of subsidies, and the final disgorging of the empire were not compelled by actual or anticipated East European unrest and national resistance. Rather than failing to extract resources or to maintain control, the Soviet leadership simply stopped trying for other reasons. This account of Soviet policy toward Eastern Europe can hardly be considered definitive, since newly opened archives in the Soviet Union and Eastern Europe promise to shed further light on these important questions. But the evidence available now on these policy shifts provides little support to the quagmire view.

THE SOVIET BALANCE SHEET

The Soviet Union did have considerable success in extracting resources and maintaining control when it was determined to do so. While it exploited all of Eastern Europe in the early cold-war years, Germany was the main target of resource extraction. Between 1945 and 1953, the Soviet Union took 20–30 percent of East German GNP, along with a lot of booty, slave labor, and technology. In addition, the Soviet Union appears to have gained considerable military collaboration as well; although East European armies were never battle-tested, they were used to maintain Soviet hegemony and were at least believed to supplement Soviet military power. Against such benefits must be weighed the costs of control, but these were not great because the Soviet forces deployed in Eastern Europe had a primarily external function. Eastern Europe's long-run value as a military-industrial base, however, was diminished by sluggish growth rates in the last decade of the cold war.

Exploitation, 1945–1956

From the moment it entered German territory through 1946, the Red Army began pillaging military, industrial, and transport equipment, as well as agricultural and industrial stocks.[27] Nonmilitary dismantling teams also swept into Germany in the spring of 1945, removing mining equipment, railway repair shops, and power plants, as well as optical, locomotive, and electrical factories. Metallurgical, chemical, and metalworking industries were especially hard hit, but even the remaining basic and consumer-goods industries lost about a quarter of their prewar capacity. One third of all East German railway track was torn up to rebuild the Soviet network. Soviet teams also dismantled plant to a lesser extent in the other two defeated enemy states, Romania and Hungary. But the Soviet gain was much less than what East Germany, Hungary, and Romania lost. The dismantling and reassembling costs were high, and Soviet disorganization and transport problems resulted in equipment being damaged en route or being left to rust on rail sidings. Western experts estimate that two-thirds of the plundered plant was wasted.[28]

As a result, the Soviet Union canceled removal plans for many plants and assumed control of them on site instead. Over two hundred "Soviet enterprises" (*Sowjetische Aktien-Gesellschaften*, or SAGs) provided the Soviet Union with a considerable share of East German production. Labor and materials expenses, additional German labor hired for various purposes, and the costs of reparations orders from non-SAG firms were all covered by the East German budget. The economics section of the fledgling East German administration was ordered to "supervise the punctual realization . . . of commodity deliveries designated as reparations, as well as the satisfaction of the needs of the Soviet occupation forces in Germany . . . under the supervision of the Soviet Military Administration."[29]

SAGs such as Wismut, a massive uranium-mining complex near the Czech border, dominated the East German economy.[30] Together they accounted for between a quarter and a third of total industrial output; even the Communist party mouthpiece, *Neues Deutschland*, admitted that the SAGs were "the very heart of the economy and the most productive of all plants."[31] Basic and metal-working products made up more than three-quarters of the combined deliveries, with an increasing proportion of chemicals, heavy machinery, and electro-technical equipment.[32] As much as two-thirds of SAG output was diverted to Soviet purposes, whether delivered to the Soviet Union as "reparations" or to the Soviet Military Administration in Germany as "occupation costs" (the latter were often transshipped to the Soviet Union). Minor SAGs were sold back to the GDR in 1947, more in 1950, and still more in 1952.[33] In late 1953, the Soviet Union returned for nothing the rest of the SAGs (except for the uranium mines, which became a joint Soviet-German enterprise), canceled further reparations, reduced occupation costs, and granted the GDR emergency credits and aid.[34]

Additional but incalculable benefits were gained from the labor provided by hundreds of thousands of German prisoners of war held in the Soviet Union after the war. Tens of thousands of scientists and technicians were also drafted from East Germany to work in the Soviet Union, and thousands of German blueprints and patents were appropriated.[35]

East German SAGs had their analogue in Hungary, Romania, and Bulgaria. As agreed at Potsdam, the Soviet Union confiscated German assets in these countries and contributed them to "joint" enterprises. Although the bloc partner provided most of the labor, raw material, and often the capital as well, control over joint enterprises remained in Soviet hands, allowing an unfair division of profits. Joint enterprises were most substantial in Romania, mainly in oil and coal extraction, transport, metalworking, banking, and insurance. Soviet-Hungarian bauxite, oil, and transport enterprises, and Soviet-Bulgarian mining, aviation, shipbuilding, and construction enterprises provided further gains. The Soviet Union gradually sold its shares in these joint enterprises above worth to the host countries. After 1956, Hungary, Romania, and Bulgaria were given the Soviet shares in remaining joint enterprises, and unpaid debts for already liquidated shares were forgiven.[36]

Another, though poorly documented, means of Soviet exploitation in the early postwar period was the arbitrary determination of exchange rates and commodity prices.[37] Soviet political dominance allowed it to buy goods at below world market prices from Eastern Europe and to sell its own goods there at a premium. The imposed bilateral trading patterns meant that the Soviet Union could even take a cut on intra–East European trade—for example, by buying Hungarian bauxite at $7 per ton and selling it to Czechoslovakia and East Germany for $12 per ton.[38] The most blatant example of price discrimination was the agreement by the "Muscovite" Polish leaders to sell millions of tons of coal per year to the Soviets at a tenth of market price. (This was supposed to be in return for a share of German reparations that the Soviets never delivered.) But in 1956 the Soviet Union canceled a Polish debt of $626 million dollars (an amount supposedly equivalent to past Soviet profits on underpriced Polish coal) and gave Poland $216 million in aid (in the form of low interest loans).[39]

The mechanisms and results of exploitation in Soviet-occupied eastern Austria are worth mention in passing. After an initial trophy campaign, the Soviet Union expropriated German businesses, oil fields, and other holdings that in total produced almost a third of industrial output in the region. But because of the autonomy of the Austrian government, the Soviet Union was unable to force it to foot the bill as it had East Germany. Instead, the Soviets bought this output at just above cost. While the profit margin is hard to ascertain, U.S. officials estimated that the Soviet Union was draining roughly $100 million a year from the Austrian economy, while annual occupation expenses were only $1.4 million.[40] In 1955, the Austrians had to buy out the Soviet sector for $150 million as a condition of the Soviet departure.[41] Total Soviet profits from Austria may have reached $2 billion.[42]

TABLE 7-1
Soviet Exactions and Aid, Eastern Europe, 1945-1960
(Millions of Dollars)

	Booty	Deliveries	Sale of SAG/JEs	Gross Gain	Aid	Soviet Net Gain
GDR	1,333	15,063	453	16,849	62	16,787
Romania	333	880	200	1,413	58	1,355
Hungary	333	449	150	977	99	878
Poland	unknown	626		626	842	−216
Bulgaria			6	6	89	−83
Czech					16	−16
total	2,000	17,018	809	19,871	1,166	18,705

Source: Marer, "Soviet Economic Policy," 161–62.

The magnitude and distribution of the measurable Soviet gains from Eastern Europe are summarized in table 7-1. The total, not including control costs, was comparable to the $20 billion provided Western Europe by the United States under the Marshall Plan. Nine-tenths of the burden fell on East Germany, and most of this had been transferred by the end of 1953. The omission of burdens on other countries due to insufficient data on Czech and Hungarian uranium and on deliveries to the Red Army in Hungary and Romania somewhat inflates East Germany's share. On the other hand, only East Germany lost thousands of workers to Soviet forced-labor camps. Dismantled capital ("Booty") is assessed in terms of its deeply depreciated value to the Soviet Union. Since there is little information on price discrimination other than the extreme case of Polish coal, only the latter is included in table 7-1 (under "Deliveries").

German reparations data, based on leaked official East German documents analyzed by Heinz Köhler, are displayed in figure 7-1.[43] The Soviet share of German economic output—not counting pillaged equipment, stocks, and intellectual property, labor in the Soviet Union, or price discrimination—totaled 43 billion 1938 marks. Two-thirds of this amount consisted of uranium and other goods shipped to the Soviet Union, a quarter was delivered directly to the Soviet occupation forces, and the rest covered additional local labor services.

Although the East German economy had been drained by war and plunder, the Soviet Union managed to achieve relatively high rates of extraction. Between 1945 and 1953, when the Soviet Union scaled back reparations drastically, they averaged 23 percent of the prewar GNP of East Germany. Because the East German economy did not recover to 1936 levels until 1954, reparations represented an even greater drain on current output. In 1950, the first postwar year for which income data is available, reparations amounted to 29 percent of East German GNP, and

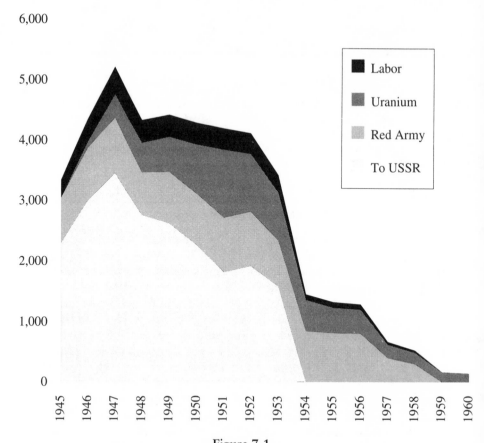

Figure 7-1.
Reparations from East German Production, 1945–1960 (millions of
1938 marks). *Source*: Köhler, *Economic Integration*, 25–28, 257.
Note: SAG inventories transferred in 1952–1953 are included
under deliveries to USSR.

the extraction rate might have been as high as 33 percent in 1947. A
constant flow of reparations represented a declining proportion of a re-
covering East German GNP, which dwindled rapidly after reparations
were reduced in 1953 (see figure 7-2).[44]

Military Collaboration and Economic Subsidies

The Soviet Union also gained from East European military collaboration,
which added three-quarters of a million men to Soviet-dominated Warsaw Pact forces (see table 7-2). The reliability of these forces, and thus

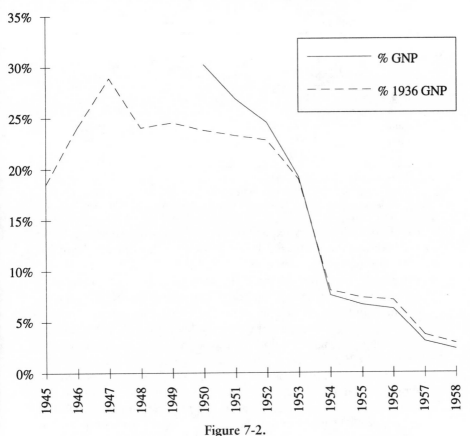

Figure 7-2.
East German Reparations, Percentage of Current and 1936 GNP.
Sources: Köhler, *Economic Integration*, 25–28, 257; Wolfgang F.
Stolper, *The Structure of the East German Economy* (Cambridge: Harvard University Press, 1960), 418.

their contribution to Soviet power, is hard to judge. The more alarmist U.S. cold war studies suggested that the northern tier forces represented "a significant contribution to Soviet military power . . . earmarked for an active mechanized ground-and-air combat role" in "a Soviet-led, rapid, massive, offensive strike into NATO territory."[45] Analysts considered the East German military most reliable; the Polish, Czechoslovak, and Hungarian militaries were considered less so, mainly because of past actual or threatened Soviet intervention in their countries.[46] There was little real basis for making an accurate assessment. But the Soviet leadership, having encouraged the creation, maintenance, and modernization of East European militaries, must have found them at least somewhat valuable.[47]

TABLE 7-2
Contributions to the Warsaw Pact by Northern Tier Countries

	Men in 1978	Avg. Annual Military Spending 1974-1984 (billions of 1983 $)	Avg. Military Spending/GNP
GDR	157,000	8.9	6.0%
Czech	186,000	6.6	5.7%
Poland	306,500	11.7	5.4%
Hungary	114,000	3.1	4.4%
Total	763,500	30.3	5.5%

Sources: International Institute for Strategic Studies, *The Military Balance, 1978–79* (London: IISS, 1978); U.S. Arms Control and Disarmament Agency, *World Military Expenditures and Arms Transfers, 1986* (Washington, D.C.: GPO, 1987).

East European military expenditures were compensated in part by Soviet subsidies in the 1970s and 1980s. Long-term, low-interest loans represented an implicit subsidy of $17.5 billion (1984 dollars) by 1984.[48] Much greater were implicit trade subsidies, arising largely from artificially low prices of Soviet oil and other raw materials. In 1974, Soviet–East European trade agreements pegged intrabloc prices of raw materials to moving, five-year averages of world-market prices. Oil prices charged to Eastern Europe lagged behind when world prices skyrocketed between 1973 and 1982, resulting in opportunity costs for fuel that could have been sold more lucratively on the world market. Some analysts also contend that the opportunity costs of Soviet trade with Eastern Europe were increased further by artificially high prices for East European manufactured exports.[49] Uncertainties about prices, exchange rates, and the "real" value of goods exchanged make it difficult to determine the total resources transferred, and leave considerable room for interpretation of the extent of the subsidies. Michael Marrese and Jan Vanous have estimated the subsidies to Eastern Europe at $97 billion (1984 dollars) from 1970 through 1984, an average of well under 1 percent of Soviet GNP.[50] Other experts have estimated the trade subsidies at only around $30–40 billion for the same period.[51]

Even if the larger estimates are accurate, the subsidies did not represent a net imperial deficit for the Soviet Union. At peak levels between 1974 and 1984, the implicit trade subsidies to Czechoslovakia, East Germany, Hungary, and Poland amounted to only a quarter of their combined military expenditures.[52] If East European militaries were worth to the Soviet Union at least a quarter of what Eastern Europe was paying for them, the subsidies did not represent a net drain on Soviet power. In the end, the subsidies dwindled sharply during the 1980s with falling world market oil prices.

TABLE 7-3
Soviet Forces in Eastern Europe, 1978

	Troops
GDR	400,000
Czechoslovakia	60,000
Poland	30,000
Hungary	50,000
Total	540,000

Source: J. F. Brown, *Eastern Europe and Communist Rule* (Durham: Duke University Press, 1988), 37.

Costs of Control

By far the largest part of the Soviet control apparatus was the Soviet military presence in Eastern Europe (see table 7-3); the number of administrators and spies remains uncertain but represented at most a small fraction of Soviet troops. Even all four hundred thousand Soviet troops deployed in East Germany cost little more than a quarter of what the Soviet Union was extracting in reparations up to 1953.[53] Of course, East German reparations, the chief source of Soviet economic gains in the empire, dwindled in that year. But it is obvious that these forces were not all needed for pacification. The fact that Soviet forces in Germany were so much larger than those in the rest of Eastern Europe combined can only be explained by the fact that Germany would be the focal point of any conceivable East-West war. (Although there is some evidence of the policing and economic functions of the Red Army in the GDR before 1953, the fact that they remained after that shows that larger forces were not posted just to enforce German reparations.)[54] To the extent these forces were a significant liability to the Soviet Union, they represented an external rather than internal cost of empire.

As with all occupation troops, Soviet forces had a dual role of dealing with both internal rebellion and foreign threats. While the actual military requirements for deterring East European rebellion remain a mystery, the actual energy devoted to suppressing rebellion was quite small. Soviet military intervention was required only three times.[55] Soviet occupation troops suppressed widespread East German demonstrations against wage cuts on June 17, 1953.[56] On November 4, 1956, two hundred thousand Soviet troops descended on Budapest, crushing thirty thousand rebels and the disloyal Hungarian regime within twenty-four hours.[57] On August 20, 1968, four hundred thousand Soviet and other Warsaw Pact troops invaded Czechoslovakia forcing the Czech regime to reverse its liberal reforms, to purge the party and the military, and to replace its maverick leader, Alexander Dubcek, with the more pliant Gustav Husak. Most of the invading forces withdrew by December, leaving fifty thousand to seventy-five thousand permanently behind.[58] Soviet forces appeared to prepare for an invasion of Poland during the Solidarity crisis of 1980–81, until the Polish regime conducted its own crackdown.

Growth and Stagnation, 1945–1985

The Soviet Empire's record of economic growth is mixed. Until about 1960, Czechoslovakia, Hungary, and Poland matched the growth rates of the more developed West European market economies. East Germany, held back initially by industrial dismantling and other reparations transfers, also achieved high growth rates in the 1950s.[59] This was accomplished through rapid extensive development, the often brutal mobilization of human and material resources from small-scale farming into industrial investment and production. In the 1960s the development gap widened, except for East Germany, which was able to keep up. In the 1970s, Poland and Hungary were able to keep pace with the help of massive Western loans, which nevertheless could not keep the more developed East German and Czechoslovak economies from losing more

TABLE 7-4

Development Levels, Selected Soviet Bloc and Western Countries, 1938 and 1980 (1980 Dollars, and Percentage of West Germany)

	1937		1980	
	GNP/Capita (dollars)	GNP/Capita (percentage of Germany)	GNP/Capita (dollars)	GNP/Capita (percentage of West Germany)
Germany/				
West Germany	2,736	100	13,590	100
Austria	1,807	66	10,230	75
Germany/				
East Germany	2,736	100	5,910	43
Czechoslovakia	1,948	71	4,740	35
Hungary	1,599	58	4,390	32
Poland	1,372	50	3,730	27
USSR	1,303	48	4,190	31

Sources: Figures for 1937 from Mark Harrison, "GDPs of the USSR and Eastern Europe: Towards an Interwar Comparison," *Europe-Asia Studies* 46, no. 2 (1994), 246, 253; 1980 figures from Paul Marer, *Dollar GNPs of the U.S.S.R. and Eastern Europe* (Baltimore: Johns Hopkins University Press for the World Bank, 1985), 18–19, 86–87, 104–5.

ground.[60] In the 1980s, with the end of this temporary impetus, growth slowed further, especially in Poland, whose GNP actually declined between 1979 and 1982.

Despite the early boom period, communist rule resulted in a cumulative net loss of overall growth for Eastern Europe. All East European countries, as well as the Soviet Union, lost ground to most Western capitalist countries, as comparisons between development levels in 1937 and 1980 show (see table 7-4).[61] This decline was even steeper in the 1980s, after the flow of Western loans dried up. Between 1981 and 1988, real GNP growth averaged 0.9 percent per year in Poland, 1.1 percent in Hungary, 1.4 percent in Czechoslovakia, 1.7 percent in East Germany, and 2.1 percent in the USSR. Over the same period, GNP growth averaged 1.8 percent per year in West Germany, 2.1 percent in France, 2.4 percent in Italy, 3.3 percent in the United States, 3.4 percent in Britain, and 4.0 percent in Japan.[62] Eastern Europe's economic base, as well as the homeland's, was gradually losing its usefulness as a source of military-industrial power to the Soviet state.

COLLABORATION AND RESISTANCE

From the initial Soviet occupation until the upheavals of 1989, East European societies showed few outward signs of political or economic resistance. This is evident from table 7-5, which catalogues all the significant episodes of rebellious collective action in the northernmost East European countries prior to 1989. The only serious challenges to Soviet hegemony arose in East Germany in 1953, Hungary in 1956, Czechoslovakia in 1968, and Poland in 1980–81. The remaining episodes were relatively minor outbreaks of strikes and riots.[63]

This passivity is rather astounding considering the intensity of German, Czechoslovak (or Czech and Slovak), Hungarian, and Polish nationalism. It can be explained only by coercion and repression. Nearly every major rebellion coincided with apparent cracks in the armor of Soviet or satellite resolve, and the most ruthlessly repressive states were also the most politically stable. Repression was particularly efficient because of the advanced level of development of East European societies, and the most advanced of these were also the most passive. The fact that East European societies provided a suboptimal degree of resistance also suggests that they suffered a severe free-riding problem. Thus, although collaboration was facilitated to a degree by small "fifth-columns" of communist believers, it would probably have occurred even without them.

The Soviet system of compulsion involved a threat of Soviet military intervention as well as domestic repression performed by satellite re-

TABLE 7-5
Unrest in Eastern Europe, 1945–1988

	Dates	Actions
East Germany	June 1953	Strikes and demonstrations
Hungary	October 1956	Abortive revolution
Czechoslovakia	June 1953	Pilsen demonstrations
	Spring 1968	Abortive revolution
Poland	June 1956	Poznan
	March 1968	Warsaw demonstrations
	December 1970–	
	January 1971	Lodz strikes
	June 1976	Radom riots
	July 1980–	
	December 1981	Strikes, demonstrations
	Spring, Fall 1988	Strikes

gimes. As with all coercive systems, perceived resolve was essential for compelling collaboration and deterring resistance. The threat of intervention had to be credible to deter satellite regimes from liberalizing or defecting from the Warsaw Pact. Of course, most East European communist officials also had private incentives for avoiding change. Since their rank depended largely on loyalty to Moscow and an unpopular ideology, their political careers depended on maintaining the status quo. But to the extent that Moscow seemed ambivalent about intervention, truly patriotic officials would be tempted to test the waters of autonomy and even hardliners would worry about the continued loyalty of their bureaucracies and police. East European publics had to consider the reaction of both Moscow and their own governments to resistance. Opportunities for opposition were few when both seemed resolute, greater when only one appeared so, and still greater when neither seemed ready to punish resistance.

The Soviet threat to intervene against disloyal regimes and rebels was made credible by the stationing of Soviet troops in Eastern Europe, control over East European militaries, and the well-remembered military interventions of 1953, 1956, and 1968. Forces based in the western Soviet Union also cast their shadow over Eastern Europe, and in fact were used in Hungary in 1956 and Czechoslovakia in 1968. (Threatened economic sanctions, such as reduced sales of Soviet fuel or grain to recalcitrant regimes, were also occasionally used.)[64]

The Soviet Union took steps to ensure that East European military forces would not face east. Initially, Soviet officers and advisers, most of whom had respective national origins but had become Soviet citizens and served in the Red Army during World War II, were put in command of East European armies. Soviet officials also oversaw all important ministries, and indigenous communists were purged from positions of authority in the late 1940s and early 1950s to ensure that the remaining national leaders would be dependent on Moscow. Stalin's successors loosened the bonds somewhat, trading abject subservience for expertise and legitimacy. But while overt supervision of ministries was terminated and the East European militaries were "renationalized," the latter remained closely watched. Soviet advisers were attached to each high-ranking officer and each ministry of defense, and East European officers received training in Soviet military academies.[65] The ability of East European militaries to defend against Soviet intervention was further hamstrung by Soviet insistence on joint military planning and exercises stressing offensive operations, on regional specialization (e.g., engineering and bridge-building for the Hungarian Army), and on Soviet control over military communications systems.[66] It is little surprise that the outnumbered, unprepared, and penetrated Hungarian and Czechoslovak armies stayed in their barracks in 1956 and 1968.

The Soviet Union also insisted that the satellite regimes repress anticommunist and anti-Soviet activity, organization, and expression by their own populations. Noncommunist organizations were generally banned, with the important exceptions of churches and, briefly, Poland's Solidarity labor union. Police surveillance permitted the quick capture and punishment of opposition activity. For example, by the end of the cold war, the East German secret police had compiled 168 kilometers of records and computerized dossiers on over 6 million people, or almost a third of the entire population. Deterrence was so effective that 98 to 99 percent of all police sanctions involved criminal rather than political crimes.[67] Thus, as two Hungarian dissidents pointed out in the late 1970s, "the working class is as incapable of organizing itself as [is] any other social group. While rare moments of cataclysmic crisis in the system give rise to strike committees and workers' council, these organizational results of popular uprising never succeed in consolidating."[68] The communist-run organizations that consumed the "organizational space" of East European society, like official labor unions, provided no substitute for autonomous social mobilization. As a result, collective protests or strikes rarely occurred on a scale large enough to lower individual risks, gain mass attention, and snowball into a threat to the state.

The resistance that did occur during the cold war coincided with perceived weaknesses in this coercive system. The massive East German demonstrations of June 17, 1953, followed signs of uncertainty by the Soviet forces and the ruling Socialist Unity Party (SED). Four days earlier, during a period of especially acute food shortages, the Soviet Army's German-language newspaper blamed the Eastern German regime for "a series of errors in the past."[69] The SED reversed several coercive measures on the next day, and its official newspaper declared that planned work-quota increases should be implemented not dictatorially but only after persuading workers of their necessity. The Berlin construction workers who started the protests on June 16 had passed this article from hand to hand the day before.[70] Their initial demonstrations were permitted to escalate because local Soviet occupation authorities inexplicably denied the East German police permission to suppress them.[71]

Likewise, the initial protests that escalated into a mass rebellion in Hungary in 1956 were possible only because the regime had permitted students to organize and demonstrate. Party chief Matyas Rakosi, under pressure from Moscow and lower officials to repudiate earlier purges, blamed the political police and forbade them from persecuting party members. University students took advantage of this divisiveness and resulting tolerance of dissent to form independent organizations and stage heated mass meetings. The absence of an immediate crackdown encouraged the formation of workers councils, which declared a strike until the students' demands were met.[72]

In Czechoslovakia in 1968, it was the Prague Spring reforms that weakened repression and permitted an increasingly nationalistic and prodemocracy public debate. The week-long protests that followed Soviet military intervention were possible because of the disarray of the Czech regime, and in fact were encouraged by Communist party organizations sympathetic to Dubcek.[73] Cleavages in the Polish regime in 1956, 1970, and 1980 permitted the outbreaks of unrest in those years. The most widespread disturbances, during 1980–81, occurred after the deadlocked regime's legalization of an independent trade union in 1980 and disappeared when the new Polish leader, Gen. Wojciech Jaruzelski, under intense Soviet pressure, outlawed Solidarity and declared martial law in December 1981.[74] In all these cases, popular or regime resistance melted away after domestic or Soviet crackdowns. (Concessions were also granted in most cases, usually to be rescinded later.)

Reduced coercion and repression were also responsible for the ultimate dissolution of Soviet hegemony and communist rule in 1989 and 1990. By calling for radical reform in the Soviet Union in 1986, Gorbachev made it known that major reform in Eastern Europe would now be permitted. Two years later, in the summer of 1988, he promised that the Soviet Union would no longer interfere in East European domestic affairs: "The imposition of a social system, way of life, or policies from outside by any means, let alone military, is a dangerous trapping of the past period. . . . Any interference in internal affairs, or any attempt to limit the sovereignty of states—including friends and allies, or anyone else—are impermissible."[75] Well-connected Soviet academics and pundits openly condemned past interventions and declared the Brezhnev Doctrine dead, and at the end of the year Gorbachev announced the demobilization of 250,000 Soviet troops stationed in Eastern Europe and the western Soviet Union.

Once the Soviet threat had abated, the Polish and Hungarian regimes moved quickly to liberalize themselves. After obtaining Moscow's approval, Jaruzelski opened negotiations with Solidarity in February 1989, leading to the June elections that ended communist rule. Also in February, Hungary legalized independent political parties and paved the way for elections the following year. Soviet acquiescence to these changes dispelled all lingering doubts about Soviet intentions. The East German and Czechoslovak regimes refused to liberalize, but their publics had new reason to doubt that resistance would still be ruthlessly crushed. Indeed, when demonstrations broke out in East Germany in October and Czechoslovakia in November, the regimes became internally divided over whether to crack down and soon disintegrated.[76]

The effectiveness of compulsion is also evident in the fact that it correlated with stability across Eastern Europe as well as in time. Post-1953 East Germany and post-1968 Czechoslovakia were the most quiescent countries; indeed, some Western specialists thought the GDR was "one of the world's most stable regimes" as late as 1988.[77] By most measures, these two countries also had the most repressive regimes; East Germany also hosted the most Soviet troops.[78]

In contrast, unrest was so chronic and widespread in Poland that some scholars even credit it with the "self-liberation" of civil society.[79] An opposition movement developed in Poland during the late 1970s, flourished in 1980–81, and continued to survive underground after the imposition of martial law. But this can be explained by the relative moderation of the regime, evident in the long toleration of an autonomous Catholic Church, the relatively lenient treatment of Solidarity's leaders, and deep internal divisions within the Communist party.[80] The lack of prior Soviet intervention in Poland, the size of Poland's army, and its partial mobilization in support of a regime change in 1956 may have increased the perceived costs of Soviet military action, giving the Polish regime more bargaining room vis-à-vis Moscow.

The tectonic processes of modernization also do not appear to have made resistance more effective. The two most loyal and stable East European countries—post-1953 East Germany and post-1968 Czechoslovakia—were also the two most highly developed in the northern tier throughout this period (see table 7-4). Poland, with the most chronic unrest, also had the least advanced economy. Since regime repressiveness and level of modernization co-vary, it is difficult to tell which had the greater effect. But this crossnational pattern—and the absence of increasing resistance over time—suggests that modernization does not strongly increase social power, and that it might even undermine it in the face of repression.

East European passivity also indicates the prevalence of free-riding. The national costs of open rebellion were significant but not devastating, as was learned in the aftermath of 1953, 1956, and 1968. Military intervention, moreover, involved nontrivial costs from the Soviet perspective, at the very least in the form of worsened relations with countries outside the empire. Given their unhappiness with communist rule, it is hard to see how average citizens could have concluded that national submission was a lesser evil than at least intermittent conflict. If most people were highly motivated by the national interest, resistance would have been far more common.

Rational-choice theory also gains support from the fact that most other outbreaks of collective action began spontaneously in large factories (or construction sites, as on June 16 in East Berlin) where direct, face-to-face communication between large numbers of workers helped to overcome atomization. The June 17 strikes were more prevalent among older plants in East Germany, where the cohesiveness of the work force—due to longer periods working together—made collective action easier.[81] East European disturbances were also more common in isolated industrial centers like Lodz, which tended to have tight-knit communities.[82] The inability to organize also dictated that disturbances would follow discrete "triggering" events that helped atomized masses coordinate their actions, such as price hikes, wage cuts, and news of disturbances in other regions spread by Western radio broadcasts. The details of these exceptions further underline the difficulty of collective action in the face of atomizing repression.

East European collaboration and acquiescence may have been somewhat facilitated by ideological predispositions. Despite longstanding anti-Russian and anti-Soviet sentiment, especially in Germany and Poland, many East Europeans welcomed communist rule. But while they were relatively more numerous than right-wingers in prewar Western Europe, they remained a small minority in their populations. East European societies were already highly nationalistic, and blatant intervention and the presence of Soviet troops made the subordination of the East German, Czechoslovak, Polish, and Hungarian communists to the Soviet Union obvious. True nationalists could hardly support regimes that owed rank to and took marching orders from Moscow.

As a result, East European communist regimes commanded little popular support when they took power, and even less toward the end of their rule. By 1949 the communist-led SED had gained power in East Germany, while communists could obtain only 6 percent of the vote in free elections in the rest of Germany. Almost 3 million (of 19 million) East Germans voted with their feet from 1949 to 1961, when the Berlin Wall ended the option of exit.[83] Stalin himself had remarked in 1944 that "introducing communism in Poland would be like saddling a cow" and he warned his Polish stooges that "when the Red Army has left, they will shoot you as traitors."[84] Hungarian Communists received 17 percent of the vote in November 1945; Czechoslovak Communists got 38 percent in May 1946 elections, but subsequent polls showed a sharp decline in support prior to the 1948 coup that consolidated Communist party rule.[85]

Surveys of traveling Czechs, Poles, and Hungarians conducted in the 1970s and early 1980s found that less than 10 percent favored communist rule.[86] A 1979–80 survey of the same nationalities found that a U.S. victory in a hypothetical war with the Soviet Union was favored by a margin of 6 to 1.[87] The first true test of popular preferences, the open elections of 1989–90, revealed support for communist rule to be almost nonexistent. In June 1989 Solidarity won 92 of 100 upper house seats and 160 of the open 161 lower house seats, and none of the unopposed communist candidates even received the minimum 50 percent needed to gain their "guaranteed" lower house seats.[88] In March 1990, as East Germans voted overwhelmingly for reunification, the Communist party (renamed the Party of Democratic Socialism) received only 16 percent of the vote.[89] Communists gained only 15 percent of the Hungarian vote and 13 percent of the Czechoslovak vote in elections later that year.[90]

Some have conjectured that economic development and social mobility increased support for communist rule in the 1950s and 1960s.[91] But the evidence for this is thin and is contradicted by the abortive revolutions in Hungary in 1956 and Czechoslovakia in 1968, as well as by the little polling data that exists.[92] Further research in newly opened archives may reveal more about the course of popular preferences. But given the fact that the satellite states were seen by the vast majority of their populations as illegitimate at the beginning and at the end of their existence, it is reasonable to assume that this was true in between as well.

SOURCES OF STAGNATION

The dwindling growth rates in the Soviet Union's "Greater East European Co-Stagnation Sphere," as well as in the Soviet homeland, seem to suggest that conquered economies are wasting assets. Three mechanisms might support this notion: workers engage in politically motivated economic resistance, repression interferes with economically vital information flows, and bloated police forces drain resources. But there is little evidence that these mechanisms had a major impact in Eastern Europe. Rather, East European stagnation was caused by the inefficiency of centrally planned economic systems, and was thus not an inherent consequence of foreign domination.

The notion that skilled East Europeans refused to use their economic talents in detested political systems is popular among democratization theorists.[93] But strikes were too few and far between, except in Poland in 1980–81, to constitute a significant drain. Labor turnover plagued all Soviet-type economies but was due to tight labor markets rather than political outrage.[94] Extensive black-market activities were motivated by the pursuit of easy profits in economies marked by extreme shortages of consumer goods and services; moreover, they may have helped rather than hindered economic growth.[95] Finally, the lost labor of imprisoned, emigrating, or exiled dissidents could not have been very significant. Even though most were young and highly skilled, their total numbers were too small to have an impact, except for the German immigration that was halted by the construction of the Berlin Wall.[96] It thus remains to be shown that East European workers made personal sacrifices that slowed economic growth just to frustrate their communist rulers.

Several writers have suggested that the repression of communication practices and technologies hampers economic growth in all modern authoritarian societies. For example, Steven Van Evera contends that "Soviet means of political control now collide with the imperatives of post-industrial economic productivity . . . the police measure required to sustain the Bolshevik dictatorship would also stifle Soviet efforts to escape the smokestack age."[97] But the expense of personal computers and photocopiers assure their scarcity in the Soviet bloc in the 1980s, regardless of their subversive potential. Politically motivated controls existed, but the extent to which they constrained economically important information flows is uncertain.[98] Officials at least tried to facilitate the flow of nonpolitical information, in the belief that "information in the form of scientific and technological data is connected with ideology only indirectly," while a "substantial part of [other] information . . . directly expresses class interests and is inseparably linked with the waging of the ideological struggle."[99]

A more likely link between political discontent and economic performance is that the totalitarian apparatus of repression might drain scarce resources. During the 1980s, for example, the East German apparatus included ninety-six thousand regular police, eighty-five thousand secret political police (the Stasi), and fifty thousand border troops.[100] Counting half of the border troops for internal functions leaves one policeman for every eighty East German citizens, or nearly four times the density of police in West Germany.[101] It thus appears that the East German police involved in political repression (total police minus the proportion typical of free societies) required the unproductive diversion of nearly 2 percent of the work force. However nontrivial, this represented a relatively small drain on the East German economy, especially considering the fact that the East German per capita work force was more than 10 percent greater than West Germany's.[102]

In general, all arguments linking repression to economic stagnation run up against the fact that the most repressive East European nations—East Germany and post-1968 Czechoslovakia—were also the most economically developed at the end of the cold war (see table 7-4). Their average growth rates over the whole period were somewhat lower, particularly in East Germany, where reparations took a heavy toll. But during the 1980s, growth was higher in East Germany and Czechoslovakia than in Hungary and Poland.[103]

In fact it was the economic rather than political structure of Eastern Europe and the Soviet Union that produced such sluggish economic performance. Governmental bureaucracies have some comparative advantages in mobilizing resources for extensive growth, but they are ill-equipped to generate further gains in economic efficiency. Prices in centrally planned economies do not reflect relative scarcities, and as a result planners and producers lack the information needed to improve efficiency. Because efficiency is difficult to measure, it is also difficult for planners to reward. Inefficiency is often rewarded instead. As Khrushchev himself complained: "It has become the tradition to produce not beautiful chandeliers to adorn homes, but the heaviest chandeliers possible. This is because the heavier the chandeliers produced, the more a factory gets since its output is calculated in tons."[104] At the level of individual workers, the leveling of salaries reduces incentives to acquire and apply skills, regardless of political motivations. Most specialized studies on Soviet-type economies lay the blame for their poor performance squarely on central planning.[105] Administrative incompetence and mismanagement, like that of the Polish regime in the late 1970s, only make matters worse.

Perhaps tyrannical rule over modern industrial societies can function only with centralized economic control. If so, then the kind of stagnation observed throughout the Soviet bloc would be an inherent liability of industrial empires. Such a conclusion might seem supported by Gorbachev's decision to introduce glasnost and perestroika before attempting to decentralize the Soviet economy.[106] But Gorbachev's timing may have been a miscalculation; certainly the Chinese leaders inching toward market authoritarianism would think so. And even if centrally planned economies become too bureaucratically entrenched to be undone without political liberalization, that does not mean that authoritarian rule over advanced societies requires central planning in the first place.

CONCLUSIONS

The decline and fall of the Soviet Empire has been seen by many as proof of the futility of conquest. But many aspects of Soviet hegemony over Eastern Europe support the argument that industrial resources are cumulative. The Soviet Union was able to maintain political control inexpensively by coercing collaborating regimes; these in turn used repression to keep nationalistic industrial societies atomized and passive for forty years. In addition, the extraction of heavy reparations from East Germany in the early postwar period adds to the list of industrial economies that have been intensively exploited.

For most of Eastern Europe, and for East Germany after 1953, the Soviet Union adopted a fattening strategy. The Soviet Union did not need to extract East European resources throughout the postwar peace, and given the ease of maintaining control, it made more sense to build these economies in case of war down the road. This strategy failed primarily because the Soviet Union had imposed its own self-obsolescing economic structure on Eastern Europe at the outset.

If the lessons concerning long-term productivity are ambiguous, there remains ample support for several hypotheses about coercion, repression, and modernization. First, resistance correlates inversely with the perceived resolve of the Soviet Union to intervene militarily and of the East European regimes to suppress opposition. Second, neither resistance nor control costs appear to correlate positively with level of development. Resistance did not increase over time except in Poland, where decreasing repressiveness appeared to play a role, and the most highly developed countries were also the most passive. Costs per capita are difficult to establish because Soviet military deployments had a predominantly strategic role. But even if they were relatively high in East Germany, the home of most Soviet troops, they were not in the next-most developed country, Czechoslovakia. The Soviet Union did not have to intervene more frequently or increase its military deployments as Eastern Europe developed, although more research is needed on how the costs of the indigenous repressive apparatuses changed over time.

The chief liability of the Soviet Empire, like the Japanese Empire, was that it provoked the hostility of a much more powerful Western coalition. The Soviet leaders, unlike the Japanese, recognized the international system's constraints on expansion and enjoyed new security due to the nuclear revolution. It gave up the empire not because "people power" has made conquest and empire unprofitable but because new thinking in Soviet foreign policy suggested that even cumulative acquisitions could be political liabilities.

CHAPTER 8

The Spoils of Conquest

THIS BOOK began by identifying the implications of the cumulativity of industrial resources for international politics. A lack of systematic research on this subject has resulted in longstanding theoretical and foreign-policy debates that can be traced to contrary assumptions about whether conquest pays. Drawing from literatures on international coercion and domestic collective action, I identified sources of collaboration and resistance that might affect the size of imperial profit margins.

To briefly summarize, I argued that modernization increases the surplus states create while decreasing the costs of extracting that surplus. This is because the division of labor within modern societies makes it difficult for them to return to subsistence production while at the same time centralizing financial control over the economy. Coercion is made more efficient by the fact that wealth gives societies more to lose from resistance. Also, modern roads, communications, and population densities facilitate surveillance and power projection. This too makes coercion more efficient, while lowering the cost of the repression needed to eliminate uncontrolled organizations and crowds. But ruthless regimes, making a relatively modest investment in coercion and repression and providing low-cost incentives for collaboration will be able to maintain productivity and extract substantial economic resources from even highly nationalistic societies.

The case-study chapters attempted to measure the profitability of several occupations and empires, and put the hypotheses on collaboration and resistance to the test. They reveal that nationalism and other aspects of modernization create a great *potential* for widespread resistance, but that the potential can be defused by ruthless invaders. This concluding chapter provides an opportunity to review this evidence, draw lessons from it for theoretical and policy debates, and consider avenues for further, fruitful research.

FINDINGS

First, history shows that industrial nations can be profitably exploited in the short term. Germany successfully mobilized Luxembourg during the First World War; the extraction rate is unknown, but wartime industrial output suggests that it was substantial. France and Belgium netted about 14 percent of the economic potential of Germany's Ruhr and Rhineland in the nine months after the collapse of the Ruhrkampf. Nazi-occupied West European nations surrendered between 19 percent and 44 percent of their prewar national incomes, and enough slave labor and booty besides to cover German control costs. The available evidence suggests that Japan was able to mobilize Korea, Taiwan, and Manchuria during World War II as well, within the limits of their less-developed economic potential. Finally, the Soviet Union succeeded in extracting an average of 23 percent of East German GNP in reparations for eight years after the end of World War II; control costs appeared to represent a small fraction of this amount.

How do these rates compare to the mobilization rates of committed, independent nations? Taking 50 percent of prewar national income (the average mobilization of Britain and Germany during World War II) as a benchmark, the Nazi-occupied Belgian, Dutch, and Norwegian economies—the most intensively exploited in this book—appear to have been roughly 85 percent cumulative, despite suffering fuel shortages, deported labor, and scant advance preparation. The reparations extracted from 1924 Ruhr-Rhineland and postwar East Germany were lower, but these economies had been wracked by years of grinding warfare, as well as hyperinflation in the former and collectivization in the latter. Counting a vassal as worth economically half of a committed ally would seem a conservative estimate for the profitability of conquest.

It is difficult to sustain the quagmire view of conquest in light of these cases. No one would deny that the occupied populations were politically hostile to exploitative invaders. But in these cases, hostility did not result in mass political or economic resistance. Control costs remained low in all cases, at least when compared to the economic gains extracted. While economic productivity suffered in some cases, much of the decline can be attributed to raw material shortages. Nationalistic economic resistance was not enough to make a significant dent in the conqueror's profits. Nor did repression appear to have damaging economic results, at least in the short term.

Not all the cases examined in this book were as profitable. Nationalistic resistance paralyzed occupied Belgium during World War I and the Ruhr-Rhineland during most of 1923, making them virtually useless to the invader (see table 8-1). But this can be explained by the theories of coercion and collective action advanced in chapter 2. In particular, the unsuccessful occupations lacked a "work or starve" threat to compel economic collaboration by industrial workers. German and Belgian food shortages during World War I forced Germany to allow an international relief effort to provide strike pay for unemployed Belgian labor. Similarly,

TABLE 8-1

Conquerors' Successes and Failures in Economic Extraction

Successes	Failures
Luxembourg, 1914–18	Belgium, 1914–18
Ruhr-Rhineland, 1924	Ruhr-Rhineland, 1923
Western Europe, 1940–44	
Japanese Empire, 1940–44[a]	
East Germany, 1945–1953	

[a] Estimate has high uncertainty.

Berlin smuggled strike-sustaining funds into occupied Germany until the autumn of 1923, a situation that the French tolerated because they feared Britain's reaction to draconian economic countermeasures.

Further weaknesses in coercion in both cases included expectations of resumed national sovereignty and the tolerance of opposition organizations. Nationalistic relief-distribution networks helped maintain social solidarity, and citizens in the second case were even permitted to openly organize and demonstrate against the occupation. (This does not appear to be sufficient for economic resistance, at least when other coercive weapons are strong, as the collaboration of World War I Luxembourg and the Ruhr-Rhineland in 1924 both show.) In addition, the war was so closely fought from the outset that Belgians had good reason to expect resumed sovereignty, and France clearly intended the Ruhr occupation to be temporary. Because citizens in both cases anticipated the resumption of national sovereignty, they had to weigh the immediate advantages of collaboration against later punishment.

But in two cases, World War I Luxembourg and 1924 Ruhr-Rhineland, economic coercion appears to have been sufficient to obtain collaboration, even without severe repression. The latter case is especially telling, because even the high probability of renewed sovereignty was not sufficient to sustain resistance in occupied Germany after Berlin's unemployment relief dwindled. The Weimar government did finally revoke its resistance decrees, so collaboration no longer guaranteed eventual punishment, but only because citizens in the occupied territory were about to defect massively under the pressure of French economic coercion.

The effects of coercion were evident in other cases as well. Resistance generally dwindled when or where coercion was intensified. The Belgian coal provision to the German Army during World War I reflects Germany's greater bargaining power over that commodity and suggests that collaboration to obtain the basic necessities of life is inevitable. Ruthless violent coercion by the Japanese crushed the initial popular resistance in Taiwan, Manchuria, and Korea, as well as its momentary, nonviolent resurgence in Korea in 1919. Likewise, the German terror campaign in Belgium during World War I stamped out all partisan activity. Conversely, reduced coercion was followed by increased resistance. The wave of resistance that swept Nazi-occupied Europe on the eve of the Allied landings reflected the fact that the odds-on, imminent Allied campaign diminished the likelihood of German reprisals and increased the chances that resistance might have an impact. Denmark was coerced less and mobilized less than the other occupied countries until it lost its "model protectorate" status in the summer of 1943. The vicissitudes of Soviet hegemony over Eastern Europe also show the effectiveness of coercion. Nationalistic discontent in Eastern Europe erupted into anti-Soviet political action only after Soviet leaders or their East European puppets appeared to be relaxing their grip.

These cases do not provide a very rigorous test of the rational-choice hypothesis that most individuals, being self-interested, will fail to resist without selective incentives. Resistance, even when it can contribute to liberation, is not always in the national interest. The resulting costs for the society at large, whether from invaders' reprisals or from economic shortages caused by strikes and sabotage, may be too high. Still, the extreme lack of resistance in the "profitable" cases seems explicable only by widespread free-riding. It is hard to see how Germany could have maintained control over occupied Europe if its inhabitants had risen up at once against the very small number of German occupation troops. The same could be said for the Japanese and Soviet Empires.

Relatively high economic activity in the successful cases point to the same conclusion. Economic resistance can be harmful to one's own nation in cases, for example, where occupiers demand an absolute amount or a fixed percentage of output. But where the occupiers make virtually unlimited demands, as in Nazi-occupied Europe, they leave very little incentive for the society as a whole to maximize productivity. Yet productivity there can only be considered high in light of the raw material shortages, pillaging, and clumsy policies their economies suffered. Likewise, firms and workers whose only customer is the occupier cannot honestly believe that their productivity is in the national interest. Thus the performance of East German SAGs, some of which were working fully for the Soviets, provides further evidence that individuals are more concerned about their own income than national objectives. In addition, the chapter on Nazi-occupied Europe reported anecdotal evidence of economic collaboration by self-interested businessmen who seemed little troubled by questions of national duty.

Not only is it clear that modern societies can be mobilized by conquerors, but the case studies lend some modest support to the hypothesis that modernization makes coercion and repression more efficient. Germany profited more from its industrial than its agrarian conquests, and armed guerrillas were more prevalent in the less developed nations and regions of Europe. Manchuria, Korea, and Taiwan were more easily pacified by Japan than less-developed China. Likewise, the populations of relatively advanced East Germany and (post-1968) Czechoslovakia were more submissive than their poorer Polish neighbors. But the impact of modernization on the cumulativity of resources is complex. Some less-developed societies, like Korea at the time of Japanese annexation, were also very easily pacified. Additional theorizing and more fine-grained measurements are needed to more fully explore this connection.

The evidence is more ambiguous on the long-term productivity of conquered economies. The declining output of most of the short-term cases reveals only the predictable effects of raw-material shortages and pillaging. Both the Japanese and Soviet Empires succeeded in achieving high rates of imperially managed smokestack industrialization without provoking rebellion. But World War II terminated the Japanese Empire at still low development levels, while the imposition of inefficient economic structures makes the Soviet case an imperfect test. Still, the fact that East Germany and Czechoslovakia reached higher levels of development than the Soviet Union itself suggests that nationalism had little to do with growth. Capitalist economic development, with intervention but not total control by the state, seemed to work in the Japanese Empire. It is difficult to know whether Taiwan, Korea, and Manchukuo could have maintained such high growth, especially in the absence of Japanese investment, once they became as industrialized as, say, 1970 Poland. It is also unclear whether Japan could have maintained such a firm grip on its colonies, a grip much tighter than that of the Soviet Union over Eastern Europe. But there is also no evidence to refute these possibilities.

Soviet hegemony over Eastern Europe, which always relied more heavily on repression and coercion than on communist legitimacy, might have been even more stable if better performing capitalist economies had been imposed. One could argue that the imposition of centrally planned economies was necessary for maintaining political control, because private capital would inevitably gain political power and the Soviet-imposed communist regimes would lose the margin of legitimacy afforded by enforced social equality. But the bargaining leverage of private capital, when atomized by political repression, amounted to little in Nazi-occupied Europe.

Nationalism, however, does generate intense political hostility and can survive decades of political and cultural oppression. As the cases of World War I Belgium and 1923 Ruhr-Rhineland show, conquerors that are morally or otherwise restrained do face costly political and economic resistance by modern societies. An important implication of this is that liberal states are unlikely to make effective conquerors, and will even have difficulties extracting sizable reparations. Liberal states' constitutions are based on respect for fundamental human rights and freedoms. While liberal states have in the past engaged in severe coercion and repression (for example, the French use of torture in Algeria), they are in general hesitant to do so. Conquest does not pay in a world of democratic states.

The hypotheses on time, size, and trade mentioned in Chapter 2 are too indeterminate for systematic testing, but some observations can be made. Time posed few obstacles to Japanese political and economic purposes in Taiwan, Korea, and Manchuria. It was less so in Soviet-dominated Eastern Europe, but here the conflating factor of central planning once again muddies the implications. Sheer size may explain Japan's difficulty in mastering occupied China; further research is needed to explore this matter. Trading gains or losses depend on speculative counterfactual assumptions about trade barriers as well as growth rates of the subjugated economies. But because development rates were so high in Taiwan, Korea, and Manchuria, it is difficult to imagine how Japan could have earned greater trading gains with these possessions by not conquering them. In sum, industrial economies are highly cumulative resources for ruthless conquerors or occupiers. Conquered nations are not as efficient as independent ones, in terms of growth or the ability to mobilize resources, but they can be compelled to perform nearly as well.

This does not make conquest a wise policy. The external costs imposed on conquerors by the international system make most efforts at expansion dangerous and unprofitable. Wilhelmine Germany's invasion of Belgium provoked the British to enter the First World War on the side of the Entente, with devastating consequences. Hitler's aggression also resulted in the defeat and dismemberment of Germany, despite resource cumulativity, because the countervailing coalition was still more powerful. Japanese expansion into Southeast Asia led to a clash with the United States, whose military-industrial strength greatly outweighed that of Japan—not to mention that of the empire. And Soviet domination over Eastern Europe led to the creation of a potent rival alliance, NATO, and a costly arms race. When external costs are taken into account, conquest pays only when unopposed.

IMPLICATIONS

That unopposed and ruthless conquest pays may seem an anachronistic and overgloomy conclusion, more than fifty years after the last great-power war and following the recent dissolution and democratization of the world's last great multinational empire. But these findings help understand these developments by dispelling an appealing and popular, but misguided explanation: that modern "people power" has made conquest and empire unprofitable and obsolete. In addition to having important implications for the causes of war and the vitality of empire, these finding also offer useful lessons about balance-of-power theory and strategy and about sources and strategies of mass resistance.

First, the cumulativity of industrial economies confirms an important premise of power-balancing grand strategies. Geopoliticians' assumption of frictionless transfer of resources may have been simplistic, but their basic point was not far from the mark. Based on the World War II cases, a conquered country is worth more than half of a fully committed ally. Thus the German conquest of Europe had to be rolled back because it did in fact greatly augment the geopolitical might of an aggressive power.

The architects of postwar containment were also correct in thinking that a Soviet-dominated Eurasia would have been a military-industrial giant. If the Soviet Union had conquered Japan and NATO Europe in the last decade of the cold war, and gained the equivalent of half their (and Eastern Europe's) GNPs, NATO North America would have found itself outstripped in economic potential by a fifth (see table 8-2). Worst-case planners might reasonably drop the discount, resulting in a 2-to-1 ratio. Kennan was right: a Soviet Eurasia would have been a geopolitical Goliath, although the imposition of central economic planning would have mitigated this somewhat over time. Such a shift in the balance of power would have made a huge difference to the outcome of another world war—if long and nonnuclear like the first two, both of which were ultimately won by the coalition with greater economic-industrial muscle. A "contained" Soviet Union, by contrast, commanded less GNP than either the United States or Western Europe, not to mention the two combined.

Of course, a full assessment of containment or any other balancing strategy also requires analyzing the external and noneconomic consequences of expansion, as well as the fact that the nuclear revolution has eroded the significance to security of economic size. In general, however, the continued profitability of conquest should encourage world and regional powers to balance against expansionist competitors.

A second important consequence of these findings are for our understanding of the causes of expansionism and war. Since coercive and repressive regimes can still make conquest pay, it is unlikely that nationalism by itself has rendered war among developed nations obsolete. If great-power expansion has disappeared since the onset of the cold war, it is not because industrial resources are noncumulative. Rather, the continued profitability of conquest suggests that the world should be thankful for other causes of peace, like deterrence and the spread of democracy. Unwarranted optimism about the powers of nationalistic resistance should not lead to neglect of the real pillars of peace in the modern world.

TABLE 8-2
GNP of Various Countries and Regions, 1986

	GNP (billions of $)
United States	4,161
Canada	446
Total: NATO, North America	4,607
West Germany	908
France	763
United Kingdom	720
Italy	644
Spain	353
Netherlands	189
Belgium	133
Total: NATO, Europe	3,710
Japan	1,658
Soviet Union	2,357
Eastern Europe	874
Total: Warsaw Pact	3,231

Source: Central Intelligence Agency, *Handbook of Economic Statistics, 1987* (Washington: GPO, 1987), 34–35.

Although ruthless, twentieth-century conquerors have found industrial economies to be cumulative, it is interesting to note that they sought raw materials, markets, and territory more often than industrial capacity. Wilhelmine Germany developed ambitions for continental aggrandizement only during World War I, and even then economic aims focused mainly on raw material supplies and markets. French territorial ambitions prior, during, and after the war appear to have been even more strongly moderated by a lack of interest in acquiring German-speaking citizens. Both Japanese and Nazi imperialism were motivated largely by geopolitical appetites, but for farmland and raw materials rather than factories per se. Japan's victims were all pre-industrial and potentially assimilable. Hitler did not seek a multinational empire but a Germanic one. "Aryan" races could be molded into citizens and soldiers of the thousand-year Reich, but the rest would eventually be expelled, enslaved, or exterminated. It is possible that Stalin seized Eastern Europe for its industry as well as its territory, but he risked only a "cold" war in doing so.

Still, Japanese and German expansionism reveals the dangerous effects of beliefs in the profitability of conquest. World War I made leaders of both countries acutely aware of the importance of economic size and autarky to security. "One of the most important lessons of the First World War for the German armed forces was [that Germany] should not be caught unprepared for war again, critically short of vital raw materials and war capacity."[1] Japan's military planners drew the same lessons from World War I, and more logically too, since the Japanese economy was more dependent on trade. Along with the belief that conquest paid, the expectation of total wars led Japanese and German leaders in the 1930s to put a high premium on size and autarky, which in turn became a rationale for aggressive expansion.

This suggests a disquieting paradox: the prospect of long wars can sometimes prompt states to start them preventively by seizing vulnerable assets. Defense dominance is believed to be strictly peace-causing in realist theory.[2] But because it makes prolonged economic mobilization more important to survival, it exacerbates states' economic insecurity. If war is likely to be short and decisive, it will be over so fast that only standing forces and existing munitions stockpiles would matter. Economic strength would still be important to security but autarky would not. But if war is likely to require a protracted, intensive economic mobilization under conditions of blockade or embargo, expansion becomes a plausible and perhaps even necessary means to security. This effect is especially pernicious when defense dominance prevails among contending powers but not between powers and nearby prey. Without concluding that defense dominance was a sufficient cause for Japanese and German expansionism, it does appear less reassuring, especially in nonnuclear worlds.

This underscores the importance of reducing the perceived risk of protectionism and war in the international system, for these factors increase the value of autarky and size to economic and military security. As economic interdependence continues to grow, future crises could tempt powerful states to reduce their dependence by conquest.[3] Rather than dismissing this problem by enshrining the myth that conquest no longer pays, it remains important to focus on real solutions to living under anarchy. Grounds for optimism can be found in the fact that democracies are unlikely to fight each other or to make conquest pay. Their continued stability and increasing numbers provides much reassurance. So does deterrence, especially nuclear deterrence, by increasing the costs of war beyond any imaginable gain.

The findings of this study also give insight into the sources of rebellious collective action and the effectiveness of guerrilla- and civilian-based defense strategies. The fact that nationalism does not prevent ruthless tyrants from pacifying and exploiting foreign nations provides greater support for theories stressing coercion and free-rider problems than for those stressing mass preferences. This study also provides evidence against the argument that development inherently strengthens the hand of civil societies against authoritarian regimes. In drawing analogies from imperial to domestic tyrannies, however, two important differences must be recognized. On the one hand, the absence of national differences reduces political hostility and increases the ranks of potential loyal collaborators. On the other, the likelihood of coups and factional divisions increases because political elites have opportunities to bid for public support through defection, and because militaries and police forces are more hesitant to brutalize their fellow citizens than foreigners. Thus the main challenge to imperial rule is low-level but protracted resistance from below, while modern native tyrants are threatened mainly by divisiveness within their own ranks.

If coercion and repression work, then popular-resistance strategies, violent or nonviolent, are unlikely to work or even be implemented against ruthless invaders. Passive resistance did prevent high economic profits in two cases—Belgium in World War I and the Ruhr-Rhineland in 1923. But these involved special circumstances that constrained the invader from applying coercion and repression. In both instances, outside parties were willing and able to provide the support so essential to maintain protracted general strikes. The invaders, moreover, were restrained from suppressing this support because of either food shortages or international pressures and limited aims. In both cases, especially in the latter, the odds of liberation were at least even, and this further weakened the repressive capability of the occupiers. These extraordinary circumstances could conceivably recur. But it would be dangerous to adopt a defense policy that depended on them.

The past failures of spontaneous efforts do not by themselves preclude the possibility that preparation and training might, as resistance strategists claim, significantly increase the effectiveness of social power. But theories of coercion and collective action suggest that planning and training are unlikely to make societies better able or more likely to resist. Coercion theory points to the importance of threats and the resolve of both sides in the conflict. Preparation and training are unlikely to increase the defeated nation's raw desire for independence, nor can they protect it from the invader's reprisals. States that distribute weapons secretly can also collaborate in their recall when faced with invaders' dire threats. No amount of training can put food in the mouths of the hungry families of striking workers. Supply stockpiles are liable to be discovered and seized, and it is hard to imagine a system that could distribute food to cities, or allow for a mass return to the land, in the face of a conqueror's opposition.

It is also hard to see how preparation could overcome the collective action problem. Proponents have recognized the importance of resistance organizations to the direction and sustenance of passive resistance.[4] But organizations, no matter how well trained, can be penetrated and dismantled by repressive conquerors. During World War II, the one resistance organization that predated Nazi occupation, the Czech Obrana Naroda (based on Czech military intelligence personnel), was rapidly suppressed precisely because of its high level of previous organization. It is a first principle among revolutionaries that size and centralization cannot be reconciled with secrecy. But decentralization into small "cells" impairs the effectiveness of organizations in coordinating collective action.

Might civilian-based or guerrilla-based defenses still be recommended to countries so small and weak that they have no hope of military defense? Weak countries might use popular resistance to demonstrate to the international community their desire for independence and thus invite an intervention by potential liberators. Peoples who lay down their own lives for national independence, rather than collaborating openly are more likely to arouse other nations to make sacrifices in the name of collective self-defense. But given the difficulty of mobilizing resistance against coercive and repressive regimes, a doomed conventional defense would probably do more to achieve this goal.

Given the vulnerability of societies once occupied, it appears that the best way to prevent resource extraction by an invader is self-sabotage, organized by the retreating state, before an occupation is complete. Thus Stalin's scorched-earth policy in 1941, like Tsar Alexander's similar strategy against Napoleon, succeeded in reducing Hitler's immediate economic gains from occupied Russia. A declared self-immolation policy might also deter aggression motivated by greed for economic resources. In fact, the Swiss threatened to blow up their Alpine tunnels upon any breach of their neutrality by Nazi Germany.[5] Calls in the United States to seize Saudi oil fields following the 1974 OPEC price hike were rebutted in a congressional study that emphasized how the Saudis could cripple production for months by blowing up its wells and refineries. (A similar threat, however, failed to deter the United States from evicting Iraq from Kuwait in 1991.)[6]

Popular-resistance strategies are, however, likely to be much more effective against invaders who are not very ruthless. The most oft-mentioned successes of national civilian resistance were, in fact, against liberal or liberalizing regimes (for example, the Ruhr-Rhineland versus the French Third Republic, Gandhi's national liberation movement versus Britain, Eastern Europe in 1989–90). Nations surrounded by stable, liberal regimes thus might safely adopt national-resistance strategies. But if one is going to trust in the good will of neighbors, perhaps no defense is needed at all.

A FINAL WORD ON FURTHER RESEARCH

I hope this book has demonstrated that collaboration and resistance not only deserve study but also can be studied rigorously and productively. And although I have attempted to examine most of the relevant published sources, much work remains to be done. Among the historical studies of individual occupations and empires, relatively few directly focus on the sources and economic effects of collaboration and resistance. The looting of art treasures garners greater attention, no doubt because of continuing repatriation disputes, even though economic exploitation has a much more costly (though less tangible) legacy.

This lacuna in historical and social science research may be due in part to an aversion to difficult truths. The cruelty, collaboration, and treason that one often finds in hostile occupations and empires cast a shadow on national pride in past aggressor states and occupied states alike. American and British historians, for instance, subjected Vichy France to searching scrutiny earlier than their German and especially French colleagues. (Indeed, the French government refused to allow Marcel Ophuls's 1968 documentary, *The Sorrow and the Pity*, on television until 1981.) The problem may go beyond national honor as well, for collaboration and exploitation also embarrass cherished notions about human nature and the economic superiority of democracy. The subject's interdisciplinary nature, laying between international and comparative politics, may also explain social scientists' relative neglect of the subject.

Deeper examination of the episodes studied in this book will surely lead to important discoveries. There is much that remains to be learned about the economics of the Japanese Empire, especially during the war. The opening of Soviet and East European archives is sure to provide a wealth of relevant evidence on the Soviet East European empire, such as the calculations motivating Soviet reparations and subsidies policies. The role of non-Russian republics in the Soviet economy should also have lessons for the cumulativity of resources. Other cases worth studying might be the West Bank in Israel since 1967, the Saar under French control in the 1920s, Alsace-Lorraine between 1871 and 1918, and even earlier episodes. Whatever the cases chosen, structured comparisons across time, across borders, and between regions, tailored to test hypotheses about collaboration and resistance, will be especially fruitful.

Notes

Chapter 1
Does Conquest Pay?

1. On domestic mobilization, see Alan C. Lamborn, *The Price of Power: Risk and Foreign Policy in Britain, France, and Germany* (Boston: Unwin Hyman, 1991). For theories of imperialism and overexpansion, see Michael Doyle, *Empires* (Ithaca: Cornell University Press, 1986); Jack Snyder, *Myths of Empire* (Ithaca: Cornell University Press, 1991); Charles Kupchan, *The Vulnerability of Empire* (Ithaca: Cornell University Press, 1994).

2. Comparative assessments of nonindustrial empires include Grover Clark, *The Balance Sheets of Imperialism* (New York: Columbia University Press, 1936), and Carlo M. Cipolla, ed., *The Economic Decline of Empires* (London: Methuen, 1970). For earlier comparative studies of occupied industrial economies, which touch on some of the issues under analysis here, see Alan Milward, *War, Economy and Society, 1939–1945* (Berkeley: University of California Press, 1977), chap. 5; Henry S. Bloch and Bert F. Hoselitz, *The Economics of Military Occupation*, rev. ed. (Chicago: University of Chicago Press, 1944); Vladimir Petrov, *Money and Conquest: Allied Occupation Currencies in World War II* (Baltimore: Johns Hopkins Press, 1967); and Ramon H. Myers and Mark R. Peattie, eds., *The Japanese Colonial Empire, 1895–1945* (Princeton: Princeton University Press, 1984).

3. See, e.g., Hans J. Morgenthau, *Politics among Nations: The Struggle for Power and Peace* (New York: Knopf, 1948); Ludwig Dehio, *The Precarious Balance: Four Centuries of European Power Struggle*, trans. C. Fullman (New York: Knopf, 1962); Edward Vose Gulick, *Europe's Classical Balance of Power* (New York: W. W. Norton, 1955); Kenneth N. Waltz, *Theory of International Politics* (New York: Random House, 1979); Williamson Murray, *The Change in the European Balance of Power, 1938–1939: The Path to Ruin* (Princeton: Princeton University Press, 1984); and Stephen M. Walt, *The Origins of Alliances* (Ithaca: Cornell University Press, 1987).

4. Cumulativity refers to potential rather than actual extraction rates, because resources can be husbanded as well as expended. This use of the term *cumulativity of resources* was coined by Stephen Van Evera, "Causes of War" (Ph.D. diss., University of California, Berkeley, 1984), 80–87, 180–83.

5. Robert Gilpin, while holding that nationalism has made conquest economically futile, outlines general reasons for a U-shaped cost curve in *War and Change in World Politics* (Cambridge: Cambridge University Press, 1981), 147–85.

6. Thucydides, *The History of the Peloponnesian War*, trans. Rex Warner (New York: Penguin Books, 1972), 132, 76; see also 93–95, 105–106, 607–13.

7. Charles Tilly, "War Making and State Making as Organized Crime," in *Bringing the State Back In*, ed. Peter B. Evans, Dietrich Rueschemeyer, and Theda Skocpol (Cambridge: Cambridge University Press, 1985), 169–91.

8. Quoted in Bernadotte Schmitt, *The Coming of the War in 1914* (New York: Howard Fertig, 1968), 2:115.

9. Quoted in Alton Frye, *Nazi Germany and the American Hemisphere, 1933–1941* (New Haven: Yale University Press, 1967), 190.

10. Eugene Staley, "The Myth of the Continents," *Foreign Affairs* 19 no. 3 (April 1941): 488. Emphasis in original. For other wartime geopolitical comparisons, see R. H. M. Worsley, *Europe versus America: Implications of the "New Order"* (London: Jonathan Cape, 1942), and Horst Mendershausen, *The Economics of War*, rev. ed. (New York: Prentice-Hall, 1943).

11. Walter Lippmann, *U.S. Foreign Policy: Shield of the Republic* (Boston: Little, Brown, 1943), 109. See also William L. Langer and S. Everett Gleason, *The Challenge to Isolation* (New York: Harper, 1952); idem, *The Undeclared War* (New York: Harper, 1953); Robert Dallek, *Franklin D. Roosevelt and American Foreign Policy, 1932–1945* (New York: Oxford University Press, 1979), esp. 173, 181, 214–15, 219, 228, 231, 256, 266. According to Sumner Welles (quoted in Ibid., 321), Roosevelt's grasp of geopolitics was "almost instinctive."

12. John Lewis Gaddis, *Strategies of Containment: A Critical Appraisal of Postwar American National Security Policy* (Oxford: Oxford University Press, 1982); Melvyn P. Leffler, *A Preponderance of Power: National Security, the Truman Administration, and the Cold War* (Stanford: Stanford University Press, 1992), esp. 10–15.

13. George F. Kennan, *American Diplomacy, 1900–1950* (Chicago: University of Chicago Press, 1951), 5.

14. "The Position of the United States with Respect to Soviet-Directed World Communism," NSC 7, March 30, 1948, reprinted in Thomas H. Etzold and John Lewis Gaddis, *Containment: Documents on American Policy and Strategy, 1945–1950* (New York: Columbia University Press, 1978), 164–69; quote is on p. 165. The final policy statement signed by Truman in November 1948, while acknowledging that U.S. psychological warfare could promote unrest in Soviet conquests, concluded that expansion "would ultimately enhance the Soviet war potential, if sufficient time were allowed and Soviet leaders were able to consolidate Russian control and to integrate Europe into the Soviet system. This would permit an eventual concentration of hostile power which would pose an unacceptable threat to the security of the United States." "U.S. Objectives with Respect to the USSR to Counter Soviet Threats to U.S. Security," NSC 20/4, November 23, 1948, reprinted in Ibid., 203–11; quote is on p. 206.

15. George Bush, *National Security Strategy of the United States, 1990–1991* (New York: Brassey's, 1990), 5.

16. Quoted in Gaddis, *Strategies of Containment*, 30; see also George F. Kennan, *The Realities of American Foreign Policy* (Princeton: Princeton University Press, 1954), 63–65.

17. Quoted in Eliot A. Cohen, "Do We Still Need Europe?" *Commentary* 81, no. 1 (January 1986): 29.

18. "The Position of the United States with Respect to Asia," NSC 48/1, Dec. 23 1949, reprinted in Etzold and Gaddis, *Containment*, 252–69; quote is on p. 253.

19. Barry Posen and Stephen Van Evera, "Defense Policy and the Reagan Ad-

ministration: Departure from Containment," *International Security* 8, no. 1 (Summer 1983): 3–45; and Stephen Walt, "The Case for Finite Containment: Analyzing U.S. Grand Strategy," *International Security* 14, no. 1 (Summer 1989): 17–18.

20. Emerson M. S. Niou, Peter C. Ordeshook, Gregory F. Rose, *The Balance of Power: Stability in International Systems* (Cambridge: Cambridge University Press, 1989), 47–51, 192–93, 332.

21. Halford J. Mackinder, "The Geographical Pivot of History," *Geographic Journal* 23, no. 4 (April 1904): 436. See also idem, *Democratic Ideals and Reality* (New York: Henry Holt, 1919); Geoffrey Parker, *Western Geopolitical Thought in the Twentieth Century* (London: Croom Helm, 1985); and G. R. Sloan, *Geopolitics in United States Strategic Policy, 1890–1987* (New York: St. Martin's Press, 1988).

22. Mackinder, "Geographical Pivot of History," 437.

23. Nicholas J. Spykman, *America's Strategy in World Politics: The United States and the Balance of Power* (New York: Harcourt, Brace, 1942), 24; see also Nicholas J. Spykman, *The Geography of the Peace*, ed. Helen R. Nicholl (New York: Harcourt, Brace & World, 1944; reprint, Hamden, Conn.: Archon Books, 1969).

24. Morgenthau, *Politics among Nations*, 44, 81; on world empire, see 298–301.

25. Waltz, *Theory of International Politics*, 172.

26. Adam Smith, *The Wealth of Nations*, (1776; reprint, New York: Modern Library, 1937), 899; for Smith's general critique of empire, see 557–96. For other early liberal views of conquest, see Klaus E. Knorr, *British Colonial Theories, 1570–1850* (Toronto: University of Toronto Press, 1944); Donald Winch, *Classical Political Economy and Colonies* (London: G. Bell and Sons, 1965); and Alan S. Milward, *The New Order and the French Economy* (Oxford: Clarendon, 1970), 3–17.

27. Richard Cobden, *Speeches on Questions of Public Policy*, ed. John Bright and James Rogers (London: Macmillan, 1870), 1:484. See also idem, *Political Writings* (New York: D. Appleton, 1867), 1:191–98, 244–52, 262–66, 463; and Peter Cain, "Capitalism, War and Internationalism in the Thought of Richard Cobden," *British Journal of International Studies* 5, no. 3 (1979): 229–47.

28. Norman Angell, *The Great Illusion: A Study of the Relation of Military Power to National Advantage*, 4th rev. and enl. ed. (New York: G. P. Putnam's Sons, 1913), 45; cf. 107–130. For a contemporary critique, see J. H. Jones, *The Economics of War and Conquest: An Examination of Mr. Norman Angell's Economic Doctrines* (London: P. S. King & Son, 1915). On Angell's impact, see J. D. B. Miller, *Norman Angell and the Futility of War* (London: Macmillan, 1986), esp. 4–10, 37–39.

29. One of the first was Klaus M. Knorr, in *On the Uses of Military Power in the Nuclear Age* (Princeton: Princeton Unversity Press, 1966), 21–34; see also his *The Power of Nations: The Political Economy of International Relations* (New York: Basic Books), 123–26. For similar claims, see Raymond Aron, *Peace and War: A Theory of International Relations*, trans. Richard Howard and Annette Baker Fox (New York: Praeger, 1968), 257; Alastair Buchan, "Technology and

World Politics," in *The Aberystwyth Papers: International Politics, 1919–1969*, ed. Brian Porter (Oxford: Oxford University Press, 1972), 160–82; Kenneth E. Boulding, "Introduction," in *Economic Imperialism*, ed. Boulding and Tapan Mukerjee (Ann Arbor: University of Michigan Press, 1972), ix–xviii, and "The Economics and Noneconomics of the World War Industry," *Contemporary Policy Issues* 4, no. 4 (October 1986): 12–21; Gilpin, *War and Change*, 106–185, 221–23; Richard Rosecrance, *The Rise of the Trading State: Commerce and Conquest in the Modern World* (New York: Basic Books, 1986); Robert O. Keohane and Joseph S. Nye, *Power and Interdependence*, 2d ed. (Boston: Scott, Foresman, 1989), 29, 228; John Mueller, *Retreat from Doomsday: The Obsolescence of Major War* (New York: Basic Books, 1989), 222–23; Carl Kaysen, "Is War Obsolete? A Review Essay" *International Security* 14, no. 4 (Spring 1990): 48–64; Martin C. McGuire, "The Revolution in International Security," *Challenge* (March–April 1990): 4–10; Ted Hopf, "Polarity, the Offense-Defense Balance, and War," *American Political Science Review* 85, no. 2 (June 1991): 489.

30. Knorr, *Power of Nations*, 124–25.

31. Kaysen, "Is War Obsolete?" 54; McGuire, "Revolution in International Security," 8.

32. Gilpin, *War and Change*, 111.

33. Ibid., 117.

34. Waltz explains that foreign "governors, being few in number, depend for the exercise of their rule on the more or less willing assent of their subjects. If sullen disregard is the response to every command, no government can rule." *Theory of International Politics*, 172, 188. Kennan falls into the same inconsistency when he writes that "one must not be too frightened of those who aspire to world domination" because of "the continued and undiminished relevance in the modern world of Gibbon's assertion that 'there is nothing more contrary to nature than the attempt to hold in obedience distant provinces.'" *Memoirs, 1925–1950* (New York: Pantheon Books, 1967), 129–30.

35. Jeremy Bentham, "A Plan for a Universal and Perpetual Peace," in *The Works of Jeremy Bentham*, ed. John Bowring (London: Simpkin, Marshall, 1843), 2:557. On overseas colonies, see ibid., 2:457, and "Emancipate Your Colonies! Shewing the Uselessness and Mischievousness of Distant Dependencies to an European State," in ibid. 4:407–18.

36. Paul Kennedy, *The Rise and Fall of the Great Powers: Economic Change and Military Conflict from 1500 to 2000* (New York: Random House, 1987), 537.

37. See, e.g., Waltz, *Theory of International Politics*, 172; Klaus Knorr, *The Power of Nations: The Political Economy of International Relations* (New York: Basic Books, 1975), 45–69. This is not to suggest that realists overlook other sources of power. See Waltz, *Theory of International Politics*, 131; Knorr, *Power of Nations*, 69–78; Morgenthau, *Politics among Nations*, 80–108; and for an analysis stressing extraction capability, see A. F. K. Organski and Jacek Kugler, *The War Ledger* (Chicago: University of Chicago Press, 1980), 64–103.

38. Bruce Russett, *No Clear and Present Danger: A Skeptical View of the United States Entry into World War II* (New York: Harper & Row, 1972), 33–34, 62. See also Lawrence Dennis, "The Economic Consequences of American

Intervention," in *In Danger Undaunted: The Anti-Interventionist Movement of 1940–1941 as Revealed in the Papers of the America First Committee*, ed. Justus D. Doenecke (Stanford: Hoover Institution Press, 1990), 200–205. Most isolationists, however, stressed the difficulty of intercontinental power projection, rather than of economic mobilization. See Manfred Jonas, *Isolationism in America, 1935–1941* (Ithaca: Cornell University Press, 1966).

39. Christopher Layne, "Atlanticism without NATO," *Foreign Policy*, no. 67 (Summer 1987): 38; Earl C. Ravenal, "Europe without America: The Erosion of NATO," *Foreign Affairs* 63, no. 5 (Summer 1985): 1034; Jerry Sanders, "Security and Choice," *World Policy Journal* 1, no. 4 (Summer 1984): 713. One who favored containment on moral grounds nevertheless agreed: Stanley Kober, "Can NATO Survive?" *International Affairs* 59, no. 3 (Summer 1983): 343–45.

40. Balancing may also occur if successful conquest causes other states to bandwagon or to fall like dominos, even where the immediate geopolitical stakes are nil. But the profitability of conquest is relevant to this behavior, because if resources are not cumulative, then the subsequent loss of richer regions becomes less dangerous.

41. See Jonas, *Isolationism in America*; Robert J. Art, "A Defensible Defense: America's Grand Strategy after the Cold War," *International Security* 15, no. 4 (Spring 1991): 10–18.

42. Robert Tucker, *A New Isolationism: Threat or Promise* (New York: Universe, 1972), 39–54; John Mueller, "The Essential Irrelevance of Nuclear Weapons: Stability in the Postwar World," *International Security* 13, no. 2 (Fall 1988): 65; Art, "Defensible Defense," 18–23.

43. Glenn Snyder, "The Balance of Power and the Balance of Terror," in *The Balance of Power*, ed. Paul Seabury (San Francisco: Chandler, 1965), 184–201. For a critique, see Robert Jervis, *The Illogic of American Nuclear Strategy* (Ithaca: Cornell University Press, 1984), 148–57, and idem, *The Meaning of the Nuclear Revolution: Statecraft and the Prospect of Armageddon* (Ithaca: Cornell University Press, 1989), chap. 1.

44. Gilpin, *War and Change*, 106–55; David A. Lake, "Powerful Pacifists: Democratic States and War," *American Political Science Review* 86, no. 1 (March 1992): 24–37.

45. Gilpin, *War and Change*, 138.

46. Emphasizing the cumulativity of resources in general theories of war are Van Evera, "Causes of War"; Hopf, "Polarity, Offense-Defense Balance"; Barry R. Posen, "The Security Dilemma and Ethnic Conflict," in *Ethnic Conflict and International Security*, ed. Michael E. Brown (Princeton: Princeton University Press, 1993), 103–25; Lake, "Powerful Pacifists."

47. Kaysen, "Is War Obsolete?;" McGuire, "Revolution in International Security;" Mueller, *Retreat from Doomsday*, 221–23; Gilpin, *War and Change*, 219–23; Robert Jervis, "The Future of World Politics: Will It Resemble the Past?" *International Security* 16, no. 3 (Winter 1991–92): 48–50; and, relating to the postindustrial era, Stephen Van Evera, "Primed for Peace: Europe after the Cold War," *International Security* 15, no. 3 (Winter 1990–91): 14–16.

48. I am indebted to Robert Powell for discussion on this point. On buck-passing, see Thomas J. Christensen and Jack Snyder, "Chain Gangs and Passed

Bucks: Predicting Alliance Patterns in Multipolarity," *International Organization* 44, no. 2 (Spring 1990): 137–68. On misperception and miscalculation, see Robert Jervis, *Perception and Misperception in International Politics* (Princeton: Princeton University Press, 1976), pt. 3; Geoffrey Blainey, *The Causes of War* (New York: Free Press, 1973).

49. For examples of these theories, see Kenneth N. Waltz, "The Origins of War in Neorealist Theory," *Interdisciplinary History* 18, no. 4 (Spring 1988): 615–28; Robert Jervis, "Cooperation under the Security Dilemma," *World Politics* 30, no. 2 (January 1978): 167–214; and idem, *Nuclear Revolution*; Michael Doyle, "Liberalism and World Politics," *American Political Science Review* 80, no. 4 (December 1986): 1151–69; Snyder, *Myths of Empire*; and Mueller, *Retreat from Doomsday*. For applications to the postwar and post–cold war eras, see Sean Lynn-Jones, ed., *The Cold War and After: Prospects for Peace* (Princeton: Princeton University Press, 1991).

50. Misha Glenny, *The Fall of Yugoslavia: The Third Balkan War*, rev. ed. (New York: Penguin, 1993), 151.

51. Randall Collins and David Waller, "What Theories Predicted the State Breakdowns and Revolutions in the Soviet Bloc?" *Research in Social Movements, Conflicts and Change* 14 (1992): 31–47.

52. For overviews of research on rebellion, see James Rule, *Theories of Civil Violence* (Berkeley: University of California Press, 1988); on authoritarianism, see Juan Linz, "Totalitarian and Authoritarian Regimes," in *Macropolitical Theory*, vol. 3 of *Handbook of Political Science*, ed. Fred Greenstein and Nelson Polsby (Reading, Mass.: Addison-Wesley, 1975), 175–412; Guillermo O'Donnell and Philippe C. Schmitter, *Transitions from Authoritarian Rule: Tentative Conclusions about Uncertain Democracies* (Baltimore: Johns Hopkins University Press, 1986).

53. Walter Laqueur, ed., *The Guerrilla Reader: A Historical Anthology* (Philadelphia: Temple University Press, 1977); Adam Roberts, *Nations in Arms: The Theory and Practice of Territorial Defence*, 2d ed. (London: Macmillan, 1986). Interestingly, Kennan once proposed in a controversial 1957 radio talk that Europe adopt guerrilla-type forces. George F. Kennan, *Russia, the Atom and the West* (New York: Harper & Brothers, 1958), 63.

54. Stephen King Hall, *Defense in the Nuclear Age* (London: Victor Gallancz, 1958), 145–59; Adam Roberts, ed., *Civilian Resistance as a National Defence: Non-Violent Action against Aggression*, 2d ed. (Harmondsworth: Penguin Books, 1969); Anders Boserup and Andrew Mack, *War without Weapons: Non-Violence in National Defense* (New York: Schocken, 1975); Gene Keyes, "Strategic Non-Violent Defense: The Construct of an Option," *Journal of Strategic Studies* 4, no. 2 (June 1981): 125–51; Gene Sharp, *Making Europe Unconquerable: The Potential of Civilian-Based Deterrence and Defense* (Cambridge, Mass.: Ballinger, 1985), and idem, *Civilian-based Defense* (Princeton: Princeton University Press, 1990); Peter Ackerman and Christopher Kruegler, *Strategic Nonviolent Conflict: The Dynamics of People Power in the Twentieth Century* (Westport, Conn.: Praeger, 1994).

55. Sharp (*Civilian-based Defense*, 83) even claims that preparation and training would produce "an effective power (conservatively estimated) at least ten

times greater than that demonstrated in the most powerful of the past cases of improvised nonviolent struggle."

56. E.g., Stephen J. Flanagan, "Nonprovocative and Civilian-based Defenses," in *Fateful Visions: Avoiding Nuclear Catastrophe*, ed. Joseph S. Nye, Jr., Graham T. Allison, and Albert Carnesale (Cambridge, Mass.: Ballinger, 1988), 105–9.

57. The United States did extract much technological knowledge, especially from occupied Germany. See John Gimbel, *Science, Technology, and Reparations: Exploitation and Plunder in Postwar Germany* (Stanford: Stanford University Press, 1990).

58. Because of the trade-off between extraction rates and growth, extraction strategies depend a great deal on the state's needs and time-horizons. See Margaret Levi, *Of Rule and Revenue* (Berkeley: University of California Press, 1988); Kennedy, *Rise and Fall of the Great Powers*. Qualifications about this trade-off are suggested by Miles Kahler, "External Ambition and Economic Performance," *World Politics* 40, no. 4 (July 1988): 419–51.

59. Arend Lijphart, "Comparative Politics and the Comparative Method," *American Political Science Review* 65 (September 1981): 682–93; Harry Eckstein, "Case Study and Theory in Political Science," in *Strategies of Inquiry*, vol. 7 of *Handbook of Political Science*, ed. Fred Greenstein and Nelson Polsby (Reading, Mass.: Addison Wesley, 1975), 79–137; and Alexander George, "Case Studies and Theory Development," in *Diplomacy: New Approaches in History, Theory and Policy*, ed. Paul Lauren (New York: Free Press, 1979), 43–68.

Chapter 2
When Does Conquest Pay?

1. For an overview of violent methods, see Walter Laqueur, *Guerrilla: A Historical and Critical Study* (Boston: Little, Brown, 1976); for nonviolent resistance methods, see Gene Sharp, *The Politics of Nonviolent Action* (Boston: Porter Sargent, 1973), part 2.

2. Robert Summers and Alan Heston, "A New Set of International Comparisons of Real Product and Price Levels Estimates for 130 Countries, 1950–1985," *Review of Income and Wealth* 34, no. 1 (March 1988), table 2.

3. Michael Mann, "The Autonomous Power of the State," *Archives Européenes de Sociologie* 25, no. 2 (1984): 209; Mark Harrison, "Resource Mobilization for World War II," *Economic History Review*, 2d ser., 41 (1988): 184–85.

4. Gilpin, *War and Change*, 142; Rosecrance, *Rise of the Trading State*, 34. Rosecrance equivocates about whether repression can make conquest pay; cf. pp. 34–35, 135, 176. See also Kaysen, "Is War Obsolete?" 52.

5. Knorr, *Power of Nations*, 112.

6. Ernest Gellner, *Nations and Nationalism* (Ithaca: Cornell University Press, 1983).

7. Barry R. Posen, "Nationalism, the Mass Army, and Military Power," *International Security* 18, no. 2 (Fall 1993): 80–124.

8. Karl W. Deutsch, *Nationalism and Social Communication*, 2d ed. (Cambridge: MIT Press, 1966).

9. Rosecrance, *Rise of the Trading State*, 36; cf. Kaysen, "Is War Obsolete?" 56. On premodern collaboration by corrupt, class-based elites, see Ronald Robinson, "Non-European Foundations of European Imperialism: Sketch for a Theory of Collaboration," in *Studies in the Theory of Imperialism*, ed. Roger Owen and Bob Sutcliff (London: Longman, 1972), 117–42; Doyle, *Empires*.

10. Disunity is used to explain variations in bandwagoning behavior in Deborah Welch Larson, "Bandwagon Images in American Foreign Policy: Myth or Reality?" in *Dominoes and Bandwagons: Strategic Beliefs and Great Power Competition in the Eurasian Rimland*, ed. Jack Snyder and Robert Jervis (New York: Oxford University Press, 1991), 85–111.

11. Thomas Schelling, *Arms and Influence* (New Haven: Yale University Press, 1966), esp. 1–34, 69–91, 170–84. On asymmetric bargaining and coercion, see also Paul Kecskemeti, *Strategic Surrender: The Politics of Victory and Defeat* (Stanford: Stanford University Press, 1958); Andrew Mack, "Why Big Nations Lose Small Wars: The Politics of Asymmetric Conflict," *World Politics* 27, no. 2 (January 1975): 175–200; Glenn H. Snyder and Paul Diesing, *Conflict among Nations: Bargaining, Decision Making, and System Structure in International Crises* (Princeton: Princeton University Press, 1977), 122–24, 183–281; and Jeffrey L. Hughes, "On Bargaining," in *Dominant Powers and Subordinate States: The United States in Latin America and the Soviet Union in Eastern Europe*, ed. Jan Triska (Durham: Duke University Press, 1986), esp. 174–88.

12. Stephen M. Walt, *The Origins of Alliances* (Ithaca: Cornell University Press, 1987), esp. 28–33; 172–78.

13. Schelling, *Arms and Influence*, 12–13.

14. A seminal work distinguishing collaboration for *raison d'état* from ideological "collaborationism" is Stanley Hoffmann, *Decline or Renewal: France since the 1930s* (New York: Viking Press, 1974), chap. 2.

15. James C. Davies, "Toward a Theory of Revolution," *American Sociological Review* 6, no. 1 (February 1962): 5–19; Ted Robert Gurr, *Why Men Rebel* (Princeton: Princeton University Press, 1970); Ted Robert Gurr, Ivo K. Feierabend, and Rosalind L. Feierabend, eds., *Anger, Violence, and Politics: Theories and Research* (Englewood Cliffs, N.J.: Prentice-Hall, 1972). For a critical review essay, see James Rule, *Theories of Civil Violence* (Berkeley: University of California Press, 1988), 200–23.

16. E.g., Charles Tilly, Louise Tilly, and Richard Tilly, *The Rebellious Century, 1830–1930* (Cambridge: Harvard University Press, 1975); Charles Tilly, *From Mobilization to Revolution* (Reading, Mass.: Addison-Wesley, 1978).

17. In contrast, semirepressive regimes experience backlash from their discrete coercive sanctions. Edward N. Muller and Erich Weede, "Cross-National Variation in Political Violence," *Journal of Conflict Resolution* 34, no. 4 (December 1990): 624–51; Dipak K. Gupta, Harinder Singh, Tom Sprague, "Government Coercion of Dissidents: Deterrence or Provocation?" *Journal of Conflict Resolution* 37, no. 2 (June 1993): 301–39.

18. On the importance of military loyalty and cohesion, see Katherine Chorley, *Armies and the Art of Revolution* (London: Faber & Faber, 1943) and D. E. H. Russell, *Rebellion, Revolution, and Armed Force* (New York: Academic Press, 1974). On the impact of international strain, see Theda Skocpol, *States and*

NOTES TO CHAPTER 2 167

Social Revolutions: A Comparative Analysis of France, Russia, and China (Cambridge: Cambridge University Press, 1979).

19. Guillermo O'Donnell and Philippe C. Schmitter, *Transitions from Authoritarian Rule: Tentative Conclusions about Uncertain Democracies* (Baltimore: Johns Hopkins University Press, 1986), 21.

20. On collective goods theory, see Mancur Olson, Jr., *The Logic of Collective Action,* 2d ed. (Cambridge: Harvard University Press, 1971); Russell Hardin, *Collective Action* (Baltimore: Johns Hopkins University Press, 1982); and Gerald Marwell and Pamela Oliver, *The Critical Mass in Collective Action: A Micro-Social Theory* (Cambridge: Cambridge University Press, 1993). Applications of the theory to revolutions include Gordon Tullock, "The Paradox of Revolution," *Public Choice* 11 (Fall 1971): 89–99; Samuel L. Popkin, *The Rational Peasant: The Political Economy of Revolution in Vietnam* (Berkeley: University of California Press, 1979), chap. 6; Michael Taylor, "Rationality and Revolutionary Collective Action," in *Rationality and Revolution,* ed. Michael Taylor (Cambridge: Cambridge University Press, 1988), 63–97.

21. Taylor, "Rationality and Revolutionary Collective Action."

22. On the importance of selective incentives and their provision by revolutionaries, see Popkin, *Rational Peasant,* chap. 6; Mark I. Lichbach, "What Makes Rational Peasants Revolutionary? Dilemma, Paradox, and Irony in Peasant Collective Action," *World Politics* 46, no. 3 (April 1994): 383–418.

23. See, e.g., V. I. Lenin, *What Is to Be Done?,* in *The Lenin Anthology,* ed. Robert C. Tucker (New York: W. W. Norton, 1975), 67–96, 107–112; Tilly, *From Mobilization to Revolution,* esp. 62–69.

24. Thomas Schelling, *Micromotives and Macrobehavior* (New York: Norton, 1978), 83–133; Marwell and Oliver, *Critical Mass in Collective Action.* Bandwagoning dynamics, along with the habitual concealment of real preferences in repressive political systems, explain why revolutions erupt so unexpectedly. Timur Kuran, "Sparks and Prairie Fires: Theory of Unanticipated Revolutions," *Public Choice* 61, no. 1 (April 1989): 41–74.

25. Schelling, *Arms and Influence,* 30.

26. Stefano Fenoaltea, "Slavery and Supervision in Comparative Perspective: A Model," *Journal of Economic History* 44, no. 3 (September 1984), esp. 635–68; Thráinn Eggertsson, *Economic Behavior and Institutions* (Cambridge: Cambridge University Press, 1990), 203–23.

27. Robert Dahl, *Polyarchy: Participation and Opposition* (New Haven: Yale University Press, 1971), 77.

28. Morgenthau, *Politics among Nations,* 299; Stanislav Andreski, *Military Organizaton and Society* (Berkeley: University of California Press, 1968), 35–36; and Anthony Giddens, *The Nation-State and Violence* (Berkeley: University of California Press, 1987), 181–97.

29. Versions of this argument can be found in studies of imperialism, totalitarianism, guerrilla warfare, political sociology, and economic theories of the state. For examples of each, see Daniel R. Headrick, *The Tools of Empire: Technology and European Imperialism in the Nineteenth Century* (New York: Oxford University Press, 1981); Carl J. Friedrich and Zbigniew K. Brzezinski, *Totalitarian Dictatorship and Autocracy* (New York: Praeger, 1956), 11; Nathan Leites and

Charles Wolf, Jr., *Rebellion and Authority: An Analytic Essay on Insurgent Conflicts* (Chicago: Markham, 1970), 132–48; Andreski, *Military Organization*, 79–80; Giddens, *Nation-State and Violence*, 295–310; and Richard D. Auster and Morris Silver, *The State as a Firm: Economic Forces in Political Development* (Boston: Martinus Nijhoff, 1979), 33–36, 41–42.

30. Morganthau, *Politics among Nations*, 299. On the evolution of military transport, see Martin Van Crevald, *Supplying War: Logistics from Wallenstein to Patton* (Cambridge: Cambridge University Press, 1977).

31. Edward E. Rice, *Wars of the Third Kind: Conflict in Underdeveloped Countries* (Berkeley and Los Angeles: University of California Press, 1988), chap. 2; Laqueur, *Guerrilla*, esp. 395.

32. Rosecrance, *Rise of the Trading State*, 36–37; cf. 128, 135, 176.

33. Dahl, *Polyarchy*, 77. Dahl points out, however, that development is neither necessary nor sufficient for polyarchy. Cf. 68–71.

34. Robert H. Bates, "The Economics of Transitions to Democracy," in *PS: Political Science & Politics* 24, no. 1 (March 1991): 24–27.

35. Fenoaltea, "Slavery and Supervision in Comparative Perspective."

36. John K. Galbraith, *The New Industrial State*, 4th ed. (Boston: Houghton Mifflin, 1985), 136–47. On the weak effect of morale on assembly-line productivity, see Charles Perrow, *Complex Organizations*, 3d ed. (New York: Random House, 1986), 86–87.

37. McGuire, "Revolution in International Security," 8; Kaysen, "Is War Obsolete?" 53.

38. On the general importance of strike pay for effective collective bargaining, see Colin Crouch, *Trade Unions: The Logic of Collective Action* (Glasgow: Fontana, 1982), 89–93.

39. Reproduced in Robert C. Tucker, ed., *The Marx-Engels Reader*, 2d ed. (New York: W. W. Norton, 1978), 480–81.

40. See Leites and Wolf, *Rebellion and Authority*, 132–48; Giddens, *Nation-State and Violence*, 295–310; Brian Chapman, *Police State* (New York: Praeger, 1970), 81–94.

41. Van Evera, "Primed for Peace," 14–15; see also George Shultz, "The Future of American Foreign Policy," in United States, Department of State, *Department of State Bulletin* 85, no. 2096 (March 1985): 13–20. This problem should be greater for "post-industrial" economies, but they should exist to a lesser extent in "smokestack" economies as well.

42. Auster and Silver, *State as a Firm*, 27–42; Gilpin, *War and Change*, 107, 147–55; Kennedy, *Rise and Fall of the Great Powers*.

43. Gilpin, *War and Change*, 156–85.

44. Rosecrance, *Rise of the Trading State*, 139. Also making this claim are Angell, *Great Illusion*, 50–67; Knorr, *Uses of Military Power*, 21–34; Aron, *Peace and War*, 257; Buchan, "Technology and World Politics," 177; Gilpin, *War and Change*, 127–44; David A. Baldwin, *Economic Statecraft* (Princeton: Princeton University Press, 1985), 116; Boulding, "Economics and Noneconomics," 14–17; Kaysen, "Is War Obsolete?" 56–57.

45. Lionel Robbins, *The Economic Basis of Class Conflict and Other Essays*

in Political Economy (London: Macmillan, 1939), 81–106; Gilpin, *War and Change*, 140–41.

46. Dependence on particular raw materials, with the exception of oil, is reduced by substitute-generating technologies, according to Eric Larson, Marc Ross, and Robert Williams, "Beyond the Era of Materials," *Scientific American* (June 1986): 34–41; and Peter F. Drucker, "The Changed World Economy," *Foreign Affairs* 64, no. 4 (Spring 1986): 768–91.

47. Although strategic resources increase in value preceeding and during war, especially if normal sources of supply are cut off by embargo or blockade, tracking substitution costs is immensely difficult. Normal peacetime prices, adjusted for inflation, will have to suffice in measuring the profitability of conquest. Controls on prices and wages have to be considered if they add to the conqueror's gains; this may be the main form of exploitation. See David S. Landes, "Some Thoughts on the Nature of Economic Imperialism," *Journal of Economic History* 21, no. 4 (December 1961): 499.

48. For the potential of what might be done, see Lance E. Davis and Robert A. Huttenback, *Mammon and the Pursuit of Empire: The Economics of British Imperialism* (Cambridge: Cambridge University Press, 1988).

49. Gross domestic product (GDP) is the best measure of national income for assessing exploitability because it includes the total income, foreign and domestic, from all domestic assets. Gross national product will also suffice, although it includes domestic income from assets abroad (which a conqueror wouldn't control) and excludes foreign income from assets at home (which he would) as a measure of national income. Net national income, which excludes capital depreciation and indirect taxes, will also be used when data on it is more reliable or available.

50. See Angela Raspin, *The Italian War Economy 1940–1943, with Particular Reference to Italian Relations with Germany* (New York: Garland, 1986).

51. Popkin, *Rational Peasant*, chap. 6; Taylor, "Rationality and Revolutionary Collective Action."

52. Stephen Van Evera, "The Cult of the Offensive and the Origins of the First World War," *International Security* 9, no. 1 (Summer 1984): 58–107.

Chapter 3
Nazi-Occupied Western Europe, 1940–1945

1. Theodore Ropp, *War in the Modern World* (New York: Collier, 1962), 319.

2. Although Bohemia-Moravia is typically considered part of Central Europe, for convenience this chapter refers to it as part of Western Europe.

3. See Alexander Dallin, *German Rule in Russia, 1941-1945* (New York: Oxford University Press, 1957); Jan Gross, *Polish Society under the German Occupation: The General Government, 1939–45* (Princeton: Princeton University Press, 1979); and Norman Rich, *The Establishment of the New Order*, vol. 2 of *Hitler's War Aims* (New York: Norton, 1974), chaps. 4, 9, 11.

4. Quoted in Rich, *Hitler's War Aims* 2: 86.

5. Dallin, *German Rule in Russia*, esp. 376–80; and Timothy P. Mulligan, *The Politics of Illusion and Empire: German Occupation Policy in the Soviet Union, 1942–1943* (New York: Praeger, 1988), 107–21.

6. Raul Hilberg, *The Destruction of the European Jews*, rev. ed., 3 vols. (New York: Holmes and Meier, 1985).

7. On Hitler's plans and motivations for conquest, see William Carr, *Arms, Autarky, and Aggression: A Study in German Foreign Policy, 1933–1939* (London: Edwin Arnold, 1972); Norman Rich, *Ideology, the Nazi State, and the Course of Expansion*, vol. 1 of *Hitler's War Aims* (New York: Norton, 1973); Klaus Hildebrand, *The Foreign Policy of the Third Reich*, trans. A. Fothergill (Berkeley and Los Angeles: University of California Press, 1973); Woodruff D. Smith, *The Ideological Origins of Nazi Imperialism* (New York: Oxford University Press, 1986); Geoffrey Stoakes, *Hitler and the Quest for World Domination* (Leamington Spa: Berg, 1986).

8. Hans-Erich Volkmann, "The National Socialist Economy in Preparation for War," in *The Build-Up of German Aggression*, vol. 1 of *Germany and the Second World War*, ed. Wilhelm Deist et al. (Oxford: Clarendon, 1990), 173–94, 309–15.

9. Rich, *Hitler's War Aims*, 2:420–22.

10. In a November 1937 conference recorded in the Hossbach Memorandum, Hitler explained that taking Austria and Czechoslovakia would "remove the threat to our flank in any possible operation against the West . . . [and] mean an acquisition of foodstuffs . . . shorter and better frontiers, the freeing of forces for other purposes, and the possibility of creating . . . about twelve divisions." Rich, *Hitler's War Aims*, 1:97.

11. Quoted in Overy, *Goering: The "Iron Man"* (Boston: Routledge & Kegan Paul, 1984), 82. On the economic utilization of Austria and Czechoslovakia, see Volkmann, "National Socialist Economy," 323–40; and Williamson Murray, *The Change in the European Balance of Power, 1938–1939: The Path to Ruin* (Princeton: Princeton University Press, 1984), 16, 149–53, 291–3.

12. Hans-Erich Volkmann, "Autarkie, Grossraumwirtschaft und Aggression: Zur ökonomischen Motivation der Besetzung Luxemburgs, Belgiens und der Niederlande 1940," *Militärgeschichtliche Mitteilungen* 1 (1976): 51–76.

13. Quoted in Alan S. Milward, *The New Order and the French Economy* (Oxford: Clarendon, 1970), 71.

14. For the Blitzkrieg interpretation, see Burton H. Klein, *Germany's Economic Preparations for War* (Cambridge: Harvard University Press, 1959), chap. 8; Alan S. Milward, "The End of the Blitzkrieg," *Economic History Review*, 2d ser., vol. 16 (1963–64): 499–518; idem, *The German Economy at War* (London: Athalone Press, 1965); idem, *The New Order and the French Economy* (Oxford: Clarendon, 1970); and Tim W. Mason, "The Primacy of Politics—Politics and Economics in National Socialist Germany," in *Nazism and the Third Reich*, ed. Henry A. Turner (New York: Quadrangle, 1972), 175–200. For the alternative view, see Berenice Carroll, *Design for Total War: Arms and Economics in the Third Reich* (The Hague: Mouton, 1968), 213–50; Richard J. Overy, "Hitler's War and the German Economy: A Reinterpretation," *Economic History Review* 2d ser., vol. 35 (1982); idem, "Mobilization for Total War in Germany, 1939–

1941," *English Historical Review* 103, no. 408 (July 1988): 613-39. See also the debate between Richard J. Overy, Tim Mason, and David Kaiser in *Past and Present* 116 (1987): 138–68 and *Past and Present* 122 (1989): 200–40, and Charles S. Maier, *In Search of Stability: Explorations in Historical Political Economy* (Cambridge: Cambridge University Press, 1987), 104–16. More research is needed to resolve this issue, and in particular how it affected policy in the occupied territories.

15. Milward, *New Order*, 160.

16. Ibid., 58.

17. See Harald Winkel, "Die wirtschaftlichen Beziehungen Deutschlands zu Dänemark in den Jahren der Besetzung, 1940–45,"in *Probleme der national-sozialistischen Wirtschaftspolitik*, Gesellschaft für Wirtschafts- und Sozialwissenschaften, Neue Folge Band 89, ed. Friedrich-Wilhelm Henning (Berlin: Duncker & Humblot, 1976), 119–74.

18. The German occupation scrip initially used by the invading troops was redeemed by local banks for native currency and charged to the national "occupation costs" account.

19. Milward, *New Order*, 54–77.

20. Ibid, 59.

21. Ibid, 125–28. See also Matthew Simon Karter, "Coercion and Resistance—Dependence and Compliance: The Germans, Vichy, and the French Economy" (Ph.D diss., University of Wisconsin, Madison, 1976), chaps. 7–9.

22. Milward, *New Order*, 86, 94–95, 144–45, 151, 161–62.

23. Forschungsstelle für Wehrwirtschaft, "Die finanziellen Leistungen der besetzten Gebiete bis Ende März 1944," October 1944, reproduced with commentary in Christoph Buchheim, "Die besetzten Länder im Dienste der deutschen Kriegswirtschaft während des Zweiten Weltkriegs," *Vierteljahrshefte für Zeitgeschichte* 34, no. 2 (April 1986): 117–45.

24. Detlef Brandes, *Die Tschechen unter deutschem protektorat* (Munich: R. Oldenbourg, 1969), 1:154; E. A. Radice, "Changes in Property Relationships and Financial Arrangements," in *Interwar Policy, the War, and Reconstruction*, vol. 2 of *The Economic History of Eastern Europe, 1919–1975*, ed. M. C. Kaser and E. A. Radice (Oxford: Clarendon, 1986), 347–48.

25. Overy, *Goering*, 111–16. See also Richard J. Overy, "German Multinationals and the Nazi State in Occupied Europe," in *Multinational Enterprise in Historical Perspective*, ed. Alice Teichova, Maurice Lévy-Leboyer, and Helga Nussbaum (Cambridge: Cambridge University Press, 1986), 299–325, and Radice, "Changes in Property Relationships," 353–56.

26. Other indicators of the Czech mobilization rate suggest that it was quite high. As shown below, Bohemia-Moravia's GNP increased slightly during the war, while GNP declined in most of the other occupied countries. In addition, the Czech export surplus with Germany and its satellites—which does not include German spending on local occupation and transportation expenses—rose to 32 percent of GNP by 1943, while private consumption shrank to 56 percent. Jaroslav Krejčí, "Bohemian-Moravian War Economy," in *Economic History of Eastern Europe, 1919-1975*, ed. M. C. Kaser and E. A. Radice, 2:461.

27. Or 273 billion 1938 francs. France, Présidence du Conseil, Commission

Consultative des Dommages et des Reparations. *Dommages subis par la France et l'Union Française du fait de la guerre et de l'occupation ennemie (1939–1945), Part imputable à l'Allemagne* (Paris: Imprimerie Nationale, 1947–1951) [cit. CCDR, *Dommages*], 1:379, 1:407–10. Milward, *New Order*, 82.

28. On the captured Czech arms, appraised at 77 million RM, see Voijech Mastny, *The Czechs under Nazi Rule: The Failure of National Resistance, 1939–1942* (New York: Columbia University Press, 1971), 65–67. On their subsequent use by Germany, see Charles K. Kliment and Hilary Louis Doyle, *Czechoslovak Armoured Fighting Vehicles, 1918–1945: Development for Czechoslovakia, Exploitation by Germany* (Watford: Argus, 1979), 38, 56–59; Alfred Meglen, "Les chars tcheques dans l'armée d'Hitler," *Revue historique de l'Armée* 21, no. 2 (1965): 151–54.

29. David E. Griffin, "The Battle of France, 1940: The Role of the French Air Force," *Aerospace Historian* 21, no. 3 (September 1974): 144–53.

30. Albert Seaton, *The German Army, 1933–1945* (New York: St. Martins Press, 1982), 160, 174.

31. Hans-Erich Volkmann, "National Socialist Economy," 325–6, 334–5. Murray, *Change*, 150–51, 291–93.

32. Arthur L. Smith, Jr., *Hitler's Gold: The Story of the Nazi War Loot* (Oxford: Berg, 1989), 27.

33. Milward, *New Order*, 80, 280–81.

34. W. G. Jensen, "The Importance of Energy in the First and Second World Wars," *Historical Journal* 11, no. 3 (1968): 548–9.

35. Some of this was leased, though at dictated rates.

36. CCDR, *Dommages*, vol. 8, reports T.C.1 and T.C.3. Some was leased, though for token amounts. Paul Durand, *La SNCF pendant la guerre* (Paris: Presses Universitaires de France, 1969), 216ff.

37. United States Strategic Bombing Survey [cit. USSBS], *The Effects of Strategic Bombing on German Transportation*, report no. 200 (Washington, D.C., 1947), 74–76; and idem, *The German Locomotive Industry*, report no. 203 (Washington, D.C., 1947), 5–17.

38. Milward, *New Order*, 77.

39. Edward L. Homze, *Foreign Labor in Nazi Germany* (Princeton: Princeton University Press, 1967); Hans Pfahlmann, *Fremdarbeiter und Krigsgefangene in der deutschen Kriegswirtschaft 1939–1945* (Darmstadt: Wehr und Wissen Verlagsgesellschaft, 1968); Ulrich Herbert, *Fremdarbeiter: Politik und Praxis des "Ausländer-Einsatzes" in der Kriegswirtschaft des dritten Reiches* (Bonn: Dietz, 1985); Ulrich Herbert, *A History of Foreign Labor in Germany, 1880–1980: Seasonal Workers/Forced Laborers/Guest Workers*, trans. William Templer (Ann Arbor: University of Michigan Press, 1990), 127–92.

40. Homze, *Foreign Labor*, 23–56.

41. Gerhard Hirshfeld, *Nazi Rule and Dutch Collaboration: The Netherlands under German Occupation, 1940–1945*, trans. L. Willmot (New York: Berg, 1988), 211–23; Werner Warmbrunn, *The Dutch under German Occupation, 1940–1945* (Stanford: Stanford University Press, 1963), 72–77, 125; Peter F. Klemm, "German Economic Policies in Belgium from 1940 to 1944" (Ph.D. diss., University of Michigan, 1973), 296–99, 473–77, 485.

42. Homze, *Foreign Labor*, 177–203; Milward, *New Order*, 110–25, 165–76; Jacques Evrard, *La Déportation des travailleurs français dans le IIIe Reich* (Paris: Fayard, 1972), pt. 1.

43. Herbert, *History of Foreign Labor*, 154; Homze, *Foreign Labor*, 232.

44. Homze, *Foreign Labor*, 260–62.

45. Homze, *Foreign Labor*, 240–63; Pfahlmann, *Fremdarbeiter und Krigsgefangene*, 229; Herbert, *Fremdarbeiter*, 206–7, 273–78.

46. Homze, *Foreign Labor*, 234–40; Pfahlmann, *Fremdarbeiter und Krigsgefangene*, 232.

47. Bernard P. Bellon, *Mercedes in Peace and War: German Automobile Workers, 1903–1945* (New York: Columbia University Press, 1990), 230–31, 238–53.

48. Herbert, *Fremdarbeiter*, 207; cf. 273, 278.

49. H. L. Ansbacher, "Testing, Management and Reactions of Foreign Workers in Germany during World War II," *American Psychologist* 5 (February 1950): 45.

50. Homze, *Foreign Labor*, 262–63.

51. Herbert, *Fremdarbeiter*, 207.

52. France, Institute National de la Statistique et des Etudes Economiques [cit. INSEE], *Mouvement Economique en France de 1938 à 1948* (Paris: Imprimerie Nationale, 1950), 200.

53. The French Reparations Commission estimated the prewar value of France's lost labor at 63 billion 1938 francs. Their calculations did not include ordinary POW labor, but assumed a high seventy-two-hour work week. About 6 billion 1938 francs worth of their salaries was included in French payments to Germany (for remittances sent home), and thus should not be double counted as part of Germany's gain. CCDR, *Dommages*, 1:375–79.

54. *The Goebbels Diaries, 1942–1943*, trans. and ed. Louis Lochner (Garden City, N.Y.: Doubleday, 1948), 464.

55. CCDR, *Dommages*, 2:375.

56. Olav Riste, "German Occupation of Norway in World War II," in *Armies of Occupation*, ed. R. A. Prete and A. H. Ion (Waterloo, Ontario: Wilfred Laurier University Press, 1984), 145–55; Chester Wilmot, *The Struggle for Europe* (London: Collins, 1952), 207. Unsurprisingly, Germany's economic gains from Norway were virtually exhausted by the occupation army. Alan S. Milward, *The Fascist Economy in Norway* (Oxford: Clarendon, 1972), 279–86.

57. Allied Command, German Military Documents Section (combined British-Canadian-U.S. staff), *German Manpower: A Study of the Employment of German Manpower from 1933–1945*, U.S. National Archives, Record Group 242 (Studies, Reports and Reference Material), chart 54. The total number of Gestapo agents, in the occupied territories as well as in Germany, was forty thousand, according to Edward Crankshaw, *Gestapo: Instrument of Tyranny* (repr., London: Greenhill, 1990), 95.

58. Gerhard Hirschfeld, *Nazi Rule and Dutch Collaboration: The Netherlands under German Occupation 1940–1945*, trans. L. Willmot (New York: Berg, 1988), 46; Rich, *Hitler's War Aims*, 2:208.

59. Estimate for 1941 based on the 22 francs/day/man cost of French soldiers

given by Milward, New Order, 61, 287. Estimates for 1943–44 based on For-schungsstelle für Wehrwirtschaft, "Die finanziellen Leistungen," 129, 135.

60. Useful overviews of European resistance include Henri Michel, *The Shadow War: European Resistance, 1939–1945*, trans. Richard Barry (New York: Harper and Row, 1972); M. R. D. Foot, *Resistance: European Resistance to Nazism, 1940–1945* (New York: McGraw-Hill, 1977); and Jørgen Haestrup, *European Resistance Movements, 1939–1945: A Complete History* (Westport, Conn.: Meckler, 1981). See also Walter Laqueur, *Guerrilla: A Historical and Critical Study* (Boston: Little, Brown, 1976), esp. 204–5.

61. Robert O. Paxton, *Vichy France: Old Guard and New Order, 1940–1944* (New York: Columbia University Press, 1972), 294–95; and Gordon Wright "Reflections on the French Resistance," *Political Science Quarterly* 77, no. 3 (September 1962): 337–39. John Sweets's criticism of this figure (*Choices in Vichy France: The French under Nazi Occupation* [New York: Oxford University Press, 1986], 225–30) is based on his sample from the mountainous (and thus resistance-conducive) Auvergne, and a broad definition of resister.

62. Warmbrunn, *Dutch under German Occupation*, 266.

63. Martin G. Sorge, *The Other Price of Hitler's War: German Military and Civilian Losses Resulting from World War II* (New York: Greenwood Press, 1986), 55; Haestrup, *European Resistance Movements*, 444–60.

64. Joanna K. M. Hanson, *The Civilian Population and the Warsaw Uprising of 1944* (New York: Cambridge University Press, 1982), 202.

65. Foot, *Resistance*, 57.

66. The refusal of railroad workers to repair the damage caused by saboteurs and Allied bombing further hurt German rail transport at the final, critical stage of the occupation. M. R. D. Foot, *S.O.E. in France: An Account of the Work of the British Special Operations Execuitve in France, 1940–44*, rev. ed. (London: HMSO, 1968), 411, 440; Haestrup, *European Resistance Movements*, 431. These authors would appear to overstate the significance of sabotage, since only half a billion of the 15 billion francs' worth of damage inflicted on the French railroads in 1944 was due to sabotage. Paul Durant, *La SNCF pendant la guerre* (Paris: Presses Universitaires de France, 1969), 282.

67. It replied with the massacre of two thousand villagers. Max Hastings, *Das Reich: Resistance and the March of the 2nd SS Panzer Division through France, 1944* (London: Michael Joseph, 1981), 217–18.

68. SHAEF report, 18 July 1945, quoted in Foot, *S.O.E. in France*, 442.

69. Haestrup, *European Resistance Movements*, 132–46.

70. Hirschfeld, *Nazi Rule and Dutch Collaboration*, 173, cf. 162–81.

71. Quoted in Hsi-Huey Liang, *The Rise of Modern Police and the European State System from Metternich to the Second World War* (Cambridge: Cambridge University Press, 1988), 299.

72. Paxton, *Vichy France*, 294. Sweets (*Choices in Vichy France*, 224–30, 175), argues that French resisters outnumbered French oppressors, while acknowledging that this made little difference to German military and economic interests. See also Rich, *Hitler's War Aims*, 2:207–10, 227; and John F. Sweets, "La police et la population dans la France de Vichy: une Etude de cas conforme et fidèle," *Revue d'histoire de la deuxième guerre mondiale*, no. 155 (July 1981):

63–73. On Belgium, see Rudi Van Doorslaer,"La police belge et le maintien de l'ordre en Belgique occupée," *Revue du Nord*, no.2—special series (1987): 73–101.

73. Hirschfeld, *Nazi Rule and Dutch Collaboration*, 162–81, esp. 173.

74. Robert O. Paxton and Michael R. Marrus, *Vichy France and the Jews* (New York: Schocken, 1981).

75. British and German mobilization rates were about the same. Anthony Adamthwaite, *France and the Coming of the Second World War, 1936–1939* (London: Cass, 1977), 164.

76. The official wholesale price index shows an increase of 11 percent between 1938 and 1944, although there is evidence that this index is biased downward. See John J. Klein, "German Money and Prices, 1932–1944," in *Studies in the Quantity Theory of Money*, ed. Milton Friedman (Chicago: University of Chicago Press, 1956), 121–59.

77. CCDR, *Dommages*, 2:151. Milward, *New Order*, 110–46.

78. Klein, *Germany's Economic Preparations*, 207, cf. 206–35. See also Milward, *German Economy at War*, and Overy, *Goering*.

79. On the rationalization measures in occupied France, see Milward, *New Order*, 147–62; and Adrian Jones, "Illusions of Sovereignty: Business and the Organization of Committees of Vichy France," *Social History* 11 (January 1986): 1–31.

80. Milward, *Fascist Economy*, 36, 95, 281.

81. John Gillingham, *Belgian Business in the Nazi New Order* (Gent: Jan Dhondt Stichting, 1977), 127–28. See also his *Industry and Politics in the Third Reich: Ruhr Coal, Hitler and Europe* (London: Methuen, 1985), 141, 152.

82. Etienne Dejonghe, "Pénurie charbonnière et répartition en France (1940–1944)," *Revue d'histoire de la deuxième guerre mondiale*, no. 102 (April 1976): 53.

83. British sources alone had also supplied over half of France's prewar jute, rubber, tin, and raw wool requirements, and a third of coke and manganese imports. Robert J. Young, *In Command of France: French Foreign Policy and Military Planning, 1933–1940* (Cambridge, Mass.: Harvard University Press, 1978), 22.

84. Sven-Olof Olsson, *German Coal and Swedish Fuel, 1939–1945*, Publications of the Institute of Economic History, no. 36 (Göteborg: Göteborg University, 1975), 120–23, 135–41. Coal was the limiting factor in German wartime steel production. See Martin Fritz, *German Steel and Swedish Iron Ore, 1939–1945*, Publications of the Institute of Economic History, no. 29 (Göteborg: Göteborg University, 1974), 17–28; cf. Klein, *Germany's Economic Preparations*, 114–35.

85. Milward, *New Order*, 195; INSEE, *Mouvement Economique en France de 1938 à 1948* (Paris: Imprimerie Nationale, 1950), 211.

86. Belgium, Administration des Mines, *Annales des Mines de Belgique* 47, no. 3 (1948): 849. Prewar but not wartime data include Luxembourg's coal consumption, biasing these percentages downward. See also Klemm, "German Economic Policies," 169–72, 349–53.

87. Milward, *Fascist Economy*, 151; Olsson, *German Coal*, 123.

88. On German coal consumption, see Olsson, *German Coal*, 115–20.

89. The U.S. Strategic Bombing Survey noted that "existing inventories were under-utilized and most of German industry worked only a single shift throughout the course of the war." USSBS, *Machine Tool Industry in Germany*, report no. 55 (Washington, D.C., 1947), 3.

90. Protectorate data, for 1939, from Krejčí, "Bohemian-Moravian War Economy." All other data for 1938, income from Colin Clark, *The Conditions of Economic Progress*, 3d ed. (London: Macmillan, 1957); and trade from Brian R. Mitchell, *International Historical Statistics: Europe, 1750–1988*, 3d ed. (New York: Stockton Press, 1992), table E2.

91. Milward, *New Order*, 195. INSEE, *Mouvement Economique*, 243–45. German share increased from 66 percent of total traffic in December 1941 to 85 percent in January 1944. Milward, *New Order*, 281–82.

92. For an overview, see Karl Brandt, *Management of Agriculture and Food in the German-Occupied and other Areas of Fortress Europe: A Study in Military Government* (Stanford: Stanford University Press, 1953).

93. INSEE, *Mouvement Economique*, 68. Milward, *New Order*, 255–68.

94. Pierre Barral, "Agriculture and Food Supply in France during the Second World War," in *Agriculture and Food Supply in the Second World War*, ed. Bernd Martin and Alan S. Milward (Ostfildern: Scripta Murcaturae Verlag, 1985), 94, 98–100. See also Milward, *New Order*, 258, 266.

95. Milward, *New Order*, 238–39, 241–43. Construction materials, on the other hand, fell to half of prewar levels, leather goods to 40 percent, and textiles and rubber to 25 percent. INSEE, *Mouvement Economique*, 211–39.

96. Hans-Erich Volkmann, "L'importance économique de la Lorraine pour le IIIe Reich," *Revue d'histoire de la deuxième guerre mondiale*, no. 120 (1980): 69–93; Milward, *New Order*, 213–15, 232.

97. By iron content; Sweden provided about a third. Milward, *New Order*, 219, 226.

98. Olsson, *German Coal*, 99; Milward, *New Order*, 186–89; France figures exclude Lorraine production.

99. Olsson, *German Coal*, 104. Gillingham, *Belgian Business*, 131–39. Milward, *New Order*, 198–209 (on iron, 229–34); Gillingham (*Industry and Politics*, 155; cf. 124, 153–57) claims that "the continued failure to provide adequate rations was the chief cause of the steady decline in miner productivity." On British coal problems, see Correlli Barnett, *The Pride and the Fall: The Dream and Illusion of Britain as a Great Nation* (New York: Free Press, 1986), 63–86.

100. On the Czech arms industry and its wartime performance, see M. Hauner, "Military Budgets and the Armaments Industry," in *Economic History of Eastern Europe*, ed. M. C. Kaser and E. A. Radice, 2:49–116, esp. 72–89; Kliment and Doyle, *Czechoslovak Armoured Fighting Vehicles*.

101. Michaël de Vlaminick, "L'industrie de l'armement en Belgique sous l'occupation (1940–1944)," *Revue du Nord*, no. 2 spécial hors-série (1987), 379–96; Klemm, "German Economic Policies," 482–83. Hirschfeld, *Nazi Rule and Dutch Collaboration*, 183–84, 191.

102. Hirschfeld, *Nazi Rule and Dutch Collaboration*, 189fn, 211–13; Rémy Desquesnes, "'Atlantikwall' et 'Südwall'. La défense allemande sur le littoral

français (1941–1944)" (Thèse d'Etat, University of Caen, 1987), 161–233. See also Alan F. Wilt, *The Atlantic Wall: Hitler's Defenses in the West, 1941–1944* (Ames: Iowa State University Press, 1975).

103. Hirschfeld, *Nazi Rule and Dutch Collaboration*, 183–92.

104. Gillingham, *Belgian Business*, 151.

105. For an overview, see Haestrup, *European Resistance Movements*, 401–44.

106. Haestrup (ibid., 427) admits that "the members of the Resistance, with the support from the majority of the Resistance historians, are inclined to attribute greater results to sabotage and, particularly, greater potential than the examination of realities can justify."

107. Foot, *S.O.E. in France*, 437; cf. 505–17. As Webster and Frankland note in the official British history of the bombing offensive, "The total effect of the damage in France was not very important. There were in most cases other plants which could supply what was necessary and in any event these factories were soon to be overrun by the allied armies." Charles Webster and Noble Frankland, *The Strategic Air Offensive against Germany, 1939–1945* (London: HMSO, 1961), 2:293.

108. Quoted in Alan S. Milward, "The Economic and Strategic Effectiveness of Resistance," in *Resistance in Europe, 1939–1945*, ed. Stephen Hawes and Ralph White (London: Allen Lane, 1975), 197. Speer hastily retracted his statement, but he makes no reference to French sabotage in his memoirs.

109. Milward, "Economic and Strategic Effectiveness of Resistance," 191.

110. Haestrup, *European Resistance Movements*, 92–132.

111. Milward, *New Order*, 165; cf. Homze, *Foreign Labor*, 190.

112. Gillingham, *Belgian Business*, 152. See also Haestrup, *European Resistance Movements*, 132–146; Milward, *New Order*, 288, 290, 293; Milward, "Economic and Strategic Effectiveness of Resistance," 199–200; Klemm, "German Economic Policies," 477ff.; cf. 199–200; Etienne Verhoeyen, "Les grands industriels belges entre collaboration et résistance: Le moindre mal," *Cahiers* (Centre de Recherches et d'Etudes Historique de la Seconde Guerre Mondiale) 10 (November 1986): 96–97, 103–104.

113. Patrick Fridenson, "Automobile Workers in France and Their Work, 1914–83," in *Work in France: Representations, Meaning, Organization, and Practice*, ed. Steven L. Kaplan and Cynthia J. Koepp (Ithaca: Cornell University Press, 1986), 529.

114. Rich, *Hitler's War Aims*, 2:68–105.

115. Adolph Hitler, *Hitler's Table Talk, 1941–1944* (London: Weidenfeld and Nicholson, 1953), 558.

116. Haestrup, *European Resistance Movements*, 444–60; Michel, *Shadow War*, 217–24.

117. Quoted in Hirschfeld, *Nazi Rule and Dutch Collaboration*, 149. Emphasis in original.

118. Ibid., 205. The motivation of the Belgian Secretaries-General was the same; see Gillingham, *Belgian Business*; Verhoeyen, "Grands industriels belges," 57–114.

119. Hirschfeld, *Nazi Rule and Dutch Collaboration*, 141–2, 150–54.

Warmbrunn, *Dutch under German Occupation*, 121–27, 267–75. On the final traumatic winter, in which twenty thousand Dutch perished of starvation, see Henri Van Der Zee, *The Hunger Winter: Occupied Holland, 1944–45* (London: Jill Norman & Hobhouse, 1982).

120. Quoted in Paxton, *Vichy France*, 16.

121. Ibid., 41–44.

122. Hirschfeld, *Nazi Rule and Dutch Collaboration*, 5, 57, 312.

123. Paul Struye, *L'Evolution du sentiment public en Belgique sous l'occupation allemande* (Brussels, 1945), cited in Gillingham, *Belgian Business*, 30.

124. Hirschfeld, *Nazi Rule and Dutch Collaboration*, 209–11. On Belgium, see Gillingham, *Belgian Business* and Verhoeyen, "Grands industriels belges," esp. 112–13.

125. Rich, *Hitler's War Aims* 2:423. See also Jean-Pierre Azéma, *From Munich to the Liberation, 1938–1944*, trans. Janet Lloyd (Cambridge: Cambridge University Press, 1984), 69; Warmbrunn, *Dutch under German Occupation*, 262; and Hirschfeld, *Nazi Rule and Dutch Collaboration*, 10, 317–19.

126. On varied backgrounds of French resisters, see H. R. Kedward, *Resistance in Vichy France* (New York: University of Oxford Press, 1978).

127. Paxton, *Vichy France*, 234–41.

128. Rosecrance, *Rise of the Trading State*, 36. Kaysen ("Is War Obsolete?" 56) makes a similar claim.

129. Quoted in Azéma, *Munich to Liberation*, 121. See also M. L. Smith, "The Anti-Bolshevik Crusade and Europe," in *Making the New Europe: European Unity and the Second World War*, ed. M. L. Smith and Peter M. R. Stirk (New York: Pinter, 1990), 46–65.

130. Juan J. Linz, "Comparative Study of Fascism," in Walter Laqueur, ed., *Fascism: A Reader's Guide* (Berkeley and Los Angeles: University of California Press, 1976): 3–121, esp. 90. For all of Europe, see also Stanley G. Payne, "Fascism in Western Europe," in Ibid., 295–311; and David Littlejohn, *The Patriotic Traitors: A History of Collaboration in German Occupied Europe, 1940–45* (Garden City, N.Y.: Doubleday, 1972).

131. Victor S. Mamatey, "The Development of Czechoslovak Democracy, 1920–1938," in *A History of the Czechoslovak Republic, 1918–1948*, ed. Radomir Luza and Victor S. Mamatey (Princeton: Princeton University Press, 1973), 99–166, esp. 154; Gotthold Rhode, "The Protectorate of Bohemia and Moravia, 1939–1945," in Ibid., 296–321, esp. 309. The German security apparatus did recruit heavily from Germanic Czechs, to take advantage of their familiarity with the country and the language. Radomir Luza, "The Czech Resistance Movement," in *A History of the Czechoslovak Republic, 1918–1948*, ed. Radomir Luza and Victor S. Mamatey (Princeton: Princeton University Press, 1973), 349–50.

132. Hirschfeld, *Nazi Rule and Dutch Collaboration*, 242–66.

133. Jean Stengers, "Belgium," in *The European Right: A Historical Profile*, ed. Hans Rogger and Eugen Weber, (Berkeley and Los Angeles: University of California Press, 1965): 128–67; E. H. Kossman, *The Low Countries, 1780–1940* (Oxford: Clarendon, 1978), 624–30, 637–49.

134. Payne, "Fascism in Western Europe," 298.

135. Bertram Gordon, *Collaborationism in France during the Second World War* (Ithaca: Cornell University Press, 1980), 326–27; Hirschfeld, *Nazi Rule and Dutch Collaboration*, 284–85. Figures on Norway and Belgium from Littlejohn, *Patriotic Traitors*, 20, 159.

136. Paxton, *Vichy France*, 221–28, 291–98; Sweets, *Choices in Vichy France*, 92–96; Gordon, *Collaborationism in France*, 166–95 and 257–59.

137. Kenneth W. Estes, "A European Anabasis: Western European Volunteers in the German Army and SS, 1940–1945" (Ph.D diss., University of Maryland, 1984), 200. Estes (p. 204–8) judges the Danes and Flemish as having performed better than the Dutch, Norwegian, French, and Wallon units. See also Gordon, *Collaborationism in France*, 244–78.

138. Stanley Hoffmann drew this important distinction for France in "Self-Ensnared: Collaboration with Nazi Germany," *Journal of Modern History* (September 1968), reprinted in *Decline or Renewal? France Since the 1930s* (New York: Viking Press, 1974), 26–44.

139. François Darnand became the French minister of "internal order" in December 1943. In Belgium, VNV members became secretaries-general for Interior and Economic Affairs; in the Netherlands, NSB members eventually replaced seven of ten secretaries-general, but "the number of NSB members in public service increased only gradually . . . without exerting any decisive ideological influence on the work of the administration in general." Hirschfeld, *Nazi Rule and Dutch Collaboration*, 153.

140. For an overview, see Rich, *Hitler's War Aims*, vol. 2.

141. Quoted in Gordon, *Collaborationism in France*, 17.

142. The French Third Republic had thirteen individuals per cabinet post between the wars, in contrast to only five to six in Belgium, the Netherlands, and Britain. Kossman, *Low Countries*, 572.

143. Foot, *Resistance*, 63–69; Haestrup, *European Resistance Movements*, 31–33; Brian Chapman, "The German Counter Resistance," in *Resistance in Europe, 1939–1945*, ed. Stephen Hawes and Ralph White (London: Allen Lane, 1975), 170–85; and Jacques Delarue, *Gestapo: A History of Horror*, trans. M. Savill (London: Macdonald, 1964).

144. Luza, "Czech Resistance Movement," 343–61.

145. Werner Rings, *Life with the Enemy: Collaboration and Resistance in Hitler's Europe, 1939–1945*, trans. J. M. Brownjohn (Garden City, N.Y.: Doubleday, 1982), 274.

146. Hirschfeld, *Nazi Rule and Dutch Collaboration*, 206–207.

147. For several such examples, see Klemm, "German Economic Policies," 213–32.

148. Milward, *New Order*, 75, 82, 87–88.

149. The Volkswagenwerke began supervising Peugeot in 1943. Jean-Louis Loubet, *Automobiles Peugeot: Une réussite industrielle, 1945–1974* (Paris: Economica, 1990), 21.

150. Ibid., 265.

151. Jean-Louis Loubet, "La Societé Anonyme André Citroën, 1924–1968, Etude historique" (Thèse de doctorat de 3ème cycle, Université de Paris X, 1979), 333.

152. Quoted in Fernand Picard, *L'Epopée de Renault* (Paris: Albin Michel, 1976), 129.

153. Picard, *Epopée de Renault*, 153.

154. Quoted in Gilbert Hatry, *Louis Renault, patron absolu* (Paris: Editions Lafourcade, 1982), 390.

155. Quoted in Ted Morgan, *An Uncertain Hour: The French, the Germans, the Jews, the Barbie Trial, and the City of Lyon, 1940–1945* (New York: William Morrow, 1990), 119. See also Gérard Declas, "Les usines Berliet, 1895–1949," pt. 2, *De Renault Frères* 3 (December 1979), 326–33.

156. On Chambon-sur-Lignon, see Phillip Hallie, *Lest Innocent Blood Be Shed* (New York: Harper & Row, 1979).

157. Karl-Heinz Schlarp, *Wirtschaft und Besatzung in Serbien, 1941–1944: Ein Beitrag zur nationalsozialistischen Wirtschaftspolitik in Südosteuropa* (Stuttgart: Franz Steiner Verlag Weisbaden, 1986), 221, 245.

158. A. F. Freris, *The Greek Economy in the Twentieth Century* (London: Croom Helm, 1986), 119.

159. E. A. Radice, "Agriculture and Food," in *Economic History of Eastern Europe*, ed. M. C. Kaser and E. A. Radice, 2:366–97.

160. Stavros B. Thomadakis, "Black Markets, Inflation, and Force in the Economy of Occupied Greece," in *Greece in the 1940s: A Nation in Crisis*, ed. John O. Iatrides (Hanover, N.H.: University Press of New England, 1981), 61–80; Mark Mazower, *Inside Hitler's Greece: The Experience of Occupation, 1941–44* (New Haven: Yale University Press, 1993), 23–72.

161. Luza, "Czech Resistance Movement," 349–50.

162. Haestrup, *European Resistance Movements*, 474.

163. John L. Hondros, *Occupation and Resistance: The Greek Agony, 1941–44* (New York: Pella, 1983), 63, 85–89, 153–62.

164. Fritz, *German Steel*; Milward, *New Order*, 210–34.

165. George F. Kennan, *Memoirs, 1925–1950* (New York: Pantheon Books, 1967), 129.

166. Theo J. Schulte, *The German Army and Nazi Policies in Occupied Russia* (Oxford: Berg, 1988); Omer Bartov, *Hitler's Army: Soldiers, Nazis, and War in the Third Reich* (New York: Oxford University Press, 1991); Gerald Reitlinger, *The SS: Alibi of a Nation, 1922–1945* (New York: Viking Press, 1957), 125–380.

Chapter 4
Belgium and Luxembourg, 1914–1918

1. Of its prewar population of 3.7 million, occupied France retained only 2.1 million, and those mainly women, children, and older men. Pierre Boulin, *L'organisation du travail dans la région envahie de la France pendant l'occupation* (Paris: Les Presses Universitaires de France, 1927), 3. Labor was no problem in Belgium, for although a million Belgians fled during the invasion, mainly into the Netherlands, all but a half-million returned after the dust settled. In 1918 there were 325,000 Belgian refugees in France, 163,000 in Britain, and 101,000 in the Netherlands. Belgium, *Annuaire statistique de la Belgique et du Congo belge, 1915–1919* 46 (1922): 114–17.

2. Germany also conquered a huge expanse of western Russia, as well as (with Austria-Hungary) Serbia and Romania. But these regions were less industrialized than Belgium and Luxembourg, and much less is known about their wartime economic history.

3. The borders in Belgium between the general government and the military zones fluctuated somewhat over the course of the occupation. A tiny strip of channel coast behind the Yser River was held tenaciously by the Belgian king and army throughout the war.

4. On German prewar aims, see Fritz Fischer, *War of Illusions*, trans. M. Jackson (New York: W. W. Norton, 1975); Imanuel Geiss, *German Foreign Policy, 1871–1914* (London: Routledge & Kegan Paul, 1976); and V. R. Berghahn, *Germany and the Approach of War in 1914* (New York: St. Martin's Press, 1973). On wartime aims, see Fritz Fischer, *Germany's Aims in the First World War* (New York: W. W. Norton, 1967); Hans W. Gatzke, *Germany's Drive to the West (Drang nach Westen): A Study of Germany's Western War Aims during the First World War* (Baltimore: Johns Hopkins University Press, 1966); L. L. Farrar, Jr., *Divide and Conquer: German Efforts to Conclude a Separate Peace, 1914–1918* (New York: Columbia University Press, 1978).

5. Quoted in Fischer, *Germany's Aims*, 95.

6. John F. V. Keiger, *France and the Origins of the First World War* (New York: St. Martin's, 1983), 5–10, 68–81.

7. For a summary, see James Joll, *Origins of the First World War* (New York: Longman, 1984), chap. 7.

8. Fischer, *War of Illusions*, chap. 11; Woodruff D. Smith, *The Ideological Origins of Nazi Imperialism* (New York: Oxford University Press, 1986), chap. 4–7; Gerd Hardach, *The First World War, 1914–1918* (Berkeley: University of California Press, 1977), 227–37.

9. Quoted in Stephen Van Evera, "The Cult of the Offensive and the Origins of the First World War," *International Security* 9, no. 1 (Summer 1984), 67.

10. Quoted in David E. Kaiser, "Germany and the Origins of the First World War," *Journal of Modern History* 55 (September 1983): 455–56.

11. Quoted in Andreas Hillgruber, *Germany and the Two World Wars*, trans. W. Kirby (Cambridge: Harvard University Press, 1981), 23; cf. 38. See also Kaiser, "Germany and the Origins," 468.

12. Bethmann Hollweg in 1917, quoted in Fischer, *War of Illusions*, 468.

13. Some have argued that that Bethmann Hollweg's July 29 offer to London to refrain from annexing Belgian and French soil (leaving their colonies fair game) in return for British neutrality demonstrates German expansionism. But there is little reason to think that these ambitions were critical in his decision to provoke or risk war, much less that the result was a war of conquest. For a discussion of this issue, see Geiss, *German Foreign Policy*, 174–75.

14. Quotations from the September Program, reproduced in Fischer, *Germany's Aims*, 103–105.

15. Fischer, *Germany's Aims*, 283–304, 298–309.

16. Quoted in ibid., 195.

17. Conservatives thus warned the government that "a government which, without urgent necessity . . . relinquishes Belgium, will lose support of the largest

and best sections of the German people and thus endanger the monarchy."
Gatzke, *Germany's Drive to the West*, 22.

18. Fischer, *Germany's Aims*, 394–404. Mass opinion had already shifted
against the war in 1916; see Gatzke, *Germany's Drive to the West*, 293; L. L.
Farrar, Jr., *Divide and Conquer: German Efforts to Conclude a Separate Peace,
1914–1918* (New York: Columbia University Press, 1978), 11–12, 109–10.

19. Smith (*Ideological Origins*, 174–85) portrays the Pan-German quest for
Lebensraum as an old Junker ploy to divert peasant attention from their wealth
and power. But the conquest of so much agricultural land would have threatened
Junker interests, unless they could gain actual ownership.

20. Hillgruber, *Germany and the Two World Wars*, 44–45.

21. Quoted in Fischer, *Germany's Aims*, 259; cf. 164–73, 273, 591; Gatzke,
Germany's Drive, 30–38.

22. Bethmann Hollweg, quoted by Fischer, *Germany's Aims*, 104. He was
even more circumspect about hegemony over the Netherlands: "in view of the
Dutch character, this closer relationship must leave them free of any feeling of
compulsion, [and] must alter nothing in the Dutch way of life." Ibid., 105.

23. Bethmann Hollweg, quoted by Fischer, *Germany's Aims*, 453. On Belgium, see 260–71; on Poland, see 203, 236–44, 353–56, 450–56.

24. Fischer, *Germany's Aims*, 261–62.

25. The German population was higher in Latvia (then called Livonia and
Courland) and Estonia than in Lithuania. Fischer, *Germany's Aims*, 456–63; cf.
273–77, 605.

26. Fischer, *Germany's Aims*, 603.

27. Quoted in Reinhold Zilch, "Die Memoranden Karl Helfferichs vom 28.
und 29. August 1914 über die finanzielle Unterdrückung und Ausplünderung
Belgiens," *Jahrbuch für Wirtschaftsgeschichte*, no. 4 (1980): 194.

28. With a base of 1913 = 100, production fell to 63 in 1915, and recovered
to 73–74 during 1916–18. Leo Grebler and Wilhelm Winkler, *The Cost of the
World War to Germany and to Austria-Hungary* (New Haven: Yale University
Press, 1940), 27.

29. Gerd Hardach, *The First World War, 1914–1918* (Berkeley: University of
California Press, 1977), 62, 70ff. See also Gerald Feldman, *Army, Industry and
Labor in Germany, 1914–1918* (Princeton: Princeton University Press, 1966),
301.

30. Hardach, *First World War*, 70–72. R. B. Armeson, *Total Warfare and
Compulsory Labor* (The Hague: Ninjoff, 1965), 29–40. Grebler and Winkler,
Cost of the War, 27–36.

31. Hardach, *First World War*, 55–73.

32. Certain industrialists opposed proposals from the head of the German
War Raw Materials Department's iron section to reactivate French and Belgian
plants, fearing they would eat into their own profits. Feldman, *Army, Industry
and Labor*, 385. But the German exploitation of Luxembourg's industry, which
was only party German-owned, suggests that it was not the opposition of German
industry that prevented the reactivation of Belgian production.

33. The Société Générale became the national bank of emission after the Ger-

mans shut down the Belgian National Bank, which had whisked its metal reserves to London during the invasion. The "war contributions" totaled 2.3 billion Belgian francs by the end of the war. Fernand Baudhuin, *Histoire économique de la Belgique, 1914–1939*, 2d ed. (Bruxelles: Emile Bruylant, 1946), 1:41–42, 73.

34. Baudhuin, *Histoire économique*, 1:43, 51–52; Henry L. Shepherd, *The Monetary Experience of Belgium, 1914–1936* (Princeton: Princeton University Press, 1936), 10–11.

35. Joseph Steichen, *Exposé de la situation économique et financière du Grand-Duché de Luxembourg* (Luxembourg: Gieser, 1920), 3.

36. Index based on coal, steel, iron, beer, and sugar, from Karel Veraghtert, "Le développement industriel," in *L'industrie en Belgique: deux siècles d'évolution 1780–1980*, ed. G. L. De Brabander et al. (Gent: Snoeck-Ducaju & Zoon, 1981), 149.

37. Belgium, *Extrait de la Statistique des Industries*, 4–7; Ludwig von Köhler, *The Administration of the Occupied Territories*, trans. W. Dittmar (New York: Carnegie Endowment for International Peace, 1942), 170–71. The drop in total output in 1917 was due to the loss of miners conscripted for work in more efficient German mines. Henri Pirenne, *La Belgique et la Guerre Mondiale* (Paris: Presses Universitaires Français, 1928), 197; Raymond Riley, *Belgium* (Boulder: Westview, 1976), 31.

38. Charles Kerchove de Denterghem, *L'industrie belge pendant l'occupation allemande, 1914–1918* (Paris: Presses Universitaires Français, 1927), 147; Belgium, Commission d'enquête sur les violations des règles du droit des gens, des lois et des coutumes de la guerre, *Rapport sur les mesures prises par les allemands a l'égard de l'industrie belge pendant l'occupation*, vol. 3 of *Rapports et Documents d'Enquête* (Bruxelles: Thone, 1921), 53, 259 [cit. *Rapport*].

39. *Rapport*, 57.

40. Kerchove, *Industrie belge*, 58, 73ff; von Köhler, *Administration*, 152. After public pressure stopped French textile factories from making sandbags for the German Army until in June 1916, only German-run factories continued to work in northern France. Boulin, *Organisation du travail*, 14, 17–22, 39.

41. *Rapport*, 48–9. Belgians got 224 million in neutral exports, and German exports must have been low because they consisted mainly of agricultural machinery, mining accessories, and other small manufactured items. Von Köhler, *Administration*, 164.

42. For the first half of 1917. Von Köhler, *Administration*, 150, 161.

43. Hans A. Schmitt, "Violated Neutrals: Belgium, the Dwarf States, and Luxemburg," in *Neutral Europe between War and Revolution, 1917–23*, ed. Hans A. Schmitt (Charlottesville: University Press of Virginia, 1988), 218.

44. By 1917, fifty-three hundred Luxembourgeois and seven hundred Belgians had taken the place of forty-two hundred Italians and twenty-two hundred Germans. M. E. Faber, *La métallurgie du Luxembourg: Etude de géographie physique, sociale et économique* (Luxembourg: Editions Luxembourgeoises, 1927), 56, 149.

45. Average iron ore output per miner increased from thirteen hundred tons in 1913 to fifteen hundred tons in 1916, and then fell to eleven hundred tons in

1917. Calculated from data from Carlo Hemmer, *L'économie du Grand-Duché de Luxembourg* (Luxembourg: Beffort, 1948), 1:80; Faber, *Métallurgie du Luxembourg*, 149.

46. Brian R. Mitchell, *International Historical Statistics: Europe, 1750–1988*, 3d ed. (New York: Stockton Press, 1992), table D9. See also Schmitt, "Violated Neutrals," 219; Grand-Duché de Luxemembourg, Commission d'étude des problèmes économiques posés par la guerre et ses conséquences éventuelles, *Travaux de la Commission sur l'orientation économique du Grand-Duché de Luxembourg* (Luxembourg: Imprimerie Victor Bück, 1919), annexes 5 and 6.

47. Gilbert Trausch, *Contributions à l'histoire sociale de la question du Luxembourg, 1914–1922* (Luxembourg: Saint-Paul, 1974), 49–56.

48. Trausch, *Contributions*, 47–49. Camille Wagner, *La sidérurgie luxembougeoise sous les régimes du Zollverein et de l'union économique belgo-luxembourgeoise* (Luxembourg: Artistique Luxembourgeoise, 1931), 27.

49. Schmitt, "Violated Neutrals," 218–20.

50. Kerchove, *Industrie belge*, 23–24.

51. Memorandum from Governor General von Bissing to von Hindenburg, 25 Nov. 1916, reproduced in Kerchove, *Industrie belge*, 153–5. Baudhuin, *Histoire économique*, vol.1, 72.

52. June 1915, quoted in *Rapport*, 49.

53. WUMBA (Waffen- und Munitions-beschaffungsamt, or Arms and Munitions Procurment Bureau) organized the seizure of all the useful machinery in the condemned plants. Its sister organization ROHMA (Rohmaterial-Beshaffungstelle, or Raw Material Procurement Bureau) was responsible for demolishing the remaining furnaces, machinery, and structures—anything that might yield a few tons of scrap metal. Several private German companies, so-called Demolition Groups, carried out the actual dismantling and pulverizing work, with only 170 Germans overseeing 1,300 Russian and Italian POW laborers. Kerchove, *Industrie belge*, 164–8.

54. Ibid., 165, 170–73.

55. Ibid., 170–73.

56. Grebler and Winkler, *Cost of the War*, 75.

57. On forced labor, see Fernand Passelecq, *Deportation et travail forcé des ouvriers et de la population civile de la Belgique occupée (1916–1918)* (Paris: Presses Universitaires Français, 1928); Gerhard Ritter, *The Tragedy of Statesmanship—Bethmann Hollweg as War Chancellor, 1914–1917*, vol. 3 of *The Sword and the Scepter: The Problem of Militarism in Germany*, trans. H. Norden (Coral Gables, Fla: University of Miami Press, 1972), 361–70; Ulrich Herbert, *A History of Foreign Labor in Germany, 1880–1980: Seasonal Workers / Forced Laborers / Guest Workers*, trans. William Templer (Ann Arbor: University of Michigan Press, 1990), 87–120. On forced labor in occupied France, see Boulin, *Organisation du travail*.

58. von Köhler, *Administration*, 186; Pirenne, *Belgique et la Guerre*, 44.

59. Ritter, *Tragedy of Statesmanship*, 361–62; von Köhler, *Administration*, 188–92.

60. Herbert, *History of Foreign Labor*, 92.

61. Quoted in Armeson, *Total Warfare and Compulsory Labor*, 30–32.

62. Ritter, *Tragedy of Statesmanship*, 361–65; von Köhler, *Administration*, 194–201.

63. Ritter, *Tragedy of Statesmanship*, 368–69; von Köhler, *Administration*, 202–15.

64. Ritter, *Tragedy of Statesmanship*, 369–70.

65. Pirenne, *Belgique et la Guerre*, 196; Pirenne himself was victim of German labor conscription.

66. Passelecq, *Deportation et travail forcé*, 325–346; cf. Ritter, *Tragedy of Statesmanship*, 366, 368, 372; Pirenne, *Belgique et la Guerre*, 194–5.

67. Von Köhler, *Administration*, 211, 216.

68. Pirenne, *Belgique et la Guerre*, 54–65. Brand Whitlock, *Belgium: A Personal Narrative* (New York: D. Appleton, 1919), 1:151–234.

69. Ritter, *Tragedy of Statesmanship*, 361, 367. Von Köhler even claimed that "in no instance was [active] resistance offered." *Administration*, 212.

70. Whitlock, *Belgium*, 1:134–35.

71. Emile Wanty, "La vie militaire," in *Histoire de la Belgique contemporaine, 1914–1970* (Bruxelles: La Renaissance du Livre, 1975), 352–53.

72. The governors general were von der Goltz (August 1914–December 1914), von Bissing (December 1914–April 1917), and von Falkenhausen (April 1917–November 1918). On the administrative structure of the general government, see von Köhler, *Administration*, 16–58, and Pirenne, *Belgique et la Guerre*, 90–111.

73. Adolf Solansky, "German Administration in Belgium" (Ph.D. diss., Columbia University, 1928), 21–22.

74. Whether for age, sex, or infirmity, only a third of civilian staffers were subject to military draft, and only 3 percent were eligible for active service. Hans von Winterfeldt, "Die Deutsche Verwaltung des Generalgouvernments in Belgien 1914–1918," in *Der grosse Krieg, 1914–1918*, ed. M. Schwarte (Leipzig: J. Barth, 1923), 10:11, 42; Ritter, *Tragedy of Statesmanship*, 361. On recruitment, see von Köhler, *Administration*, 18–20.

75. Grand-Duché de Luxembourg, *Neutralité du Grand-Duché pendant la guerre de 1914–1918: Attitude des pouvoirs publics* (Luxembourg: Imprimerie Victor Buck, 1919); Jean Mounier, *L'état actuel de la question du Luxembourg* (Paris: Jouve, 1920), 27–57.

76. Quoted in Ernest Faber, *Luxemburg im Kriege, 1914–1918* (Mersch: Faber, 1933), 35.

77. Trausch, *Contributions*, 45, 53. Only eighty-six Luxembourgeois had been put under German arrest by February 1915, over the period with the peak arrest rate. Three thousand did escape to fight (and perish) with the French Army. Mounier, *Etat actuel*, 56–57.

78. Whitlock, *Belgium*, 1:125. Herbert Hoover complained that Whitlock spent most of the war writing, "shrank from the rough stuff of dealing with the German officials, and had to be prodded constantly." Herbert C. Hoover, *The Relief of Belgium and Northern France, 1914–1930*, vol. 1 of *An American Epic* (Chicago: Henry Regnery, 1959), 40–41.

79. Quoted in Faber, *Luxemburg im Krieg*, 53.

80. Ibid., 54; cf. 83.

81. Hsi-Huey Liang, *The Rise of Modern Police and the European State System from Metternich to the Second World War* (Cambridge: Cambridge University Press, 1988), 200.

82. *Rapport*, 11–17.

83. Kerchove, *Industrie belge*, 160.

84. Von Köhler, *Administration*, 168–69. Of the sixty-six more iron-related enterprises closed in the first half of 1918, only four were closed for resistance. Kerchove, *Industrie belge*, 123–5.

85. Kerchove, *Industrie belge*, 58–59, 73ff.

86. Kerchove, *Industrie belge*, 11–20, 68.

87. Despite the fact that the critical Briey iron mines were not severely hampered by military problems, French ore production fell to a fifth of prewar levels. Boulin, *Organisation du travail*, 26, 30. See also M. F. Leprince-Ringuet, *Rapport sur l'industrie minière en Meurthe-et-Moselle pendant les années 1914 à 1918* (Nancy: Imprimerie Berger-Levrault, 1919); S. Pesquiès-Courbier, "Le bassin ferrifère de Briey durant la guerre de 1914–1918," *Revue historique des armées* no. 2 (1981): 99–128.

88. Kerchove, *Industrie belge*, 28–29.

89. On quarries, see Kerchove, *Industrie belge*, 77, 85–86, 130–34; on workshops, see 59.

90. Although Germany was nearly 90 percent self-reliant in food-stuffs before the war, the call-up of men and horses into the army, and the loss of crucial imported fertilizers sent German agriculture into a slump. Government efforts to increase grain and potato cultivation, at the expense of less calorie-efficient livestock, were largely frustrated by profiteers and greedy farmers who sold meat at astronomical prices in a burgeoning black market. Hardach, *First World War*, 112–23. On the role of hunger in Germany's collapse, see Avner Offer, *The First World War: An Agrarian Interpretation* (Oxford: Clarendon, 1989), pt. 1.

91. Quoted in Hoover, *Relief*, 9.

92. For accounts of the relief effort, see Hoover, *Relief*; Albert Henry, *La ravitaillement de la Belgique pendant l'occupation allemande* (Paris: Presses Universitaires de France, 1924); and Pirenne, *Belgique et la Guerre*, chap. 6.

93. Hoover, *Relief*, 120, 412; for a detailed accounting of provisions, see George I. Gay, *The Commission for Relief in Belgium: Statistical Review of Relief Operations* (Stanford: Stanford University Press, 1925).

94. Quoted in George I. Gay and H. H. Fisher, *Public Relations of the Commission for Relief in Belgium* (Stanford: Stanford University Press, 1929), 1:v.

95. The Food Committee of Northern France (Comité Nationale de Secours et d'Alimentation du Nord de la France) had a proportionately similar cadre of relief workers. Hoover, *Relief*, 415; Pirenne, *Belgique et la Guerre*, 164.

96. See, e.g., Hoover, *Relief*, esp. 154–60.

97. Karl Bittmann, *Im besezten Belgien (1914–1917)*, vol. 3 of *Werken und Wirken: Erinnerungen aus Industrie und Staatsdienst* (Karlsruhe in Baden: Verlag C. J. Müller, 1924), 140.

98. Herbert Hoover to Lloyd George, 17 Feb. 1915, reproduced in Hoover, *Relief*, 76.

99. Hoover, *Relief*, 154.

100. Pirenne, *Belgique et la Guerre*, chap. 3; Wanty, "La vie militaire," 352–53.

101. Pirenne, *Belgique et la Guerre*, 164.

102. Kerchove, *Industrie belge*, 54.

103. Pirenne, *Belgique et la Guerre*, 197; von Köhler, *Administration*, 220; Baudhuin, *Histoire économique*, 1:33.

104. Pirenne, *Belgique et la Guerre*, 179–80; 197.

105. Trausch, *Contributions*, 26–27.

106. Ibid., 32.

107. Wagner, *La sidérurgie luxembougeoise*, 26. On industrialists' profits, see Luxembourg, Chambre de Commerce, *Rapport général sur la situation de l'industrie et due commerce pendant l'année 1918* (Luxembourg: Victor Buck, 1919), 22; Schmitt, "Violated Neutrals," 221.

108. Quoted in Trausch, *Contributions*, 41.

109. Ibid., 63.

110. Schmitt, "Violated Neutrals," 220.

111. James Newcomer, *The Grand Duchy of Luxembourg: The Evolution of Nationhood, 963 A.D. to 1983* (New York: University Press of America, 1984), 231.

112. Faber, *Luxemburg im Krieg*, 95. For other reports on public opinion, see Mounier, *L'état actuel*, and Francis Gribble, *In Luxembourg in Wartime* (London: Headly Brothers, 1916).

Chapter 5
The Ruhr-Rhineland, 1923–1924

1. Walter A. McDougall, *France's Rhineland Diplomacy, 1914–1924: The Last Bid for a Balance of Power in Europe* (Princeton: Princeton University Press, 1978), 15–57.

2. Quoted in ibid., 27.

3. On reparations diplomacy leading up to the Ruhr invasion, see Bruce Kent, *The Spoils of War: The Politics, Economics, and Diplomacy of Reparations, 1918–1932* (Oxford: Clarendon, 1989); Marc Trachtenberg, *Reparation in World Politics: France and European Diplomacy, 1916–1923* (New York: Columbia University Press, 1980); McDougall, *France's Rhineland Diplomacy*; Hermann J. Rupieper, *The Cuno Government and Reparations, 1922–1923: Politics and Economics* (The Hague: Martinus Nijhoff, 1979); Sally Marks, *Innocent Abroad: Belgium at the Paris Peace Conference of 1919* (Chapel Hill: University of North Carolina Press, 1981); Anne Orde, *British Policy and European Reconstruction after the First World War* (Cambridge: Cambridge University Press, 1990).

4. Quoted in McDougall, *France's Rhineland Diplomacy*, 6.

5. Trachtenberg (*Reparation*, 77–84, 107–9, 337–42) shows that this "transfer problem," while real, was exaggerated in the interwar period.

6. Trachtenberg, *Reparation*, 122–23.

7. McDougall, *France's Rhineland Diplomacy*, 104.

8. The customs arrangement, from which the United States abstained, lasted

through September and recouped 270 million francs. Paul Tirard, *La France sur le Rhin: Douze années d'occupation rhénane* (Paris: Librarie Plon, 1930), 332–42.

9. John Maynard Keynes, *The Economic Consequences of the Peace* (London: Macmillan, 1920).

10. Gerald D. Feldman, *The Great Disorder: Politics, Economics, and Society in the German Inflation, 1914–1924* (New York: Oxford University Press, 1993), 329.

11. Trachtenberg, *Reparation*; McDougall, *France's Rhineland Diplomacy*; Stephen A. Schuker, *The End of French Predominance in Europe: The Financial Crisis of 1924 and the Adoption of the Dawes Plan* (Chapel Hill: University of North Carolina Press, 1976), and idem, *American "Reparations" to Germany, 1919–1933: Implications for the Third-World Debt Crisis*, Princeton Studies in International Finance no. 61 (July 1988). For an earlier critique of Keynes (by a French economist who perished fighting with De Gaulle in 1944), which placed the reparations problem in the perspective of Nazi gains from occupied Europe, see Etienne Mantoux, *The Carthaginian Peace, or the Economic Consequences of Mr. Keynes* (London: Oxford University Press, 1946).

12. Charles Kindleberger, *A Financial History of Western Europe* (London: Allen & Unwin, 1984), 232–51; Trachtenberg, *Reparation*, 67–68.

13. Schuker, *End of French Predominance*, 25–26. For further details on reparations payments, see Trachtenberg, *Reparation*, 205–6, and Etienne Weill-Raynal, *Les réparations allemandes et la France* (Paris: Nouvelles Editions Latines, 1947), 1:493–535; on the costs of the occupation, see Feldman, *Great Disorder*, 670, 939 n. 4.

14. Rupieper, *Cuno Government*, 31–77; Kent, *Spoils of War*, 141–208.

15. Quoted in Trachtenberg, *Reparation*, 214.

16. Gerald D. Feldman, *Iron and Steel in the German Inflation, 1916–1923* (Princeton: Princeton University Press, 1974), 351.

17. On French strategy, see Trachtenberg, *Reparation*; McDougall, *France's Rhineland Diplomacy*; Jon Jacobson, "Strategies of French Foreign Policy after World War I," *Journal of Modern History* 55, no. 1 (March 1983): 88–117.

18. Rupieper, *Cuno Government*, 100.

19. Feldman, *Iron and Steel*, 474–75; Great Britain, Dept. of Overseas Trade (J. W. F. Thelwall and C. J. Kavanagh), *Report on the Economic and Financial Conditions in Germany, revised to April 1924* (London: Department of Overseas Trade, 1924), 114–117.

20. Seydoux expected the occupation to cost 100 million gold marks and earn 450 million from coal taxes and 400–600 million from taxes on other industries and customs. McDougall, *France's Rhineland Diplomacy*, 225. On the evolution of planning for the Ruhr occupation, see Trachtenberg, *Reparation*, chap. 7.

21. Quoted in McDougall, *France's Rhineland Diplomacy*, 226.

22. Quoted in Trachtenberg, *Reparation*, 267.

23. McDougall, *France's Rhineland Diplomacy*, esp. 237, 244–49, 259–64, 288; Trachtenberg, *Reparation*, 260–75.

24. Trachtenberg, *Reparation*, 100–109.

25. Lloyd George, August 1922, quoted in Trachtenberg, *Reparation*, 254.

26. This account of the Ruhr occupation relies mainly on the works cited in note 3, as well as Feldman, *Iron and Steel* and *Great Disorder*; Jean-Claude Favez, *Le Reich devant l'occupation franco-belge de la Ruhr en 1923* (Geneva: Librarie Droz, 1969); François-André Paoli, *La phase de fermeté (11 janvier 1920–17 juin 1924)*, vol. 2 of *L'armée française de 1919 à 1939* (Paris: Service historique de l'armée, 1969), 257–65; Weill-Raynal, *Réparations allemandes*, vol. 2; General Degoutte, *L'Occupation de la Ruhr*, Rapport d'ensemble du Général Degoutte, personal and secret, Imprimerie de l'Armée du Rhin, July 1924 (French War Ministry Archives, Vincennes). Also useful are Alfred E. Cornbise, "Some Aspects of the German Response to the Ruhr Occupation, January–September 1923" (Ph.D. diss., University of North Carolina, Chapel Hill, 1965); Donald B. Saunders, "Stresemann vs. Poincaré: The Conduct of Germany's Western Policy during Gustav Stresemann's Chancellorship, August–November 1923" (Ph.D diss., University of North Carolina, Chapel Hill, 1974); John F. Flynn, "The 1923 Ruhr Crisis as a Two-front War" (Ph.D. diss., Ohio State University, 1977).

27. For a summary of the passive resistance decrees, see Favez, *Occupation franco-belge*, 101–114.

28. H. Breaud, *La régie des chemins de fer des territoires occupés, 1923–1924* (Paris: Chaix, 1938), 24–29, 85–86; see also Tirard, *France sur le Rhin*, 360–73.

29. Of the five hundred thousand miners in occupied territory, eighty-two thousand were foreign workers (fifty-three thousand Poles). Paoli, *Phase de fermeté*, 263–64.

30. McDougall, *France's Rhineland Diplomacy*, 277. Trachtenberg, *Reparation*, 304.

31. Trachtenberg, *Reparation*, 301, 303. On similarly futile French efforts to utilize German domainal forests, see Tirard, *France sur le Rhin*, 378–83.

32. McDougall, *France's Rhineland Diplomacy*, 277–78. McDougall claims that half of all French furnaces were blown by March out for lack of fuel, but industrial production figures show increasing steel production.

33. Breaud, *Régie*, 28.

34. The size of the French occupation force peaked in April 1923 at 163,000 (57,000 in the Ruhr); they dropped down to 100,000 in January 1924. About 5,000 troops British troops were stationed in the Rhineland during the entire period. Paoli, *Phase de fermeté*, 309, annexe IV.

35. The French government reported net profits of 525.2 million francs at the end of September 1923. But the occupation of the Ruhr had cost France alone around 810 million francs (40 million per month for the Rhineland, and another 50 million francs per month for the Ruhr). Great Britain, Dept. of Overseas Trade, *Economic and Financial Conditions*, 118; France, Ministère des Finances, *Rapport du Comité des Experts chargé de préparer la conférence des ministres des finances du 7 janvier 1925* (Paris: Imprimerie Nationale, 1925), 71; McDougall, *France's Rhineland Diplomacy*, 278.

36. Weill-Raynal, *Réparations allemandes*, 2:458–61.

37. Feldman, *Iron and Steel*, 405–27.

38. Alfred J. Toynbee, *Survey of International Affairs, 1924* (London: Oxford University Press, 1926), 299–300.

39. This accounting does not differentiate plundered goods from extorted output; a portion of the total gains were delivered to Italy and the United States. Weill-Raynal's figures cited in table 5–1 are based largely on Reparations Commission, *Annex* no. 2624D, 14 Jan. 1925, which can be consulted in the U.S. National Archives, Records of the United States Unofficial Delegation to the Reparations Commission, Record Group 43, entry 26. This report was written by Thomas N. Perkins for the Second Committee of Experts, as part of the Dawes Plan's reevaluation of Germany's capacity to pay reparations. Weill-Raynal's figures are more comprehensive, since Perkins (probably for purposes of Reparations accounting) did not include the full costs of the Ruhr troops and excluded the Rhineland troops and their currency seizures altogether.

The extraction rate calculation is based on a very uncertain £300 million (or 5.67 billion gold marks) estimate for "minimum annual wealth production" in the occupied territories by Great Britain, Dept. of Overseas Trade, *Economic and Financial Conditions*, 113.

40. None of these take into account the operation's opportunity costs; assuming that Germany would otherwise have maintained its 1922 pace of coal deliveries, the French and Belgians lost 17 million tons of reparations coal during 1923. McDougall, *France's Rhineland Diplomacy*, 273; France, Armée du Rhin, *An d'Occupation*, 40.

41. Quoted by Schuker, *End of French Predominance*, 171.

42. Trachtenberg, *Reparation*, 329.

43. Rupieper, *Cuno Government*, 113.

44. Feldman, *Iron and Steel*, 351–92.

45. Quoted in Kent, *Spoils of War*, 211.

46. Feldman, *Great Disorder*, 670, 939 n. 4.

47. Quoted by McDougall, *France's Rhineland Diplomacy*, 272.

48. McDougall, *France's Rhineland Diplomacy*, esp. 280–86, 299–359; K. P. Jones, "Stresemann, the Ruhr Crisis, and Rhenish Separatism: A Case Study of *Westpolitik*," *European Studies Review* 7 (1977): 318–19.

49. Harold J. Gordon, Jr., *The Reichswehr and the German Republic, 1919–1926* (Princeton: Princeton University Press, 1957), 255–56; Cornbise, "German Response," 70–72.

50. Gordon, *Reichswehr*, 348; Cornbise, "German Response," 144–45, 150–54.

51. Favez, *Occupation franco-belge*, 361.

52. Rupieper, *Cuno Government*, 101, 144.

53. Paoli, *Phase de fermeté*, 288.

54. Trachtenberg, *Reparation*, 314–29; Feldman, *Iron and Steel*, 405–22.

55. Trachtenberg, *Reparation*, 265–75, 298–305.

56. Trachtenberg, *Reparation*, 334. Kent (*Spoils of War*, 209) also claims that a stronger policy would have worked. On the tentative steps toward implementing a Rhenish mark during 1923, see McDougall, *France's Rhineland Diplomacy*, 262–63, 324–25; Feldman, *Great Disorder*, 687, 769–70, 788, 823–24.

57. The small British zone of occupation around Cologne refrained from executing new Franco-Belgian decrees, but did cooperate with transport through the zone. McDougall, *France's Rhineland Diplomacy*, 253–56.

58. Rupieper, *Cuno Government*, 230–31, 234–54.

59. Trachtenberg, *Reparation*, 331–35.

60. Schuker, *End of French Predominance*, chaps. 1–2, 6–9; McDougall, *France's Rhineland Diplomacy*, 293–99, 360–79.

61. Schuker, *End of French Predominance*, 385.

62. Wolfgang Sternstein, "The *Ruhrkampf* of 1923: Economic Problems of Civilian Defence," in *Civilian Resistance as a National Defence*, ed. Adam Roberts (Harmondsworth: Penguin, 1969), 149–50, 157; Peter Ackerman and Christopher Kruegler, *Strategic Nonviolent Conflict: The Dynamics of People Power in the Twentieth Century* (Westport, Conn.: Praeger, 1993), 99–155.

63. Quoted by Schuker, *End of French Predominance*, 388.

Chapter 6
The Japanese Empire, 1910–1945

1. James B. Crowley, "Japan's Military Foreign Policies," in *Japan's Foreign Policy, 1868–1941: A Research Guide*, ed. James W. Morley (New York: Columbia University Press, 1974), 12–13.

2. Hilary Conroy, *The Japanese Seizure of Korea, 1868–1910: A Study of Realism and Idealism in International Relations* (Philadelphia: University of Pennsylvania Press, 1960), 17–77.

3. Quoted in W. G. Beasley, *Japanese Imperialism, 1894–1945* (Oxford: Clarendon, 1987), 60. On Taiwan, see Edward I-te Chen, "Japan's Decision to Annex Taiwan: A Study of Ito-Mutsu Diplomacy," *Journal of Asian Studies* 37, no. 1 (November 1977): 61–72. On Japan's aims in Korea at this time, see Conroy, *Japanese Seizure of Korea*, 169–324.

4. Peter Duus, "Economic Dimensions of Meiji Imperialism: The Case of Korea, 1895–1910," in *The Japanese Colonial Empire, 1895–1945*, ed. Ramon H. Myers and Mark R. Peattie (Princeton: Princeton University Press, 1984) [cit. *JCE*], 128–71.

5. Beasley, *Japanese Imperialism*, 69–90; Conroy, *Japanese Seizure of Korea*, 325–82.

6. Quoted in Beasley, *Japanese Imperialism*, 166.

7. Ibid., 91–97.

8. Ibid., 156–74; Toshiyuki Mizoguchi, "The Changing Pattern of Sino-Japanese Trade, 1884–1937," in *The Japanese Informal Empire in China, 1895–1937*, ed. Peter Duus, Ramon H. Myers, and Mark R. Peattie (Princeton: Princeton University Press, 1989) [cit. *JIEC*], 10–30; Banno Junju, "Japanese Industrialists and Merchants and the Anti-Japanese Boycotts in China, 1919–1928," in *JIEC*, 314–29.

9. Beasley, *Japanese Imperialism*, 188–90; cf. 118, 158; Ramon H. Myers, "Japanese Imperialism in Manchuria: The South Manchuria Railway Company, 1906–1933," in *JIEC*, 101–32. See also, Akira Iriye, "The Failure of Economic Expansionism: 1918–1931," in *Japan in Crisis*, ed. Bernard Silberman and Harry Harootunian (Princeton: Princeton University Press, 1974), 237–69.

10. Michael A. Barnhart, *Japan Prepares for Total War: The Search for Economic Security, 1919–1941* (Ithaca: Cornell University Press, 1988), 22–33.

11. Mark R. Peattie, *Ishiwara Kanji and Japan's Confrontation with the West* (Princeton: Princeton University Press, 1975), 67–74, 96–110.

12. James B. Crowley, *Japan's Quest for Autonomy: National Security and Foreign Policy 1930–1938* (Princeton: Princeton University Press, 1966), 82–121; Peattie, *Ishiwara Kanji*, 87–181.

13. Hochin Choi, *The Economic History of Korea: From the Earliest Times to 1945* (Seoul: Freedom Library, 1971), 223–40.

14. Jerome B. Cohen, *Japan's Economy in War and Reconstruction* (Minneapolis: University of Minnesota Press), 114.

15. Crowley, *Japan's Quest for Autonomy*, 187–243, 280–300; Barnhart, *Japan Prepares for Total War*, 39–49; Takafusa Nakamura, "Japan's Economic Thrust into North China, 1933–1938: Formation of the North China Development Corporation," in *The Chinese and the Japanese*, ed. Akira Iriye (Princeton: Princeton University Press, 1980), 220–53.

16. Crowley, *Japan's Quest for Autonomy*, 187–243, 280–300.

17. Ibid., 301–78.

18. Colonel Ishiwara Kanji, quoted in Barnhart, *Japan Prepares for Total War*, 89; cf. 39–49, 77–90.

19. Barnhart, *Japan Prepares for Total War*, 91–114, 136–61.

20. Cohen, *Japan's Economy in War*, 135.

21. Naval Chief of Staff Admiral Nagano, October 1941, quoted in Crowley, "Military Policies," 97.

22. John H. Boyle, *China and Japan at War, 1937–1945: The Politics of Collaboration* (Stanford: Stanford University Press, 1972). Japan did promise independence to China, the Philippines, Burma, and Thailand—but not to Indonesia or Malaya; but Japan's conception of "independence" had already been demonstrated in "independent Manchukuo." On Southeast Asia, see Jan Pluvier, *South-East Asia from Colonialism to Independence* (Kuala Lumpur: Oxford University Press, 1974), 191–284, and Willard H. Elsbree, *Japan's Role in Southeast Asian Nationalist Movements, 1940 to 1945* (New York: Russell and Russell, 1953), 15–75.

23. December 1941 cabinet paper, quoted in Beasely, *Japanese Imperialism*, 245.

24. The irrationality of Japanese policy has been analyzed by Jack L. Snyder, *Myths of Empire* (Ithaca: Cornell University Press, 1991), chap. 4, and Charles A. Kupchan, *The Vulnerability of Empire* (Ithaca: Cornell University Press, 1994), 297–358.

25. The figures on Korea and Taiwan (1912–1937) are from Samuel Pao-San Ho, "Colonialism and Development: Korea, Taiwan, and Kwantung," in *JCE*, 359, and that for Manchuria (1929–1941) is from Kang Chao, *The Economic Development of Manchuria: The Rise of a Frontier Economy*, Michigan Papers in Chinese Studies, no. 43 (Ann Arbor: Center for Chinese Studies, University of Michigan, 1983), 14. For further details on Taiwanese and Korean development, see Samuel Pao-San Ho, *Economic Development of Taiwan, 1860–1970* (New Haven: Yale University Press, 1978); Chang-chul Suh, *Growth and Structural Changes in the Korean Economy, 1910–1940* (Cambridge: Harvard University Press, 1978); Toshiyuki Mizoguchi and Yuzo Yamamoto, "Capital Formation in

Taiwan and Korea," in *JCE*, 399–419; Toshiyuki Mizoguchi and Mataji Umemura, *Basic Economic Statistics of Former Japanese Colonies, 1895–1938* (Tokyo: Toyo Keizai Shinposha, 1988). On Manchurian growth, see Elizabeth B. Schumpeter, ed., *The Industrialization of Japan and Manchuko, 1930–1940: Population, Raw Materials, and Industry* (New York: Macmillan, 1940), 271–476; Ramon H. Myers, *The Japanese Economic Development of Manchuria, 1932–1945* (1959; New York: Garland, 1982); Ann Rasmussen Kinney, *Japanese Investment in Manchurian Manufacturing, Mining, Transportation and Communications, 1931–1945* (1962; New York: Garland, 1982); and Katsuji Nakagane, "Manchukuo and Economic Development," in *JIEC*, 133–57.

26. Paul Bairoch, *The Economic Development of The Third World since 1900*, trans. Cynthia Postan (Berkeley and Los Angeles: University of California Press, 1975), 184.

27. Ho, "Colonialism and Development," 356–57; Toshiyuki Mizoguchi and Yuzo Yamamoto, "Capital Formation in Taiwan and Korea," in *JCE*, 404–11; Choi, *Economic History of Korea*, 282–90. Corporate investors controlled two-thirds of Japanese assets in Korea by 1945. Dennis L. McNamara, *The Colonial Origins of Korean Enterprise, 1910–1945* (Cambridge: Cambridge University Press, 1990), 51.

28. Initially under the supervision of the South Manchuria Railway, later under the Nissan-Manchukuo conglomerate (Mangyo). Katsuji Nakagane, "Manchukuo and Economic Development," in *JIEC*, 133–57; Myers, *Japanese Economic Development of Manchuria*, 32–73; Kinney, *Japanese Investment in Manchuria*, 85–123.

29. On banking, see Mitsuhiko Kimura, "Financial Aspects of Korea's Economic Growth under Japanese Rule," *Modern Asian Studies* 20, no. 4 (1986): 793–820.

30. By the end of the 1930s, railways grew to five thousand kilometers in Korea and ten thousand kilometers in Manchukuo. See Schumpeter, ed., *Industrialization of Japan and Manchuko*, 372–73; F. C. Jones, *Manchuria since 1931* (New York: Oxford University Press, 1949), 100–122; Myers, "Japanese Imperialism in Manchuria," 101–32; Conroy, *Japanese Seizure of Korea*, 476–79, 486; and McNamara, *Colonial Origins*, 48.

31. Ramon H. Myers and Yamada Saburo, "Agricultural Development in the Empire," in *JCE*, 427–46; Ho, "Colonialism and Development," 359–64.

32. Since pig-iron filled a third of the shipping space needed for the amount of ore and coal to make it, smelting iron on location reduced transportation costs. Jerome B. Cohen, *Japan's Economy in War and Reconstruction* (Minneapolis: University of Minnesota Press, 1949), 121.

33. Ho, "Colonialism and Development," 377.

34. Supreme Commander for the Allied Powers, Natural Resources Section [cit. SCAP], *Iron and Steel Metallurgy of the Japanese Empire*, Report no. 50, (Tokyo, 1946), 39–40, 52–53; Myers, *Japanese Economic Development of Manchuria*, 129, 283.

35. Barbara Molony, "Noguchi Jun and Nichitsu: Colonial Investment Strategy in a High-Technology Enterprise," in *Managing Industrial Enterprise: Cases from Japan's Prewar Experience*, ed. William D. Wray (Cambridge, Mass.: Har-

vard University Press for the Harvard Council on East Asian Studies: 1989): 229–63. Korean food and textile processing had fallen from 57 percent to 45 percent of manufacturing output, according to Ho, "Colonialism and Development," 394–95.

36. SCAP, *Aluminum Metallurgy in the Japanese Empire*, Report no. 87 (Tokyo, 1947), 66.

37. Ho, "Colonialism and Development," 353–55.

38. E. Patricia Tsurumi, "Colonial Education in Korea and Taiwan," in *Japanese Colonial Empire*, ed. Ramon H. Myers and Mark Peattie, 275–311; Wonmo Dong, "Assimilation and Social Mobilization in Korea," in *Korea under Japanese Colonial Rule: Studies of the Policy and Techniques of Japanese Colonialism*, ed. Andrew C. Nahm (Kalamazoo, Mich.: Center for Korean Studies, Western Michigan University, 1973), 155–61; Jones, *Manchuria since 1931*, 45–49.

39. Cohen, *Japan's Economy in War*, 115–16, 159, 175.

40. Ramon H. Myers, "Creating a Modern Enclave Economy: The Economic Integration of Japan, Manchuria, and North China, 1932–1945," in *The Japanese Wartime Empire*, ed. Peter Duus, Ramon H. Myers, and Mark R. Peattie (Princeton: Princeton University Press, forthcoming).

41. Chao, *Economic Development of Manchuria*, 32.

42. Ho, *Economic Development of Taiwan*, 285.

43. Chong-sik Lee, *Japan and Korea: The Political Dimension* (Stanford: Hoover Institution Press, 1985), 13–20; Cohen, *Japan's Economy in War*, 300–301, 324–26; Ching-chih Chen, "Police and Community Control Systems in the Empire," in *JCE*, 232; Shiota Shobei, "A Ravaged People: The Koreans in World War II," *Japan Interpreter* 7 (1971): 43–53.

44. George Hicks, "The Comfort Women," in *Japanese Wartime Empire*, ed. Peter Duus, Ramon H. Myers, and Mark R. Peattie.

45. Cohen, *Japan's Economy in War*, 140–47.

46. Ibid., 121–22, 129.

47. Ibid., 128, 165. The shipping shortage was compounded by U.S. air attacks on the Yangtze river, hampering transport within China. W. N. Medlicott, *The Economic Blockade* (London: HMSO, 1959), 2:406–7.

48. Choi, *Economic History of Korea*, 307–8. For an example of what extensive research can accomplish, see Lance E. Davis and Robert A. Huttenback, *Mammon and the Pursuit of Empire: The Economists of British Imperialism* (Cambridge: Cambridge University Press, 1988).

49. Barnhart, *Japan Prepares for Total War*, 58–63, 115–16, 271.

50. Schumpeter, ed., *Industrialization of Japan and Manchukuo*, 384–5, 854–61.

51. Ho, "Colonialism and Development," 382.

52. Japan, Ministry of Foreign Affairs, Special Survey Committee, *Postwar Reconstruction of the Japanese Economy*, ed. Saburo Okita (Tokyo: University of Tokyo Press, 1992), 48. The $20 billion figure is from John W. Dower, "The Useful War," *Daedalus* 119, no. 3 (Summer 1990), 52.

53. Okita, ed., *Postwar Reconstruction*, 46.

54. Ho, "Colonialism and Development," 378–79, 387–88, 398; Toshiyuki Mizoguchi, "Consumer Prices and Real Wages in Taiwan and Korea under Japa-

nese Rule," *Hitotsubashi Journal of Economics* 13, no. 1 (June 1972): 40–56; Mizoguchi and Umemura, *Basic Economic Statistics*, 235, 239.

55. Per capita annual rice consumption fell in Taiwan from 130 to 100 kilos and from 100 to 75 kilos in Korea, so that the Japanese could enjoy their 160 kilo-level. Ho, "Colonialism and Development," 379.

56. Chao, *Economic Development of Manchuria*, 34. Myers, *Japanese Economic Development of Manchuria*, 127, 193–96.

57. Ho, "Colonialism and Development," 374–75.

58. Ho, "Colonialism and Development," 357–58; Myers, *Japanese Economic Development of Manchuria*, 220–61; Government-General of Chosen, *Annual Report on the Madministration of Chosesn, 1937–38* (Tokyo, 1938), 53–59.

59. Nisaburo Murakushi, *The Transfer of Coal-Mining Technology from Japan to Manchuria and Manpower Problems—Focusing on the Development of the Fushun Coal Mines*, United Nations University HSDP-JE Series, vol. 47 (Tokyo: United Nations University, 1981), 83. Although output declined after 1937, labor resistance does not appear to have been a factor. See SCAP, *Fushun Coal Field, Manchuria*, Report no. 68 (Tokyo: 1947), 10–11.

60. The lower estimate is from Young-Iob Chung, "Japanese Investment in Korea, 1904–1945," in Andrew C. Nahm, ed., *Korea under Japanese Colonial Rule*, 89–90; the higher from Suh, *Korean Economy*, 127–29. Lower capital accumulation figures and thus higher proportion of imported capital for Korea, are given by Mizoguchi and Yamamoto, "Capital Formation in Taiwan and Korea," 418.

61. Carter J. Eckert, *Offspring of Empire: The Koch'ang Kims and the Colonial Origins of Korean Capitalism, 1876–1945* (Seattle: University of Washington Press, 1991), 77, 114–22, 126.

62. Mizoguchi and Yamamoto, "Capital Formation in Taiwan and Korea," 408–11; Nakagane, "Manchukuo and Economic Development," 152–53; Jamese W. Morley, ed., *The China Quagmire: Japan's Expansion on the Asian Continent, 1933–1941* (New York: Columbia University Press, 1983), 6; Myers, *Japanese Economic Development of Manchuria*, 154–55; Irving I. Kramer, *Japan in Manchuria* (Tokyo: Foreign Affairs Association, 1954), 29–32.

63. Ho, "Colonialism and Development," 371–74; Mizoguchi and Yamamoto, "Capital Formation in Taiwan and Korea," 419.

64. Ho, "Colonialism and Development," 386; Alice H. Amsden, "The State and Taiwan's Economic Development," in *Bringing the State Back In*, ed. Peter B. Evans, Dietrich Rueschemeyer, and Theda Skocpol (Cambridge: Cambridge University Press, 1985), 78–106.

65. Korea accumulated a trade deficit of over 1 billion yen by 1937, and Manchukuo's trade balance with Japan amounted to a third of a billion yen in that year alone. Long-term capital flowing into Korea and Manchukuo covered these deficits. The balance is slightly worse if invisibles are included. Mizoguchi and Yamamoto, "Capital Formation in Taiwan and Korea," 408–11; Nakagane, "Manchukuo and Economic Development," 152–53.

66. Mizoguchi and Yamamoto, "Capital Formation in Taiwan and Korea," 408–11.

67. Ho, *Economic Development of Taiwan*, 83–90.

68. However, Taiwanese sugar couldn't have been all that uncompetitive, since production continued after 1945. Ho, *Economic Development of Taiwan*, 73–74, 85–86, 357. On the rice trade, see Yujiro Hayami and V. W. Ruttan, "Korean Rice, Taiwan Rice, and Japanese Agricultural Stagnation: An Economic Consequence of Colonialism," *Quarterly Journal of Economics* 84, no. 4 (November 1970): 562–89.

69. Molony, "Noguchi Jun and Nichitsu," 263, 250–59.

70. Aikawa's Nissan joined the Kwantung Army in the crash industrialization of Manchukuo and also in the expectation of high profits. Manchukuo guaranteed a return of 6 percent to its shareholders, but it was earning 13.6 percent by 1940. Aikawa only threw up his hands in 1942 when Army interference had become intolerable. Kinney, *Japanese Investment in Manchuria*, 20–23; Myers, *Japanese Economic Development of Manchuria*, 262–70; Cohen, *Japan's Economy in War*, 39.

71. On subsidies to strategic industries, see Cohen, *Japan's Economy in War*, 2–3, 25–28. See also Chalmers Johnson, *MITI and the Japanese Miracle: The Growth of Industrial Policy, 1925–1975* (Stanford: Stanford University Press, 1982); Dower, "Useful War."

72. Chalmers A. Johnson, *Japan's Public Policy Companies* (Washington, D.C.: American Enterprise Institute, 1978); Richard J. Samuels, *The Business of the Japanese State: Energy Markets in Comparative and Historical Perspective* (Ithica: Cornell University Press, 1987).

73. Myers, "Creating a Modern Enclave Economy."

74. Harry Lamley, "The 1895 Taiwan War of Resistance: Local Chinese Efforts against a Foreign Power," in *Taiwan: Studies in Local Chinese History*, ed. Leonard Gordon (New York: Columbia University Press, 1970): 23–76; Chen, "Japan's Decision to Annex Taiwan," 62.

75. Chong-sik Lee, *The Politics of Korean Nationalism* (Berkeley and Los Angeles: University of California Press, 1963), 79–85.

76. Chong-sik Lee, *Revolutionary Struggle in Manchuria: Chinese Communists and Soviet Interest, 1922–1945* (Berkeley and Los Angeles: University of California Press, 1983), 269–320; idem, *Counter-insurgency in Manchuria: The Japanese Experience, 1931–1940*, Rand Memorandum RM-5012-ARPA (Santa Monica: Rand, January 1967), 1–78, 189. Pacification costs (1931–37) were reportedly ¥1.4 billion, according to Jones, *Manchuria since 1931*, 138.

77. Chen, "Police and Community Control," 213–39; Gregory Henderson, *Korea: the Politics of the Vortex* (Cambridge: Harvard University Press, 1968), 72–112.

78. The figure for Taiwan is higher if the aboriginal population and the police required to control them are included. See Ching-Chih Chen, "Japanese Socio-Political Control in Taiwan, 1895–1945, (Ph.D. diss., Harvard University, 1973), 258–63; Chen, "Police and Community Control," 218–20, 229; Dong, "Assimilation and Social Mobilization," 179; and idem, "Japanese Colonial Policy," 226, 305–6, 362. Repression had increased in Japan since 1911, when the police density was 0.8 per thousand, according to Edward J. Baker, "The Role of Legal Reforms in the Japanese Annexation and Rule of Korea, 1905–1919," in *Studies on Korea in Transition*, ed. D. R. McCann et al. (Honolulu: University of Hawaii, 1979), 38–41.

79. Dong, "Assimilation and Social Mobilization in Korea," 164.

80. Koreans made up 18–30 percent of the high officials, 32–40 percent of the junior officials, and 39–57 percent of the rest of the employees between 1915–42. Dong, "Assimilation and Social Mobilization in Korea," 164; see also Lai Tse-Han, Ramon H. Myers, and Wei Wou, *A Tragic Beginning: The Taiwan Uprising of February 28, 1947* (Stanford: Stanford University Press, 1991), 42; Chen, "Japanese Colonialism: Political Control," 148; Nakagane, "Manchukuo and Economic Development," 138; Jones, *Manchuria since 1931*, 32–33.

81. Chen, "Police and Community Control Systems," 215–18, 225–27, 233–34.

82. Figures for 1938 are from Ho, *Economic Development of Taiwan*, 312; Dong, "Japanese Colonial Policy," 497; *The Manchukuo Year Book* (Hsinking, Manch.: Manchukuo Year Book, 1942), 117.

83. Troops in Korea in 1941, from Saburo Hayashi and Alvin D. Coox, *Kogun: The Japanese Army in the Pacific War* (Quantico, Va.: Marine Corps Assoc., 1959), 173. Taiwan figure extrapolated from division strength, from Alvin D. Coox, "The Kwantung Army Dimension," in *JIEC*, 408.

84. Barker, "Role of Legal Reform;" and Chen, "Policing and Community Control," 222.

85. Alvin D. Coox, *Nomonhan: Japan against Russia, 1939* (Stanford: Stanford University Press, 1985), 1:66–67, 84

86. Lee, *Revolutionary Struggle in Manchuria*; Lee, *Counter-insurgency in Manchuria*.

87. Economic development expenditures have been excluded from budget data drawn from Government-General of Chosen, *Annual Report on Administration of Chosen, 1937–38* (Tokyo, 1938), 52–53, and Myers, *Japanese Economic Development of Manchuria*, 245–47. Figures may not be strictly comparable due to different accounting categories. Korean administrative and policing expenses had remained fairly constant since 1919, according to Choi, *Economic History of Korea*, 299–304.

88. Ho, "Colonialism and Development," 358; Choi, *Economic History of Korea*, 299–304.

89. A similar judgment is reached by Miles Kahler, "External Ambition and Economic Performance," *World Politics* 40, no. 4 (July 1988), 436–38.

90. Nakamura, *Economic Growth in Prewar Japan*, 6–7.

91. Ibid., 263–310.

92. Mark Selden, *The Yenan Way in Revolutionary China* (Cambridge: Harvard University Press, 1971), chap. 4–6. On the North China Army's grain requisitions, see Lincoln Li, *The Japanese Army in North China, 1937–1941: Problems of Political and Economic Control* (Tokyo: Oxford University Press, 1975), 180–86.

93. Chalmers Johnson, *Peasant Nationalism and Communist Power: The Emergence of Revolutionary China, 1937–1945* (Stanford: Stanford University Press, 1962), 73–74.

94. Lyman P. Van Slyke, ed., *The Chinese Communist Movement: A Report of the United States War Department, July 1945* (Stanford: Stanford University Press, 1968), 116–17.

95. Boyle, *China and Japan at War*, 83ff; Li, *Japanese Army in North China*,

64–90. In North China, armed puppet forces amounted to 180,000, but since most of these were needed for local policing, the number available for antiguerrilla operations was only 41,000. Ibid., 210–11.

96. Johnson, *Peasant Nationalism*, 55–69, 73. See also Walter Laqueur, *Guerrilla: A Historical and Critical Study* (Boston: Little, Brown, 1976), 239–62.

97. Li, *Japanese Army in North China*, 144, 162–66.

98. Quoted in Boyle, *China and Japan at War*, 149. Cf. Cohen, *Japan's Economy in War*, 45.

99. On precolonial Korean identity, see Michael Edson Robinson, *Cultural Nationalism in Colonial Korea, 1920–1925* (Seattle: University of Washington Press, 1988), 14–37; Chong-sik Lee, *The Politics of Korean Nationalism* (Berkeley and Los Angeles: University of California Press, 1963), 3–85.

100. On the March First Movement, see Dae-yeol Ku, *Korea under Colonialism: The March First Movement and the Anglo-Japanese Relations* (Seoul: Seoul Computer Press for the Royal Asiatic Society, Korea Branch, 1985), 65–98; Lee, *Korean Nationalism*, 101–26.

101. Edward I-te Chen, "Formosan Political Movements under Japanese Colonial Rule, 1914–1937," *Journal of Asian Studies* 31, no. 3 (May 1972), 477–97.

102. Chen, "Formosan Political Movements," 477–97; George H. Kerr, *Formosa: Licensed Revolution and the Home Rule Movement, 1895–1945* (Honolulu: University Press of Hawaii, 1974).

103. On the administrative structure, and relationship to Tokyo, of the governments-general, see Edward I-te Chen, "Japanese Colonialism in Korea and Formosa: A Comparison of the Systems of Political Control," *Harvard Journal of Asiatic Studies* (1970): 126–58.

104. Y. Tak Matsusaka, "Managing Occupied Manchuria, 1931–1934," in *Japanese Wartime Empire*, ed. Peter Duus, Ramon Myers, and Mark Peattie.

105. Quoted in Chen, "Police and Community Control Systems," 236. See also Henderson, *Korea*, 107.

106. Eckert, *Offspring of Empire*, 254; Daniel S. Juhn, "Nationalism and Korean Businessmen," in *Korea's Response to Japan: The Colonial Period, 1910–1945* ed. C. I. Eugene Kim and Dorothea Mortimore (Kalamazoo, Mich.: Center for Korean Studies, Western Michigan University, 1977): 45–51.

107. Quoted in Eckert, *Offspring of Empire*, 264, see 243–47.

108. Quoted in Tsurumi, "Colonial Education," 296.

109. Based on official Japanese figures; Korean nationalist figures are much higher. Only 9 Japanese were killed and 186 injured. Lee, *Korean Nationalism*, 114.

110. Government-General of Chosen, *Annual Report, 1937–38*, 178, 181.

111. Chen, "Police and Community Control"; Lee, *Korean Nationalism*, 89–93; Henderson, *Korea*, 72–112, esp. 111. On censorship, see Michael E. Robinson, "Colonial Publication Policy and the Korean Nationalist Movement," in *JCE*, 312–43.

112. Michael Edson Robinson, *Cultural Nationalism in Colonial Korea, 1920–25* (Seattle: University of Washington, 1988); Lee, *Korean Nationalism*, 237–73; Chen, "Formosan Political Movements," 489.

113. Chen, "Formosan Political Movements," 496; Lee, *Korean Nationalism*, 255.

114. Eckert, *Offspring of Empire*, 234; see also Juhn, "Nationalism and Korean Businessmen."

115. Dong, "Assimilation and Social Mobilization in Korea," 169; Ho, *Economic Development of Taiwan*, 33, 82–83, 319, 322; Jones, *Manchuria since 1931*, 206–7; Chao, *Economic Development of Manchuria*, 34–35. GDP per capita had increased 20 percent since the onset of Japanese rule.

116. United Nations, *Growth of the World's Urban and Rural Population, 1920–2000* (New York: United Nations, 1969), 106.

117. Dong, "Assimilation and Social Mobilization," 176.

118. Henderson, *Korea*, 104–12; Dong, "Japanese Colonial Policy," 341.

119. Lai, Myers, and Wou, *Tragic Beginning*, 27; Chen, "Japanese Socio-Political Control," 258–59.

120. Tsurumi, "Colonial Education;" Jones, *Manchuria since 1931*, 45–49.

121. Lai, Myers, and Wou, *Tragic Beginning*, 35; Dong, "Assimilation and Social Mobilization, 158–59.

122. Lai, Myers, and Wou, *A Tragic Beginning*, 32–36.

123. Lai, Myers, and Wou, *Tragic Beginning*, 29–49. On pro-Japanese associations in Manchukuo, see Jones, *Manchuria since 1931*, 50–54; Coox, *Nomonhan*, 65.

124. Quoted in Eckert, *Offspring of Empire*, 231; for other examples, see 224–52. Henderson (*Korea*, 106) estimates that there were ten thousand Korean collaborationists.

125. Wan-yao Chou, "The Kominka Movement in Taiwan and Korea: Comparisons and Interpretations," in *Wartime Japanese Empire*, ed. Peter Duus, Ramon Myers, and Mark Peattie; Lee, *Korean Nationalism*, 264–73; Lee, *Japan and Korea*, 7–13.

126. Two-thirds of all Taiwanese children were getting a primary education, compared to one-third of Korean children in 1940. Dong, "Assimilation and Social Mobilization," and Ho, *Economic Development of Taiwan*, 321. On precolonial education in Korea, see Dennis L. McNamara, "Comparative Colonial Response: Korea and Taiwan, 1895–1919," *Korean Studies* 10 (1986): 54–59; Tsurumi, "Colonial Education," 294–301. Taiwanese rice consumption was nearly comparable to consumption in Japan proper and roughly double Korean consumption. Industrial wages were also higher in Taiwan than in Korea and on average were closer to the wages of Japanese colonists in comparable trades. Edward I-te Chen, "Japanese Colonialism in Korea and Formosa: A Comparison of its Effects upon the Development of Nationalism," (Ph.D diss., University of Pennsylvania, 1968), 210–14, 241–44.

127. Kerr, *Formosa*, 134, 165; Chen, "Police and Community Control," 229.

128. Although it contained a small fraction of China's population and area, Manchuria in 1943 produced 60–70 percent of China's soda ash, ammonium sulfate, and cement, 50 percent of its coal and iron ore, and 85–95 percent of the electricity, pig-iron, steel, and machinery. Chao, *Economic Development of Manchuria*, 19–21; Myers, *Japanese Economic Development of Manchuria*, 3–5.

129. Michael Lindsay, *The Unknown War: North China, 1937–1945* (London: Bergström & Boyle Books, 1975), 6; Chong-sik Lee, *Revolutionary Struggle in Manchuria*, 276–91, 319–20. On village cohesiveness, see Michael Taylor, "Rationality and Revolutionary Collective Action," 74–76; Philip C. C. Huang,

Peasant Economy and Social Change in North China (Stanford: Stanford University Press, 1985), 29–30, 249–91; Jones, *Manchuria since 1931*, 9, 171–2.

130. Lee, *Korean Nationalism*, 261.

131. François Caron, *An Economic History of Modern France*, trans. Barbara Bray (New York: Columbia University Press, 1979), 13–24.

Chapter 7
The Soviet Empire, 1945–1989

1. "United States Objectives and Programs for National Security," NSC 68, 14 Apr. 1950, reprinted in Thomas H. Etzold and John Lewis Gaddis, *Containment: Documents on American Foreign Policy and Strategy, 1945–1950* (New York: Columbia University Press, 1978), 385–442; quote is from 385. For a later articulation of this view, see Richard Pipes, "Militarism and the Soviet State," *Daedalus* 109, no. 4 (1980): 1–12; and idem, "Soviet Global Strategy," *Commentary* 69, no. 4 (April 1980): 31–39.

2. The classic statement is William Appleman Williams, *The Tragedy of American Diplomacy*, rev. ed. (New York: Norton, 1988). For recent scholarly works stressing Soviet weakness and security concerns, see Matthew A. Evangelista, "Stalin's Postwar Army Reappraised," *International Security* 7, no. 3 (Winter 1982–83): 110–38, and R. Craig Nation, *Black Earth, Red Star: A History of Soviet Security Policy, 1917–1991* (Ithaca: Cornell University Press, 1992). For an analysis of the debate over Stalin's prewar policies, see Barry Posen, "Competing Images of the Soviet Union," *World Politics* 39, no. 4 (July 1987): 579–97.

3. For examples of the former view, see Richard Pipes, "Militarism and the Soviet State," *Daedalus* 109, no. 4 (1980): 1–12; and idem, "Soviet Global Strategy," *Commentary* 69, no. 4 (April 1980): 31–39. Examples of the latter include Raymond L. Garthoff, *Detente and Confrontation: American-Soviet Relations from Nixon to Reagan*, rev. ed. (Washington, D.C.: Brookings, 1994); and Nation, *Black Earth*.

4. Zdenek Mlynar, *Nightfrost in Prague: The End of Humane Socialism*, trans. Paul Wilson (New York: Karz, 1980), 239–40.

5. Alec Nove, *An Economic History of the U.S.S.R.* (New York: Viking Penguin, 1982), 289–95; Susan J. Linz, "World War II and Soviet Economic Growth," in *The Impact of World War II on the Soviet Union*, ed. Susan J. Linz (Totowa, N.J.: Rowman & Allanheld, 1985), 11–37.

6. Bruce Kuklick, *American Policy and the Division of Germany: The Clash with Russia over Reparations* (Ithaca: Cornell University Press, 1972), chaps. 4–7; John H. Backer, *The Decision to Divide Germany* (Durham: Duke University Press, 1978), chap. 3. Hungary and Romania agreed in separate armistice agreements with Stalin to deliver reparations goods worth $200 million and $300 million, respectively. See Nicolas Spulber, *The Economics of Communist Eastern Europe* (New York: John Wiley & Sons, 1957), 39–40, 167.

7. Ann L. Phillips, *Soviet Policy toward East Germany Reconsidered: The Postwar Decade* (New York: Greenwood Press, 1986), 65–71; Alec Cairncross, *The Price of War: British Policy on German Reparations, 1941–1949* (New York: Basil Blackwell, 1986), 194–207.

8. William Taubman, *Stalin's American Policy: From Entente to Détente to Cold War* (W. W. Norton, 1982), 193–227; Nation, *Black Earth, Red Star*, 173–201.

9. Quoted by Paul Marer, "The Political Economy of Soviet Relations with Eastern Europe," in *Soviet Policy in Eastern Europe*, ed. Sarah Meiklejohn Terry (New Haven: Yale University Press, 1984), 158. Marer suggests (159) that Stalin may also have been motivated by the example of the Soviets' own "great leap forward" of the 1930s, or by the desire to make Eastern Europe dependent on Soviet raw materials.

10. Phillips, *Soviet Policy toward East Germany*, 13–64, 115–49; Rolf Steininger, *The German Question: The Stalin Note of 1952 and the Problem of Reunification*, trans. Jane T. Hedges, ed. Mark Cioc (New York: Columbia University Press, 1990); James Richter, "Soviet Policy towards Germany in 1953,"*Europe-Asia Studies* 45, no. 4 (1993): 671–75.

11. Richter, "Soviet Policy," 680–85; Hope Harrison, "The Bargaining Power of Weaker Allies in Bipolarity and Crisis: The Dynamics of Soviet–East German Relations, 1953–61" (Ph.D. diss., Columbia University, 1993), chap. 2.

12. Valerie Bunce, "The Empire Strikes Back: The Evolution of the Eastern Bloc from a Soviet Asset to a Soviet Liability," *International Organization* 39, no. 1 (Winter 1985): 1–46; 30 (quote). See also Steven White, "Economic Performance and Communist Legitimacy," *World Politics* 38, no. 3 (April 1986), 462–82; Walter Connor, *Socialism's Dilemmas: State and Society in the Soviet Bloc* (New York: Columbia University Press, 1988), 192; Charles Gati, *The Bloc that Failed: Soviet-East European Relations in Transition* (Bloomington: Indiana University Press, 1990), 113–124; J. F. Brown, *Surge to Freedom: The End of Communist Rule in Eastern Europe* (Durham: Duke University Press, 1991), 28–31.

13. W. Brus, "1953 to 1956: The 'Thaw' and the 'New Course,'" in *Institutional Change within a Planned Economy*, vol. 3 of *The Economic History of Eastern Europe, 1919–1975*, ed. M. C. Kaser (Oxford: Clarendon Press, 1986), 64.

14. Already, the lengthening of time-horizons from the extreme uncertainty of the immediate postwar period led to a shift in reparations policy from the plunder binge of 1945 and 1946 to a more sustainable mobilization of ongoing German production. Vladimir Rudolf, "The Administrative Organization of Soviet Control, 1945–1948: The Agencies of Control: Their Organization and Policies," in *Soviet Economic Policy in Postwar Germany: A Collection of Papers by Former Soviet Officials*, ed. Robert Slusser (New York: Research Program on the USSR, 1953), 19. Alan Rousso, "Tipping the Balance of Power: The Political Economy of Intra-Alliance Trade in the Nuclear Age" (Ph.D. diss., Columbia University, 1994), chap. 5.

15. Spulber, *Economics of Communist Eastern Europe*, 167–70.

16. Heinz Köhler, *Economic Integration in the Soviet Block with an East German Case Study* (New York: Praeger, 1965), 46–47.

17. Richter, "Soviet Policy," 676; Harrison, "Bargaining Power," chap. 2.

18. Quoted in Harrison, "Bargaining Power," 43.

19. Ibid., 56.

20. By subsidy-per-GNP: Bulgaria, GDR, Czechoslovakia, Hungary, Poland

and Romania. Michael Marrese and Jan Vanous, "The Content and Controversy of Soviet Trade Relations with Eastern Europe, 1970–1984," in *Economic Adjustment and Reform in Eastern Europe and the Soviet Union*, ed. Josef Brada, Ed A. Hewett, and Thomas A. Wolf (Durham: Duke University Press, 1988), 202–3.

21. Marrese and Vanous, "Content and Controversy," 192–201; William M. Reisinger, *Energy and the Soviet Bloc: Alliance Politics after Stalin* (Ithaca: Cornell University Press, 1992), esp. 70–127.

22. Stephen M. Walt, *The Origins of Alliances* (Ithaca: Cornell University Press, 1987), 273–81.

23. William C. Wohlforth, *The Elusive Balance: Power and Perceptions during the Cold War* (Ithaca, N.Y.: Cornell University Press, 1993), chaps. 8–9; Coit D. Blacker, *Hostage to Revolution: Gorbachev and Soviet Security Policy, 1985–1991* (New York: Council on Foreign Relations, 1993).

24. Raymond L. Garthoff, *Deterrence and the Revolution in Soviet Military Doctrine* (Washington, D.C.: Brookings Institute, 1990), chap. 3. For a generational-cognitive explanation, see Robert Legvold, "War, Weapons, and Soviet Foreign Policy," in *Gorbachev's Russia and American Foreign Policy*, ed. Seweryn Bialer and Michael Mandelbaum (Boulder: Westview, 1988): 105. For a domestic-political explanation, see Jack L. Snyder, *Myths of Empire: Domestic Politics and International Ambition* (Ithaca: Cornell University Press, 1991), chap. 6.

25. Nation, *Black Earth*, 285–310; Garthoff, *Deterrence*, 119–20, 159–60, 192. Garthoff, however, vacillates between saying that doctrinal change permitted the loss of Eastern Europe and vice-versa.

26. Karen Dawisha, *Eastern Europe, Gorbachev, and Reform: The Great Challenge*, 2d ed. (Cambridge: Cambridge University Press, 1990), 197–224; Steven Kull, *Burying Lenin: The Revolution in Soviet Ideology and Foreign Policy* (Boulder: Westview Press, 1992), 131–57.

27. J. P. Nettl, *The Eastern Zone and Soviet Policy in Germany, 1945–50* (London: Oxford University Press, 1951), 199–207; Vassily Yershov, "Confiscation and Plunder by the Army of Occupation," and Vladimir Alexandrov, "The Dismantling of German Industry," in *Soviet Economic Policy*, ed. Robert Slusser, 1–17; Köhler, *Economic Integration*, 10–17.

28. Paul Marer, "Soviet Economic Policy in Eastern Europe," in U.S. Congress, Joint Economic Committee, *Reorientation and Commercial Relations of the Economies of Eastern Europe* (Washington, D.C.: GPO, 1974), 139, 144, 161; Köhler, *Economic Integration*, 16–17.

29. Soviet Military Administration of Germany, Order no. 32, February 1948, quoted by Köhler, *Economic Integration*, 43 n. 2. On the Soviet and East German agencies of this period, see Nettl, *Eastern Zone*, 56–73, 114–43; and the articles in *Soviet Economic Policy*, ed. Robert Slusser, 18–86.

30. Nikolai Grishin, "The Saxony Uranium Mining Operation ("Vismut")," in *Soviet Economic Policy*, ed. Slusser, 127–53.

31. Quoted in Köhler, *Economic Integration*, 18. See also Nettl, *Eastern Zone*, 219–25.

32. Köhler, *Economic Integration*, 19–23.

33. Ibid., 46–47.

34. The GDR decisions were announced in the August following the June uprising. See Phillips, *Soviet Policy*, chap. 5.

35. Bruce Parrott, *Politics and Technology in The Soviet Union* (Cambridge: MIT Press, 1983), 104–5. On U.S. exploitation of West German technology, see John Gimbel, *Science, Technology, and Reparations: Exploitation and Plunder in Postwar Germany* (Stanford: Stanford University Press, 1990).

36. Spulber, *Economics of Communist Eastern Europe*, 182–94; Marer, "Soviet Economic Policy," 141–43, 162; Marshall I. Goldman, *Soviet Foreign Aid* (New York: Praeger, 1967), chap. 2; and Janos Horvath, "Grant Elements in Intra-bloc Aid Programs," *ASTE Bulletin* 13, no. 3 (Fall 1971): 1–17.

37. Marer, "Soviet Economic Policy," 147. On East German terms of trade, see Köhler, *Economic Integration*, 346–58.

38. Jan Wszelaki, *Communist Economic Strategy: The Role of East-Central Europe* (New York: National Planning Association, 1959), 60.

39. Spulber, *Economics of Communist Eastern Europe*, 176–78; Marer, "Soviet Economic Policy," 140.

40. Raelynn J. Hillhouse, "A Reevaluation of Soviet Policy in Central Europe: The Soviet Union and the Occupation of Austria," *Eastern European Politics and Societies* 3, no. 1 (Winter 1989), 91–102.

41. Audrey Kurth Cronin, *Great Power Politics and the Struggle over Austria, 1945–1955* (Ithaca: Cornell University Press, 1986), 154.

42. Günter Bischof, "Between Responsibility and Rehabilitation: Austria in International Politics, 1940–1950," (Ph.D. diss., Harvard University, 1989), 238–69, 306–32, 454–66.

43. Köhler's data is widely accepted in the literature. It is used by Marer, "Soviet Economic Policy;" Horvath, "Grant Elements;" and Hartmut Zimmermann, ed., *DDR Handbuch*, 3d ed. (Köln: Verlag Wissenschaft und Politik, 1985), 1121–22.

44. Köhler, *Economic Integration*, 34.

45. A. Ross Johnson, "The Warsaw Pact: Soviet Military Policy in Eastern Europe," in *Soviet Policy in Eastern Europe*, ed. Terry, 262, 266.

46. Enthusiastic about the East German Army were A. Ross Johnson, Robert W. Dean, and Alexander Alexiev, *East European Military Establishments: The Warsaw Pact Northern Tier* (New York: Crane Russak, 1982), and Douglas A. MacGregor, *The Soviet-East German Military Alliance* (New York: Cambridge University Press, 1989); more hedged was Henry Krisch, "German Democratic Republic," in *Soviet Allies: The Warsaw Pact and the Issue of Reliability*, ed. Daniel N. Nelson (Boulder: Westview Press, 1983). Experts became notably more skeptical about the reliability of the Polish Army after the imposition of martial law in 1981; see Jan B. de Weydenthal, "Martial Law and the Reliability of the Polish Military," in *Soviet Allies*, ed. Daniel N. Nelson, 225–49, and Dale R. Herspring, "The Soviets, the Warsaw Pact, and the Eastern European Militaries," in *Central and Eastern Europe: The Opening Curtain?* ed. William E. Griffith (Boulder: Westview Press, 1989), 130–55. Most commentators were cautious about post-1968 Czech and post-1956 Hungarian reliability as well.

47. Christopher D. Jones suggests that national armies legitimated the presence of Soviet troops, but this explains neither the size nor the modernization of

204 NOTES TO CHAPTER 7

these armies. "National Armies and National Sovereignty," in *Warsaw Pact: Alliance in Transition?* ed. David Holloway and Jane M. O. Sharp (Ithaca: Cornell University Press, 1984), 102–10. On East European force modernization, see Johnson et al., *East European Military Establishments.*

48. Keith Crane, *The Soviet Economic Dilemma of Eastern Europe,* Rand report R-3368-AF (Santa Monica: Rand Corporation, May 1986), 10; cf. Marer, "Political Economy," 173.

49. Manufactures tend to be overpriced in Soviet–East European trade, Marrese and Vanous argue, because—unlike for raw materials—there was considerable ambiguity in equivalent world market prices for these goods. CMEA negotiators were able to exaggerate the value of their manufactures by comparing them to analogous but higher quality Western products.

50. Marrese and Vanous, "Content and Controversy," 196 ("baseline" estimate). This updates estimates made in their original *Implicit Subsidies and Non-Market Benefits in Soviet Trade with Eastern Europe* (Berkeley and Los Angeles: University of California Press, 1983). Accepting the methodology if not the interpretation of the Marrese-Vanous study are Franklyn D. Holzman, "The Significance of Soviet Subsidies to Eastern Europe," *Comparative Economic Studies* 28, no. 1 (Spring 1986): 54–65, and 28, no. 3 (Fall 1986): 59–64; Josef C. Brada, "Soviet Subsidization of Eastern Europe: The Primacy of Economics over Politics?" *Journal of Comparative Economics* 9 (1985): 80–92; Thomas A. Wolf, "Estimating 'Foregone Gains' in Soviet–East European Trade: A Methodological Note," *Comparative Economic Studies* 27, no. 3 (Fall 1985): 83–98; and the RAND studies summarized in Charles Wolf, Jr., "The Costs and Benefits of the Soviet Empire," in *The Future of the Soviet Empire,* ed. Henry S. Rowen and Charles Wolf, Jr. (New York: St. Martin's Press, 1987), 121–40.

51. Marer, "Political Economy," 174–80; Kazimierz Poznanski, "Opportunity Cost in Soviet Trade with Eastern Europe: Discussion of Methodology and New Evidence," *Soviet Studies* 40, no. 2 (April 1988), 290–307; Raimund Dietz, "Soviet Foregone Gains in Trade with the CMEA Six: A Reappraisal," *Comparative Economic Studies* 27, no. 2 (Summer 1986): 69–94.

52. Military expenditures estimated at $334 billion by United States, Arms Control and Disarmament Agency, *World Military Expenditures and Arms Transfers, 1986* (Washington, D.C.: GPO, 1987); Marrese and Vanous, "Content and Controversy," 196 ("baseline" estimate).

53. Based on reparations figures from Köhler, *Economic Integration,* and East German wages from Wolfgang F. Stolper, *The Structure of the East German Economy* (Cambridge: Harvard University Press, 1960), 431.

54. This evidence is summarized in Evangelista, "Stalin's Postwar Army Reappraised," 283–311.

55. For an overview, see Michel Tatu, "Intervention in Eastern Europe," in *Diplomacy of Power: Soviet Armed Forces as a Political Instrument,* ed. Stephen S. Kaplan (Washington, D.C.: Brookings Institution, 1981), 205–64.

56. Arnulf Baring, *Uprising in East Germany: June 17, 1953,* trans. G. Onn (Ithaca: Cornell University Press, 1972); Heinz Brandt, *The Search for a Third Way: My Path Between East and West,* trans. Salvator Attanasio (Garden City, N.Y.: Doubleday, 1970), 183–220.

57. Paul Kecskemeti, *The Unexpected Revolution: Social Forces in the Hungarian Uprising* (Stanford: Stanford University Press, 1961).

58. H. Gordon Skilling, *Czechoslovakia's Interrupted Revolution* (Princeton: Princeton University Press, 1976); Jiri Valenta, *The Soviet Invasion of Czechoslovakia, 1968: Anatomy of a Decision*, rev. ed. (Baltimore: Johns Hopkins Press, 1991).

59. Edwin M. Snell and Marilyn Harper, "Postwar Economic Growth in East Germany: A Comparison with West Germany," in U.S. Congress, Joint Economic Committee, ed., *Economic Developments in Countries of Eastern Europe* (Washington, D.C.: GPO, 1970), 568–75; Paul Gregory and Gert Leptin, "Similar Societies under Differing Economic Systems: The Case of the Two Germanys," *Soviet Studies* 29, no. 4 (October 1977), 519–42.

60. Marer, "Economies and Trade of Eastern Europe," in *Central and Eastern Europe*, ed. William E. Griffith, 48–52.

61. This pattern was somewhat obscured during the cold war by overestimation of East European and Soviet GNPs. Frequently cited experts, including Thad Alton and PlanEcon, revised their estimates downward dramatically after 1989, to levels comparable to those in table 7-4. See Elio Lancieri, "Dollar GNP Estimates for Central and Eastern Europe 1970–90: A Survey and a Comparison with Western Countries," *World Development* 21, no. 1 (1993), 161–75. For a more favorable analysis of East European growth, based on lower 1937 GNP estimates, see Eva Ehrlich, "Contest between Countries, 1937–1986," *Soviet Studies* 43, no. 5 (1991): 875–96.

62. Lancieri, "Dollar GNP Estimates," table 11 (Alton figures); Organisation for Economic Co-operation and Development, *Main Aggregates*, vol. 1 of *National Accounts, 1960–1990* (Paris: OECD, 1991), part 5.

63. J. M. Montias, "Economic Conditions and Political Instability in Communist Countries: Observations on Strikes, Riots, and Other Disturbances," *Studies in Comparative Communism* 13, no. 4 (Winter 1980): 283–99; Alex Pravda, "Industrial Workers: Patterns of Dissent, Opposition and Accommodation," in *Opposition in Eastern Europe*, ed. Rudolf L. Tokes (Baltimore: Johns Hopkins University Press, 1979), 241–50; Connor, *Socialism's Dilemmas*, chap. 9.

64. Dawisha, *Eastern Europe, Gorbachev, and Reform*, 46, 70, 113–14, 128.

65. Tatu, "Intervention in Eastern Europe," 239–49; Condoleeza Rice, "The Military as an Instrument of Influence and Control," in *Dominant Powers and Subordinate States: The United States in Latin America and the Soviet Union in Eastern Europe*, ed. Jan Triska (Durham: Duke University Press, 1986), 248–50.

66. Christopher D. Jones, *Soviet Influence in Eastern Europe: Political Autonomy and the Warsaw Pact* (New York: Praeger, 1981); Rice, "Military as an Instrument," 249; Dawisha, *Eastern Europe, Gorbachev, and Reform*, 101–6. Jones argues (79–92) that Yugoslavian, Romanian, and Albanian capabilities for national defense deterred Soviet intervention and allowed them national autonomy. Poland, too, may have deterred invasion in 1956 because its internal security forces and part of the army were prepared to fight, although the Polish regime's subsequent subservience to Moscow makes this an unclear case.

67. Nancy Travis Wolfe, *Policing a Socialist Society: The German Democratic Republic* (New York: Greenwood Press, 1992), 5. On opposition in general, see

Jane Leftwich Curry, ed., *Dissent in Eastern Europe* (New York: Praeger, 1983), and Rodolf L. Tokes, ed., *Opposition in Eastern Europe* (Baltimore: Johns Hopkins University Press, 1979).

68. Quoted in Connor, *Socialism's Dilemmas*, 180.

69. Quoted in Baring, *Uprising*, 27. See also Phillips, *Soviet Policy*, 126–33.

70. Baring, *Uprising*, 30–34.

71. Brandt, *Search for a Third Way*, 213.

72. Kecskemeti, *Unexpected Revolution*; Brzezinksi, *Soviet Bloc*, chap. 10.

73. Skilling, *Czechoslovakia's Interrupted Revolution*, chap. 22.

74. Timothy Garton Ash, *The Polish Revolution: Solidarity, 1980–82* (London: Jonathan Cape, 1983); Bartlomiej Kaminski, *The Collapse of State Socialism: The Case of Poland* (Princeton: Princeton University Press, 1992).

75. Quoted in Mark Kramer, "Beyond the Brezhnev Doctrine: A New Era in Soviet-East European Relations?" *International Security* 14, no. 3 (Winter 1989–90): 39–41. See also Dawisha, *Eastern Europe, Gorbachev, and Reform*, 197–224; Hannes Adomeit, "Gorbachev and German Unification: Realignment of Power," *Problems of Communism* 39 (July–August 1990): 1–23.

76. Elizabeth Pond, "A Wall Destroyed: The Dynamics of German Unification in the GDR," *International Security* 15, no. 2 (Fall 1990); Ash, *We the People*; Judy Batt, *East-Central Europe: From Reform to Transformation* (New York: Council on Foreign Relations, 1991); Brown, *Surge to Freedom*.

77. David Childs, *The GDR: Moscow's German Ally*, 2d ed. (London: Unwin Hyman, 1988), xii.

78. Raymond D. Gastil, *Freedom in the World: Political Rights and Civil Liberties, 1987–1988* (New York: Greenwood Press, 1988), 56–63; Curry, ed., *Dissent in Eastern Europe*; Tokes, ed., *Opposition in Eastern Europe*; Michael Bernhard, "Civil Society and Democratic Transition in East Central Europe," *Political Science Quarterly* 108, no. 2 (Summer 1993): 307–26.

79. E.g., Bernhard, "Civil Society and Democratic Transition," 314–17.

80. Sabrina P. Ramet, *Social Currents in Eastern Europe: The Sources and Meaning of the Great Transformation* (Durham: Duke University Press, 1991), 29, 155–72.

81. Baring, *Uprising*, 56–67; Montias, "Economic Conditions and Political Instability," 283–99.

82. Pravda, "Industrial Workers," 224.

83. Childs, *GDR*, 25, 64, 142.

84. Quoted in Norman H. Davies, *God's Playground: A History of Poland in Two Volumes* (Oxford: Clarendon Press, 1981), 2:558, 574.

85. Joseph A. Rothschild, *Return to Diversity: A Political History of East Central Europe since World War II*, 2d ed. (New York: Oxford University Press, 1993), 92, 99.

86. Henry O. Hart, "The Tables Turned: If East Europeans Could Vote," *Public Opinion* 6, no. 5 (October–November 1983), 53–57; Connor, *Socialism's Dilemmas*, 219–20.

87. Radio Free Europe, "Czechoslovak, Hungarian and Polish Attitudes toward a 'Serious Conflict' between the United States and the Soviet Union," *East European Area Audience and Opinion Research* (December 1981).

88. Batt, *East-Central Europe*, 119–20.

89. Pond, "A Wall Destroyed," 65.

90. Batt, *East-Central Europe*, 122–26.

91. An example of this argument can be found in Connor, *Socialism's Dilemmas*, chap. 7.

92. Dawisha, *Eastern Europe, Gorbachev, and Reform*, 60.

93. Robert H. Bates, "The Economics of Transitions to Democracy," *PS: Political Science & Politics* 24, no. 1 (March 1991): 24–27.

94. Gordon S. Bergsen and Russell Bova, "Worker Power Under Communism: The Interplay of Exit and Voice," *Comparative Economic Studies* 32, no. 1 (Spring 1990): 61–62.

95. Kaminski, *Collapse of State Socialism*, 179–86.

96. In East Germany, for example, political prisoners in the early 1980s numbered about forty-five hundred, and immigrants averaged fifteen thousand per year. Michael J. Sodaro, "Limits to Dissent in the GDR: Fragmentation, Cooptation, and Repression," in *Dissent in Eastern Europe*, ed. Curry, 92; H. G. Peter Wallach and Ronald H. Francisco, *United Germany: The Past, Politics, Prospects* (Westport, Conn.: Greenwood Press, 1992), 31.

97. Steven Van Evera, "Primed for Peace: Europe after the Cold War," *International Security* 15, no. 3 (Winter 1990–91): 15.

98. Paul Snell, "Soviet Microprocessors and Microcomputers," in *Technical Progress and Soviet Economic Development*, ed. Ronald Amann and Julian Cooper (New York: Basil Blackwell, 1986): 62–63; Seymour Goodman, "Information Technologies and the Citizen: Toward a 'Soviet-Style Information Society'?" in *Science and the Soviet Social Order*, ed. Loren R. Graham (Cambridge: Harvard University Press, 1990), esp. 371–72, n. 10; Gary L. Geipel, A. Tomasz Jarmoszko, and Seymour E. Goodman, "The Information Technologies and East European Societes," *East European Politics and Societies* 5, no. 3 (Fall 1991): 394–438.

99. Soviet official V. Korbeinikov, quoted in Erik P. Hoffmann and Robbin F. Laird, *Technocratic Socialism: The Soviet Union in the Advanced Industrial Era* (Durham: Duke University Press, 1985), 156.

100. These were assisted by hundred of thousands of volunteer police "helpers" and Stasi informants. Zimmermann, *DDR Handbuch*, 275–76; and Wolfe, *Policing a Socialist Society*, 3–100. On the Stasi, see also Karl Wilhelm Fricke, *MfS intern: Macht, Strukturen, Auflösung der DDR-Staatssicherheit, Analyse und Dokumentation* (Cologne: Verlag Wissenschaft und Politik, 1991), 21–38; David Gill and Ulrich Schröter, *Das Ministerium für Staatssicherheit: Anatomie des Mielke-Imperiums* (Berlin: Rowohlt, 1991), 31–94; Peter Joachim Lapp, *Frontdienst im Frieden—die Grenztruppen der DDR: Entwicklung Struktur, Auggaben*, 2d ed. (Koblenz: Bernard & Graefe Verlag, 1987).

101. Erika S. Fairchild, *German Police: Ideals and Reality in the Post-war Years* (Springfield: C. C. Thomas, 1988): 51–53.

102. For example, by mobilizing greater numbers of women and older people into the work force, East Germany's rate was 15 percent higher than West Germany's in the late 1960s. Gregory and Leptin, "Similar Societies under Differing Economic Systems," 529–30.

103. Lancieri, "Dollar GNP Estimates," 169.

104. Quoted in Charles E. Lindblom, *Politics and Markets: The World's Polit-ical-Economic Systems* (New York: Basic Books, 1977), 71.

105. Paul R. Gregory and Robert C. Stuart, *Soviet Economic Structure and Performance*, 3d ed. (New York: Harper & Row, 1986), chaps. 7, 8, 11; on innovation and technology in particular, see Joseph S. Berliner, *The Innovation Decision in Soviet Industry* (Cambridge: MIT Press, 1976); R. Amman and J. Cooper, eds., *Industrial Innovation in the Soviet Union* (New Haven: Yale University Press, 1982).

106. A pre-Gorbachev Soviet version of this argument is Tatanya Zaslavskaya, "The Novisibirsk Report," *Survey* 28, no. 1 (Spring 1984): 88–108. But Judy Batt argues that the "marketisation [of communist societies] is possible without the collapse of one-party rule and democratic revolution; and that the costs of avoiding democratic political transformation need not be intolerably high." Batt, *Economic Reform and Political Change in Eastern Europe: A Com-parison of the Czechoslovak and Hungarian Experiences* (New York: St. Mar-tin's, 1988), 45.

Chapter 8
The Spoils of Conquest

1. Richard J. Overy, "Mobilization for Total War in Germany 1939–1941," *English Historical Review* 103, no. 408 (July 1988): 614.

2. Jervis, "Cooperation under the Security Dilemma."

3. John Mearsheimer, "Back to the Future: Instability in Europe after the Cold War," *International Security* 15, no. 1 (Summer 1990): 42–48; Anne Uchitel, "Interdependence and Instability," in *Coping with Complexity in the Interna-tional System*, ed. Jack Snyder and Robert Jervis (Boulder: Westview Press, 1992), 243–64.

4. See, e.g., Theodor Ebert, "Organization in Civilian Defence," in *Civilian Resistance*, ed. Adam Roberts, 295–315.

5. M. R. D. Foot, *Resistance: European Resistance to Nazism, 1940–1945* (New York: McGraw-Hill, 1977), 213.

6. U.S. Congress, House Committee on International Relations, *Report on Oil Fields as Miltiary Objectives: A Feasibility Study*, prepared by John M. Collins and Clyde R. Mark, 94th Congress, 1st sess. (Washington, D.C.: GPO, 1975). See also Robert W. Tucker, "Oil: The Issue of American Intervention," *Commentary*, January 1975, 21–31; and Miles Ignotus (pseud.), "Seizing Arab Oil," *Harpers*, March 1975, 45–62.

Works Cited

General
(Chapters 1, 2, and 8)

Ackerman, Peter, and Christopher Kruegler. *Strategic Nonviolent Conflict: The Dynamics of People Power in the Twentieth Century.* Westport, Conn.: Praeger, 1994.

Alternative Defense Commission (Great Britain). *Defense without the Bomb.* London: Taylor & Francis, 1983.

Andreski, Stanislav. *Military Organizaton and Society.* Berkeley: University of California Press, 1968.

Angell, Norman. *The Great Illusion: A Study of the Relation of Military Power to National Advantage.* 4th rev. and enl. ed. New York: G. P. Putnam's Sons, 1913.

Aron, Raymond. *Peace and War: A Theory of International Relations.* Translated by Richard Howard and Annette Baker Fox. New York: Praeger, 1968.

Art, Robert J. "A Defensible Defense: America's Grand Strategy after the Cold War." *International Security* 15, no. 4 (Spring 1991): 5–53.

Auster, Richard D., and Morris Silver, *The State as a Firm: Economic Forces in Political Development.* Boston: Martinus Nijhoff, 1979.

Baldwin, David A. *Economic Statecraft.* Princeton: Princeton University Press, 1985.

Bates, Robert H. "The Economics of Transitions to Democracy." *PS: Political Science and Politics* 24, no. 1 (March 1991): 24–27.

Bentham, Jeremy. *The Works of Jeremy Bentham.* Edited by John Bowring. 11 vols. London: Simpkin, Marshall, 1843.

Bisceglia, Louis. *Norman Angell and Liberal Internationalism in Britain, 1931–1935.* New York: Garland, 1982.

Blainey, Geoffrey. *The Causes of War.* New York: Free Press, 1973.

Bloch, Henry S., and Bert F. Hoselitz. *The Economics of Military Occupation.* Rev. ed. Chicago: University of Chicago Press, 1944.

Boserup, Anders, and Andrew Mack. *War without Weapons: Non-Violence in National Defense.* New York: Schocken, 1975.

Boulding, Kenneth. "The Economics and Noneconomics of the World War Industry." *Contemporary Policy Issues* 4, no. 4 (October 1986): 12–21.

―――. "Introduction." In *Economic Imperialism*, edited by Kenneth E. Boulding and Tapan Mukerjee, ix–xviii. Ann Arbor: University of Michigan Press, 1972.

Buchan, Alastair. "Technology and World Politics." In *The Aberystwyth Papers: International Politics 1919–1969*, edited by Brian E. Porter, 160–82. Oxford: Oxford University Press, 1972.

Cain, Peter. "Capitalism, War and Internationalism in the Thought of Richard Cobden." *British Journal of International Studies* 5, no. 3 (1979): 229–47.

Chao, Kang. *The Economic Development of Manchuria: The Rise of a Frontier Economy*. Michigan Papers in Chinese Studies no. 43. Ann Arbor: Center for Chinese Studies, University of Michigan, 1983.

Chapman, Brian. *Police State*. New York: Praeger, 1970.

Chorley, Katherine. *Armies and the Art of Revolution*. London: Faber & Faber, 1943.

Christensen, Thomas J., and Jack Snyder. "Chain Gangs and Passed Bucks: Predicting Alliance Patterns in Multipolarity." *International Organization* 44, no. 2 (Spring 1990): 137–68.

Cipolla, Carlo M., ed. *The Economic Decline of Empires*. London: Methuen, 1970.

Clark, Colin. *The Conditions of Economic Progress*. 3d ed. London: Macmillan, 1957.

Clark, Grover. *The Balance Sheets of Imperialism*. New York: Columbia University Press, 1936.

Cobden, Richard. *Political Writings*, vol. 1. New York: D. Appleton, 1867.

———. *Speeches on Questions of Public Policy*, edited by John Bright and James Rogers, vol. 1. London: Macmillan, 1870.

Cohen, Eliot A. "Do We Still Need Europe?" *Commentary* 81, no. 1 (January 1986): 28–35.

Compton, James V. *The Swastika and the Eagle: Hitler, the United States, and the Origins of World War II*. Boston: Houghton Mifflin, 1967.

Crouch, Colin. *Trade Unions: The Logic of Collective Action*. Glasgow: Fontana, 1982.

Dahl, Robert. *Polyarchy: Participation and Opposition*. New Haven: Yale University Press, 1971.

Dallek, Robert. *Franklin D. Roosevelt and American Foreign Policy, 1932–1945*. New York: Oxford University Press, 1979.

Davies, James C. "Toward a Theory of Revolution." *American Sociological Review* 6, no. 1 (February 1962): 5–19.

Davis, Lance E., and Robert A. Huttenback. *Mammon and the Pursuit of Empire: The Economics of British Imperialism*. Cambridge: Cambridge University Press, 1988.

De Nardo, James. *Power in Numbers*. Princeton: Princeton University Press, 1985.

Dehio, Ludwig. *The Precarious Balance: Four Centuries of European Power Struggle*. Translated by C. Fullman. New York: Knopf, 1962.

Dennis, Lawrence. "The Economic Consequences of American Intervention." In *In Danger Undaunted: The Anti-Interventionist Movement of 1940–1941 as Revealed in the Papers of the America First Committee*, edited by Justus D. Doenecke, 200–205. Stanford: Hoover Institution Press, 1990.

Deutsch, Karl W. *Nationalism and Social Communication: An Inquiry into the Foundations of Nationality*. 2d ed. Cambridge: MIT Press, 1966.

Doyle, Michael. *Empires*. Ithaca: Cornell University Press, 1986.

———. "Liberalism and World Politics." *American Political Science Review* 80, no. 4 (December 1986): 1151–69.

Drucker, Peter F. "The Changed World Economy." *Foreign Affairs* 64, no. 4 (Spring 1986): 768–91.

Ebert, Theodor. "Organization in Civilian Defence." In *Civilian Resistance*, edited by Adam Roberts, 295–315.

Eckstein, Harry. "Case Study and Theory in Political Science." in *Strategies of Inquiry*, vol. 7 of *Handbook of Political Science*, edited by Fred Greenstein and Nelson Polsby, 79–137. Reading, Mass.: Addison Wesley, 1975.

Eggertsson, Thráinn. *Economic Behavior and Institutions*. Cambridge: Cambridge University Press, 1990.

Feierabend, Ivo K., Rosalind L. Feierabend, and Ted Robert Gurr, eds. *Anger, Violence, and Politics: Theories and Research*. Englewood Cliffs, N.J.: Prentice-Hall, 1972.

Fenoaltea, Stefano. "Slavery and Supervision in Comparative Perspective: A Model." *Journal of Economic History* 44, no. 3 (September 1984): 635–68.

Flanagan, Stephen J. "Nonprovocative and Civilian-based Defenses." In *Fateful Visions: Avoiding Nuclear Catastrophe*, edited by Joseph S. Nye, Jr., Graham T. Allison, and Albert Carnesale, 393–410. Cambridge, Mass.: Ballinger, 1988.

Friedrich, Carl J., and Zbigniew K. Brzezinski, *Totalitarian Dictatorship and Autocracy*. New York: Praeger, 1956.

Frye, Alton. *Nazi Germany and the American Hemisphere, 1933–1941*. New Haven: Yale University Press, 1967.

Gaddis, John Lewis. *Strategies of Containment: A Critical Appraisal of Postwar American National Security Policy*. Oxford: Oxford University Press, 1982.

Galbraith, John K. *The New Industrial State*. 4th ed. Boston: Houghton Mifflin, 1985.

Gellner, Ernest. *Nations and Nationalism*. Ithaca: Cornell University Press, 1983.

George, Alexander. "Case Studies and Theory Development." In *Diplomacy: New Approaches in History, Theory and Policy*, edited by Paul Lauren, 43–68. New York: Free Press, 1979.

Giddens, Anthony. *The Nation-State and Violence*. Berkeley: University of California Press, 1987.

Gilpin, Robert. *War and Change in World Politics*. Cambridge: Cambridge University Press, 1981.

Gimbel, John. *Science, Technology, and Reparations: Exploitation and Plunder in Postwar Germany*. Stanford: Stanford University Press, 1990.

Glenny, Misha. *The Fall of Yugoslavia: The Third Balkan War*. Rev. ed. New York: Penguin, 1993.

Grand Duchy of Luxembourg, Ministère de l'Economie. *Statistiques historiques, 1839–1989*. Luxembourg: Service Central de la Statistique et des Etudes Economiques, 1990.

Gulick, Edward Vose. *Europe's Classical Balance of Power*. New York: W. W. Norton, 1955.

Gupta, Dipak K., Harinder Singh, and Tom Sprague. "Government Coercion of Dissidents: Deterrence or Provocation?" *Journal of Conflict Resolution* 37, no. 2 (June 1993): 301–39.

Gurr, Ted Robert. *Why Men Rebel*. Princeton: Princeton University Press, 1970.

Hall, Stephen King. *Defense in the Nuclear Age*. London: Victor Gallancz, 1958.

Hardin, Russell. *Collective Action*. Baltimore: Johns Hopkins University Press, 1982.

Harrison, Mark. "GDPs of the USSR and Eastern Europe: Towards an Interwar Comparison." *Europe-Asia Studies* 46, no. 2 (1994): 243–59.

———. "Resource Mobilization for World War II." *Economic History Review*, 2d ser., 41 (1988): 171–92.

Harvey, S. "Mobilisation économique et succès militaires pendant la seconde guerre mondiale." *Revue de la deuxième guerre mondiale et conflits contemporaines*, no. 142 (April 1986): 19–35.

Headrick, Daniel R. *The Tools of Empire: Technology and European Imperialism in the Nineteenth Century.* New York: Oxford University Press, 1981.

Hoffmann, Stanley. *Decline or Renewal: France since the 1930s.* New York: Viking Press, 1974.

Hopf, Ted. "Polarity, the Offense-Defense Balance, and War." *American Political Science Review* 85, no. 2 (June 1991): 475–93.

Hughes, Jeffrey L. "On Bargaining." In *Dominant Powers and Subordinate States: The United States in Latin America and the Soviet Union in Eastern Europe*, edited by Jan Triska, 168–99. Durham: Duke University Press, 1986.

Ignotus, Miles (pseud.). "Seizing Arab Oil." *Harpers* (March 1975): 45–62.

Jervis, Robert. "Cooperation under the Security Dilemma." *World Politics* 30, no. 2 (January 1978): 167–214.

———. *The Illogic of American Nuclear Strategy.* Ithaca: Cornell University Press, 1984.

———. *The Meaning of the Nuclear Revolution: Statecraft and the Prospect of Armageddon.* Ithaca: Cornell University Press, 1989.

———. *Perception and Misperception in International Politics.* Princeton: Princeton University Press, 1976.

Jonas, Manfred. *Isolationism in America, 1935–1941.* Ithaca: Cornell University Press, 1966.

Jones, J. H. *The Economics of War and Conquest: An Examination of Mr. Norman Angell's Economic Doctrines.* London: P. S. King & Son, 1915.

Kahler, Miles. "External Ambition and Economic Performance." *World Politics* 40, no. 4 (July 1988): 419–51.

Kaysen, Carl. "Is War Obsolete? A Review Essay." *International Security* 14, no. 4 (Spring 1990): 48–64.

Kecskemeti, Paul. *Strategic Surrender: The Politics of Victory and Defeat.* Stanford: Stanford University Press, 1958.

Kennan, George F. *American Diplomacy 1900–1950.* Chicago: University of Chicago Press, 1951.

———. *Memoirs 1925–1950.* New York: Pantheon Books, 1967.

———. *Realities of American Foreign Policy.* Princeton: Princeton University Press, 1954.

———. *Russia, the Atom and the West.* New York: Harper & Bros., 1958.

Kennedy, Paul. *The Rise and Fall of the Great Powers: Economic Change and Military Conflict from 1500 to 2000.* New York: Random House, 1987.

Keohane, Robert O. *After Hegemony: Cooperation and Discord in the World Political Economy.* Princeton: Princeton University Press, 1984.

Keohane, Robert O., and Joseph S. Nye. *Power and Interdependence.* 2d ed. Boston: Scott, Foresman, 1989.

Keyes, Gene. "Strategic Non-Violent Defense." *Journal of Strategic Studies* 4, no. 2 (June 1981): 125–51.

Kindleberger, Charles P. *A Financial History of Western Europe*. Boston: George Allen & Unwin, 1984.

Knorr, Klaus E. *British Colonial Theories, 1570–1850*. Toronto: University of Toronto Press, 1944.

———. *On the Uses of Military Power in the Nuclear Age*. Princeton: Princeton Unversity Press, 1966.

———. *The Power of Nations: The Political Economy of International Relations*. New York: Basic Books, 1975.

Kober, Stanley. "Can NATO Survive?" *International Affairs* 59 (Summer 1983): 343–45.

Kupchan, Charles. *The Vulnerability of Empire*. Ithaca: Cornell University Press, 1994.

Kuran, Timur. "Sparks and Prairie Fires: Theory of Unanciticpated Revolutions." *Public Choice* 61, no. 1 (April 1989): 41–74.

Lamborn, Alan C. *The Price of Power: Risk and Foreign Policy in Britain, France, and Germany*. Boston: Unwin Hyman, 1991.

Landes, David S. "Some Thoughts on the Nature of Economic Imperialism." *Journal of Economic History* 21, no. 4 (December 1961): 496–512.

Langer, William L., and S. Everett Gleason. *The Challenge to Isolation*. New York: Harper for the Council on Foreign Relations, 1952.

———*The Undeclared War, 1940–1941*. New York: Harper for the Council on Foreign Relations, 1953.

Laqueur, Walter. *Guerrilla: A Historical and Critical Study*. Boston: Little, Brown, 1976.

Laqueur, Walter, ed. *The Guerrilla Reader: A Historical Anthology*. Philadelphia: Temple University Press, 1977.

Larson, Deborah Welch. "Bandwagon Images in American Foreign Policy: Myth or Reality?" in *Dominoes and Bandwagons*, edited by Jack Snyder and Robert Jervis, 85–111.

Larson, Eric, Marc Ross, and Robert Williams. "Beyond the Era of Materials." *Scientific American* (June 1986): 34–41.

Layne, Christopher. "Atlanticism Without NATO." *Foreign Policy* no. 67 (Summer 1987): 22–45.

Leffler, Melvyn P. *A Preponderance of Power: National Security, the Truman Administration, and the Cold War*. Stanford: Stanford University Press, 1992.

Leites, Nathan, and Charles Wolf, Jr. *Rebellion and Authority: An Analytic Essay on Insurgent Conflicts*. Chicago: Markham, 1970.

Levi, Margaret. *Of Rule and Revenue*. Berkeley: University of California Press, 1988.

Levy, Jack S. "The Offensive/Defensive Balance of Military Technology: A Theoretical and Historical Analysis." *International Studies Quarterly* 28 (1984): 219–38.

Lichbach, Mark I. "What Makes Rational Peasants Revolutionary? Dilemma, Paradox, and Irony in Peasant Collective Action." *World Politics* 46, no. 3 (April 1994): 383–418.

Lijphart, Arend. "Comparative Politics and the Comparative Method." *American Political Science Review* 65 (September 1981): 682–93.

Linz, Juan. "Totalitarian and Authoritarian Regimes." In *Macropolitical Theory*, vol. 3 of *Handbook of Political Science*, edited by Fred Greenstein and Nelson Polsby, 175–412. Reading, Mass.: Addison-Wesley, 1975.

Lippmann, Walter. *U.S. Foreign Policy: Shield of the Republic*. Boston: Little, Brown, 1943.

Lynn-Jones, Sean, ed. *The Cold War and After: Prospects for Peace*. Princeton: Princeton University Press, 1991.

Machiavelli, Niccolo. *The Prince and the Discourses*. New York: Modern Library, 1950.

Mackinder, Halford J. *Democratic Ideals and Reality*. New York: Henry Holt, 1919.

———. "The Geographical Pivot of History." *Geographic Journal* 23, no. 4 (April 1904): 421–44.

Maddison, Angus. *The World Economy in the 20th Century*. Paris: OECD, 1989.

Mann, Michael. "The Autonomous Power of the State." *Archives Européennes de Sociologie* 25, no. 2 (1984): 185–213.

Marer, Paul. *Dollar GNPs of the U.S.S.R. and Eastern Europe*. Baltimore: Johns Hopkins Press for the World Bank, 1985.

Marwell, Gerald, and Pamela Oliver. *The Critical Mass in Collective Action: A Micro-Social Theory*. Cambridge: Cambridge University Press, 1993.

Marx, Karl. *Manifesto of the Communist Party* (1848) In *The Marx-Engels Reader*, 2d ed., edited by Robert C. Tucker, 480–81. New York: W. W. Norton, 1978.

McGuire, Martin C. "The Revolution in International Security." *Challenge*, March–April 1990, 4–10.

Mearsheimer, John. "Back to the Future: Instability in Europe after the Cold War." *International Security* 15, no. 1 (Summer 1990): 5–56.

Mendershausen, Horst. *The Economics of War*. Rev. ed. New York: Prentice Hall, 1943.

Miller, J. D. B. *Norman Angell and the Futility of War*. London: Macmillan, 1986.

Milward, Alan S. *The New Order and the French Economy*. Oxford: Oxford University Press, Clarendon Press, 1970.

———. *War, Economy and Society, 1939–1945*. Berkeley: University of California Press, 1977.

Mitchell, Brian R. *International Historical Statistics: Europe, 1750–1988*. 3d ed. New York: Stockton Press, 1992.

Mizoguchi, Toshiyuki, and Mataji Umemura. *Basic Economic Statistics of Former Japanese Colonies, 1895–1938*. Tokyo: Toyo Keizai Shinposha, 1988.

Modelski, George. "Agraria and Industria: Two Models of the International System." In *The International System*, edited by Klaus Knorr and Sidney Verba, 118–43. Princeton: Princeton University Press, 1961.

Morgenthau, Hans J. *Politics among Nations: The Struggle for Power and Peace*. New York: Knopf, 1948.

Mueller, John. *Retreat from Doomsday: The Obsolescence of Major War.* New York: Basic Books, 1989.

Muller, Edward N., and Erich Weede. "Cross-National Variation in Political Violence." *Journal of Conflict Resolution* 34, no. 4 (December 1990): 624–51.

Murray, Williamson. *The Change in the European Balance of Power, 1938–1939: The Path to Ruin.* Princeton: Princeton University Press, 1984.

Myers, Ramon H., and Mark Peattie, eds. *The Japanese Colonial Empire, 1895–1945.* Princeton: Princeton University Press, 1984.

Niou, Emerson M. S., Peter C. Ordeshook, and Gregory F. Rose. *The Balance of Power: Stability in International Systems.* Cambridge: Cambridge University Press, 1989.

O'Donnell, Guillermo, and Philippe C. Schmitter. *Transitions from Authoritarian Rule: Tentative Conclusions about Uncertain Democracies.* Baltimore: Johns Hopkins University Press, 1986.

Olson, Mancur, Jr. *The Logic of Collective Action.* 2d ed. Cambridge: Harvard University Press, 1971.

Organski, A. F. K., and Jacek Kugler. *The War Ledger.* Chicago: University of Chicago Press, 1980.

Parker, Geoffrey. *Western Geopolitical Thought in the Twentieth Century.* London: Croom Helm, 1985.

Perrow, Charles. *Complex Organizations.* 3d ed. New York: Random House, 1986.

Petrov, Vladimir. *Money and Conquest: Allied Occupation Currencies in World War II.* Baltimore: Johns Hopkins University Press, 1967.

Popkin, Samuel L. *The Rational Peasant: The Political Economy of Revolution in Vietnam.* Berkeley: University of California Press, 1979.

Posen, Barry R. "Nationalism, the Mass Army, and Military Power." *International Security* 18, no. 2 (Fall 1993): 80–124.

———. "The Security Dilemma and Ethnic Conflict." In *Ethnic Conflict and International Security,* edited by Michael E. Brown, 103–25. Princeton: Princeton University Press, 1993.

Posen, Barry R., and Stephen Van Evera. "Defense Policy and the Reagan Administration: Departure from Containment." *International Security* 8, no. 1 (Summer 1983): 3–45.

Ravenal, Earl C. "Europe without America: The Erosion of NATO." *Foreign Affairs* 63, no. 5 (Summer 1985): 1020–35.

Rice, Edward E. *Wars of the Third Kind: Conflict in Underdeveloped Countries.* Berkeley and Los Angeles: University of California Press, 1988.

Robbins, Lionel. *The Economic Causes of War.* London: Jonathan Cape, 1939.

Roberts, Adam, ed. *Civilian Resistance as a National Defence: Non-Violent Action against Aggression.* 2d ed. Harmondsworth: Penguin Books, 1969.

———. *Nations in Arms: The Theory and Practice of Territorial Defence.* 2d ed. London: Macmillan, 1986.

Robinson, Ronald. "Non-European Foundations of European Imperialism: Sketch for a Theory of Collaboration." In *Studies in the Theory of Imperialism,* edited by Roger Owen and Bob Sutcliff, 117–40. London: Longman, 1972.

Rosecrance, Richard. *The Rise of the Trading State: Commerce and Conquest in the Modern World.* New York: Basic Books, 1986.

Rule, James B. *Theories of Civil Violence.* Berkeley: University of California Press, 1988.

Russell, D. E. H. *Rebellion, Revolution, and Armed Force.* New York: Academic Press, 1974.

Russett, Bruce. *No Clear and Present Danger: A Skeptical View of the United States Entry into World War II.* New York: Harper & Row, 1972.

Sanders, Jerry. "Security and Choice." *World Policy Journal* 1, no. 4 (Summer 1984): 677–722.

Schelling, Thomas. *Arms and Influence.* New Haven: Yale University Press, 1966.

———. *Micromotives and Macrobehavior.* New York: Norton, 1978.

Schmitt, Bernadotte. *The Coming of the War in 1914.* 2 vols. New York: Howard Fertig, 1968.

Sharp, Gene. *Civilian-Based Defense.* Princeton: Princeton University Press, 1990.

———. *Making Europe Unconquerable: The Potential of Civilian-Based Deterrence and Defense.* Cambridge, Mass.: Ballinger, 1985.

———. *The Politics of Nonviolent Action.* Boston: Porter Sargent, 1973.

Shultz, George. "The Future of American Foreign Policy." *Department of State Bulletin* 85, no. 2096 (March 1985): 13–20.

Skocpol, Theda. *States and Social Revolutions: A Comparative Analysis of France, Russia, and China.* Cambridge: Cambridge University Press, 1979.

Sloan, G. R. *Geopolitics in United States Strategic Policy, 1890–1987.* New York: St. Martin's Press, 1988.

Smith, Adam. *The Wealth of Nations* (1776). New York: Modern Library, 1937.

Snyder, Glenn H., and Paul Diesing. *Conflict Among Nations: Bargaining, Decision Making, and System Structure in International Crises.* Princeton: Princeton University Press, 1977.

Snyder, Glenn. "The Balance of Power and the Balance of Terror." In *The Balance of Power,* edited by Paul Seabury, 184–201. San Francisco: Chandler, 1965.

Snyder, Jack. *Myths of Empire: Domestic Politics and International Ambition.* Ithaca: Cornell University Press, 1991.

Snyder, Jack, and Robert Jervis, eds. *Dominoes and Bandwagons: Strategic Beliefs and Great Power Competition in the Eurasian Rimland.* New York: Oxford University Press, 1991.

Spykman, Nicholas J. *America's Strategy in World Politics: The United States and the Balance of Power.* New York: Harcourt, Brace, 1942.

———. *The Geography of the Peace,* edited by Helen R. Nicholl. New York: Harcourt, Brace & World, 1944; repr., Hamden, Conn.: Archon Books, 1969.

Staley, Eugene. "The Myth of the Continents." *Foreign Affairs* 19, no. 3 (April 1941): 481–94.

Summers, Robert, and Alan Heston. "A New Set of International Comparisons of Real Product and Price Levels Estimates for 130 Countries, 1950–1985." *Review of Income and Wealth* 34, no. 1 (March 1988): 1–25.

Taber, Robert. *The War of the Flea: A Study of Guerrilla Warfare Theory and Practice.* New York: Citadel, 1970.

Taylor, Michael. "Rationality and Revolutionary Collective Action." In *Rationality and Revolution,* edited by Michael Taylor, 63–97. Cambridge: Cambridge University Press, 1988.

Thucydides, *The History of the Peloponnesian War.* Translated by Rex Warner. New York: Penguin Books, 1972.

Tilly, Charles. *From Mobilization to Revolution.* Reading, Mass.: Addison-Wesley, 1978.

———. "War Making and State Making as Organized Crime." In *Bringing the State Back In,* edited by Peter B. Evans, Dietrich Rueschemeyer, and Theda Skocpol, 169–91. Cambridge: Cambridge University Press, 1985.

Tilly, Charles, Louise Tilly, and Richard Tilly. *The Rebellious Century, 1830–1930.* Cambridge: Harvard University Press, 1975.

Tucker, Robert. *A New Isolationism: Threat or Promise.* New York: Universe, 1972.

———. "Oil: The Issue of American Intervention." *Commentary,* January 1975, 21–31.

Tullock, Gordon. "The Paradox of Revolution." *Public Choice* 11 (Fall 1971): 89–99.

Uchitel, Anne. "Interdependence and Instability." In *Coping with Complexity in the International System,* edited by Jack Snyder and Robert Jervis, 243–64. Boulder, Colo.: Westview Press, 1992.

United States, Central Intelligence Agency. *Handbook of Economic Statistics, 1987.* Washington, D.C.: Government Printing Office, 1987.

United States, Congress, House Committee on International Relations. *Report on Oil Fields as Miltiary Objectives: A Feasibility Study,* prepared by John M. Collins and Clyde R. Mark. 94th Congress, 1st sess. Washington, D.C.: U.S. Government Printing Office, 1975.

Van Crevald, Martin. *Supplying War: Logistics from Wallenstein to Patton.* Cambridge: Cambridge University Press, 1977.

Van Evera, Stephen. "Causes of War." Ph.D. diss., University of California, Berkeley, 1984.

———. "The Cult of the Offensive and the Origins of the First World War." *International Security* 9, no. 1 (Summer 1984): 58–107.

———. "Primed for Peace: Europe after the Cold War." *International Security* 1, no. 3 (Winter 1990–91): 7–57.

Walt, Stephen M. "The Case for Finite Containment: Analyzing U.S. Grand Strategy." *International Security* 14, no. 1 (Summer 1989): 5–49.

———. *The Origins of Alliances.* Ithaca: Cornell University Press, 1987.

Waltz, Kenneth N. "The Origins of War in Neorealist Theory." *Interdisciplinary History* 18, no. 4 (Spring 1988): 615–28.

———. *Theory of International Politics.* New York: Random House, 1979.

Wight, Martin. *Power Politics.* Edited by H. Bull and C. Holbraad. New York: Holmes & Meier, 1978.

Winch, Donald. *Classical Political Economy and Colonies.* London: G. Bell and Sons, 1965.

Worsley, R. H. M. *Europe versus America: Implications of the "New Order."* London: Jonathan Cape, 1942.

Zamagni, Vera. *The Economic History of Italy, 1860–1990.* Oxford: Clarendon Press, 1993.

Nazi-Occupied Western Europe, 1940–1944
(Chapter 3)

Adamthwaite, Anthony. *France and the Coming of the Second World War, 1936–1939.* London: Cass, 1977.

Allied Command, German Military Documents Section (combined British-Canadian-U.S. staff). *German Manpower: A Study of the Employment of German Manpower from 1933–1945.* U.S. National Archives. Record Group 242, Studies, Reports and Reference Material.

Ansbacher, H. L. "Testing, Management and Reactions of Foreign Workers in Germany during World War II." *American Psychologist* 5 (February 1950): 38–49.

Aukrust, Odd, and P. J. Bjerve. *Hva kriegen kostet Norge.* Oslo: Dreyers, 1945.

Azéma, Jean-Pierre. *From Munich to the Liberation 1938–1944.* Translated by Janet Lloyd. Cambridge: Cambridge University Press, 1984.

Bank for International Settlements, *Fourteenth Annual Report.* Basle, 1944.

Barbera, Henry. *Rich Nations and Poor in Peace and War: Continuity and Change in the Development Hierarchy of Seventy Nations from 1913 through 1952.* Lexington, Mass.: Lexington Books, 1973.

Barnett, Correlli. *The Pride and the Fall: The Dream and Illusion of Britain as a Great Nation.* New York: Free Press, 1986.

Barral, Pierre. "Agriculture and Food Supply in France during the Second World War." In *Agriculture and Food Supply in the Second World War,* edited by Bernd Martin and Alan S. Milward, 89–102. Ostfildern: Scripta Murcaturae Verlag, 1985.

Bartov, Omer. *Hitler's Army: Soldiers, Nazis, and War in the Third Reich.* New York: Oxford University Press, 1991.

Bellon, Bernard P. *Mercedes in Peace and War: German Automobile Workers, 1903–1945.* New York: Columbia University Press, 1990.

Best, Werner. "Die deutschen Aufsichtsverwaltungen in Frankreich, Belgien, den Niederlanden, Norwegen, Dänemak, und im Protektorat Böhmen und Mähren." September 1941. U.S. National Archives. Captured German Documents, Records of German Field Commands, Record Group 242, T-501, Roll 101.

Bochove, Cornelis A. van, and Wim van Sorge. "Constant Wealth National Income: Accounting for War Damage with an Application to the Netherlands, 1940–45." *Review of Income and Wealth* 35, no. 2 (June 1989): 187–208.

Brandes, Detlef. *Die Tschechen unter deutschem protektorat.* 2 vols. Munich: R. Oldenbourg, 1969.

Brandt, Karl. *Management of Agriculture and Food in the German-Occupied and other Areas of Fortress Europe: A Study in Military Government.* Stanford: Stanford University Press, 1953.

Buchheim, Christoph. "Die besetzten Länder im Dienste der deutschen Kriegswirtschaft während des Zweiten Weltkriegs." *Vierteljahrshefte für Zeitgeschichte* 34, no. 2 (April 1986): 117–45.

Carr, William. *Arms, Autarky, and Aggression: A Study in German Foreign Policy, 1933–1939.* London: Edwin Arnold, 1972.

Carroll, Berenice. *Design for Total War: Arms and Economics in the Third Reich.* The Hague: Mouton, 1968.

Chapman, Brian. "The German Counter Resistance." In *Resistance in Europe, 1939–1945*, edited by Stephen Hawes and Ralph White, 170–85. London: Allen Lane, 1975.

Crankshaw, Edward. *Gestapo: Instrument of Tyrrany.* London: Greenhill, 1990.

Dallin, Alexander. *German Rule in Russia 1941–1945.* New York: Oxford University Press, 1957.

Declas, Gérard. "Les usines Berliet, 1895–1949." *De Renault Frères* 3 (December 1979): 326–33.

Dejonghe, Etienne. "Pénurie charbonnière et répartition en France (1940–1944)." *Revue d'histoire de la deuxième guerre mondiale*, no. 102 (April 1976): 21–55.

Delarue, Jacques. *Gestapo: A History of Horror.* Translated by M. Savill. London: Macdonald, 1964.

Desquesnes, Rémy. "'Atlantikwall' et 'Südwall.' La défense allemande sur le littoral français (1941–1944)." Thèse d'Etat, University of Caen, 1987.

de Vlaminick, Michaël. "L'industrie de l'armement en Belgique sous l'occupation (1940–1944)." *Revue du Nord*, no. 2 spécial hors-série (1987): 379–96.

Duic, Mario. "Widerstand gegen Aggressoren in Industriestaaten am Beispiel Westeuropas im Zweiten Weltkrieg." *Osterreichische Militarische Zeitschrift* 11, no. 3 (1983): 326–31; and 12, no. 1 (1984): 43–47.

Durand, Paul. *La SNCF pendant la guerre.* Paris: Presses Universitaires de France, 1969.

Estes, Kenneth W. "A European Anabasis: Western European Volunteers in the German Army and SS, 1940–1945." Ph.D diss., University of Maryland, 1984.

Evrard, Jacques. *La déportation des travailleurs français dans le IIIe Reich.* Paris: Fayard, 1972.

Foot, M. R. D. *Resistance: European Resistance to Nazism, 1940–1945.* New York: McGraw-Hill, 1977.

———. *S.O.E. in France: An Account of the Work of the British Special Operations Executive in France, 1940–44.* Rev. ed. London: Her Majesty's Stationery Office, 1968.

France. Institute National de la Statistique et des Etudes Economiques. *Annuaire statistique, 1966.* Paris: Imprimerie Nationale, 1967.

———. Institute National de la Statistique et des Etudes Economiques. *Mouvement économique en France de 1938 à 1948.* Paris: Imprimerie Nationale, 1950.

———. Présidence du Conseil, Commission Consultative des Dommages et des Reparations. *Dommages subis par la France et l'Union Française du fait de la guerre et de l'occupation ennemie (1939–1945), Part imputable à l'Allemagne.* 9 vols. Paris: Imprimerie Nationale, 1947–1951.

Freris, A. F. *The Greek Economy in the Twentieth Century*. London: Croom Helm, 1986.

Fridenson, Patrick. "Automobile Workers in France and Their Work, 1914–83." In *Work in France: Representations, Meaning, Organization, and Practice*, edited by Steven L. Kaplan and Cynthia J. Koepp, 514–47. Ithaca: Cornell University Press, 1986.

Fritz, Martin. *German Steel and Swedish Iron Ore, 1939–1945*. Publications of the Institute of Economic History, no. 29. Göteborg: Gothenburg University, 1974.

Germany. Supreme Command, Research Office for Military Economy (OKW, Forschungsstelle für Wehrwirtschaft). "Die finanziellen Leistungen der besetzten Gebiete bis Ende März 1944," October 1944. Reproduced with commentary in Christoph Buchheim, "Die besetzten Länder im Dienste der deutschen Kriegswirtschaft während des Zweiten Weltkriegs." *Vierteljahrshefte für Zeitgeschichte* 34 (April 1986): 117–45.

Gillingham, John. *Belgian Business in the Nazi New Order*. Gent: Jan Dhondt Stichting, 1977.

———. "How Belgium Survived: The Food Supply Problems of an Occupied Nation." In *Agriculture and Food Supply in the Second World War*, edited by Bernd Martin and Alan S. Milward, 69–86. Ostfildern: Scripta Murcaturae Verlag, 1985.

———. *Industry and Politics in the Third Reich: Ruhr Coal, Hitler and Europe*. London: Methuen, 1985.

Goebbels, Joseph. *The Goebbels Diaries, 1939–1941*. Translated and edited by F. Taylor. New York: Penguin, 1982.

———. *The Goebbels Diaries, 1942–943*. Translated and edited by L. Lochner. Garden City, N.Y.: Doubleday & Co., 1948.

Gordon, Bertram. *Collaborationism in France during the Second World War*. Ithaca: Cornell University Press, 1980.

Griffin, David E. "The Battle of France, 1940: The Role of the French Air Force." *Aerospace Historian* 21, no. 3 (September, 1974): 144–53.

Gross, Jan. *Polish Society under the German Occupation: the General Government 1939–45*. Princeton: Princeton University Press, 1979.

Haestrup, Jørgen. *European Resistance Movements, 1939–1945: A Complete History*. Westport, Conn.: Meckler, 1981.

Hallie, Phillip. *Lest Innocent Blood Be Shed*. New York: Harper & Row, 1979.

Hanson, Joanna K. M. *The Civilian Population and the Warsaw Uprising of 1944*. Cambridge: Cambridge University Press, 1982.

Harrison, Mark. "GDPs of the USSR and Eastern Europe: Towards an Interwar Comparison." *Europe-Asia Studies* 46, no. 2 (1994): 243–59.

Hastings, Max. *Das Reich: Resistance and the March of the 2nd SS Panzer Division through France, 1944*. London: Michael Joseph, 1981.

Hatry, Gilbert. *Louis Renault, patron absolu*. Paris: Editions Lafourcade, 1982.

Hauner, M. "Military Budgets and the Armaments Industry." In *Interwar Policy, the War, and Reconstruction*, edited by M. C. Kaser and E. A. Radice, 49–116.

Herbert, Ulrich. *Fremdarbeiter: Politik und Praxis des "Ausländer-Einsatzes" in der Kriegswirtschaft des dritten Reiches*. Bonn: Dietz, 1985.

———. *A History of Foreign Labor in Germany, 1880–1980: Seasonal Workers / Forced Laborers / Guest Workers*. Translated by William Templer. Ann Arbor: University of Michigan Press, 1990.

Hildebrand, Klaus. *The Foreign Policy of the Third Reich*. Translated by A. Fothergill. Berkeley and Los Angeles: University of California Press, 1973.

Hirschfeld, Gerhard. "Nazi Propaganda in Occupied Western Europe: The Case of the Netherlands." In *Nazi Propaganda: The Power and the Limitations*, edited by David Welch. Beckenham: Croom Helm, 1983.

Hoffmann, Stanley. *Decline or Renewal: France since the 1930s*. New York: Viking Press, 1974.

Homze, Edward L. *Foreign Labor in Nazi Germany*. Princeton: Princeton University Press, 1967.

Hondros, John L. *Occupation and Resistance: The Greek Agony, 1941–44*. New York: Pella, 1983.

Jensen, W. G. "The Importance of Energy in the First and Second World Wars." *Historical Journal* 11, no. 3 (1968): 538–54.

Jones, Adrian. "Illusions of Sovereignty: Business and the Organization of Committees of Vichy France." *Social History* 11 (January 1986): 1–31.

Karter, Matthew Simon. "Coercion and Resistance—Dependence and Compliance: The Germans, Vichy, and the French Economy." Ph.D diss., University of Wisconsin, Madison, 1976.

Kaser, M. C., and E. A. Radice, eds. *Interwar Policy, the War, and Reconstruction*. Vol. 2 of *The Economic History of Eastern Europe, 1919–1975*. Oxford: Clarendon, 1986.

Kedward, H. R. *Resistance in Vichy France*. New York: University of Oxford Press, 1978.

Kennan, George F. *Memoirs 1925–1950*. New York: Pantheon Books, 1967.

Klein, Burton. *Germany's Economic Preparations for War*. Cambridge: Harvard University Press, 1959.

Klein, John J. "German Money and Prices, 1932–1944." In *Studies in the Quantity Theory of Money*, edited by Milton Friedman, 121–59. Chicago: University of Chicago Press, 1956.

Klemm, Peter F. "German Economic Policies in Belgium from 1940 to 1944." Ph.D. diss., University of Michigan, 1973.

Kliment, Charles K., and Hilary Louis Doyle, *Czechoslovak Armoured Fighting Vehicles, 1918–1945: Development for Czechoslovakia, Exploitation by Germany*. Watford: Argus, 1979.

Kossman, E. H. *The Low Countries, 1780–1940*. Oxford: Clarendon, 1978.

Krejčí, Jaroslav. "The Bohemian-Moravian War Economy." In *Interwar Policy, the War, and Reconstruction*, edited by M. C. Kaser and E. A. Radice, 452–92.

———. *Social Change and Stratification in Postwar Czechoslovakia*. London: Macmillan, 1972.

Liang, Hsi-Huey. *The Rise of Modern Police and the European State System from Metternich to the Second World War*. Cambridge: Cambridge University Press, 1988.

Linz, Juan J. "Comparative Study of Fascism." In *Fascism: A Reader's Guide*, edited by Walter Lacqueur, 3–121. Berkeley and Los Angeles: University of California Press, 1976.

Littlejohn, David. *The Patriotic Traitors: A History of Collaboration in German Occupied Europe, 1940–45.* Garden City, N.Y.: Doubleday, 1972.

Loubet, Jean-Louis. *Automobiles Peugeot: Une réussite industrielle 1945–1974.* Paris: Economica, 1990.

———. "La Societé Anonyme André Citroën, 1924–1968, étude historique." Thèse de doctorat de 3ème cycle, Université de Paris X, 1979.

Luza, Radomir. "The Czech Resistance Movement." In *A History of the Czechoslovak Republic, 1918–1948,* edited by Radomir Luza and Victor S. Mamatey, 343–61. Princeton: Princeton University Press, 1973.

Maier, Charles S. *In Search of Stability: Explorations in Historical Political Economy.* Cambridge: Cambridge University Press, 1987.

Mamatey, Victor S. "The Development of Czechoslovak Democracy, 1920–1938." In *A History of the Czechoslovak Republic, 1918–1948,* edited by Radomir Luza and Victor S. Mamatey, 99–166. Princeton: Princeton University Press, 1973.

Martin, Bernd, and Alan S. Milward, eds. *Agriculture and Food Supply in the Second World War.* Ostfildern: Scripta Murcaturae Verlag, 1985.

Mason, Tim W. "The Primacy of Politics—Politics and Economics in National Socialist Germany." In *Nazism and the Third Reich,* edited by Henry A. Turner, 175–200. New York: Quadrangle, 1972.

Mastny, Voijech. *The Czechs under Nazi Rule: The Failure of National Resistance 1939–1942.* New York: Columbia University Press, 1971.

Meglen, Alfred. "Les chars tcheques dans l'armée d'Hitler." *Revue historique de l'Armée* 21, no. 2 (1965): 151–54.

Michel, Henri. *The Shadow War: European Resistance, 1939–1945.* Translated by Richard Barry. New York: Harper & Row, 1972.

Milward, Alan S. "Could Sweden have Stopped the Second World War?" *Scandinavian Economic History Review* 15, nos. 1–2 (1967): 127–38.

———. "The Economic and Strategic Effectiveness of Resistance." In *Resistance in Europe, 1939–1945,* edited by Stephen Hawes and Ralph White, 186–203. London: Allen Lane, 1975.

———. "The End of the Blitzkrieg." *Economic History Review,* 2d ser., vol. 16 (1963–1964): 499–518.

———. *The Fascist Economy in Norway.* Oxford: Clarendon, 1972.

———. *The German Economy at War.* London: Athalone Press, 1965.

———. *The New Order and the French Economy.* Oxford: Clarendon, 1970.

———. *War, Economy and Society, 1939–1945.* Berkeley and Los Angeles: University of California Press, 1977.

Mitchell, Brian R. *International Historical Statistics: Europe, 1790–1988.* 3d ed. New York: Stockton Press, 1992.

Morgan, Ted. *An Uncertain Hour: The French, the Germans, the Jews, the Barbie Trial, and the City of Lyon, 1940–1945.* New York: William Morrow, 1990.

Mulligan, Timothy P. *The Politics of Illusion and Empire: German Occupation Policy in the Soviet Union, 1942–1943.* New York: Praeger, 1988.

Murray, Williamson. *The Change in the European Balance of Power, 1938–1939: The Path to Ruin.* Princeton: Princeton University Press, 1984.

Olsson, Sven-Olof. *German Coal and Swedish Fuel 1939–1945.* Publications of the Institute of Economic History, no. 36. Göteborg: Gothenburg University, 1975.

Overy, Richard J. "German Multinationals and the Nazi State in Occupied Europe." In *Multinational Enterprise in Historical Perspective*, edited by Alice Teichova, Maurice Lévy-Leboyer, and Helga Nussbaum, 299–325. Cambridge: Cambridge University Press, 1986.

———. "Germany, 'Domestic Crisis' and War in 1939." *Past and Present*, no. 116 (1987): 138–68.

———. *Goering: The "Iron Man."* Boston: Routledge & Kegan Paul, 1984.

———. "Hitler's War and the German Economy: A Reinterpretation." *Economic History Review*, 2d ser., vol. 35 (1982): 272–91.

———. "Mobilization for Total War in Germany 1939–1941." *English Historical Review* 103, no. 408 (July 1988): 613–39.

Overy, Richard J., David Kaiser, and Tim Mason. "Debate: Germany, 'Domestic Crisis' and War in 1939." *Past and Present*, no. 122 (1989): 200–240.

Payne, Stanley G. "Fascism in Western Europe." In *Fascism: A Reader's Guide*, edited by Walter Lacqueur, 295–311. Berkeley and Los Angeles: University of California Press, 1976.

Paxton, Robert O. *Vichy France: Old Guard and New Order, 1940–1944.* New York: Columbia University Press, 1972.

Paxton, Robert O., and Michael R. Marrus. *Vichy France and the Jews.* New York: Schocken, 1981.

Pfahlmann, Hans. *Fremdarbeiter und Kriegsgefangene in der deutschen Kriegswirtschaft 1939–1945.* Beiträge zur Wehrforschung, vol. 16/17. Darmstadt: Wehr und Wissen Verlagsgesellschaft, 1968.

Picard, Fernand. *L'Epopée de Renault.* Paris: Albin Michel, 1976.

Radice, E. A. "Agriculture and Food." In *Interwar Policy, the War, and Reconstruction*, edited by M. C. Kaser and E. A. Radice, 366–97.

———. "Changes in Property Relationships and Financial Arrangements." In *Interwar Policy, the War, and Reconstruction*, edited by M. C. Kaser and E. A. Radice, 329–65.

———. "Territorial Changes, Population Movements and Labor Supplies." In *Interwar Policy, the War, and Reconstruction*, edited by M. C. Kaser and E. A. Radice, 309–28.

Raspin, Angela. *The Italian War Economy, 1940–1943, with Particular Reference to Italian Relations with Germany.* New York: Garland, 1986.

Reitlinger, Gerald. *The SS: Alibi of a Nation, 1922–1945.* New York: Viking Press, 1957.

Rhode, Gotthold. "The Protectorate of Bohemia and Moravia, 1939–1945." In *A History of the Czechoslovak Republic, 1918–1948*, edited by Radomir Luza and Victor S. Mamatey, 296-321. Princeton: Princeton University Press, 1973.

Rich, Norman. *Hitler's War Aims.* 2 vols. New York: Norton, 1973, 1974.

Rings, Werner. *Life with the Enemy: Collaboration and Resistance in Hitler's Europe, 1939–1945.* Translated by J. M. Brownjohn. Garden City, N.Y.: Doubleday, 1982.

Riste, Olav. "German Occupation of Norway in World War II." In *Armies of*

Occupation, edited by R. A. Prete and A. H. Ion, 145–55. Waterloo, Ontario: Wilfred Laurier University Press, 1984.

Ropp, Theodore. *War in the Modern World.* New York: Collier, 1962.

Schlarp, Karl-Heinz. *Wirtschaft und Besatzung in Serbien 1941–1944: Ein Beitrag zur nationalsozialistischen Wirtschaftspolitik in Südosteuropa.* Stuttgart: Franz Steiner Verlag Weisbaden, 1986.

Schulte, Theo J. *The German Army and Nazi Policies in Occupied Russia.* Oxford: Berg, 1988.

Seaton, Albert. *The German Army, 1933–1945.* New York: St. Martins Press, 1982.

Smith, Arthur L., Jr. *Hitler's Gold: The Story of the Nazi War Loot.* Oxford: Berg, 1989.

Smith, M. L. "The Anti-Bolshevik Crusade and Europe." In *Making the New Europe: European Unity and the Second World War,* edited by M. L. Smith and Peter M. R. Stirk, 46–65. New York: Pinter, 1990.

Smith, Woodruff D. *The Ideological Origins of Nazi Imperialism.* New York: Oxford University Press, 1986.

Sorge, Martin G. *The Other Price of Hitler's War: German Military and Civilian Losses Resulting from World War II.* New York: Greenwood Press, 1986.

Stengers, Jean. "Belgium." In *The European Right: A Historical Profile,* edited by Hans Rogger and Eugen Weber, 128–67. Berkeley and Los Angeles: University of California Press, 1965.

Stoakes, Geoffrey. *Hitler and the Quest for World Domination.* Leamington Spa: Berg, 1986.

Sweets, John F. *Choices in Vichy France: The French under Nazi Occupation.* New York: Oxford University Press, 1986.

———. "La police et la population dans la France de Vichy: Une étude de cas conforme et fidèle." *Revue d'histoire de la deuxième guerre mondiale,* no. 155 (July 1981): 63–73.

Thomadakis, Stavros B. "Black Markets, Inflation, and Force in the Economy of Occupied Greece." In *Greece in the 1940s: A Nation in Crisis,* edited by John O. Iatrides, 61–80. Hanover, N.H.: University Press of New England, 1981.

Umbreit, Hans. "Les pouvoirs allemands en France et en Belgique." *Revue du Nord,* no. 2—special series (1987): 5–40.

United Nations. Department of Economic and Social Affairs. *Growth of the World's Urban and Rural Population, 1920–2000.* New York: United Nations, 1969.

United States. Strategic Bombing Survey. *Reports,* nos. 55, 200, 203. Washington, D.C., January 1947.

Van Den Wijngaert, Marc. "La politique du moindre mal. La politique due Comité des Secrétaires Généraux en Belgique sous l'occupation allemande, 1940–1944." *Revue du Nord,* no. 2—special series (1987): 63–72.

Van Der Zee, Henri. *The Hunger Winter: Occupied Holland, 1944–45.* London: Jill Norman & Hobhouse, 1982.

Van Doorslaer, Rudi. "La police belge et le maintien de l'ordre en Belgique occupée." *Revue du Nord,* no.2—special series (1987): 73–101.

Volkmann, Hans-Erich. "Autarkie, Grossraumwirtschaft und Aggression: Zur ökonomischen Motivation der Besetzung Luxemburgs, Belgiens und der Niederlande 1940." *Militärgeschichtliche Mitteilungen* 1 (1976): 51–76.

———. "L'Importance économique de la Lorraine pour le IIIe Reich." *Revue d'histoire de la deuxième guerre mondiale*, no. 120 (1980): 69–93.

———. "The National Socialist Economy in Preparation for War." In *The Build-up of German Aggression*. Vol. 1 of *Germany and the Second World War*, edited by Wilhelm Deist et al., 157–372. Oxford: Clarendon, 1990.

Warmbrunn, Werner. *The Dutch under German Occupation, 1940–1945*. Stanford: Stanford University Press, 1963.

Weber, Wolfram. *Die innere Sicherheit im besetzten Belgien und Nordfrankreich 1940–44*. Düsseldorf: Droste, 1978.

Webster, Charles, and Noble Frankland. *The Strategic Air Offensive against Germany, 1939–1945*. 4 vols. London: Her Majesty's Stationery Office, 1961.

Wilmot, Chester. *The Struggle for Europe*. London: Collins, 1952.

Wilt, Alan F. *The Atlantic Wall: Hitler's Defenses in the West, 1941–1944*. Ames: Iowa State University Press, 1975.

Winkel, Harald. "Die wirtschaftlichen Beziehungen Deutschlands zu Dänemark in den Jahren der Besetzung 1940–45." In *Probleme der nationalsozialistischen Wirtschaftspolitik*, edited by Friedrich-Wilhelm Henning, 119–74. Gesellschaft für Wirtschafts- und Sozialwissenschaften, Neue Folge Band 89. Berlin: Duncker & Humblot, 1976.

Wright, Gordon. "Reflections on the French Resistance." *Political Science Quarterly* 77, no. 3 (September 1962): 336–49.

Young, Robert J. *In Command of France: French Foreign Policy and Military Planning, 1933–1940*. Cambridge: Harvard University Press, 1978.

Belgium and Luxembourg, 1914–1918
(Chapter 4)

Armeson, R. B. *Total Warfare and Compulsory Labor*. The Hague: Ninjoff, 1965.

Baudhuin, Fernand. *Histoire économique de la Belgique 1914–1939*. 2d ed. 2 vols. Bruxelles: Emile Bruylant, 1946.

Belgium. *Annuaire Statistique de la Belgique et du Congo Belge, 1915–1919*. Vol. 46. Bruxelles: 1922.

Belgium. Commission d'enquête sur les violations des règles du droit des gens, des lois et des coutumes de la guerre. *Rapport sur les mesures prises par les allemands a l'égard de l'industrie belge pendant l'occupation*. Vol. 3 of *Rapports et Documents d'Enquête*. Bruxelles: Thone, 1921.

Belgium. Ministère de l'Industrie, du Travail et du Ravitailement, Administration des Mines. *Extrait de la Statistique des Industries extractives et métallurgiques en Belgique pour les Années, 1913–1918*. Bruxelles: Narisse, 1919.

Berghahn, V. R. *Germany and the Approach of War in 1914*. New York: St. Martin's Press, 1973.

Bittmann, Karl. *Im besetzten Belgien (1914–1917)*. Vol. 3 of *Werken und Wirken: Erinnerungen aus Industrie und Staatsdienst*. Karlsruhe in Baden: Verlag C. J. Müller, 1924.

Boulin, Pierre. *L'organisation du travail dans la région envahie de la France pendant l'occupation*. Paris: Les Presses Universitaires de France, 1927.

Faber, M. E. *La métallurgie du Luxembourg: Etude de géographie physique, sociale et economique*. Luxembourg: Editions Luxembourgeoises, 1927.

Farrar, L. L., Jr. *Divide and Conquer: German Efforts to Conclude a Separate Peace, 1914–1918*. New York: Columbia University Press, 1978.

Feldman, Gerald. *Army, Industry and Labor in Germany 1914–1918*. Princeton: Princeton University Press, 1966.

Fischer, Fritz. *Germany's Aims in the First World War*. New York: W. W. Norton, 1967.

———. *War of Illusions*. Translated by M. Jackson. New York: W. W. Norton, 1975.

Fontaine, Arthur. *French Industry during the War*. New Haven: Yale University Press, 1926.

Gatzke, Hans. *Germany's Drive to the West (Drang nach Westen): A Study of Germany's Western War Aims during the First World War*. Baltimore: Johns Hopkins Press, 1966.

Gay, George I. *The Commission for Relief in Belgium: Statistical Review of Relief Operations*. Stanford: Stanford University Press, 1925.

Gay, Geroge I., and H. H. Fisher. *Public Relations of the Commission for Relief in Belgium*. Vol. 1. Stanford: Stanford University Press, 1929.

Geiss, Imanuel. *German Foreign Policy, 1871–1914*. London: Routledge & Kegan Paul, 1976.

Grand Duchy of Luxembourg. *Neutralité du Grand-Duché pendant la guerre de 1914–1918: Attitude des pouvoirs publics*. Luxembourg: Imprimerie Victor Buck, 1919.

Grand Duchy of Luxembourg. Chambre de Commerce. *Rapport général sur la situation de l'industrie et due commerce pendant l'année 1918*. Luxembourg: Imprimerie Victor Buck, 1919.

Grand Duchy of Luxembourg. Commission d'étude des problèmes économiques posés par la guerre et ses conséquences éventuelles. *Travaux de la Commission sur l'orientation économique du Grand-Duché de Luxembourg*. Luxembourg: Imprimerie Victor Buck, 1919.

Grebler, Leo, and Wilhelm Winkler. *The Cost of the World War to Germany and to Austria-Hungary*. New Haven: Yale University Press, 1940.

Gribble, Francis. *In Luxembourg in Wartime*. London: Headly Bros., 1916.

Hardach, Gerd. *The First World War, 1914–1918*. Berkeley: University of California Press, 1977.

Hemmer, Carlo. *L'économie du Grand-Duché de Luxembourg*. 2 vols. Luxembourg: Beffort, 1948.

Henry, Albert. *La ravitaillement de la Belgique pendant l'occupation allemande*. Paris: Presses Universitaires de France, 1924.

Herbert, Ulrich. *A History of Foreign Labor in Germany, 1880–1980: Seasonal Workers / Forced Laborers / Guest Workers*. Translated by William Templer. Ann Arbor: University of Michigan Press, 1990.

Hillgruber, Andreas. *Germany and the Two World Wars*. Translated by W. Kirby. Cambridge: Harvard University Press, 1981.

Hoover, Herbert C. *The Relief of Belgium and Northern France, 1914–1930.* Vol. 1 of *An American Epic.* Chicago: Henry Regnery, 1959.

Joll, James. *Origins of the First World War.* New York: Longman, 1984.

Kaiser, David E. "Germany and the Origins of the First World War." *Journal of Modern History* 55 (September 1983): 442–74.

Keiger, John F. V. *France and the Origins of the First World War.* New York: St. Martin's, 1983.

Kerchove de Denterghem, Charles. *L'industrie belge pendant l'occupation allemande, 1914–1918.* Paris: Presses Universitaires Français, 1927.

Köhler, Ludwig von. *The Administration of the Occupied Territories.* Translated by W. Dittmar. New York: Carnegie Endowment for International Peace, 1942.

Leprince-Ringuet, M. F. *Rapport sur l'industrie minière en Meurthe-et-Moselle pendant les années 1914 à 1918.* Nancy: Imprimerie Berger-Levrault, 1919.

Mitchell, Brian R. *International Historical Statistics: Europe, 1750–1988.* 3d ed. New York: Stockton Press, 1992.

Mounier, Jean. *L'état actuel de la question du Luxembourg.* Paris: Jouve, 1920.

Newcomer, James. *The Grand Duchy of Luxembourg: The Evolution of Nationhood, 963 A.D. to 1983.* New York: University Press of America, 1984.

Offer, Avner. *The First World War: An Agrarian Interpretation.* Oxford: Clarendon, 1989.

Passelecq, Fernand. *Deportation et travail forcé des ouvriers et de la population civile de la Belgique occupée (1916–1918).* Paris: Presses Universitaires Français, 1928.

Pesquiès-Courbier, S. "Le bassin ferrifère de Briey durant la guerre de 1914–1918." *Revue historique des armées,* no. 2 (1981): 99–128.

Pirenne, Henri. *La Belgique et la Guerre Mondiale.* Paris: Presses Universitaires Français, 1928.

Ritter, Gerhard. *The Tragedy of Statesmanship—Bethmann Hollweg as War Chancellor, 1914–1917.* Vol. 3 of *The Sword and the Scepter: The Problem of Militarism in Germany.* Trans. H. Norden. Coral Gables, Fla: University of Miami Press, 1972.

Schmitt, Hans A. "Violated Neutrals: Belgium, the Dwarf States, and Luxemburg." in *Neutral Europe between War and Revolution, 1917–23,* edited by Hans A. Schmitt, 204–34. Charlottesville: University Press of Virginia, 1988.

Shepherd, Henry L. *The Monetary Experience of Belgium, 1914–1936.* Princeton: Princeton University Press, 1936.

Smith, Woodruff D. *The Ideological Origins of Nazi Imperialism.* New York: Oxford University Press, 1986.

Solansky, Adolf. "German Administration in Belgium." Ph.D. diss., Columbia University, 1928.

Steichen, Joseph. *Exposé de la situation économique et financière du Grand-Duché de Luxembourg.* Luxembourg: Gieser, 1920.

Trausch, Gilbert. *Contributions à l'histoire sociale de la question du Luxembourg, 1914–1922.* Luxembourg: Saint-Paul, 1974.

Veraghtert, Karel. "Le développement industriel." In *L'industrie en Belgique: deux siècles d'évolution 1780–1980.* Gent: Snoeck-Ducaju & Zoon, 1981.

Wagner, Camille. *La sidérurgie luxembougeoise sous les régimes du Zollverein et de l'union économique belgo-luxembourgeoise.* Luxembourg: Artistique Luxembourgeoise, 1931.

Wanty, Emile. "La vie militaire." In John Bartier et al., *Histoire de la Belgique contemporaine 1914–1970*, 331–87. Bruxelles: La Renaissance du Livre, 1975.

Whitlock, Brand. *Belgium: A Personal Narrative.* 2 vols. New York: D. Appleton, 1919.

Winterfeldt, Hans von. "Die Deutsche Verwaltung des Generalgouverments in Belgien 1914–1918." In *Die Organisationen der Kriegführung.* Vol. 10 of *Der grosse Krieg, 1914–1918,* edited by M. Schwarte, 1–110. Leipzig: J. Barth, 1923.

Zilch, Reinhold. "Die Memoranden Karl Helfferichs vom 28. und 29. August 1914 über die finanzielle Unterdrückung und Ausplünderung Belgiens." *Jahrbuch für Wirtschaftsgeschichte*, no. 4 (1980): 193–212.

The Ruhr-Rhineland, 1923–1924
(Chapter 5)

Allied Powers. Reparations Commission. *Annexes.* U.S. National Archives. Records of the United States Unofficial Delegation to the Reparations Commission, Record Group 43, Entry 26.

Breaud, H. *La régie des chemins de fer des territoires occupés, 1923–1924.* Paris: Chaix, 1938.

Cornbise, Alfred E. "Some Aspects of the German Response to the Ruhr Occupation, January–September 1923." Ph.D diss, University of North Carolina, Chapel Hill, 1965.

Favez, Jean-Claude. *Le Reich devant l'occupation franco-belge de la Ruhr en 1923.* Geneva: Librarie Droz, 1969.

Feldman, Gerald. *Iron and Steel in the German Inflation, 1916–1923.* Princeton: Princeton University Press, 1974.

Flynn, John F. "The 1923 Ruhr Crisis as a Two-front War." Ph.D. diss, Ohio State University, 1977.

France. Armée du Rhin (General Joseph Degoutte). *L'Occupation de la Ruhr,* Rapport d'ensemble du Général Degoutte, personal and secret, 100 exemplaires. Düsseldorf: Imprimerie de l'Armée du Rhin, July 1924.

———. *Un an d'occupation: L'Oeuvre franco-belge dans la Ruhr en 1923.* Düsseldorf: Imprimerie de l'Armée du Rhin, February 1924.

France. Ministère des Finances. *Rapport du Comité des Experts chargé de préparer la conférence des ministres des finances du 7 janvier 1925.* Paris: Imprimerie Nationale, 1925.

Gordon, Harold J., Jr. *The Reichswehr and the German Republic, 1919–1926.* Princeton: Princeton University Press, 1957.

Great Britain. Department of Overseas Trade (J. W. F. Thelwall and C. J. Kavanagh). *Report on the Economic and Financial Conditions in Germany, Revised to April 1924.* London: Department of Overseas Trade, 1924.

Jacobson, Jon. "Strategies of French Foreign Policy after World War I." *Journal of Modern History* 55, no. 1 (March 1983): 88–117.

Jones, K. P. "Stresemann, the Ruhr Crisis, and Rhenish Separatism: A Case Study of *Westpolitik.*" *European Studies Review* 7 (1977): 318–19.

Kent, Bruce. *The Spoils of War: The Politics, Economics, and Diplomacy of Reparations, 1918–1932*. Oxford: Clarendon, 1989.

Keynes, John Maynard. *The Economic Consequences of the Peace*. London: Macmillan, 1920.

Kindleberger, Charles. *A Financial History of Western Europe*. London: Allen & Unwin, 1984.

Maier, Charles S. *Recasting Bourgeois Europe: Stabilization in France, Germany, and Italy in the Decade after World War I*. Princeton: Princeton University Press, 1975.

Mantoux, Etienne. *The Carthaginian Peace, or the Economic Consequences of Mr. Keynes*. London: Oxford University Press, 1946.

Marks, Sally. *Innocent Abroad: Belgium at the Paris Peace Conference of 1919*. Chapel Hill: University of North Carolina Press, 1981.

McDougall, Walter A. *France's Rhineland Diplomacy, 1914–1924: The Last Bid for a Balance of Power in Europe*. Princeton: Princeton University Press, 1978.

Paoli, François-André. *La phase de fermeté (11 janvier 1920 - 17 juin 1924)*. Vol. 2 of *L'Armée française de 1919 à 1939*. Paris: Service historique de l'armée, 1969.

Rupieper, Hermann J. *The Cuno Government and Reparations, 1922–1923: Politics and Economics*. The Hague: Martinus Nijhoff, 1979.

Saunders, Donald B. "Stresemann vs. Poincaré: the Conduct of Germany's Western Policy during Gustav Stresemann's Chancellorship, August–November 1923." Ph.D diss., University of North Carolina, Chapel Hill, 1974.

Schuker, Stephen A. *American "Reparations" to Germany, 1919–1933: Implications for the Third-World Debt Crisis*. Princeton Studies in International Finance, no. 61. Princeton: Princeton University Press, 1988.

———. *The End of French Predominance in Europe: The Financial Crisis of 1924 and the Adoption of the Dawes Plan*. Chapel Hill: University of North Carolina Press, 1976.

Sternstein, Wolfgang. "The *Ruhrkampf* of 1923: Economic Problems of Civilian Defence." In *Civilian Resistance as a National Defence*, edited by Adam Roberts, 128–61. Harmondsworth: Penguin, 1969.

Tirard, Paul. *La France sur le Rhin: Douze années d'occupation rhénane*. Paris: Librarie Plon, 1930.

Toynbee, Arnold J. *Survey of International Affairs, 1924*. Oxford: Oxford University Press, 1926.

Trachtenberg, Marc. *Reparation in World Politics: France and European Diplomacy 1916–1923*. New York: Columbia University Press, 1980.

Weill-Raynal, Etienne. *Les réparations allemandes et la France*. 3 vols. Paris: Nouvelles Editions Latines, 1947.

The Japanese Empire, 1910–1945
(Chapter 6)

Amsden, Alice H. "The State and Taiwan's Economic Development." In *Bringing the State Back In*. Edited by Peter B. Evans, Dietrich Rueschemeyer, and Theda Skocpol, 78–106. Cambridge: Cambridge University Press, 1985.

Bairoch, Paul. *The Economic Development of The Third World since 1900*.

Translated by Cynthia Postan. Berkeley and Los Angeles: University of California Press, 1975.

Baker, Edward J. "The Role of Legal Reforms in the Japanese Annexation and Rule of Korea, 1905–1919." In *Studies on Korea in Transition*, edited by David R. McCann, John Middleton, and Edward J. Shultz, 17–42. Honolulu: University of Hawaii, 1979.

Barnhart, Michael A. *Japan Prepares for Total War: The Search for Economic Security, 1919–1941*. Ithaca: Cornell University Press, 1988.

Beasley, W. G. *Japanese Imperialism, 1894–1945*. Oxford: Clarendon, 1987.

Bix, Herbert P. "Japanese Imperialism and the Manchurian Economy, 1900–1931." *China Quarterly*, no. 51 (July–September 1972): 425–43.

Boulding, Kenneth E., and Alan H. Gleason. "War as an Investment: The Strange Case of Japan." In *Economic Imperialism*, edited by Kenneth E. Boulding and Tapan Mukerjee, 240–61. Ann Arbor: University of Michigan Press, 1972.

Boyle, John H. *China and Japan at War, 1937–1945: The Politics of Collaboration*. Stanford: Stanford University Press, 1972.

Caron, François. *An Economic History of Modern France*. Translated by Barbara Bray. New York: Columbia University Press, 1979.

Chang, Yunshik. "Colonization as Planned Change: The Korean Case." *Modern Asian Studies* 5 (1971): 161–86.

Chao, Kang. *The Economic Development of Manchuria: The Rise of a Frontier Economy*. Michigan Papers in Chinese Studies no. 43. Ann Arbor: Center for Chinese Studies, University of Michigan, 1983.

Chen, Ching-chih. "Japanese Socio-Political Control in Taiwan, 1895–1945." Ph.D. diss., Harvard University, 1973.

———. "Police and Community Control Systems in the Empire." In *Japanese Colonial Empire*, edited by Ramon H. Myers and Mark Peattie, 213–39.

Chen, Edward I-Te. "Formosan Political Movements under Japanese Colonial Rule, 1914–1937." *Journal of Asian Studies* 31, no. 3 (May 1972): 477–97.

———. "Japanese Colonialism in Korea and Formosa: A Comparison of its Effects upon the Development of Nationalism." Ph.D. diss., University of Pennsylvania, 1968.

———. "Japanese Colonialism in Korea and Formosa: A Comparison of the Systems of Political Control." *Harvard Journal of Asiatic Studies* 30 (1970): 126–58.

———. "Japan's Decision to Annex Taiwan: A Study of Ito-Mutsu Diplomacy." *Journal of Asian Studies* 37, no. 1 (November 1977): 61–72.

Choi, Hochin. *The Economic History of Korea: From the Earliest Times to 1945*. Seoul: Freedom Library, 1971.

Chou, Wan-yao. "The Kominka Movement in Taiwan and Korea: Comparisons and Interpretations." In *Japanese Wartime Empire*, edited by Peter Duus, Ramon Myers, and Mark Peattie.

Cohen, Jerome B. *Japan's Economy in War and Reconstruction*. Minneapolis: University of Minnesota Press, 1949.

Conroy, Hilary. *The Japanese Seizure of Korea, 1868–1910: A Study of Realism and Idealism in International Relations*. Philadelphia: University of Pennsylvania Press, 1960.

s CHAPTER 6   231

Coox, Alvin D. "The Kwantung Army Dimension." In *Japanese Informal Empire*, edited by Peter Duus, Ramon Myers, and Mark Peattie, 395–428.

———. *Nomonhan: Japan against Russia, 1939.* 2 vols. Stanford: Stanford University Press, 1985.

Crowley, James B. "Japan's Military Foreign Policies." In *Japan's Foreign Policy 1868–1941: A Research Guide*, edited by James W. Morley, 3–117. New York: Columbia University Press, 1974.

———. *Japan's Quest for Autonomy: National Security and Foreign Policy, 1930–1938.* Princeton: Princeton University Press, 1966.

Cummings, Bruce. "The Northeast Asian Political Economy." *International Organization* 38, no. 1 (Winter 1984): 1–40.

Dong, Wonmo. "Assimilation and Social Mobilization in Korea." In *Korea Under Japanese Colonial Rule: Studies of the Policy and Techniques of Japanese Colonialism*, edited by Andrew C. Nahm, 146–82ed. Kalamazoo: Center for Korean Studies, Western Michigan University, 1973.

———. "Japanese Colonial Policy and Practice in Korea." Ph.D. diss., Georgetown University, 1965.

Dower, John. "The Useful War." *Daedalus* 119, no. 3 (Summer 1990): 49–70.

Duus, Peter. "Economic Dimensions of Meiji Imperialism: The Case of Korea, 1895–1910." In *Japanese Colonial Empire*, edited by Ramon H. Myers and Mark Peattie, 128–71.

Duus, Peter, Ramon H. Myers, and Mark Peattie, eds. *Japanese Informal Empire in China, 1895–1937.* Princeton: Princeton University Press, 1989.

———. *The Japanese Wartime Empire, 1931–1945.* Princeton: Princeton University Press, forthcoming.

Eastman, Lloyd E. "Facets of an Ambivalent Relationship: Smuggling, Puppets, and Atrocities during the War, 1937–1945." In *The Chinese and the Japanese: Essays in Political and Cultural Interactions*, edited by Akira Iriye, 275–303. Princeton: Princeton University Press, 1980.

Elsbree, Willard H. *Japan's Role in Southeast Asian Nationalist Movements, 1940 to 1945.* New York: Russell and Russell, 1953.

Eckert, Carter. *Offspring of Empire: The Koch'ang Kims and the Colonial Origins of Korean Capitalism, 1876–1945.* Seattle: University of Washington Press, 1991.

Hara, Akira. "L'économie japonaise pendant la deuxième guerre mondiale." *Revue d'histoire de la deuxième guerre mondiale*, no. 89 (1973): 33–56.

Hayami, Yujiro, and Vernon Ruttan. "Korean Rice, Taiwan Rice and Japanese Agricultural Stagnation: An Economic Consequence of Colonialism." *Quarterly Journal of Economics* 84, no. 4 (November 1970): 562–89.

Henderson, Gregory. *Korea: The Politics of Vortex.* Cambridge: Harvard University Press, 1968.

Hicks, George. "The Comfort Women." In *Japanese Colonial Empire*, edited by Ramon Myers and Mark Peattie.

Ho, Samuel Pao-San. "Colonialism and Development: Korea, Taiwan, and Kwantung." In *Japanese Colonial Empire*, edited by Ramon H. Myers and Mark Peattie, 347–98.

Ho, Samuel Pao-San. *Economic Development of Taiwan, 1860–1970*. New Haven: Yale University Press, 1978.

Huang, Philip C. C. *Peasant Economy and Social Change in North China*. Stanford: Stanford University Press, 1985.

Iriye, Akira. "The Failure of Economic Expansionism: 1918–1931." In *Japan in Crisis*, edited by Bernard Silberman and Harry Harootunian, 237–69. Princeton: Princeton University Press, 1974.

———. "The Failure of Military Expansionism." In *Dilemmas of Growth in Prewar Japan*, edited by James Morley, 107–38. Princeton, Princeton University Press, 1971.

Ito Misuharu. "Munitions Unlimited—The Controlled Economy." *Japan Interpreter* 7, nos. 3–4 (Summer–Autumn 1972): 353–63.

Japan. Government-General of Chosen. *Annual Report, 1937–38*. Tokyo, 1938.

Johnson, Chalmers. *Japan's Public Policy Companies*. Washington, D.C.: American Enterprise Institute, 1978.

———. *MITI and the Japanese Miracle: The Growth of Industrial Policy, 1925–1975*. Stanford: Stanford University Press, 1982.

———. *Peasant Nationalism and Communist Power: The Emergence of Revolutionary China, 1937–1945*. Stanford: Stanford University Press, 1962.

Jones, F. C. *Japan's New Order in East Asia: Its Rise and Fall*. London: Oxford University Press, 1954.

———. *Manchuria since 1931*. New York: Oxford University Press, 1949.

Junju, Banno. "Japanese Industrialists and Merchants and the Anti-Japanese Boycotts in China, 1919–1928." In *Japanese Informal Empire*, edited by Peter Duus, Ramon Myers, and Mark Peattie, 314–29.

Kerr, George H. *Formosa: Licensed Revolution and the Home Rule Movement, 1895–1945*. Honolulu: University Press of Hawaii, 1974.

Kim, C. I. Eugene, and Dorothea Mortimore, eds. *Korea's Response to Japan: The Colonial Period, 1910–1945*. Kalamazoo: Center for Korean Studies, Western Michigan University, 1977.

Kim, C. I. Eugene, and Han-kyo Kim. *Korea and the Politics of Imperialism, 1870–1910*. Berkeley and Los Angeles: University of California Press, 1967.

Kimura, Mitsuhiko. "Financial Aspects of Korea's Economic Growth under Japanese Rule." *Modern Asian Studies* 20, no. 4 (1986): 793–820.

Kinney, Ann Rasmussen. *Japanese Investment in Manchurian Manufacturing, Mining, Transportation and Communications, 1931–1945*. New York: Garland, 1982.

Kramer, Irving I. *Japan in Manchuria*. Tokyo: Foreign Affairs Association, 1954.

Kublin, Hyman. "The Evolution of Japanese Colonialism." *Comparative Studies in Society and History* 2 (October 1959): 67–84.

Lai, Tse-han, Ramon H. Myers, and Wei Wou. *A Tragic Beginning: The Taiwan Uprising of February 28, 1947*. Stanford: Stanford University Press, 1991.

Lamley, Harry. "The 1895 Taiwan War of Resistance: Local Chinese Efforts against a Foreign Power." In *Taiwan: Studies in Local Chinese History*, edited by Leonard Gordon, 23–76. New York: Columbia University Press, 1970.

Lebra, Joyce C., ed. *Japan's Greater East Asia Coprosperity Sphere*. Kuala Lumpur: Oxford University Press, 1975.

Lee, Chong-sik. *Counterinsurgency in Manchuria: The Japanese Experience, 1931–1940*. Rand Memorandum RM-5012-ARPA. Santa Monica: Rand Corporation, 1967.

———. *Revolutionary Struggle in Manchuria: Chinese Communists and Soviet Interest, 1922–1945*. Berkeley and Los Angeles: University of California Press, 1983.

———. *The Politics of Korean Nationalism*. Berkeley and Los Angeles: University of California Press, 1963.

Li, Lincoln. *The Japanese Army in North China, 1937–1941: Problems of Political and Economic Control*. Tokyo: Oxford University Press, 1975.

Lindsay, Michael. *The Unknown War: North China, 1937–1945*. London: Bergström & Boyle Books, 1975.

Lone, Stewart. "Japanese Annexation of Korea in 1910." *Modern Asian Studies* 25, no. 1 (February 1991): 143–73.

The Manchukuo Year Book. Hsinking, Manch: Manchukuo Year Book Co., 1942.

Martin, Bernd, and Alan S. Milward, eds. *Agriculture and Food Supply in the Second World War*. Ostfildern: Scripta Murcaturae Verlag, 1985.

Matsusaka, Y. Tak. "Managing Occupied Manchuria, 1931–1934." In *Japanese Wartime Empire*, edited by Peter Duus, Ramon Myers, and Mark Peattie.

McNamara, Dennis L. *The Colonial Origins of Korean Enterprise, 1910–1945*. Cambridge: Cambridge University Press, 1990.

———. "Comparative Colonial Response: Korea and Taiwan, 1895–1919." *Korean Studies* 10 (1986): 54–68.

Medlicott, W. N. *The Economic Blockade*. 2 vols. London: Her Majesty's Stationery Office, 1952, 1959.

Mizoguchi, Toshiyuki. "The Changing Pattern of Sino-Japanese Trade, 1884–1937." In *Japanese Informal Empire in China*, edited by Peter Duus, Ramon Myers, and Mark Peattie, 10–30.

———. "Consumer Prices and Real Wages in Taiwan and Korea under Japanese Rule." *Hitotsubashi Journal of Economics* 13, no. 1 (June 1972): 40–56.

———. "Economic Growth of Korea under the Japanese Occupation: Background of Industrialization of Korea." *Hitotsubashi Journal of Economics* 20, no. 1 (1979): 1–19.

———. "Foreign Trade in Taiwan and Korea under Japanese Rule." *Hitsotsubashi Journal of Economics* 14, no. 2 (February 1974): 37–53.

Mizoguchi, Toshiyuki, and Mataji Umemura. *Basic Economic Statistics of Former Japanese Colonies, 1895–1938*. Tokyo: Toyo Keizai Shinposha, 1988.

Mizoguchi, Toshiyuki, and Yūzō Yamamoto. "Capital Formation in Taiwan and Korea." In *Japanese Colonial Empire*, edited by Ramon H. Myers and Mark Peattie, 399–419.

Molony, Barbara. "Noguchi Jun and Nichitsu: Colonial Investment Strategy in a High-Technology Enterprise." In *Managing Industrial Enterprise: Cases from Japan's Prewar Experience*, edited by William D. Wray, 229–63. Cambridge: Harvard University Press for the Harvard Council on East Asian Studies: 1989.

———. *Technology and Investment: The Prewar Japanese Chemical Industry*. Cambridge: Harvard University Press for the Harvard Council on East Asian Studies: 1990.

Montgomery, Michael. *Imperialist Japan: The Yen to Dominate.* London: Christopher Helm, 1987.

Morley, James W., ed. *The China Quagmire: Japan's Expansion on the Asian Continent, 1933–1941.* New York: Columbia University Press, 1983.

———. *Dilemmas of Growth in Prewar Japan.* Princeton: Princeton Unversity Press, 1971.

Mote, Frederick W. *Japanese-Sponsored Governments in China, 1937–1945.* Stanford: Stanford University Press, 1954.

Murakushi, Nisaburo. *The Transfer of Coal-Mining Technology from Japan to Manchuria and Manpower Problems—Focusing on the Development of the Fushun Coal Mines.* United Nations University HSDP-JE Series, vol. 47. Tokyo: United Nations University, 1981.

Myers, Ramon H. "Creating a Modern Enclave Economy: The Economic Integration of Japan, Manchuria, and North China, 1932–1945." In *Japanese Wartime Empire,* edited by Peter Duus, Ramon Myers, and Mark Peattie.

———. *The Japanese Economic Development of Manchuria, 1932 to 1945.* New York: Garland, 1982.

———. "Japanese Imperialism in Manchuria: The South Manchuria Railway Company, 1906–1933." In *Japanese Informal Empire,* edited by Peter Duus, Ramon Myers, and Mark Peattie, 101–32.

Myers, Ramon H., and Mark Peattie, eds. *The Japanese Colonial Empire, 1895–1945.* Princeton: Princeton University Press, 1984.

Myers, Ramon H., and Yamada Saburo. "Agricultural Development in the Empire." In *Japanese Colonial Empire,* edited by Ramon Myers and Mark Peattie, 427–46.

Myers, Ramon H., and Thomas R. Ulie. "Foreign Influence and Agricultural Development in Northeast China: A Case Study of the Liaotung Peninsula, 1906–42." *Journal of Asian Studies* 31, no. 2 (February 1972): 329–50.

Nahm, Andrew C., ed. *Korea under Japanese Colonial Rule: Studies of the Policy and Techniques of Japanese Colonialism.* Kalamazoo: Center for Korean Studies, Western Michigan University, 1973.

Nakagane, Katsuji. "Manchukuo and Economic Development." In *Japanese Informal Empire,* edited by Peter Duus, Ramon Myers, and Mark Peattie, 133–57.

Nakamura, Takafusa. *Economic Growth in Prewar Japan.* Translated by R. A. Feldman. New Haven: Yale University Press, 1983.

———. "Japan's Economic Thrust into North China, 1933–1938: Formation of the North China Development Corporation." In *The Chinese and the Japanese: Essays in Political and Cultural Interactions,* edited by Akira Iriye, 220–53. Princeton: Princeton University Press, 1980.

Nish, Ian. *The Origin of the Russo-Japanese War.* New York: Longman, 1986.

Notar, Ernest J. "Japan's Wartime Labor Policy: A Search for Method." *Journal of Asian Studies* 44, no. 2 (February 1985): 311–28.

Ogata, Sadako N. *Defiance in Manchuria.* Berkeley and Los Angeles: University of California Press, 1964.

Peattie, Mark R. *Ishiwara Kanji and Japan's Confrontation with the West.* Princeton: Princeton University Press, 1975.

Pluvier, Jan. *South-East Asia from Colonialism to Independence*. Kuala Lumpur: Oxford University Press, 1974.

Rice, Richard. "Economic Mobilisation in Wartime Japan." *Journal of Asian Studies* 38, no. 4 (August 1979): 689–706.

Robinson, Michael Edson. "Colonial Publication Policy and the Korean Nationalist Movement." In *Japanese Colonial Empire*, edited by Ramon H. Myers and Mark Peattie, 312–43.

———. *Cultural Nationalism in Colonial Korea, 1920–25*. Seattle: University of Washington Press, 1988.

Samuels, Richard J. *The Business of the Japanese State: Energy Markets in Comparative and Historical Perspective*. Ithaca: Cornell University Press, 1987.

Schumpeter, Elizabeth B., ed. *The Industrialization of Japan and Manchuko, 1930–1940: Population, Raw Materials, and Industry*. New York: Macmillan, 1940.

Selden, Mark. *The Yenan Way in Revolutionary China*. Cambridge: Harvard University Press, 1971.

Shiota, Shobei. "A 'Ravaged' People: The Koreans in World War II." *Japan Interpreter* 7 (1971): 43–53.

Suh, Chang-chul. *Growth and Structural Changes in the Korean Economy, 1910–1940*. Harvard East Asian Monographs, no. 83. Cambridge: Harvard University Press, 1978.

Sun, Kungtu C. *The Economic Development of Manchuria in the First Half of the Twentieth Century*. Harvard East Asian Monographs, no. 28. Cambridge: Harvard University Press, 1969.

Supreme Commander for the Allied Powers, Natural Resources Section. *Aluminum Metallurgy in the Japanese Empire*, Report no. 87. Tokyo, 1947.

———. *Fushun Coal Field, Manchuria*, Report no. 68. Tokyo, 1947.

———. *Iron and Steel Metallurgy of the Japanese Empire*, Report no. 50. Tokyo, 1946.

Tsurumi, E. Patricia. "Colonial Education in Korea and Taiwan." In *Japanese Colonial Empire*, edited by Ramon H. Myers and Mark Peattie, 275–311.

Van Slyke, Lyman P. *The Chinese Communist Movement: A Report of the United States War Department, July 1945*. Stanford: Stanford University Press, 1968.

The Soviet Empire, 1945–1989
(Chapter 7)

Adomeit, Hannes. "Gorbachev and German Unification: Revision of Thinking, Realignment of Power." *Problems of Communism* 39 (July–August 1990): 1–23.

Alexandrov, Vladimir. "The Dismantling of German Industry." In *Soviet Economic Policy*, edited by Robert Slusser, 14–17.

Amman, Ronald, and Julian Cooper, eds. *Industrial Innovation in the Soviet Union*. New Haven: Yale University Press, 1982.

Ash, Timothy Garton. *The Polish Revolution: Solidarity, 1980–82*. London: Jonathan Cape, 1983.

———. *The Uses of Adversity*. Cambridge, England: Granta Books, 1989.

Ash, Timothy Garton. *We the People: The Revolution of '89.* Cambridge, England: Granta Books, 1990.

Backer, John H. *The Decision to Divide Germany: American Foreign Policy in Transition.* Durham: Duke University Press, 1978.

Baring, Arnulf. *Uprising in East Germany: June 17, 1953.* Translated by G. Onn. Ithaca: Cornell University Press, 1972.

Bates, Robert H. "The Economics of Transitions to Democracy." *PS: Political Science & Politics* 24, no. 1 (March 1991): 24–27.

Batt, Judy. *East-Central Europe: From Reform to Transformation.* New York: Council on Foreign Relations, 1991.

———. *Economic Reform and Political Change in Eastern Europe: A Comparison of the Czechoslovak and Hungarian Experiences.* New York: St. Martin's Press, 1988.

Bergsen, Gordon S., and Russell Bova. "Worker Power under Communism: The Interplay of Exit and Voice." *Comparative Economic Studies* 32, no. 1 (Spring 1990): 42–72.

Berliner, Joseph S. *The Innovation Decision in Soviet Industry.* Cambridge: MIT Press, 1976.

Bernhard, Michael. "Civil Society and Democratic Transition in East Central Europe." *Political Science Quarterly* 108, no. 2 (Summer 1993): 307–26.

Bialer, Seweryn. "Gorbachev's Move." *Foreign Policy* 68 (Fall 1987): 59–87.

———. *The Soviet Paradox: External Expansion, Internal Decline.* London: IB Tauris, 1986.

Bischof, Günter. "Between Responsibility and Rehabilitation: Austria in International Politics, 1940–1950." Ph.D. diss, Harvard University, 1989.

Blacker, Coit. *Hostage to Revolution: Gorbachev and Soviet Security Policy, 1985–1991.* New York: Council on Foreign Relations, 1993.

Brada, Josef C. "Soviet Subsidization of Eastern Europe: The Primacy of Economics over Politics?" *Journal of Comparative Economics* 9 (1985): 80–92.

Brandt, Heinz. *The Search for a Third Way: My Path between East and West.* Translated by Salvator Attanasio. Garden City, N.Y.: Doubleday, 1970.

Brown, J. F. *Eastern Europe and Communist Rule.* Durham: Duke University Press, 1988.

———. *Surge to Freedom: The End of Communist Rule in Eastern Europe.* Durham: Duke University Press, 1991.

Brus, W. "1953 to 1956: The 'Thaw' and the 'New Course,'" In *Institutional Change within a Planned Economy.* Vol. 3 of *The Economic History of Eastern Europe 1919–1975*, edited by M. C. Kaser, 40–70. Oxford: Clarendon Press, 1986.

Brzezinski, Zbigniew K. *The Soviet Bloc: Unity and Conflict.* Rev. and enlarged ed. Cambridge: Harvard University Press, 1967.

Bunce, Valerie. "The Empire Strikes Back: The Evolution of the Eastern Bloc from a Soviet Asset to a Soviet Liability." *International Organization* 39, no. 1 (Winter 1985): 1–46.

Cairncross, Alec. *The Price of War: British Policy on German Reparations, 1941–1949.* New York: Basil Blackwell, 1986.

Childs, David. *The GDR: Moscow's German Ally.* 2d ed. London: Unwin Hyman, 1988.

Connor, Walter. *Socialism's Dilemmas: State and Society in the Soviet Bloc.* New York: Columbia University Press, 1988.

Crane, Keith. *The Soviet Economic Dilemma of Eastern Europe.* Rand R-3368-AF. Santa Monica, Calif.: Rand Corporation, May 1986.

Cronin, Audrey Kurth. *Great Power Politics and the Struggle over Austria, 1945–1955.* Ithaca: Cornell University Press, 1986.

Curry, Jane Leftwich, ed. *Dissent in Eastern Europe.* New York: Praeger, 1983.

Dallin, Alexander. "The Soviet Stake in Eastern Europe." *The Annals of the American Academy of Political and Social Science* 317 (May 1958): 138–45.

Davies, Norman H. *God's Playground: A History of Poland in Two Volumes.* 2 vols. Oxford: Clarendon Press, 1981.

Dawisha, Karen. *Eastern Europe, Gorbachev, and Reform: The Great Challenge.* 2d ed. Cambridge: Cambridge University Press, 1990.

Dietz, Raimund. "Soviet Foregone Gains in Trade with the CMEA Six: A Reappraisal." *Comparative Economic Studies* 27, no. 2 (Summer 1986): 69–94.

Ebert, Theodor. "Non-Violent Resistance against Communist Regimes?" In *Civilian Resistance as a National Defence: Non-violent Action against Aggression,* edited by Adam Roberts, 204–27. Harmondsworth: Penguin, 1969.

Ehrlich, Eva. "Contest between Countries, 1937–1986." *Soviet Studies* 43, no. 5 (1991): 875–96.

Etzold, Thomas H., and John Lewis Gaddis, eds. *Containment: Documents on American Policy and Strategy, 1945–1950.* New York: Columbia University Press, 1978.

Evangelista, Matthew A. "Stalin's Postwar Army Reappraised." *International Security* 7, no. 3 (Winter 1982–83): 110–38.

Fairchild, Erika S. *German Police: Ideals and Reality in the Post-War Years.* Springfield, Ill: C. C. Thomas, 1988.

Feis, Herbert. *From Trust to Terror: The Onset of the Cold War, 1945–1950.* New York: W. W. Norton, 1970.

Fricke, Karl Wilhelm. *MfS intern: Macht, Strukturen, Auflösung der DDR-Staatssicherheit, Analyse und Dokumentation.* Cologne: Verlag Wissenschaft und Politik, 1991.

Garthoff, Raymond L. *Detente and Confrontation: American-Soviet Relations from Nixon to Reagan.* Rev. ed. Washington, D.C.: Brookings Institution, 1994.

———. *Deterrence and the Revolution in Soviet Military Doctrine.* Washington, D.C.: Brookings Institution, 1990.

Gastil, Raymond D. *Freedom in the World: Political Rights and Civil Liberties, 1987–1988.* New York: Greenwood Press, 1988.

Gati, Charles. *The Bloc that Failed: Soviet–East European Relations in Transition.* Bloomington: Indiana University Press, 1990.

Geipel, Gary L., A. Tomasz Jarmoszko, and Seymour E. Goodman. "The Information Technologies and East European Societes." *East European Politics and Societies* 5, no. 3 (Fall 1991): 394–438.

Gill, David, and Ulrich Schröter. *Das Ministerium für Staatssicherheit: Anatomie des Mielke-Imperiums.* Berlin: Rowohlt, 1991.

Gimbel, John. *Science, Technology, and Reparations: Exploitation and Plunder in Postwar Germany.* Stanford: Stanford University Press, 1990.

Goldman, Marshall I. *Soviet Foreign Aid.* New York: Praeger, 1967.

Goodman, Seymour. "Information Technologies and the Citizen: Toward a 'Soviet-Style Information Society'?" In *Science and the Soviet Social Order,* edited by Loren R. Graham, 51–67. Cambridge: Harvard University Press, 1990.

Gregory, Paul, and Gert Leptin. "Similar Societies under Differing Economic Systems: The Case of the Two Germanys." *Soviet Studies* 29, no. 4 (October 1977): 519–42.

Gregory, Paul R., and Robert C. Stuart. *Soviet Economic Structure and Performance.* 3d ed. New York: Harper & Row, 1986.

Griffith, William E., ed. *Central and Eastern Europe: The Opening Curtain?* Boulder: Westview Press, 1989.

Grishin, Nikolai. "The Saxony Uranium Mining Operation ('Vismut')." In *Soviet Economic Policy,* edited by Robert Slusser, 127–53.

Harrison, Hope. "The Bargaining Power of Weaker Allies in Bipolarity and Crisis: The Dynamics of Soviet–East German Relations, 1953–61." Ph.D diss., Columbia University, 1993.

Harrison, Mark. "GDPs of the USSR and Eastern Europe: Towards and Interwar Comparison." *Europe-Asia Studies* 46, no. 2 (1994): 243–59.

Hart, Henry O. "The Tables Turned: If East Europeans Could Vote." *Public Opnion* 6, no. 5 (October–November 1983): 53–57.

Herspring, Dale R. "The Soviets, the Warsaw Pact, and the Eastern European Militaries." In *Central and Eastern Europe,* edited by William E. Griffith, 130–55.

Hillhouse, Raelynn J. "A Reevaluation of Soviet Policy in Central Europe: The Soviet Union and the Occupation of Austria." *Eastern European Politics and Societies* 3, no. 1 (Winter 1989): 83–104.

Hoffmann, Erik P., and Robbin F. Laird. *Technocratic Socialism: The Soviet Union in the Advanced Industrial Era.* Durham: Duke University Press, 1985.

Holzman, Franklyn D. "The Significance of Soviet Subsidies to Eastern Europe." *Comparative Economic Studies* 28, no. 1 (Spring 1986): 54–65, and no. 3 (Fall 1986): 59–64.

Horvath, Janos. "Grant Elements in Intra-bloc Aid Programs." *ASTE Bulletin* 13, no. 3 (Fall 1971): 1–17.

International Institute for Strategic Studies. *The Military Balance, 1978–79.* London: International Institute for Strategic Studies, 1978.

Johnson, A. Ross. "The Warsaw Pact: Soviet Military Policy in Eastern Europe." In *Soviet Policy in Eastern Europe,* edited by Sarah Meiklejohn Terry, 255–84.

Johnson, A. Ross, Robert W. Dean, and Alexander Alexiev. *East European Military Establishments: The Warsaw Pact Northern Tier.* New York: Crane Russak, 1982.

Jones, Christopher D. "National Armies and National Sovereignty." In *The Warsaw Pact: Alliance in Transition?* edited by David Holloway and Jane M. O. Sharp, 59–86. Ithaca: Cornell University Press, 1984.

———. *Soviet Influence in Eastern Europe: Political Autonomy and the Warsaw Pact.* New York: Praeger, 1981.

Kecskemeti, Paul. *The Unexpected Revolution: Social Forces in the Hungarian Uprising.* Stanford: Stanford University Press, 1961.

Köhler, Heinz. *Economic Integration in the Soviet Bloc with an East German Case Study.* New York: Praeger, 1965.

Kramer, Mark. "Beyond the Brezhnev Doctrine: A New Era in Soviet–East European Relations?" *International Security* 14:3 (Winter 1989–90): 25–67.

Krisch, Henry. "German Democratic Republic." In *Soviet Allies,* edited by Daniel N. Nelson, 143–83.

Kuklick, Bruce. *American Policy and the Division of Germany: The Clash with Russia over Reparations.* Ithaca: Cornell University Press, 1972.

Kuran, Timur. "Now out of Never: The Element of Surprise in the East European Revolution of 1989." *World Politics* 44, no. 1 (October 1991): 7–48.

Lancieri, Elio. "Dollar GNP Estimates for Central and Eastern Europe, 1970–90: A Survey and a Comparison with Western Countries." *World Development* 21, no. 1 (1993): 161–75.

Lapp, Peter Joachim. *Frontdienst im Frieden—die Grenztruppen der DDR: Entwicklung Struktur, Aufgaben.* 2d ed. Koblenz: Bernard & Graefe Verlag, 1987.

Lindblom, Charles E. *Politics and Markets: The World's Political-Economic Systems.* New York: Basic Books, 1977.

Linz, Susan J. "World War II and Soviet Economic Growth." In *The Impact of World War II on the Soviet Union,* edited by Susan J. Linz, 11–37. Totowa, New Jersey: Rowman & Allanheld, 1985.

MacGregor, Douglas A. *The Soviet–East German Military Alliance.* Cambridge: Cambridge University Press, 1989.

Marer, Paul. *Dollar GNPs of the U.S.S.R. and Eastern Europe.* Baltimore: Johns Hopkins Press for the World Bank, 1985.

———. "The Economies and Trade of Eastern Europe." in *Central and Eastern Europe,* edited by William E. Griffith, 37–73.

———. "The Political Economy of Soviet Relations with Eastern Europe." In *Soviet Policy in Eastern Europe,* edited by Sarah Meiklejohn Terry, 174–80.

———. "Soviet Economic Policy in Eastern Europe." In U.S. Congress, Joint Economic Committee. *Reorientation and Commercial Relations of the Economies of Eastern Europe,* 135–63. Washington, D.C.: Government Printing Office, 1974.

Marrese, Michael, and Jan Vanous. "The Content and Controversy of Soviet Trade Relations with Eastern Europe, 1970–1984." In *Economic Adjustment and Reform in Eastern Europe and the Soviet Union,* edited by Josef Brada, Ed A. Hewett, and Thomas A. Wolf, 185–220. Durham: Duke University Press, 1988.

———. *Implicit Subsidies and Non-Market Benefits in Soviet Trade with Eastern Europe.* Berkeley and Los Angeles: University of California Press, 1983.

Mlynar, Zdenek. *Nightfrost in Prague: The End of Humane Socialism.* Translated by Paul Wilson. New York: Karz, 1980.

Montias, J. M. "Economic Conditions and Political Instability in Communist Countries: Observations on Strikes, Riots, and Other Disturbances." *Studies in Comparative Communism* 13, no. 4 (Winter 1980): 283–99.

Nation, R. Craig. *Black Earth, Red Star: A History of Soviet Security Policy, 1917–1991.* Ithaca: Cornell University Press, 1992.

Nelson, Daniel N., ed. *Soviet Allies: The Warsaw Pact and the Issue of Reliability.* Boulder: Westview Press, 1983.

Nettl, J. P. *The Eastern Zone and Soviet Policy in Germany, 1945–50.* New York: Oxford University Press, 1951.

Nove, Alec. *An Economic History of the U.S.S.R.* New York: Penguin, 1982.

Organisation for Economic Co-operation and Development. *Main Aggregates.* Vol. 1 of *National Accounts, 1960–1990.* Paris: OECD, 1991.

Parrott, Bruce. *Politics and Technology in The Soviet Union.* Cambridge: MIT Press, 1983.

Phillips, Ann L. *Soviet Policy Toward East Germany Reconsidered: The Postwar Decade.* New York: Greenwood Press, 1986.

Pipes, Richard. "Militarism and the Soviet State." *Daedalus* 109, no. 4 (1980): 1–12.

———. "Soviet Global Strategy." *Commentary* 69, no. 4 (April 1980): 31–39.

Pond, Elizabeth. "A Wall Destroyed: The Dynamics of German Unification in the GDR." *International Security* 15, no. 2 (Fall 1990): 35–66.

Posen, Barry R. "Competing Images of the Soviet Union," *World Politics* 39, no. 4 (July 1987): 579–97.

Poznanski, Kazimierz Z. "Opportunity Cost in Soviet Trade with Eastern Europe: Discussion of Methodology and New Evidence." *Soviet Studies* 40, no. 2 (April 1988): 290–307.

Pravda, Alex. "Industrial Workers: Patterns of Dissent, Opposition and Accommodation." In *Opposition in Eastern Europe,* edited by Rudolf L. Tokes, 209–62. Baltimore: Johns Hopkins University Press, 1979.

Radio Free Europe. East European Area Audience and Opinion Research. "Czechoslovak, Hungarian and Polish Attitudes toward a 'Serious Conflict' between the United States and the Soviet Union." December 1981.

Ramet, Sabrina P. *Social Currents in Eastern Europe: The Sources and Meaning of the Great Transformation.* Durham: Duke University Press, 1991.

Rice, Condoleezza. "The Military as an Instrument of Influence and Control." In *Dominant Powers and Subordinate States: The United States in Latin America and the Soviet Union in Eastern Europe,* edited by Jan Triska, 239–60. Durham: Duke University Press, 1986.

———. *Uncertain Allegiance: The Soviet Union and the Czechoslovak Army, 1948–1983.* Princeton: Princeton University Press, 1985.

———. "Warsaw Pact Reliability: The Czechoslovak People's Army (CLA)." In *Soviet Allies,* edited by Daniel N. Nelson, 125–42.

Richter, James. "Soviet Policy towards Germany in 1953." *Europe-Asia Studies* 45, no. 4 (1993): 671–91.

Rothschild, Joseph A. *Return to Diversity: A Political History of East Central Europe since World War II.* New York: Oxford University Press, 1989.

Rousso, Alan. "Tipping the Balance of Power: The Political Economy of Intra-Alliance Trade in the Nuclear Age." Ph.D. diss., Columbia University, 1994.

Rudolf, Vladimir. "The Administrative Organization of Soviet Control, 1945–1948: The Agencies of Control: Their Organization and Policies." In *Soviet Economic Policy in Postwar Germany,* edited by Robert Slusser, 18–35.

Shoup, Paul S. *The East European and Soviet Data Handbook: Political, Social, and Developmental Indicators, 1945–1975.* New York: Columbia University Press, 1981.

Skilling, H. Gordon. *Czechoslovakia's Interrupted Revolution.* Princeton: Princeton University Press, 1976.

Slusser, Robert, ed. *Soviet Economic Policy in Postwar Germany: A Collection of Papers by Former Soviet Officials.* New York: Research Program on the USSR, 1953.

Snell, Edwin M., and Marilyn Harper. "Postwar Economic Growth in East Germany: A Comparison with West Germany." In *Economic Developments in Countries of Eastern Europe,* edited by U.S. Congress, Joint Economic Committee, 558–607. Washington, D.C.: Government Printing Office, 1970.

Snell, Paul. "Soviet Microprocessors and Microcomputers." In *Technical Progress and Soviet Economic Development,* edited by Ronald Amann and Julian Cooper, 62–63. New York: Basil Blackwell, 1986.

Snyder, Jack L. "The Gorbachev Revolution: A Waning of Soviet Expansionism?" In *Soviet Military Policy,* edited by Sean M. Lynn-Jones and Steven E. Miller, 93–106. Cambridge: MIT Press, 1989.

Sodaro, Michael J. "Limits to Dissent in the GDR: Fragmentation, Cooptation, and Repression." In *Dissent in Eastern Europe,* edited by Jane Leftwich Curry, 82–116. New York: Praeger, 1983.

Spulber, Nicolas. *The Economics of Communist Eastern Europe.* New York: John Wiley & Sons, 1957.

Stolper, Wolfgang F. *The Structure of the East German Economy.* Cambridge: Harvard University Press, 1960.

Taubman, William. *Stalin's American Policy: From Entente to Détente to Cold War.* New York: W. W. Norton, 1982.

Tatu, Michel. "Intervention in Eastern Europe." In *Diplomacy of Power: Soviet Armed Forces as a Political Instrument,* edited by Stephen S. Kaplan, 205–64. Washington, D.C.: Brookings Institution, 1981.

Terry, Sarah Meiklejohn. "The Future of Poland: *Persestroika* or Perpetual Crisis?" In *Central and Eastern Europe: The Opening Curtain?* edited by William E. Griffith, 178–217. Boulder: Westview Press, 1989.

———, ed. *Soviet Policy in Eastern Europe.* New Haven: Yale University Press, 1984.

Ulam, Adam. *Expansion and Coexistence: Soviet Foreign Policy, 1917–73.* 2d ed. New York: Praeger, 1974.

United States. Arms Control and Disarmament Agency. *World Military Expenditures and Arms Transfers, 1986.* Washington, D.C.: Government Printing Office, 1987.

Valenta, Jiri. *Soviet Intervention in Czechoslovakia, 1968: Anatomy of a Decision.* Baltimore: Johns Hopkins University Press, 1979.

———. "Soviet Policy toward Hungary and Czechoslovakia." In *Soviet Policy in Eastern Europe,* edited by Sarah Meiklejohn Terry, 93–124.

Van Evera, Stephen. "Primed for Peace: Europe after the Cold War." *International Security* 15, no. 3 (Winter 1990–91): 7–57.

Van Oudenaren, John. "The Soviet Union and Eastern Europe: New Prospects and Old Dilemmas." In *Central and Eastern Europe: The Opening Curtain?* edited by William E. Griffith, 102–29. Boulder: Westview Press, 1989.

Volgyes, Ivan. "Hungary." in *Soviet Allies*, edited by Daniel N. Nelson, 184–224.

Wallach, H. G. Peter, and Ronald H. Francisco. *United Germany: The Past, Politics, Prospects.* Westport, Conn.: Greenwood Press, 1992.

Weydenthal, Jan B. de. "Martial Law and the Reliability of the Polish Military." In *Soviet Allies*, edited by Daniel N. Nelson, 225–49.

White, Steven. "Economic Performance and Communist Legitimacy." *World Politics* 38, no. 3 (April 1986): 462–82.

Windsor, Philip, and Adam Roberts, *Czechoslovakia and 1968: Reform, Repression, and Resistance.* New York: Columbia University Press, 1969.

Wolf, Charles Jr., and Henry S. Rowen, eds. *The Future of the Soviet Empire.* New York: St. Martin's Press, 1987.

Wolf, Thomas A. "Estimating 'Foregone Gains' in Soviet–East European Trade: A Methodological Note." *Comparative Economic Studies*, no. 27, no. 3 (Fall 1985): 83–98.

Wolfe, Nancy Travis. *Policing a Socialist Society: The German Democratic Republic.* New York: Greenwood Press, 1992.

Wszelaki, Jan. *Communist Economic Strategy: The Role of East-Central Europe.* New York: National Planning Association, 1959.

Yershov, Vassily. "Confiscation and Plunder by the Army of Occupation." In *Soviet Economic Policy*, edited by Robert Slusser, 1–14

Zaslavskaya, Tatanya. "The Novisibirsk Report." *Survey* 28, no. 1 (Spring 1984): 88–108.

Zdenek, Mlynar. *Nightfrost in Prague: The End of Humane Socialism*, translated by Paul Wilson. New York: Karz, 1980.

Zimmermann, Hartmut, ed. *DDR Handbuch.* 3d ed. Köln: Verlag Wissenschaft und Politik, 1985.

Index

Acheson, Dean, 7
Afghanistan, 13
Alexander I, Tsar, 25, 156
Algeria, 19, 113–14, 151
Alsace-Lorraine, 38, 43, 70, 72–73, 87–88, 157
Angell, Sir Norman, 9, 11, 70, 161n.28
assassination, 18, 33, 48–49, 55–56, 68, 101
Athens, 6
atrocities, 24, 55–56, 68, 79–80, 114, 151
Austria, 14, 36–38, 122, 128, 170n.10
autarky, 30, 32, 85, 99, 101–3, 107, 109, 118, 154. *See also* resource dependence; size of empire
authoritarian rule, 13, 22, 28, 154–55, 164n.52, 166n.17, 167n.29

balance-of-power strategy, 6–11, 152
balance-of-power theory, 8–11, 12–13, 152
balancing behavior, 5, 21, 125, 144, 151, 163n.40
Balfour, Lord Arthur James, 98
Balkans, 13, 20, 37, 47, 70. *See also* Serbia; Yugoslavia
Baltic states, 38, 73, 121, 182n.25
bandwagoning, 21, 125, 163n.40, 166n.10, 167n.24
Bates, Robert H., 27
Batt, Judy, 208n.106
Belgium
—in World War I: collaboration and resistance in, 80–85, 147; exploitation of, 74–80, 183n.33, 184n.53; general government of, 69, 79–80, 181n.3; German aims in, 70–74; invasion of, 69, 180n.1; National Food and Relief Committee of, 82–84
—interwar, 87–98, 147, 190n.40
—in World War II, 36–68. *See also* Nazi-occupied Western Europe
Benes, Eduard, 60
Bentham, Jeremy, 10
Beria, Lavrenti P., 123
Berliet, Marius, 63

Berlin Wall, 124, 141–42
Bethmann Hollweg, Theobald von, 70–71, 181n.13, 182n.22
Bissing, Ferdinand von, 73, 185n.72
black market, 32, 42, 46, 53, 65, 84, 142
blockade, 56, 72–73, 81, 82, 93, 98, 101, 106–7, 112, 118, 154
Bohemia-Moravia, 36–68. *See also* Nazi-occupied Western Europe
boycotts, 18, 25, 33–34, 53, 76, 81, 83–84, 93–94
Brezhnev Doctrine, 124–25, 139
Brezhnev, Leonid I., 121
Briey. *See* Longwy-Briey
buck-passing, 12, 163n.48
Bulgaria, 122
Bülow, Bernhard F. von, 70
Bunce, Valerie, 123

case-study method, 16
censorship, 73, 95, 83, 115
Central China, 102, 112
Chambon-sur-Lignon, 64
Chiang Kai-shek, 101–2, 112–13, 114, 118
China, 101, 107, 112, 143. *See also* Central China; Chiang Kai-shek; communism; Inner Mongolia; Manchuria; North China
Citroën, 63
civil disobedience. *See* passive resistance
civilian-based defense, 5, 13, 98, 154–56
Class, Heinrich, 72
clearing deficits, 41–42. *See also* financial transfers
Cobden, Richard, 9, 11
Cockerill Steel, 62
coercion: defined, 21; in Eastern Europe, 135–44, 149; economic side-effects of, 142–43, 147; effectiveness of, 14, 21–31, 34, 154; efficiency of, 5, 149–50; in the Japanese Empire, 110–18, 148–49; in Nazi-occupied Europe, 47–49, 54–66, 149; in the Ruhr-Rhineland, 95–96; willingness to engage in, 4, 23–24, 90, 98, 150–51, 155–56; in WWI Belgium